Parents and Professionals in Special Education

Library
St. Joseph's College
Patchogue, N.Y. 11772

◻ **Jane B. Schulz**
Western Carolina University

Allyn and Bacon, Inc.
Boston   London   Sydney   Toronto

**To my mother,
Tommie J. Bolton**

All photographs courtesy of Jos and Mary deWit

Copyright © 1987 by Allyn and Bacon, Inc.
7 Wells Avenue, Newton, Massachusetts 02159

All rights reserved. No part of the material protected by this copyright notice may be reproduced or utilized in any form or by any means, electronic or mechanical, including photocopying, recording, or by any information storage and retrieval system, without written permission from the copyright owner.

Series Editors: John Coleman, Martin Connor
Production Coordinator: Sue Freese
Editorial/Production Services: Grace Sheldrick, Wordsworth Associates
Cover Administrator: Linda K. Dickinson
Cover Designer: Leslie Genser

Library of Congress Cataloging-in-Publication Data

Schulz, Jane B., date
   Parents and professionals in special education.

   Includes bibliographies and index.
   1. Exceptional children—Education—United States.
2. Parents of exceptional children—United States.
3. Exceptional children—United States—Family relationships.   4. Parent-teacher relationships—United States. I. Title.
LC3965.S47   1987   371.9'0 973   86-22333
ISBN 0–205–10479–7

Printed in the United States of America
10 9 8 7 6 5 4 3 2 1   91 90 89 88 87

Contents

Preface   v

Part I   Families of Exceptional Children   1

1. The Family   3
   Family Systems   3
   Family Dynamics   11
   Family Stress and Crisis   22
   Conclusion   24
   References   25

2. The Impact of Exceptional Children on the Family   29
   Impact of Birth   30
   Impact of Child and Adolescent   34
   Conclusion   49
   References   50

3. Family Adaptation to Exceptional Children   55
   Adaptation to Handicapped Children   55
   Adaptation to Gifted Children   80
   Conclusion   82
   References   82

4. The Parents' Role in Special Education   89
   Background of Parent Involvement   89
   Parent Advocacy   92
   Legislative Action   96
   Levels of Participation   104
   Conclusion   106
   References   109

5. The Parent-Professional Relationship   115
   Areas of Conflict   116
   Parent-Professional Models   123
   Expectations   132
   Establishing a Positive Relationship   136
   Conclusion   137
   References   138

Part II The Parent-Professional Partnership 143

6 Parent-School Communication   145
  Modes of Communication   145
  The Communication Process   148
  Strategies   160
  Conclusion   172
  References   173

7 Parent-Teacher Conferences   177
  Conference Purposes   178
  Structuring the Conference   190
  Special Situations   202
  Conclusion   211
  References   212

8 Assessment of Parents' Strengths and Needs   217
  Individuality of Parents   217
  Areas of Assessment   226
  Assessment Techniques and Models   243
  Conclusion   254
  References   255

9 Parent Education Programs   259
  Rationale for Parent Education   259
  Educating Parents of Handicapped Children   261
  Educating Parents of Gifted Children   282
  Evaluating Parent Education Programs   287
  Ethical Issues   289
  Conclusion   291
  References   291

10 Teacher Education Programs   297
  Teacher Preparation   297
  Preparation of Regular Educators   319
  Conclusion   333
  References   334

  Name Index   338
  Subject Index   343

Preface

Many factors contribute to the success or failure of children and young people in school. The quality of teaching, selection of curriculum and materials, physical accommodations, and administrative philosophy all combine to create the school environment. The student's ability, physical properties, maturity, and motivation account for some of the individual variables to be considered. In addition, recent investigation has revealed a startling observation: the most critical factor in a child's education is the parent.

Educators are becoming increasingly interested in parent involvement in the educational process. Public attitudes reflect a similar interest and contribute to the idea that public schools can, by working with parents, meet educational standards that are impossible to reach without such cooperation. However, research on parent participation in children's education indicates that although family involvement is considered critical to program success, schools make little sustained effort to communicate with parents and help them assist in the instructional process.

The home is the first training place; parents are the first teachers. From the family, the child derives attitudes, personality, and a model for relationships. The establishment of a parent-school partnership is crucial to the continuous and optimal development of the child.

A positive parent-teacher relationship is important for all students; it is essential for students who are exceptional. By definition, children and adolescents who are either handicapped or gifted require more education than their normal peers require. Parents and teachers are vital to the planning, implementing, and monitoring of special programs.

Parents and Professionals in Special Education makes and develops two basic assumptions. The first assumption is that parents are essential to the education of exceptional children and adolescents and are a necessary part of the educational team. The second assumption is that parents of exceptional children, like all parents, are individuals who have unique strengths and differing needs.

Parents and Professionals in Special Education is organized into two parts. Part I forms the conceptual, informational, and attitudinal portion of the book. Within this first part, five chapters deal with the family as a system, the impact of exceptional children on the family, family adaptation to exceptional children, the parents' role in special education, and the parent-professional relationship. Part I provides a background of the structures and functions of all families and particularly families of exceptional children and young people.

Part I also develops the sequences of parent participation from a legal and a functional perspective. Chapter 5 presents typical models for parent-professional relationships and includes discussions of problems, approaches, and positive relationships between parents and professionals who work with their exceptional children.

Part II of *Parents and Professionals* deals with the practical, instructional aspects of the home-school relationship. Chapter 6 focuses on parent-teacher communication with examination of attitudes, skills, and strategies for improving communication. The importance of parent-teacher conferences is emphasized in Chapter 7, where specific steps and strategies are suggested for optimal use of this important communication and problem-solving situation. Chapter 8 stresses the individuality of parents and suggests areas and techniques for discovering their strengths and needs. Chapters 9 and 10 are concerned with parent education programs and teacher education programs. Each of these last two chapters presents rationale, models, and suggestions for better parent education programs and for programs that will help all teachers work better with exceptional children.

Partnerships are formed by people who have common concerns and common goals. They are fostered and developed through mutual understanding, communication, and acquisition of appropriate skills. The purpose of *Parents and Professionals in Special Education* is to help teachers, prospective teachers, parents, and prospective parents grow in these directions.

Acknowledgments

□ □ *Parents and Professionals in Special Education* is the result of my experiences as the parent of a son who is handicapped and of children who are gifted. It also reflects my experiences as the teacher of handicapped students and of students preparing to be special educators. The students, the family members, and the professionals with whom I have been associated have contributed greatly to my understanding and to this book. I am grateful to all of them.

I am also grateful to the individuals who reviewed my work over several stages, including Norm Bissell (University of Cincinnati), Anne Gallegos (University of Colorado at Boulder), Marci J. Hanson (Educational Consultant, Los Altos, California), Don Potter (University of South Dakota), and Ann Rogers-Warren (Peabody College/Vanderbilt University).

I am particularly indebted to the people who have shared their personal experiences with me and with the readers of this book. The contributions of Kay McLain, Barbara Matalon, Jackie Spencer, Pam Stalley, Mary Trembath, Jan Minor, Linda Bowers, Mary deWit, and Michelle Mazzucco have brought humanity to the text. Equally important are the photography of Mary and Jos deWit and the willingness of families and individuals to be photographed.

Because *Parents and Professionals* is about families, it is fitting that I acknowledge the contributions of my own family: of my daughter, Mary deWit, who has read, edited, and greatly improved the manuscript; of my daughter-in-law, Barbara Schulz, who has kept me in touch with public schools; of my son, Billy, who has provided me with unique and valuable experiences; and of all my family members, who have encouraged and strengthened me.

J. B. S.

Part I
Families of Exceptional Children

CAROLYN

Our hands reach out to hold you,
Who will tumble without our grasp.
We feed you and clothe you and bathe you,
And you sleep peacefully in your not-knowing trust.

At seven we awaken to your squeals,
Whose joy expresses more than the towhees;
We wonder that you can be so glad
To belong to a world so unmade for you.

You pass the day as all days —
Sitting, eating, scooting, smiling —
Making us laugh with your laugh,
And cry with your seizures contorting.

We dress you for bed and whisper goodnight
And return to our wise world of knowledge;
And oh, sister, daughter — our eternal baby:
In your ignorance you have taught us love.

Kay McLain, 1985

1

The Family

Philosophical, as well as semantic, differences exist between the phrases *exceptional children* and *children who are exceptional.* By the same token, it is more appropriate to refer to families of exceptional children and adolescents as "families who happen to have exceptional children."

Families who have handicapped or gifted children come from that vast, variable, and dynamic group known as the American family. Before the birth of their child, these families were no better nor less prepared for parenthood than were other families. They certainly were not prepared for the impact of a child whose needs would be different from normal expectations and for the crisis frequently accompanying the birth of such a child.

Families of exceptional children may be placed in double jeopardy; not only are they faced with a unique set of problems, but they are also subject to the same pressures and tensions every family faces (Gallagher, Beckman, & Cross, 1983). As Turnbull (1976) states, they are "parents at risk" (p. 768).

Professionals who plan to work with exceptional children and their families need a basis for knowing and understanding those families before they become at risk. They need to be aware of the developmental stages of the family members, how they interact with each other, and how they react as a family to outside forces.

This understanding begins with a knowledge of the normal family, its structure, its stages, and its relationship to society as a whole. Family organization and patterns of functioning can be investigated and interpreted by viewing the family as a system.

Family Systems

The family is frequently referred to as an institution: the basic social institution (Leslie, 1967), the oldest social institution, and the most stable institution in the social system (Nimkoff, 1965). As part of a large social system, the family interacts with other institutions—economic, religious, cultural, educational, and political. The family thus is a subsystem of the larger society; it fulfills selected tasks for the society that are highly patterned, recurrent, and organized (Eshelman, 1981).

The dictionary defines *system* as "a group of interacting, interrelated, or interdependent elements forming or regarded as forming a collective entity" (Morris, 1981, p. 1306). In a family, persons are so related and connected that they form an entity—an organic whole greater than the sum of its component parts (Chinn, Winn, & Walters, 1978).

As the family is a subsystem of a larger society, so are there subsystems within the family, such as marital, mate-selection, sexual, and child-rearing systems. There are also interrelated positions in the family, such as parent-child, husband-wife, uncle-aunt, grandparent-grandchild, father-mother, and brother-sister (Eshleman, 1981).

A system can be open or closed. An open system has room for different ideas and is constantly receptive to alternatives. An open system accepts the constant change and growth of its members. In a closed system, members see change as a threat and difference as a lack of love. They have fixed assumptions about how other family members think, feel, and behave (Luthman, 1974).

Crucial assumptions of systems theory are:

1. The parts of the family are interrelated.
2. One part of the family cannot be understood in isolation from the rest of the system.
3. Family functioning cannot be fully understood by simply understanding each of the parts.
4. A family's structure and organization are important factors determining the behavior of family members.
5. Transactional patterns of the family system shape the behavior of family members. (Epstein, Bishop, & Baldwin, 1982, p. 116)

In viewing the family as a system, interest focuses on interrelationships. The nature of the interrelationships within a particular family are dependent on the organization of that family—its structure, functions, and changes.

Family Structure

Structure is the design of roles or relationships among individuals in the family. The traditional American structure is the **nuclear** family, composed of father, mother, and children; or the **extended** family, which includes kin beyond the nuclear family. Changes in American social, marriage, and family patterns have resulted in the addition of the **one-parent** family, in which a single parent is the head of the household that includes at least one child; and the **reconstituted** family, formed when a single person with one or more children marries.

To incorporate some of the diversity encountered in modern American society, the family can be defined as "a multigenerational unit in which people live 'under the same roof' and whose family members have either a biological relationship or an irrational attachment to one another" (Karpowitz, 1980, p. 29). In the United States, however, the nuclear family is still the basic residential family unit and reflects what is considered the normal family structure.

The Nuclear Family The nuclear family is found in all known societies. It can be defined as "a group of at least two adults of opposite sex, living in a socially approved sex relationship, with their own or adopted children" (Leslie, 1967, p. 13).

The nuclear family is characterized by sexual, reproductive, residential, economic, and socialization functions. The extended family and agencies outside the family may share in the fulfillment of these tasks but never to the exclusion of the nuclear family. The immediate family is residentially independent and is relatively free from economic obligation to kin.

☐ **The family is a dynamic system in which each member functions within a specific role.**

The suggestion that the nuclear family is ideal may appear prejudicial; this conception excludes the possibility that other ethnic, racial, and cultural family structures could be considered equally acceptable. This continuing stereotype may sustain tensions between family behavior in the dominant culture and traditional patterns of the black family and immigrant families.

In defense of the traditional structure, Yorburg declares:

> Marriage and the nuclear family will continue as basic institutions in human societies, functioning imperfectly and inefficiently, and sometimes destructively, but persevering because it is not possible to offer anything more workable to provide for the basic emotional needs of human beings—young or old. (Yorburg, 1983, p. 225)

The Extended Family The nuclear family may be extended to include the parental generations and sometimes other relatives. Since early industrialization in the United States, the family trend has been toward independence and away from the extended family. The extended, or joint, relationship restricts freedom of movement and choice of opportunity since decisions are made for the welfare of the entire family.

The shift has been away from the development of close family ties and the pursuit of group goals and toward the pursuit of individual goals (Chinn, 1974). This change has resulted in dependence on social institutions other than the family.

Although most Americans do not live in an extended family, there is a traditional emphasis on the value of maintaining ties between parents and their married children (Reiss, 1971). The extended family can provide a network of stable social support, even in a modified relationship. The support of the extended family may be crucial to the functioning of one-parent families or of families experiencing crises. The original family frequently provides lodging to adult family members who are in situations of economic and social distress. Co-residence is a response to particularly difficult situations and is usually abandoned when the situation improves (Bane, 1976).

The One-parent Family According to U.S. Census Bureau statistics for 1984, single parents headed 25.7 percent of the families with children under eighteen in the United States. It is predicted that one of every three families will be headed by a single parent in 1990; it is estimated that one-fourth of fathers and mothers now married will be single parents sometime during this decade (*Newsweek*, 1985). Some people view this trend as a consequence of moral decay; others see it as a redefinition of the family.

As a type of family structure, the one-parent family can be the result of illegitimacy, death of a spouse, separation, divorce, illness, or institutionalization. The reasons for being a single parent have different impacts on the family.

The one-parent experience may be overwhelming for both the parent and the children. One major problem is task overload, which is most evident among single mothers with young children (Beal, 1982). Another problem results from the financial demands of raising a family alone, particularly among women. Nearly 90 percent of the nation's one-parent households are headed by women. According to a U.S. Commission on Civil Rights study, 54 percent of single-parent families were living below the poverty line in 1983, compared with 18 percent for all families with children. For families headed by females, the figure was 47.2 percent, compared with 19.7 percent for males (*Newsweek,* 1985). Women comprise the largest group of single parents, but men are making more claims for custody rights than in the past, with the result that father-headed households have more than doubled since 1970.

In addition to the stress of financial burdens, single parents may be isolated from the extended family and other social networks. Isolation can occur because of family rejection of illegitimacy, disagreements about divorce, or because the single parent does not have time to pursue a social life. The most dramatic effects, however, are felt by the children.

The effects of a broken home on a child or children depend on many factors, including:

- ☐ Whether the home was broken by death, desertion, or divorce.
- ☐ Age of the child.
- ☐ Quality of the child's relationship with both parents.
- ☐ Whether the parent the child is living with remarries and the quality of the child's relationship with the step-parent.
- ☐ Personality and emotional stability of the child and the parent.
- ☐ Availability of parent substitutes for the child.
- ☐ Financial situation of the one-parent family. (Stinnett & Birdsong, 1978, p. 187)

Family Functions

☐ The socially accepted functions of the family have not changed drastically through the years. These functions include:

1. Establishing accepted and internalized norms for regulating sex, reproduction, and care and socialization of the young.
2. Establishing a system for producing and distributing essential goods and services.
3. Offering protection against human destructiveness.
4. Providing recreational outlets.
5. Communicating and maintaining cultural beliefs that give meaning and purpose to life (Yorburg, 1983).

One universal function of the family is its nurturance of the newborn (Reiss, 1971). This function includes parenthood and socialization.

Parenthood The beginning of a traditional family is marriage between two persons. Each person comes from a family; the family background of each partner will be a significant factor in determining the structure, rules, and roles the couple will develop for their own family (Chinn, Winn, & Walters, 1978). Individual and joint experiences will also contribute to the values and goals of the marriage.

Although children are not essential to a marriage, most married couples want and have them. Since the mid-1950s, the birth rate in the United States has decreased, with a substantial movement toward fewer children, usually two in number (Eshleman, 1981).

The parent role is difficult and complicated. Society's expectations are greater than many parents are prepared to meet. The following inconsistencies are characteristic:

1. The role of parent in modern America is not well-defined. It is often ambiguous and hard to pin down.

2. The role is not adequately delimited. Parents are expected to succeed where even the professionals fail.

3. Modern parents are not well-prepared for their roles as fathers and mothers.

4. There is a romantic complex about parenthood. In some ways this complex is even deeper and more unrealistic than that relating to marriage.

5. Modern parents are in the unenviable position of having complete responsibility for their offspring but only partial authority over them.

6. The standards of role performance imposed on modern parents are too high. This arises from the fact that modern fathers and mothers are judged largely by professional practitioners such as psychiatrists and social workers rather than by their peers—other parents who are "amateurs" and not professionals.

7. Parents are the victims of inadequate behavioral science. They have been told repeatedly . . . that nothing determines what the child will be like but the influence of the parents. . . . This is obviously not true.

8. Parents do not choose their children unless they are adoptive parents.

9. There is no traditional model for modern parents to follow in rearing their children. The old model has been riddled by critical studies, yet no adequate new model has been developed. Instead, we have had a series of fads and fashions in child rearing based on the research of the moment. . . . Educators have been unconsciously presenting their middle-class values for all parents to emulate.

10. Contrary to what some may think, parenthood as a role does not enjoy the priority one would expect in modern America. The needs of the economic system in particular come first.

11. Other new roles have been assumed by modern parents since World War I that are not always completely compatible with the role of parent. The clearest and most striking example of this would be the occupational roles assumed by millions of American mothers.

12. The parental role is one of the few important roles in contemporary America from which one cannot honorably withdraw. Most of us can escape from our jobs if they are too frustrating; many of us escape from our parents when we marry; and a considerable number of husbands and wives manage to withdraw with some honor from marriages that they no longer find enchanting.

13. And last but not least, it is not enough for modern parents to produce children in their own image: the children have to be reared to be not only different from their fathers and mothers but also better. (LeMasters, 1974, pp. 50–53)

In spite of the ambiguities related to parenthood, the American society holds strongly to the view that to be a parent is a good thing. Parenthood is valued for five reasons:

1. It satisfies a need for attaining adult status and a social identity.
2. It establishes a continuity between the past and the future.
3. It helps expand the parents' self-concept by evoking new, previously untapped dimensions of personality.
4. It satisfies a need for affection and belonging.
5. It provides an opportunity for stimulation and fun (Eshleman, 1981).

Parenthood has a tremendous impact on the marital relationship. It results in a permanent rearrangement of emotional and economic resources as well as a realignment of the marital interaction patterns (Chinn, Winn, & Walters, 1978). As expressed by Yorburg:

> Infancy and childhood, the first major stages in the human life cycle, have dramatic implications for family functioning. The introduction of a new child into the family group is more crucial for the rearrangement and redefinition of family roles than the gradual changes that occur with puberty and middle and old age. (Yorburg, 1983, p. 53)

Socialization Nimkoff (1965) claims that the family persists because it has two essential functions that either cannot be transferred to or are not performed as well by other institutions or agencies. These functions are reproduction and the socialization of very young children.

The socialization process begins at birth and continues throughout the life span. Early parent-child interaction develops in three stages. The first stage of the process is the parent's development of a positive attachment to the child. In the second stage, the child develops a positive attachment to the parent. During the third stage, the parent and child share activities, enabling the child to develop new relationships, interests, and skills (Schaefer, 1975).

Child-rearing practices greatly influence the kind and degree of socialization that takes place. These practices can be authoritarian, or permissive, or somewhere in between (Yorburg, 1983). Authoritarian parents demand absolute obedience to external rules; in the permissive parent-child relationship, the child's needs and wishes are considered in the process of socialization. Research related to family support and control leads to the following theoretical propositions:

1. The greater the parental support, the greater the social competence in children.
2. The greater the inductive control attempts of parents, the greater the social competence in children. [Inductive control refers to voluntary compliance to parental desires.]
3. The greater the coercive control attempts of parents, the less the social competence in children. [Coercive control refers to external pressure on the child to behave according to the parents' desires.] (Rollins & Thomas, 1979, p. 334)

Children must learn their roles as defined by their family and culture. They have the basic right to expect and to receive help from their families in achieving physical, emotional, and intellectual maturity.

Family Changes

Karpowitz (1980) describes the family as a "changing, coping, developing, adapting, acting, involving social organism" (p. 28) and declares that no other social institution has adapted to such a wide variety of social changes over such an extended period of time. Indeed, the family unit is besieged by forces that alter its functioning. Table 1.1, a summary of family changes, depicts the vast transformation in family structure and life-styles that have taken place during the past decade.

The changing family reflects a changing society and demonstrates a unique characteristic of the family as a system:

TABLE 1.1 Summary of Family Changes, 1970 and 1980

Nature of Change	1970	1980	% Change
Marriages performed	2,159,000	2,317,000	+ 7.3
Divorces granted	708,000	1,170,000	+ 65.3
Married couples	44,728,00	47,662,000	+ 6.6
Unmarried (cohabitating) couples	523,000	1,346,000	+157.4
People living alone	10,851,000	17,202,000	+ 58.5
Married couples with children	25,541,000	24,625,000	− 3.6
Children living with 2 parents	58,926,000	48,295,000	− 18.0
Children living with 1 parent	8,230,000	11,528,000	+ 40.1
Families with both husand and wife working	20,327,000	24,253,000	+ 19.3

Source: James Garbarino, *CHILDREN AND FAMILIES IN THE SOCIAL ENVIRONMENT.* Copyright c 1982 (Aldine Publishing Company, New York).

Changes that have been documented in recent years represent neither the demise of the family unit nor a change in essence, but rather the flexibility and adaptation of the family to the demands of an increasingly complex society. (Chinn, 1974, p. 43)

The relationship between family changes and the forces affecting them are referred to as dynamics.

Family Dynamics

Dynamics is defined as "the physical or moral forces that produce motion and change in any field or system" (Morris, 1981, p. 407). This is a view of the family as a moving, changing system.

In describing family dynamics, two aspects of marital and family behavior have been delineated: **cohesion** and **adaptability** (Olson, Sprenkle, & Russell, 1979). Family cohesion is defined as "the emotional bonding members have with one another and the degree of individual autonomy a person experiences in the family system" (p. 5). At the extreme of high family cohesion, **enmeshment**, there is an overidentification with the family; the low extreme, **disengagement**, is indicated by low bonding and high autonomy from the family. Olson, Sprenkle, and Russell (1979) hypothesize that a **balanced** degree of family cohesion is the most conducive to effective family functioning. They suggest that these three points on the cohesion continuum can be represented conceptually by three different poems.

Family connectedness in the extreme (enmeshment) is evident in the poem "Togetherness Prayer":

> We do our thing together
> I am here to meet all your needs and expectations
> And you are here to meet mine
> We had to meet, and it was beautiful
> I can't imagine it turning out any other way.*

Family separateness in the extreme (disengagement) is expressed in "Gestalt Prayer":

> I do my thing, and you do your thing
> I am not in this world to live up to your expectations
> And you are not in this world to live up to mine

---

*"Togetherness Prayer" from MY NEEDS, YOUR NEEDS, OUR NEEDS by Jerry Gillies. Text copyright © 1973, 1974 by Jerry Gillies. Poems copyright © 1974 by Judy Altura. Reprinted by permission of Doubleday and Company, Inc.

You are you and I am I
And if by chance we meet, it's beautiful
If not, it can't be helped.*

A separate-connectedness, or balance, is portrayed in "About Marriage":

Sing and dance together and be joyous,
but let each one of you be alone
Even as the strings of a lute are alone
though they quiver with the same music
And stand together yet not too near together;
For the pillars of the temple stand apart,
And the oak tree and the cypress grow
not in each other's shadow
But let there be spaces in your togetherness
And let the winds of the heavens dance between you.**

It is hypothesized that when the levels of cohesion are balanced, the family can deal more effectively with situational stress and developmental change.

The second dimension described is family adaptability (Olson, Sprenkle, & Russell, 1979). **Adaptability** is defined as "the ability of a marital/family system to change its power structure, role relationships, and relationship rules in response to situational and developmental stress" (p. 12). Later work adds the dimension of **family communication** as a facilitating dimension, enabling couples and families to move on the other two dimensions (Olson, Russell, & Sprenkle, 1983). A combination of these dimensions resulted in the development of the circumplex model, which permits the identification and description of sixteen types of marital and family systems.

Beavers and Voeller (1983) suggest changes to the circumplex model that relate its ideas to human developmental theory. Just as a child grows toward autonomy and emotional maturity, families grow in their ability to make adaptive change. Severely disturbed families are inflexible and incapable of adapting to change. Theories of cohesion, adaptability, and balance are important concepts in observing and predicting the abilities of families to deal with stress.

Further understanding is added by Taylor (1983), who refers to the similar dimensions of **flexibility** and **resiliency**. Flexibility is defined as "uncommitted potential for change" and resiliency as "the ability to both recover from traumatic experiences and to create new values during the very process of recovery" (p. 344). The ability of a family to respond to change with flexibility and resiliency may be the determiner of that family's strength in dealing with crisis.

---

*Perls, 1969. © Real People Press 1969. All rights reserved.

**"On Marriage" from THE PROPHET by Kahlil Gibran, copyright 1968. Used by permission of Alfred A. Knopf, Inc.

An investigation of family dynamics and interrelationships leads to several questions: What are the relationships within the family; How do they change? What are the relationships between the family and other changing social systems? And most important, How does the family respond to changes within and outside the family? Answers to these questions will provide understanding of the dynamics of a particular family and its ability to deal with the impact of a child who is handicapped or gifted.

Two kinds of changes affect the family. The first type is related to the normal, developmental changes that occur in families. The second type of change reflects societal dynamics that have an impact on the family. The interaction of these two forces, as well as factors within each type of change, may produce anxiety, stress, and crisis.

Developmental Changes

☐ The family can be viewed as "a system moving through time" (McGoldrick & Carter, 1982, p. 168). Each step of the family life cycle embodies transition and change. As Table 1.2 indicates, each transition involves shifts in status, or role, for all family members.

TABLE 1.2 The Stages of the Family Life Cycle

Family life cycle stage	Emotional process of transition: Key principles	Second-order changes in family status required to proceed developmentally
1. Between families: The unattached young adult	Accepting parent-offspring separation	a. Differentiation of self in relation to family of origin b. Development of intimate peer relationships c. Establishment of self in work
2. The joining of families through marriage: The newly married couple	Commitment to new system	a. Formation of marital system b. Realignment of relationships with extended families and friends to include spouse
3. The family with young children	Accepting new generation of members into the system	a. Adjusting marital system to make space for child(ren) b. Taking on parenting roles c. Realignment of relationships with extended family to include parenting and grandparenting roles
4. The family with adolescents	Increasing flexibility of family boundaries to include children's independence	a. Shifting of parent-child relationships to permit adolescents to move in and out of system b. Refocus on midlife marital and career issues c. Beginning shift toward concerns for older generation

(continued)

TABLE 1.2 *(cont.)*

Family life cycle stage	Emotional process of transition: Key principles	Second-order changes in family status required to proceed developmentally
5. Launching children and moving on	Accepting a multitude of exits from and entries into the family system	a. Renegotiation of marital system as a dyad b. Development of adult to adult relationships between grown children and their parents c. Realignment of relationships to include in-laws and grandchildren d. Dealing with disabilities and death of parents (grandparents)
6. The family in later life	Accepting the shifting of generational roles	a. Maintaining own and/or couple functioning and interests in face of physiological decline; exploration of new familial and social role options b. Support for a more central role for middle generation c. Making room in the system for the wisdom and experience of the elderly; supporting the older generation without overfunctioning for them d. Dealing with loss of spouse, siblings, and other peers, and preparation for own death. Life review and integration.

Source: M. McGoldrick & E. A. Carter, *The family life cycle.* In Walsh, F. (ed.), *Normal family processes,* p. 176. Copyright 1982, The Guilford Press. Used with permission.

The needs of parents with their first baby are vastly different from those of a large family with children of various ages or of a family in which teenagers are about to depart from home (Karpowitz, 1980). The philosophy inherent in this approach is that as each family member progresses through predictable developmental stages, so does the family. A knowledge of the family cycle can help pinpoint and clarify some of the problems encountered at various stages of development.

Major changes within the family cycle that affect the timing of life transitions include marriage, parenthood, the empty nest, and widowhood (Hareven, 1982). The typical American family cycle is characterized by marriage in the twenties, commencement of childbearing soon after, and a small number of children. This type of pattern results in a compact period of parenthood in the middle years of life, an extended period without children and frequently with the loss of a spouse, and a period of solitary living.

Many families do not go through the normal life stages at the normal time. The changing role of women is central to shifting life patterns; their life cycles are no longer linked exclusively to child-rearing activities. More than half of mothers with school-age children and more than 40 percent of mothers with younger children work outside the home (Walsh, 1982). Many young women delay marriage and children because of their own career pursuits or in support of their husbands' early careers. In addition, 7 percent of women never marry, 4 percent never have children, and 38 percent end their marriages in divorce (McGoldrick & Carter, 1982). Other events, such as early death of a family member or the presence of a chronically ill or handicapped family member, also drastically alter the cycle.

The family is the basic unit of emotional development. By identifying and predicting the phases and course of development, professionals can understand the emotional problems that people develop as they move together through this basic process (McGoldrick & Carter, 1982).

Social Changes

☐ Any major change in the social system is reflected in the family. Attitudinal and technological changes affect role definition of family members and therefore functions of the family.

☐ *The family life cycle embodies transition and change. The young adult will eventually leave home to begin a new family cycle.*

Factors that have contributed to the changing family are the advent and effects of birth control during the last two decades, the movement for equal rights for women, acceptance of alternative life-styles, and the high incidence of single-parent families (Lillie, 1981). Concurrent with these changes, many parents experience a conflict with the values of their own parents. Family responsibilities may be quite different from those of a generation ago.

Many changing social conditions directly influence the organization and function of the American family. Three of the most dramatic forces are poverty, divorce, and family violence.

Poverty There are many kinds of poor families, and they vary as a function of race, color, language, ethnicity, and ability to cope (Colon, 1982). In affluent America, poverty confers minority and inferior status. This position, associated with the continual concerns about food, clothing, and shelter, causes constant stress on the underprivileged family (Glasser & Glasser, 1970).

Problems encountered in the poor family come from within the family organization as well as from external events. These external factors can be explained as cultural or situational:

> The cultural view emphasizes cross-generational family socialization processes that create and perpetuate the features of the poor. The situational view stresses the structural features of society that create and perpetuate those features of the occupational system that prevent the poor from ever improving their families' economic position. (Colon, 1982, p. 345)

Prolonged unemployment, irregular employment, and low income are important forces leading to a chronic family pattern. The result is a family system that is less complex and less adequately organized to cope with its needs than a comparable middle-class family.

The family life cycle is seriously affected by poverty. The average poor person leaves home, marries, has children, gets divorced, becomes a grandparent, and dies earlier than the middle-class person. Poor families are subject to more abrupt loss of membership through sudden departures, deaths, imprisonments, and substance addiction. Remaining family members are required to assume new roles and responsibilities often before they are developmentally capable (Colon, 1982).

The Joint Commission on Mental Health of Children (1970) found that the family life-styles and childbearing patterns associated with poverty were vastly different from those of middle-class families. The following practices were found in many poor families:

- ☐ Inconsistent, harsh physical punishment.
- ☐ Fatalistic attitudes and magical thinking.
- ☐ An orientation to the present.

- ☐ Rigid, authoritarian family structures with strict definitions of male and female roles.
- ☐ Constricted experiences with society and an alienated, distrustful approach to society.
- ☐ Limited verbal communication with little attention to abstract concepts.
- ☐ Human behavior seen as unpredictable.
- ☐ Low self-esteem, passivity, and acceptance of impoverished conditions.
- ☐ Distrust for the opposite sex.

The impact of poverty on children is profound. Children's future intellectual competence is critically affected by their early experiences. Environmental influences and attention by the mother have a maximum impact on the development of intelligence in the first three or four years of life (Yorburg, 1983).

Difficult socioeconomic circumstances can also influence the parents' strategies for interacting with their children. An investigation of home environments of socioculturally retarded children disclosed an absence of maternal warmth, involvement, restriction, and punishment; organization of the environment; appropriate toys; and opportunities for variety (Gallagher, Beckman, & Cross, 1983). The reason suggested was that mothers in poor families may be forced to expend much of their energy in maintaining the household and have little left to share with their children.

Lower-class family members experience more severe stressful events than members of the middle class and have fewer resources to deal with them. Miller (1970) expresses the magnitude of the problem: "Lower-class life is crisis-life, constantly trying to make-do with string where rope is needed" (p. 47).

Divorce The divorce rate in America has doubled since 1965. Presently, one-third of all marriages are likely to end in divorce. As many as four out of ten children born in the seventies are expected to spend part of their childhood in a one-parent household (Walsh, 1982), and approximately half the children born in the eighties will spend part of their childhood living with one parent (*Newsweek*, 1985). Marital disruptions and rearrangement of nuclear family structure are increasingly common experiences in the lives of many parents and their children. Although divorce may be a positive solution to destructive family functioning, it is a critical experience that affects the entire family system and the functioning and interactions of the members within that system (Hetherington, Cox, & Cox, 1982).

Divorce can be conceptualized as an interruption or dislocation of the traditional family life cycle, producing the kind of profound disequilibrium associated with shifts, gains, and losses in family membership. Divorce occurring at different stages in the family life cycle has a different impact on family structure and functioning.

In divorcing families, emotional tension peaks predictably at these points:

1. at the time of the *decision* to separate or divorce;
2. when this decision is announced to family and friends;
3. when money and custody-visitation arrangements are discussed;
4. when the physical separation takes place;
5. when the actual legal divorce takes place;
6. when separated spouses or ex-spouses have contact about money or children and at life cycle transition points of all family members;
7. as each spouse is making the initial adjustments to rebuilding a new life. (McGoldrick & Carter, 1982, p. 189)

In attempting to appraise the effects of divorce on families, two things must be kept in mind. First, the outcomes of divorce will differ for different members of the family. Stresses, support systems, and coping strategies vary for husbands, wives, and even among children in the same family. Second, divorce cannot be viewed as an event occurring at a single point in time; it represents an extended transition in the lives of parents and children (Hetherington, Cox, & Cox, 1982).

Critical events in the life cycle of divorcing families include age at the time of marriage, age at the time of divorce, and the interval between marriages. The influence of divorce on children is related to two issues: (1) The intensity of the emotional attachment and (2) conflict between parents and the degree to which the child is the focus of the family emotional processes (Beal, 1982). One child may be more sensitive to parental anxieties than other children and therefore have more difficulty dealing with divorce.

Stinnett and Birdsong outline potentially traumatic situations for children of divorcing parents:

- ☐ The necessity to adjust to the knowledge that divorce will probably take place
- ☐ Having to adjust to the fact of divorce
- ☐ The possibility that in the pre-divorce or post-divorce years, one or both parents may "use" the child as a weapon against the other
- ☐ Redefining relationships with parents
- ☐ The new status of being the child of divorced parents may necessitate new adjustments with peers
- ☐ Some children may recognize the implications of their parents' failure in marriage
- ☐ There may be problems of adjustment for the child if parents remarry. (Stinnett & Birdsong, 1978, p. 185)

Research has shown very mixed results on the consequences of divorce on children (Eshleman, 1985). Many structural variations—such as custody arrangements, remarriage of parent, presence of grandparents or other relatives, age of children, educational and neighborhood influences, economic resources, and presence of siblings—influence the consequences of a shift from a marital to a divorced parental status. One consistent consequence revealed by research is that children from disrupted marriages have a higher rate of divorce than do children from intact marriages. This finding may explain the intergenerational transmission of divorce.

Many other variables seem to relate to divorce (Reiss, 1971). There is a higher rate of divorce among couples who were married in their teens; the rate is also higher with girls who were pregnant at the time of marriage. People of poverty have high divorce rates; the life-style of couples in lower socioeconomic groups promotes the highest degree of marital strain and maladjustment.

The presence of a handicapped child also influences family stability (Canino & Reeve, 1980). The stresses of raising a handicapped child increase the risk of matrimonial disharmony and predispose the parents to divorce.

Although divorce is generally perceived as a negative situation, Hareven (1982) claims that the increase in divorce statistics is no proof of family breakdown. It is, rather, that people care enough about the quality of family life to dissolve an unsatisfactory marriage and, frequently, to replace it with a more successful one.

Regardless of the effects of divorce, research findings suggest that most family members can adapt to the stress of divorce within a few years (Hetherington, Cox, & Cox, 1982). The longer-term adjustment is related to economic, environmental, social, and emotional conditions that persist or are associated with living in a one-parent household.

Family Violence and Child Abuse In American society, people are more likely to be hit, beaten up, physically injured, or even killed in their own homes by another family member than anywhere else in their community or by anyone else (Eshleman, 1981). Because of the private nature of family violence, precise data on conjugal and parental abuse and violence are difficult to obtain.

The violence of society at large is reflected in the smaller world of the family. Mitchell (1978) claims that life has always been risky and violent; the increase of reporting violence does not necessarily mean an increase in violence. He states the problem:

> We have to come to terms with the understanding that a measure of aggressive behavior and violence is inevitable to human progress and survival, but we have to identify what is unnecessary violence, and what is preventable violence, particularly in the setting of the human family in its own internal transactions, and in its transactions with others outside itself. (Mitchell, 1978, p. 10)

A number of trends related to family violence are alarming. An increasing number of wives are physically attacked while they are pregnant (Eshleman, 1985); many women are victims, in their own homes, of male-initiated violence and social isolation; a number of children die each year because of acute battering or prolonged, systematic cruelty or neglect; an increasing number of children, especially babies and young children under two, are physically and emotionally assaulted by adults and by their parents in particular; and any child under the age of four has a real risk of being abused physically or emotionally, particularly in cultures of urbanization (Mitchell, 1978).

Child abuse and **neglect** are defined as the "physical or mental injury, sexual abuse, negligent treatment or maltreatment of a child under the age of eighteen by a person who is responsible for the child's welfare under circumstances which indicate that the child's health or welfare is harmed or threatened thereby" (Marion, 1981). In addition to the types of abuse mentioned, several kinds may be found in combination.

Three factors must be present for child abuse to occur. The first is parents or caregivers who have the potential for abusing. The second is a child who is perceived by the parents as different. The third factor is a stress situation that precipitates a crisis (Berger, 1981).

Because parents often see abused children as different and difficult to raise, handicapped children qualify as abuse risks (Canino & Reeve, 1980). The consequences of a failing marital relationship associated with the demands of raising a handicapped child could contribute to the stress situation.

Child abuse and neglect tend to occur more frequently in low-income homes. The higher incidence reported in such families may be due to greater visibility by social agencies or may be related to the higher stress level associated with economic problems. Personality traits exhibited by abusing parents include immaturity and dependence, a sense of personal incompetence, difficulty in expressing pleasure, social isolation, misperceptions of the child, fear of spoiling the child, belief in the value of punishment, and unawareness of the child's needs (Berger, 1981).

Two major areas of concern are related to child abuse and neglect: breaking the child-abusing parent cycle and providing teatment for abused and neglected children and their families (Rose & Hardman, 1981). Providing positive adult relationships for the child and education of potentially abusive parents serve to break the cycle.

Treatment for abused children and their families can be provided through the school and other social agencies. Adequate reporting of abuse must be followed by therapeutic family-oriented programs.

Working with abusive parents requires a nonpunitive point of view (Marion, 1981). The practice of permanently removing the child from the home is no longer considered the best answer to child abuse. As in other problem areas, it must be recognized that family members do not operate in isolation from each other or from society.

The problems of poverty, divorce, and violence are family problems; they are also major social issues. Society has assigned to the family the responsibilities for meeting the physical and emotional needs of its members, as well as for dealing with and operating within these and other major areas of conflict and stress. As stated by Hill:

> The modern family lives in a greater state of tension precisely because it is the great burden carrier of the social order. In a society of rapid social change, problems outnumber solutions, and the resulting uncertainties are absorbed by the members of society, who are for the most part also members of families. Because the family is the bottleneck through which all troubles pass, no other association so reflects the strains and stresses of life. (Hill, 1958, p. 40)

The final dimension of family life discussed in this chapter is stress: its definition, its causes, and its effect on the family.

☐ *A family can be affected by a wide variety of stressors that can originate from within the family or from social factors outside the family.*

Family Stress and Crisis

Definition

☐ In investigating social stress in families, Hill (1958) defines **stressor** as a crisis-provoking event or situation for which the family has little or no preparation. In a classical model, he presents a formula for crisis:

> A (the event) $\longrightarrow$ *interacting* with B (the family's crisis-meeting resources) $\longrightarrow$ *interacting* with C (the definition the family makes of the event) $\longrightarrow$ *produces* X (the crisis). (Hill, 1958, p. 141)

Definitions of the terms used in the model will clarify this ABCX formula.

Stressor events (A) differ in their sources; some originate within the family, others from outside. Crises that result from such stress as economic depression or war present different problems from those arising out of the interpersonal relations within the family, such as infidelity or divorce (Hansen & Hill, 1964). In analyzing stressful events, Holmes and Rahe (1967) found one common theme: the occurrence of each event evoked or was associated with some adaptive or coping behavior on the part of the individual involved.

Family resources (B) may include adaptability, coherence, financial stability, friends, religion, education, and health. Persons with more skills, assets, and resources, more versatile defenses, and broader experiences deal better with stress. In general, the more competence individuals have demonstrated in the past, the more likely it is they will cope with a current stressor (Rabkin & Struening, 1976).

The extent to which families define the event as a crisis (C) reflects the value system of the family and previous experience with crises. A critical factor in evaluating the impact of stressful events is the individual's perception of them (Rabkin & Struening, 1976). Perception depends on the appraisal of potentially harmful, challenging, or threatening events.

Crisis-proneness (X) is the phenomenon of experiencing stressor events (A) with greater frequency and greater severity and defining these (C) more frequently as crises.

As indicated in Figure 1.1, McCubbin and Patterson (1982) have visualized the ABCX model to show the relationship between a stressor event and the amount of crisis. In this model, the family's vulnerability, or ability to prevent a stressor event from creating a crisis, is influenced by the definition the family makes of the seriousness of the change.

In summary, **crisis** is any event that causes stress within the family. The nature of the event may be so severe that it would be a crisis in any family (such as poverty, death, or divorce); family resources influence how the event affects the family; and the definition the family makes determines how stressful it will be (as with divorce, economic stress, illness, and disability) (Chinn, 1974).

FIGURE 1.1 The ABCX Model

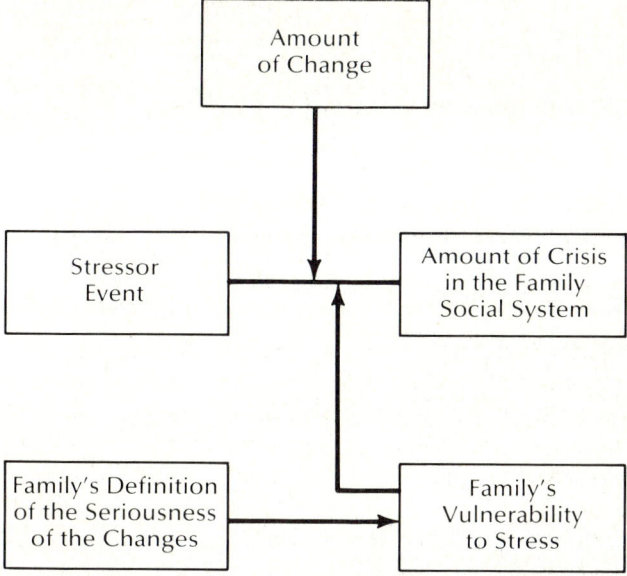

Source: From H. I. McCubbin and J. M. Patterson, Family adaptation to crises. In H. I. McCubbin, A. E. Cauble, and J. M. Patterson, (Eds.), *Family stress, coping, and social support.* 1982. Courtesy of Charles C Thomas, Publisher, Springfield, Illinois.

Causes

☐ Hill (1958) points to the vulnerability of crisis-prone families. For example, a family from a low socioeconomic group may have a quality of desperation in a financial crisis that is lacking for families who have reserves on which to draw. The low socioeconomic family is restricted in income, health, energy, space, and ideas for coping with crisis.

A wide variety of factors are also linked to stress in families of handicapped children (Gallagher, Beckman, & Cross, 1983). Increased tensions in the family, combined with the child's decreased ability to perform acceptably, create stressful events. As noted, there is also greater incidence of divorce in families of handicapped children. In addition, these families may experience increased financial difficulties resulting from the need for special equipment, medical expenses, and special programs.

Effects

☐ Within the family life cycle, the effect of stress is reflected in the vertical and horizontal flow of anxiety in a family. As illustrated in Figure 1.2, the vertical

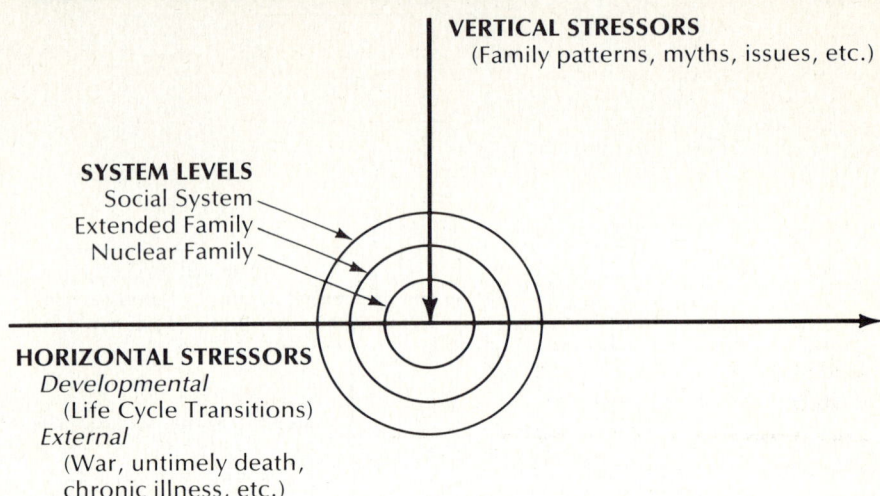

FIGURE 1.2 Horizontal and Vertical Stressors

Source: E. A. Carter & M. McGoldrick, THE FAMILY LIFE CYCLE: Figure 1.2, "Horizontal and Vertical Stresssors/The family life cycle and family therapy: An Overview." New York: Gardner Press, 1980, p. 10. Used with permission.

flow includes family patterns transmitted down the generations: the family attitudes, expectations, and issues. The horizontal flow includes the anxiety produced by stresses on the family as it moves forward through time, coping with changes of the family life cycle. It includes the predictable developmental stresses and the unpredictable events, such as an untimely death or the birth of a handicapped child (Carter & McGoldrick, 1980).

Given enough stress on the horizontal axis, any family will be dysfunctional. A small horizontal stress in which the vertical axis is full of intense stress will create great disruption in the system (Bowen, 1978).

All forms of abrupt or disjunctive changes are likely to cause crisis. Unless family members are adequately prepared, family developmental changes can result in crises (Glasser & Glasser, 1970). Knowledgeable professionals can help families anticipate and prepare for these changes.

Conclusion

The family, as a subsystem of the larger society, is subject to the changes taking place in that society. As a system, the family is built on interrelationships within as well as outside the family unit. All of these factors interact and overlap to produce stress and crisis.

The family's ability to deal with stress depends on prior experience and resources. Some families are more vulnerable than others and therefore need more help in coping with crises. Some families of exceptional children have the resources and experience to cope with this stressor; others do not. The next chapter focuses on the impact of an exceptional child on the family and on the coping strategies developed in various families.

References

Bane, M. J. (1976). *Here to stay*. New York: Basic Books.
Beal, E. W. (1982). Separation, divorce, and single-parent families. In E. A. Carter & M. McGoldrick (Eds.), *The family life cycle: A framework for family therapy*. New York: Gardner Press.
Beavers, W., & Voeller, M. N. (1983). Family models: Comparing and contrasting the Olson Circumplex Model with the Beavers Systems Model. *Family Process, 22*(9), 85–98.
Berger, E. H. (1981). *Parents as partners in education*. St. Louis: C. V. Mosby.
Bowen, M. (1978). *Family therapy in clinical practice*. New York: Jason Aronson.
Canino, D. J., & Reeve, R. E. (1980). General issues in working with parents of handicapped children. In R. R. Abidin (Ed.), *Parent education and intervention handbook*. Springfield, Ill.: Charles C Thomas.
Carter, E.A., & McGoldrick, M. (1980). The family life cycle and family therapy: An overview. In E. A. Carter & M. McGoldrick, (Eds.), *The family life cycle: A framework for family therapy*. New York: Gardner Press.
Chinn, P. C. (1974). *Child health maintenance*. St. Louis: C. V. Mosby.
Chinn, P. C., Drew, C. J., & Logan, D. R. (1979). *Mental retardation*. St. Louis: C. V. Mosby.
Chinn, P. C., Winn, J., & Walters, R. H. (1978). *Two-way talking with parents of special children*. St. Louis: C. V. Mosby.
Colon, F. (1982). The family life cycle of the multiproblem poor family. In E. A. Carter & R. McGoldrick (Eds.), *The family life cycle: A framework for family therapy*. New York: Gardner Press.
Epstein, N. B., Bishop, D. S., & Baldwin, L. M. (1982). McMaster model of family functioning: A view of the normal family. In F. Walsh (Ed.), *Normal family processes*. New York: The Guilford Press.
Eshleman, J. R. (1985). *The family* (4th ed.). Boston: Allyn and Bacon.
Eshleman, J. R. (1981). *The family* (3rd ed). Boston: Allyn and Bacon.
Gallagher, J. J., Beckman, P., & Cross, A. H. (1983). Families of handicapped children: Sources of stress and its ameliorization. *Exceptional Children 50*(1), 10–19.
Gibran, K. (1968). *The prophet*. New York: Alfred A. Knopf.
Gillies, J. (1974). *My needs, your needs, our needs*. Bergenfield, N.J.: New American Library.
Glasser, P. H., & Glasser, L. N. (1970). *Families in crisis*. New York: Harper & Row.

Hansen, D. A., & Hill, R. (1964). Families under stress. In H. T. Christensen (Ed.), *Handbook of marriage and the family* 782–819. Chicago: Rand McNally.

Hareven, T. K. (1982). American families in transition: Historical perspectives on change. In F. Walsh (Ed.), *Normal family processes*. New York: The Guilford Press.

Hetherington, E. M., Cox, M., & Cox, R. (1982). Effects of divorce on parents and children. In M. E. Lamb (Ed.), *Nontraditional familes: Parenting and child development*. Hillsdale, N.J.: Lawrence Erlbaum Associates.

Hill, R. (1958). Social stresses on the family. *Social Casework 39*, 139–150.

Holmes, T. H., & Rahe, R. H. (1967). The social readjustment rating scale. *Journal of Psychosomatic Research 11*, 213–218.

Joint Commission on Mental Health of Children. (1970). *Crisis in child mental health: Challenge for the 1970s*. New York: Harper & Row.

Karpowitz, D. H. (1980). A conceptualization of the American family. In M. J. Fine (Ed.), *Handbook on parent education*. New York: Academic Press.

LeMasters, E. E. (1974). *Parents in modern America*. Homewood, Ill.: Dorsey.

Leslie, G. R. (1967). *The family in social context*. New York: Oxford University Press.

Lillie, D. (1981). Educational and psychological strategies for working with parents. In J. D. Paul (Ed.), *Understanding and working with parents of children with special needs*. New York: Holt, Rinehart & Winston.

Luthman, S. G. (1974). *The dynamic family*. Palo Alto, Calif.: Science and Behavior Books.

McCubbin, H. I., & Patterson, J. M. (1982). Family adaptation to crises. In H. I. McCubbin, A. E. Cauble, & J. M. Patterson (Eds.), *Family stress, coping, and social support*. Springfield, Ill.: Charles C Thomas.

McGoldrick, M., & Carter, E. A. (1982). The family life cycle. In F. Walsh (Ed.), *Normal family processes*. New York: The Guilford Press.

Marion, R. L. (1981). *Educators, parents, and exceptional children*. Rockville, Md.: Aspen Systems.

Miller, S. M. (1970). The American lower classes: A typological approach. In P. H. Glasser & L. N. Glasser (Eds.), *Families in crisis*. New York: Harper & Row.

Mitchell, A. R. K. (1978). *Violence in the family*. East Sussex, England: Wayland Publishers.

Morris, W. (Ed.) (1981). *The American Heritage dictionary of the English language*. Boston: American Heritage and Houghton Mifflin.

Nimkoff, M. F. (1965). *Comparative family systems*. Boston: Houghton Mifflin.

Olson, D. H., Russell, C. S., & Sprenkle, D. H. (1983). Circumplex model of marital and family systems: VI. Theoretical update. *Family Process 22*(9), 69–83.

Olson, D. H., Sprenkle, D. H., & Russell, C. S. (1979). Circumplex model of marital and family systems: I. Cohesion and adaptability dimensions, family types, and clinical applications. *Family Process, 18*(1), 3–28.

Perls, F. S. (1969). *Gestalt therapy verbation*. Moab, Utah: Real People Press.

Playing both mother and father. (1985). *Newsweek* July 15 (3), 42–43.

Rabkin, J. G., & Struening, E. L. (1976). Life events, stress, and illness. *Science, 194*(3), 1013–1020.

Reiss, I. L. (1971). *The family system in America*. New York: Holt, Rinehart & Winston.

Rollins, B. C., & Thomas, D. L. (1979). Parental support, power and control techniques in the socialization of children. In W. R. Burr, R. Hill, F. I. Nye, & I. L.

Reiss (Eds.), *Contemporary theories about the family,* Vol. 1. New York: The Free Press.

Rose, E., & Hardman, M. L. (1981). The abused mentally retarded child. *Education and Training of the Mentally Retarded, 16*(2), 114–118.

Schaefer, E. S. (1975). Factors that impede the process of socialization. In M. J. Begab & S. A. Richardson (Eds.), *The mentally retarded and society: A social science perspective.* Baltimore: University Park Press.

Stinnett, N., & Birdsong, C. W. (1978). *The family and alternate life styles.* Chicago: Nelson Hall.

Taylor, D. (1983). Reflections on parenting: A multigenerational perspective. *Family Process, 22*(3), 341–346.

Turnbull, H. R. (1976). Report of the Parents' Committee: Families in crisis, families at risk. In T. D. Tjossem (Ed.), *Intervention strategies for high risk infants and young children.* Baltimore: University Park Press.

Walsh, F. (1982). Conceptualizations of normal family functioning. In F. Walsh (Ed.), *Normal family processes.* New York: The Guilford Press.

Yorburg, B. (1983). *Families and societies.* New York: Columbia University Press.

2

The Impact of Exceptional Children on the Family

One primary function of the family is providing a socially acceptable vehicle for producing and raising children. American society strongly believes that parenthood is an expected and enviable state; most couples share this value. Parents choose to have children for various reasons, and many children, of course, are unplanned. Only recently have couples openly expressed the choice to remain childless.

The prospect of parenthood can be positive or negative; it is frequently mixed. Couples' reactions to pregnancy depend on many factors: economic, emotional, and social. The primary factor, however, is the quality of the marital relationship.

Even when conditions are less than optimal, couples who view themselves with self-esteem and their relationship as mutually satisfying accept parenthood positively. On the other hand, if self-esteem and a satisfying relationship are lacking, the prospective parents are likely to view the situation negatively, in spite of other conditions (Chinn, Winn, & Walters, 1978).

The period of pregnancy can be one of joy or apprehension. Financial problems, physical discomfort and complications, as well as sexual adjustment, can create stress in the marital relationship. For many couples, however, pregnancy is a time of satisfaction and strengthens the marriage bond.

Prenatal attitudes are particularly important in determining the relationship between the mother and the child. Strong evidence indicates that the mother's overall reaction to the pregnancy and childbirth experience is an accurate predictor of maternal adaptation to parenthood. Prenatal attitudes also help structure early experiences with the infant, affecting attitudes toward parenting as well as adjustment to parenthood (Glass, 1983).

Prospective parents experience a wide range of emotions while awaiting the birth of a child (Suran & Rizzo, 1983). Often, they feel fulfillment and usually some anxiety regarding the birth process and potential problems. They always have various expectations about the kind of person the child will become. Even in cases of unwanted or stressful pregnancies, parents develop expectations and dreams about the unborn child. The actual birth of the child may have an impact on the family that is not commensurate with their expectations, however.

Impact of Birth

Few couples are prepared for the realities of parenthood. Glass (1983) reports that the birth of a first child can be "one of the most significant and stressful life events experienced by individuals" (p. 377). The advent of subsequent children may add to the family stress. Pregnancy and birth result in a permanent rearrangement of time schedules, emotional and economic resources, and marital interaction patterns (Chinn, Winn, & Walters, 1978).

The parents' attitudes and resources determine, to a great extent, the kind and level of impact they feel at the birth of a child. Another important determiner is the child, especially the degree to which that child fulfills the expectations of the parents. We can better understand families of exceptional children by examining the impact of the birth of a normal child as well as that of an abnormal child.

Normal Infant

"What did we do before the baby came?" is a question that parents frequently ask each other. Although it may be a welcome one, the baby does constitute an intrusion into the life of the family unit. The center of the family shifts as attention focuses on the newborn child. As an important development in the family life cycle, the addition of a child requires an adjustment in the family system. The family must make space for a child, assume parent roles, and realign relationships with the extended family to include parenting and grandparenting roles (see Chapter 1, Table 1.2). In addition, stress may be placed on the marital relationship and on the family's economic and social status.

Marital Relationship The birth of a child may draw a couple closer together as they share concerns, responsibilities, goals, and pleasures. On the other hand, the addition of a baby may cause discord and conflict. "The baby comes first" requires an adjustment in the amount and quality of time devoted to each parent by the other; sleepless nights contribute to fatigue and short tempers; and household tasks are increased and intensified.

Economic Status In many cases, the birth of a baby means the loss of an income. If the mother is career-oriented, she may resent the loss of opportunities and achievement as well as the loss of income. Even if she returns to work, the cost of child care is an additional burden.

Hospital costs, continued medical care, and food and clothing for the baby create a financial structure that is staggering. Many couples not prepared for this phenomenon may find themselves in a stressful situation even if they joyfully anticipated and received the baby.

Social Status The birth of a child brings about an immediate and dramatic change in the couple's life-style. The freedom to travel and to engage in an active social life will undoubtedly be curtailed. Because their friends may not have children and are not restricted in the same manner, couples may experience shifts in friendships. Housing needs may change and therefore neighborhood acquaintances have to be surrendered.

Although the negative aspects of parenthood are numerous, they are usually overshadowed by the excitement of the baby's first smile, first words, and first step. Most couples find that once the impact of birth is over, the joys are well worth the changes.

In sharp contrast to the fulfillment experienced by most parents, couples who have abnormal babies may find few of the typical joys that compensate for the frustrations and inconveniences imposed by a child (Chinn, Drew, & Logan, 1979). The impact of birth may be devastating and will require a life-time adjustment.

Abnormal Infant

It is important to recognize that a baby must be rather severely handicapped for the abnormality to be apparent at birth. Although slight physical defects may be detected immediately, mild learning and emotional problems, as well as indications of giftedness, are not apparent initially.

The birth of a handicapped child places the family in a cultural dilemma. Society views parenthood positively, but it views parenthood of a handicapped child negatively (Zuk, 1962). Awareness of society's ambivalence adds to the stress the family feels within itself.

The stress factors accompanying the birth of a normal child are intensified when the child is not normal. The marital relationship may suffer unduly from the added stresses of blame, guilt, and anxiety. Featherstone (1980, p. 91) identifies the process that may take place:

> A child's handicap attacks the fabric of a marriage in four ways. It excites powerful emotions in both parents. It acts as a dispiriting symbol of shared failure. It reshapes the organization of the family. It creates fertile ground for conflict.

The economic stress may be multiplied by additional hospital and medical costs. In some cases, extended surgery and prostheses are necessary.

The parents' social life could become nonexistent if they are unable to find appropriate babysitters or are reluctant to leave their child. They may be fearful of rejection by their friends.

Additional stresses are likely to occur in families of handicapped infants. In referring to common reactions and problems, it should be recognized that each family is unique in addressing these issues and also that scientific data in this area are scarce. Robinson and Robinson (1976) point out three reasons for this scarcity. First, it is futile to find too many common threads among families who constitute a group "only by virtue of a common quirk of fate" (p. 414). Second, many professionals working with families share a clinical orientation, tending to overgeneralize. Finally, much of the available research is based on parents seen in outpatient facilities, primarily white, middle-class mothers of young, severely handicapped children.

However, commonalities are observed in the initial impact of the birth of a handicapped child. Among those most frequently identified are shock, denial, and grief.

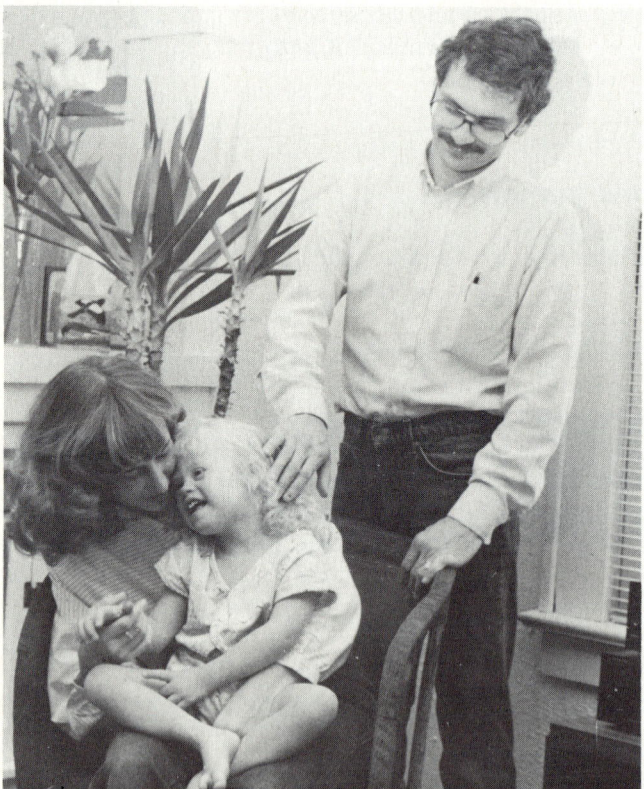

☐ *Although the initial reaction may be overwhelming, many parents accept and enjoy their handicapped child.*

Shock Although many parents eventually accept and enjoy their handicapped child, the initial reaction may be overwhelming. As one mother recalled, "I knew he had Down's Syndrome when they placed him on my stomach . . . when his condition was confirmed, I felt devastated" (Haac, 1984, p. 1). The stage of shock is likely to encompass feelings of anxiety, guilt, numbness, confusion, helplessness, anger, and despair (Hardman, Drew, & Egan, 1984). At this point, parents are less likely than at any other time to find the supportive services they need or to process information they receive. They may question their own worth or that of their child. Featherstone (1980, pp. 4–5) describes her experience when "the world fell in":

> Jody was born in late June 1972, while my husband Jay and I watched in exhausted amazement. Our older child, Liza, was then three years old. Although the baby was a month ahead of schedule, we felt no special concerns about him, because he weighed in at a healthy six and a quarter pounds and looked beautiful. We took him home after four days, infatuated with ourselves and our two wonderful children.
>
> Nine days later the world fell in: the doctor who had delivered Jody called to say that routine examination revealed a placenta infected with a disease called toxoplasmosis. Many women have this disease during pregnancy and bear totally healthy children. I was less lucky. Over the next year we learned that Jody was blind, hydrocephalic, and retarded, that he suffered from cerebral palsy and from seizures.
>
> Each week after that first telephone call brought new calamities, until we were almost numb with the pain. A specialist examined Jody's eyes and told us that they were seriously damaged: Jody would see little, if anything, of our world. Two weeks later the pediatrician noticed that his head was growing too fast. Another specialist confirmed the suspicions of the first doctor: fluid was accumulating inside Jody's skull, pressing against his brain. The infection had obviously spread beyond his eyes. Probably his brain was damaged, too. . . . I wondered whether his life held any chance of happiness. I wondered whether it was worth living.

Denial Even when they are told that their baby is not normal, some parents deny that there is a problem. Others may believe the child will outgrow the problem. One mother expressed the thought that "as soon as he begins to walk, everything will be all right." Part of the denial process may involve seeking various professional opinions, hoping to find one that disagrees with the original diagnosis.

The denial stage is especially counterproductive because it delays treatment and adjustment. It may last for weeks or for years and can ultimately result in unrealistic planning for the child.

Grief The grief stage results from the mourning reaction to the loss of the expected normal child and a simultaneous need to adjust to the infant actually born to the parents (Solnit & Stark, 1961). The fear of death of an abnormal child intensifies the reaction, so that parents withdraw from the relationship they had established with the expected child, hoping the baby will survive but preparing for the child's death at the same time (Opirhory & Peters, 1982).

The grieving process described by Kübler-Ross (1970) is frequently used to predict the stages that parents of handicapped infants will experience. These stages are denial, anger, bargaining, depression, and acceptance. Examples of this progression are projected in Figure 2.1.

In a study of the birth of sick or handicapped infants, Trout (1983) found that many parents were grieving for their lost child even as they stared at their living—but sick or handicapped—newborn. The feelings of grief are complicated by the demands of the new baby and by feelings of guilt. Olshanky (1962) views chronic sorrow and grief as natural reactions to the birth of a handicapped child. Gath (1977), in a study of babies with Down's Syndrome, reported that grief was evident in all parents at the first interview and that 90 percent still mentioned grief two years later.

Farber (1960) identified two types of crisis that parents of mentally retarded children experienced. Grief is an initial crisis precipitated at the time the child is diagnosed as handicapped. The extreme initial impact on the family is regarded as a **tragic crisis**. The second type of crisis is regarded as a **crisis of role organization**. This type of crisis suggests an inability to cope with the child over a long period of time.

Role reorganization can occur at two different points in the parent-child relationship. It can follow the impact of birth, as parents realize that their problems and adjustment are ongoing. It can also occur when parents do not become aware that their child is exceptional until the child is older.

Impact of Child and Adolescent

> Children represent both the celebration of all that is joyous in our world, and the greatest single challenge for parents, teachers, students, and others who work with children. (Hanson & Reynolds, 1980, p. vii)

As children progress from one developmental stage to the next, their parents observe them with pride, anxiety, and sometimes alarm. Parents have expectations based on societal, familial, and experiential standards. When children's behavior deviates from the established standards, family crises may develop.

Children and adolescents affect every family. The kind and degree of impact differ with the characteristics of the child as well as with the structure and resources of the family. Reactions and coping strategies can vary widely, depending on whether the child is normal, severely handicapped, mildly handicapped, or gifted.

FIGURE 2.1 Components of the Grieving Process Continuum

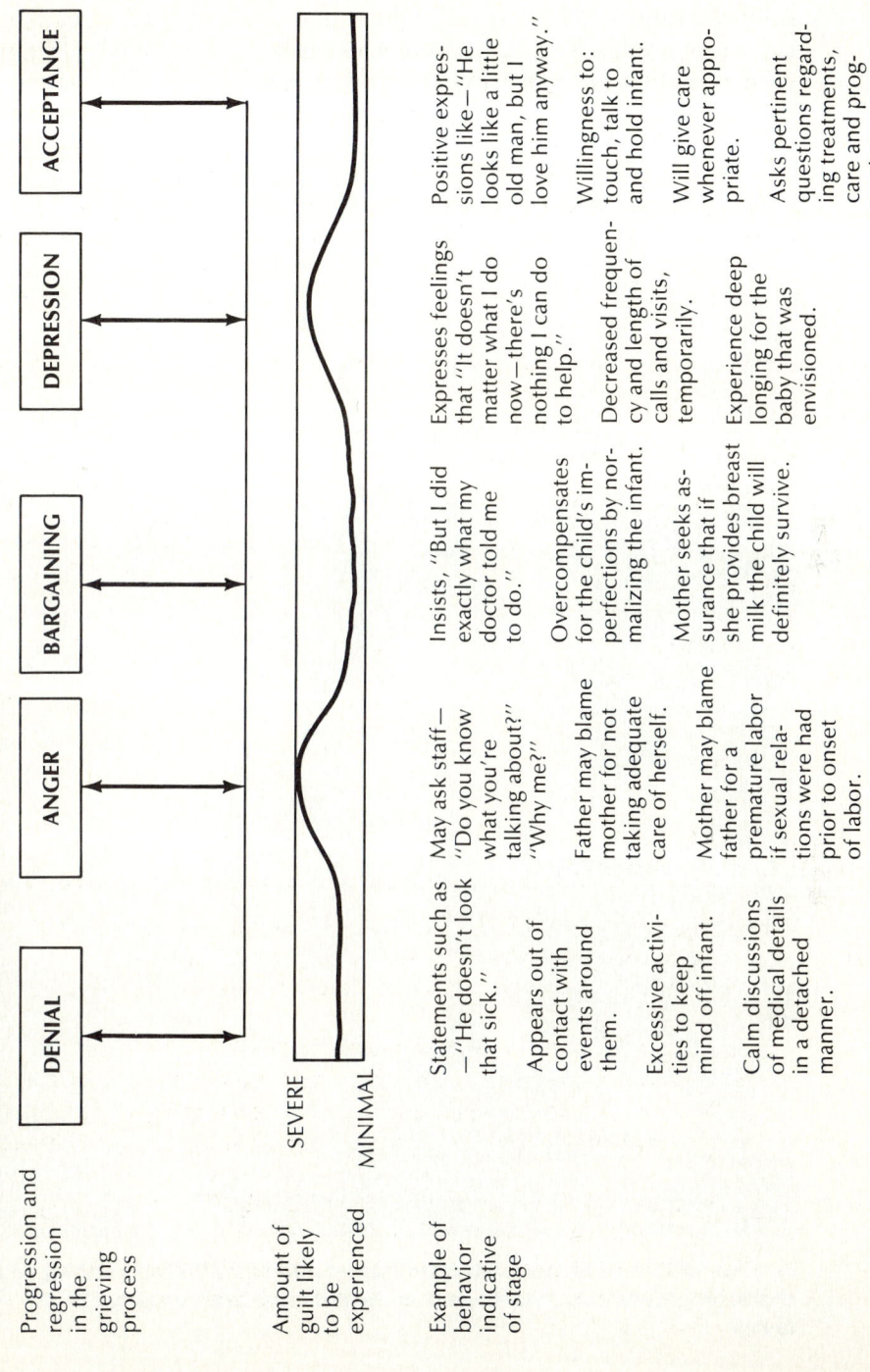

Source: Opirhory, G. & Peters, G. A. Counseling intervention strategies for families with the less than perfect newborn. *The Personnel and Guidance Journal, 60*(8), 1982 451–455. Copyright AACD. Reprinted with permission. No further reproduction authorized without further permission of AACD.

Normal Child and Adolescent

☐ **Early Childhood** The course of physical development in the young child centers around the skills of balance, locomotion, and prehension. Bromwich (1981, p. 334) identifies several issues of concern to parents during this developmental change:

> At around fifteen months developmental age, many parents feel at a loss in dealing with the child's assertive and negative behavior.
> In some homes, the physical safety of the child becomes a concern when the child begins to be mobile and starts walking.
> Mothers' feelings of isolation tend to increase. Some mothers feel "cooped up" with the child who "gets into everything!"

Cognition and language development occur at a rapid pace. Parents are aware that their children know far more than they did. Social background is

☐ *The impact an exceptional child has on a family differs according to the characteristics of the child as well as the structure and resources of the family.*

a strong variable in language learning; lower-class adults do not speak to their children as often or with as large a vocabulary as do middle-class adults. Language plays an important role in the process of thinking, especially in abstract thought (Tulkin & Kagan, 1972).

Middle Childhood The period of middle childhood is dominated by the school experience. During this period, children absorb a tremendous amount of cultural information as well as basic educational skills. They are constantly evaluated, grouped, and labeled during the school years. Although the label may have nothing to do with their potential, it does affect friendships and social status (Hanson & Reynolds, 1980).

Adolescence Adolescence, marking the transition from childhood to adulthood, is a period of wide variances in emotional, intellectual, and physical development. Although much of the development centers around school experiences, the family is the primary influence in the development of a value system. Rice (1978) identifies five factors related to the family and values: (1) the degree of parental warmth, acceptance, and trust; (2) the frequency and intensity of parent-teen interaction and communication; (3) the type and degree of discipline used; (4) the role-model parents offer the child; (5) and the independence opportunities the parents provide.

Adolescents experience many crises (or events perceived as crises). Peer acceptance is extremely important at this stage and may call for behavior contradictory to the values established earlier.

This is also a difficult time for parents. The family life cycle undergoes a tremendous change as the adolescent becomes more independent; there is a renewed focus on marital and career issues. In addition to the normal developmental factors, crises may arise concerning the adolescent and drug or alcohol abuse, sexual freedom and pregnancy, academic problems, and school dropout.

Crises, as well as triumphs, are present in every child's life. Families of children and adolescents, normal and exceptional, are affected by these events. In addition to the pressures and demands all parents experience, parents of exceptional children and adolescents must learn to deal with the exceptionality themselves, help the child and other family members deal with it, procure services for the child and, in the case of a severely handicapped child, continue the process for a lifetime.

Severely Handicapped Child and Adolescent

☐ Parents of a severely handicapped child will have many adjustments to make as the baby grows into childhood, adolescence, and adulthood. Because of their extreme physical and/or mental impairment, these children are not expected to become independent and to leave home. Such dependence represents a drastic alteration in the family life cycle. The impact felt relates to expectations, family reorganization, prolonged and intensive care, provision of services, and fear of the future.

Expectations   It is one thing to realize that an infant is less than perfect; it is quite another to watch the lack of progress and to compare the handicapped child with other normal, developing children. Parents of handicapped children are reminded of their thwarted expectations at numerous milestones. One mother told of her handicapped son's sixteenth birthday and of the sudden thought that came to her with a shock: he would be learning to drive if he were normal.

Parents of severely handicapped children do not know what to expect. The basic assumptions do not apply:

> Although parenthood is difficult, there are a number of precedents, support systems, and social institutions that provide structure and reinforcement most of the time. Most parents usually can assume that their children will fit the expectations of their particular culture, grow up to be competent citizens who share in the responsibilities and the benefits of the society, find satisfying and remunerative work, marry and produce children of their own, and along the way, receive an adequate public education. These are the basic assumptions of life. Parents of handicapped children can make no assumptions. (Schulz, 1982, p. 17)

Family Reorganization   Farber (1975, p. 252) refers to the presence of a severely handicapped child in the family as a factor in the arrest of the family life cycle. Role expectations are modified in the following ways:

> 1. In interaction with their children, parents tend to assign a status to each child commensurate with the capabilities they impute to him.
>   a. The roles embodied in the status are classified on the basis of age grading. By definition, normally, mental age is approximately equal to chronological age.
>   b. Age grading in a culture is regarded more as a psychological and social activity than as a chronological variable, e.g., the chronologically middle aged severely retarded individual is generally regarded as a "boy" or "girl" by those with whom he interacts.
> 2. As the child proceeds in his life career, the parents normally tend to revise their self-concepts and roles. With respect to their normal children, ideally, parents continually redefine their roles, obligations, and values to adjust to the changing role of the child. With respect to their retarded children, the parental role is fairly constant. Regardless of his birth order in the family, the severely handicapped child eventually becomes the youngest child socially. A very severely handicapped child at home would not engage in dating and courtship, belong to organizations, seek part-time employment, or take part in other activities characteristic of adolescents. In his progressive movement to the youngest-child status,

the severely retarded child would not merely slow down movement in the family cycle but also prevent the development of the later stages in the cycle.

Prolonged and Intensive Care The diapers, the feeding, the dressing, and other signs of the additional work of infancy remain with the family of a severely handicapped child. The care needs of handicapped children do not diminish as they do for other children (Michaelis, 1980).

In reviewing the research on the impact of a cerebral palsied child on the family unit, the hardships are categorized as altered relationships with friends, major changes in family activities, medical concerns, intrafamily strains, specialized child care needs, and time commitments (McCubbin, Cauble & Patterson, 1982). In caring for a physically handicapped child, family responsibilities and tasks shift in response to the child's changing medical needs and developmental needs.

Parents of severely handicapped children experience a major shift in the family life cycle at a time when children normally leave home. Residential facilities may be available for some adolescents; others remain at home and require parental care into adulthood. When this situation occurs, middle-aged parents do not enjoy the freedom experienced by their peers or the relief from physical and financial responsibility to be expected in midlife.

Provision of Services The needs of severely handicapped children and adolescents are overwhelming. In addition to educational services, they may need treatment of medical problems from pediatricians or neurologists; sensory handicaps require treatment from opthamologists and audiologists; physical problems may require extensive therapeutic intervention from orthopedists, physical therapists, and occupational therapists; language deficits require the services of speech and language therapists; and, as they grow older, they will need vocational trainers, counselors, and evaluators (Lyon & Preis, 1983).

Families frequently require help in determining the services needed and in locating the various agencies that are available. Without help, the services may be delayed and valuable time lost.

Fear of the Future Many parents have reported that the uncertainty of their severely handicapped child's future has caused the family deep concern and stress. Parents at this life cycle stage experience greater parent burnout, less support, less community acceptance, fewer services, and more isolation than do parents at earlier life cycle stages (Turnbull & Brotherson, 1984).

When adult group homes are available, parents are concerned about the adequacy of care and the transition process. If institutionalization is considered, feelings of guilt may arise. If the handicapped adult remains in the home, parents worry about the availability of care after their death. Legal provisions are difficult and complicated.

Although the problems and changes encountered by families of severely and moderately handicapped children seem to be overwhelming, such families frequently find satisfaction and joy in raising their children. The transition is expressed by one mother in a personal communication to the author:

> When Shannon was born Jack and I were both so shocked and disappointed, but now I can say I don't think I could love any child as much as I do Shannon. She has so much personality. She is so sweet and loving. She's Shannon, a unique individual. She has taught me the meaning of love. She has taught me about acceptance and patience. I no longer fear raising Shannon. I'm looking forward to watching her grow and being there to help along the way. (D. Summers, personal communication, August 8, 1981)

Mildly Handicapped Child and Adolescent

☐ Because of the early and sustained adjustments required of families of severely handicapped children and adolescents, much more research relates to this group than to families of mildly handicapped people. Seligman (1979) reports that significant gaps exist in the literature on unique problems faced by parents of mildly handicapped children. Nevertheless, some evidence indicates that the child with a mild handicap has more severe adjustment problems arising from disturbed parent-child relationships than does the child with a severe handicap (Ross, 1964). In addition, the visibility of a pronounced handicap makes it difficult to deny; parents may be tempted to overlook a mild handicap or to pretend it does not exist. The impact felt by the family of a mildly handicapped child or adolescent revolves around the discovery of the problem, the nature of the problem, the cause of the problem, and the treatment of the problem.

Discovery of the Problem For most handicapped children, the problem is not obvious. Differences may first become apparent to teachers and parents when children do not develop physically, socially, emotionally, or intellectually according to expectations (Paul, 1983). For many parents, the actual problem is not recognized until the child is in school and is compared with other children. The discovery may come as a surprise to parents who are not knowledgable about normal child development or who have no basis for comparison. Mild mental retardation may not manifest itself until the child is in school, fails academically, and is evaluated and declared retarded by the school psychologist (Chinn, Drew, & Logan, 1979).

In many instances, parents suspect that a problem exists and may be relieved to have a name for it. On the other hand, a label is not always helpful and may be difficult to accept. One mother, who suspected that her child was deaf and even reported her suspicions to the pediatrician, reacted with hostility to the diagnosis of a severe sensorineural loss. She recalls:

> I had a good cry by myself at home that night, then set about my task of convincing the rest of the family that it was true. This was difficult, particularly with one set of grandparents who were convinced that we should only rent hearing aids and "wait and see." (Liversidge, 1979, p. 159)

A relational problem may precede the discovery of a mild handicap. Learning disabled children, for example, are usually not identified during the early developmental period. Early symptoms are impulsivity, irritability, and limited attention span; not until the child is older do symptoms related to perception, conceptualization, language, and memory become apparent to the family (Faerstein, 1981). Because of the behavior problems, the family may have reacted adversely to the child even before a diagnosis is made.

When the discovery of a handicap is unexpected, it can have a dramatic effect on the family. Osman (1982, p. 44) presents an example:

> Diana Harris was the child of professional parents who had chosen to limit their family to one. They were devoted to Diana and had high hopes for her, so it was a crushing blow when her first-grade teacher told the Harrises that Diana was not keeping up with her class. Her parents were amazed, having assumed that Diana was easily as bright as her peers. Since she was their only child, though, they had no basis for comparison.

In many cases, parents are not surprised when a child has trouble learning. They can relate the difficulties to problems they experienced themselves or to those other family members experienced.

One advantage inherent in later discovery of a problem is that families have, in most instances, formed a close tie with the child; infancy and early childhood were not marred by the realization that the child was handicapped. A strong family bond is thus likely to be in place; the child has been accepted as a family member without a handicap.

Nature of the Problem Even with mild handicaps, the type of problem represented helps determine the impact on the family. Physical and sensory problems are visible; learning and emotional problems are not and may, therefore, be less acceptable. Society in general appears to be less tolerant of such hidden handicaps.

When parents are informed that their child is retarded, the label itself is difficult to accept. On hearing the label, parents may acknowledge the condition or they may resort to a variety of defense mechanisms in order to help their egos cope with the problem (Chinn, Drew, & Logan, 1979). The initial impact may result in a transient stress disorder, or it may have a permanent debilitating effect on the entire family.

In describing a child with learning disabilities, Osman (1982) reports that "Danny's personality was even more of a problem to the family than the mild-to-moderate learning difficulties for which I had been seeing him" (p. 33).

Since social and interactive factors are associated with learning disabilities (Whitford, Chapman, & Boersma, 1982), implications for family upheaval are clear.

Parents of children who have communication problems are caught in a vicious circle of breakdown in communication. Webster (1979, p. 149) cites the premises on which this assumption is based:

> (1) Wherever there is a speech or hearing problem there is some degree of breakdown in communication.
> (2) This breakdown leads to difficulties in interpersonal relationships.
> (3) Difficulties in interpersonal relationships lead to further breakdown in communication.

When a child has a sensory or a physical handicap, parents learn to cope with a problem of which they are constantly aware. The home environment may have to be modified or prostheses provided and maintained. Chronic illnesses or birth defects may create more family stress if guilt or blame is involved.

Chronic illnesses of various types appear to have impacts of great variability. Epilepsy, for example, has a particular set of characteristics that distinguishes it from other chronic illnesses (Ferrari, Matthews, & Barabas, 1983). The unpredictability of seizures and the high degree of passivity and unassertive behavior of epileptic children distinguish this condition from other chronic illnesses.

Ross (1964, p. 139) places parents of emotionally disturbed children and adolescents in a unique position:

> The exceptional condition of the retarded, blind, or physically handicapped child is ordinarily the result of factors which are independent of the relationship between child and parent. When the relationship becomes affected, it does so as a consequence of the child's special condition. While disturbed parent-child relationships may thus *follow* a physical disability, they are usually thought to *precede* an emotional disorder. Current psychodynamic theory views such disorders as having their origin in often subtle interaction effects involving the relationship between parent and child.

The nature of the handicap is a major factor in determining the impact of a mildly handicapped child on the family. The distinctive effects appear to be related to visibility of the handicap, status of the label, behaviors associated with the handicap, physical accommodations required, and relation to the origin of the handicap.

Cause of the Problem Three groups of children and adolescents with learning problems can be categorized as mildly handicapped: learning disabled, educable mentally retarded, and emotionally disturbed. Although the specific cause of the problem is often unknown for these children, biological factors, heredity, and environment have been cited as causes of all three conditions (Lerner, 1981). The cause of the problem, or parents' perception of the cause, contributes to the degree of impact on the family.

Many parents believe that the blame for the child's handicap rests with them. They may recall a common event of childhood, such as rolling off a bed, and attach undue significance to it because of the child's handicap. They may think that the handicap could have been averted if more financial resources had been available. They may even harbor feelings of guilt for some past wrongdoing and view the handicapped child as punishment. Couples who have had marital problems, separation, or divorce frequently attribute their child's maladjustment to the attending stress.

In some cases, parents are realistic in their belief that they are responsible, at least in part, for their child's condition. Abortion attempts, drug and alcohol abuse, automobile accidents resulting in head injuries, failure to recognize serious illnesses, and physical abuse may be contributing factors to handicapping conditions (Robinson & Robinson, 1976). Whether the responsibility is real or imagined, guilt and/or rejection may result.

Gardner (1979) reports that most parents of children with leukemia, cystic fibrosis, cerebral palsy, and brain injury exhibit at one time or another inappropriate guilt reactions concerning their child's illness. He suggests that the self-blame be interpreted as an attempt to gain control over the situation and used as a means to increase parent involvement.

Parents of emotionally disturbed children and adolescents, in particular, have been blamed for causing their child's problem. Ross (1964) states that "parents, and particularly mothers, play a crucial role in the development of emotional disturbances of children" (p. 146). As the parent of an autistic child, Warren (1978, p. 195) refutes this claim:

> No known factors in the psychological environment of a child have been shown to cause autism.
>
> That means we didn't do it. . . . It means that careful, objective, scientific people have carried out study after study, test after test, interview after interview; and have written paper after paper in journal after journal which show that we, the parents of autistic children, are just ordinary people. Not any crazier than others. Not "refrigerator parents" any more than others. Not cold intellectuals, any more than others. Not neurotic or psychopathic or sociopathic or any of those words that have been made up.

When handicaps are physical in nature, knowledge of the cause may lead to treatment of the problem. When handicaps are cognitive or emotional in nature, knowledge of the cause may bring some relief or understanding. In most cases, however, identifying the precise cause makes little difference in the life of the child. The most dramatic and lasting difference is made when parents and professionals accept the problem and take positive steps to remedy it.

Treatment of the Problem When parents realize that their child is handicapped, their first question is likely to be: What can we do about it? Sometimes, they will seek a cure; in most cases, the prospects for a complete cure are remote.

Many parents are confused and find that the professionals they encounter are unable to give advice beyond their own areas of expertise (Chinn, Drew, & Logan, 1979). Finding out what resources are available is the first step toward treatment.

A variety of services are available for mildly handicapped children and their families. They may be eligible for medical, educational, financial, and other social services provided through a broad network of national, state, and local organizations (Hardman, Drew, & Egan, 1984). Parent groups have been established to represent almost every type of disability and are helpful in providing direct services, mutual support, and assistance in locating treatment.

At the national level, a great deal of information can be obtained from the National Center for Handicapped Children and Youth. State departments of education provide information concerning identification and placement of handicapped children. If the child's problem has been discovered by local school personnel, an individual education program (IEP) will be developed by a team, including the parents.

The impact of the mildly handicapped child is much more positive when the family is satisfied with the treatment and educational programming provided. Fortunately, if parents are not satisfied, they have legal recourse to insure an appropriate education (see Chapter 4).

Gifted Child and Adolescent

> If I were to say that I had a retarded or physically handicapped child, people would believe me. No one would resent me, and most reactions would be sympathetic. Having a gifted child, however, I know I do better keeping quiet. People wouldn't believe me, and they would resent me. "Another bragging mother" I would be called.... (Coleman, 1982, p. 47)

It would be a misrepresentation of the literature on gifted children to state that gifted children are typically a problem to their families. It is also misleading to assume that gifted and talented children do not present unique challenges and problems to their families (Colangelo & Dettmann, 1983).

According to Ross (1964), child-rearing behavior of parents is largely based on expectations derived from their image of the normal or average child. When intellectual endowment is unusually high, the exceptional condition does present potential problems to the parents and to the child.

In a review of literature on parents of gifted children, four main issues emerge that are of interest to educators (Dettmenn & Colangelo, 1980, pp. 158–159):

1. First, parents are confused about their role in identifying the gifted child.
2. A second general issue reflects the deep concern and anxiety parents have with their gifted child's achievement.
3. A multitude of issues in the literature revolve around parental problems and concerns with family relationships and gifted children.
4. Finally, the issue of parents' relationships with the school was frequently referred to in the literature.

Thus, the impact of the gifted child on the family will be related to identification, achievement, family relationships, and school relationships.

Identification A review of the literature on the identification of gifted children reveals two parental concerns (Colangelo & Dettmann, 1983). First, what is the role of parents in the identification process? Second, how can parents know if their child is gifted?

Increasing evidence indicates that parents are accurate identifiers of young gifted children. A study of 465 kindergartners indicated that, at the

☐ *There is increasing evidence that parents are accurate identifiers of young gifted children.*

kindergarten level, parents are more able than teachers to assess their children's abilities (Ciha, Harris, Hoffman, & Potter, 1979). Although the study does not rule out the possibility that parents tend to overestimate their own child's ability, parental opinion of a child's academic potential is an effective means of screening at this level. It is a source of useful information at all levels.

Some parents feel that identification is the school's responsibility; others want to be involved in the process. Confusion arises over the parents' lack of knowledge about characteristics of gifted children and about identification procedures. Colangelo and Dettmann (1983, p. 24) suggest that:

> ... it is worthwhile for parents and educators to realize that giftedness is not a nine-to-three phenomenon and that giftedness can manifest itself in a variety of environments. A sharing of information between parents and educators can enhance the identification process. Also, parents will be most effective in the identification process when educators provide them with specific criteria that can be used for identification.

Parents who suspect that their children are gifted must be prepared to act as advocates for them (Maeroff, 1980).

Another issue related to identification is the effect of labeling on gifted children and their families. Fisher (1981) claims that labels of giftedness serve (1) as a justification for parents to make additional demands on the school; (2) to increase parents' expectations, aspirations, and demands on their children; (3) to increase parents' tolerance for unusual behavior and requests on the part of the gifted child; (4) to disrupt families in which there were nongifted siblings; and (5) to affect how parents view their child and their responsibility to the child.

The label itself is not anxiety producing or anxiety reducing. Rather, the parents' interpretation of what the label means for the child and for the family affects the power of the label (Fisher, 1981).

Achievement The Marland Report, in a study of gifted education, revealed that "a high percentage of dropouts were actually gifted children who left school because of boredom with a lockstep system geared to the average child" (Lyon, 1982, p. 220). A substantial proportion of gifted children never achieve the level of performance predicted by their high scores on intelligence tests.

One factor that predicts underachievement is substantial family conflict (Kirk & Gallagher, 1983). Parental pressure has been associated with both achievement and underachievement. Parents who have low expectations and who do not encourage and support their gifted child are more common among underachievers than are parents with excessive expectations (Fine, 1977). Gallagher (1975, p. 353) describes the plight of the gifted underachiever:

> One way to look at the underachiever is that he is in the middle of a circle of barbed wire . . . and all of his environment has contributed to the building of that

wire circle—his family, his friends, his school, and, most important, himself. Any movements that he attempts to get out of the barbed wire are going to be painful to him.

An investigation of high achievers indicates that they almost invariably held special family positions. Albert (1980) stresses that the child's early observed giftedness helps orient a family toward the child in a special way.

Ross (1972) claims that parents who are able to share confidences, ideas, and decisions with their children and to encourage their development without pressuring them tend to have children whose achievement is commensurate with their abilities. Healthy family relations and parent-child interaction contribute to the maximum achievement level of the gifted child.

Family Relationships   The role the gifted child assumes in the family system has an impact on the family and a reciprocal impact on the child. Hackney (1981, pp. 52–53) identifies five areas in which parents felt the family was affected by the presence of a gifted child:

1. *Normal roles in the family were altered.* Parents experienced difficulty in clarifying differences between parental roles and child roles and had problems determining whether the child should be treated as a child or as an adult.
2. *Parents' feelings about themselves were affected.* Many parents have feelings of fear, guilt, and a heavy sense of responsibility.
3. *The family was required to make special adaptations.* Many parents found that their lives were shaped by the presence of the gifted child; families have to make concessions in their lives to accommodate the gifted member.
4. *Special family/neighborhood issues were produced.* The gifted child may be missing many social experiences with peers; the child may be rejected because of maturity differences.
5. *Special family/school issues were produced.* Once the child is labeled, the responsibilities of the school and home are intensified, magnified and made more critical.

Parents have also indicated changes in the marital relationship, lack of communication with each other concerning standards for the gifted child, and fears about potential maladjustment of the child. The chief concern is that parents feel inadequate to provide for their gifted child (Dettmann & Colangelo, 1980).

Ross (1964) claims that the difference between the intellectual capacity of the gifted child and other family members will determine the degree of the problem. When the difference is dramatic, the child may be rejected by the family. The lack of understanding and the agonizing confusion possible in such situations are expressed by Potok (1972, p. 196) in his story of a very talented boy who was rejected by his father:

Asher, I know you don't want trouble. I am not accusing you, God forbid, of being an evil person. But there is something inside you I don't understand. It will bring trouble. Look at the trouble it has already brought. I don't know what you are. You are my own son, and I don't know what you are. I am ashamed of my own son.

Most parents experience pride and joy in raising a gifted child. One father described it as easy:

> Being the parent of an intelligent gifted child must certainly be much easier than ordinary parenting. There is pride, of course, in his accomplishments and a good feeling in that his teachers and peers think well of him. He has a sense of humor that is helping all of us survive the trauma of adolescence. Now that he is fifteen, he is essentially responsible for his own development. As parents, we're here to help but he comes and goes as he needs to with only token nagging on our part. He's developed the toughness necessary to stand up to his parents, yet he manages to keep the channels of communication open. He is still largely unformed but jelling fast as a personality. (T. E. Swanson, personal communication, June 15, 1984)

Moore (1982, p. 11) describes her "total experience" in raising a gifted child as positive but also adds:

> Sara's intellectual gifts have not been an outright bonus. Along with the good has come internal and external conflict in the short span of ten years. Parents alone have the motivation and intuitive knowledge of the child necessary to resolve these conflicts with the help of experts. Informed parents are the child's chief advocate and primary educator.

School Relationships   Gifted and talented children are likely to enter school with enthusiasm. If they enter a school system in which there are programs designed to meet their needs, they may keep their enthusiasm throughout their school years. Frequently, however, gifted and talented students become disenchanted for lack of challenging educational opportunities (Karnes & Karnes, 1982). A parent describes the impact of this situation:

> We, as parents, are forced to watch our children's initial enthusiasm for learning change to boredom, behavior problems, physical and emotional distress, and finally inertia. They learned early that the system only demanded regurgitation, and that is all they gave. Many of these children have reached maturity while the educators have foresworn concrete action for further study. We have witnessed and paid heavily in tax dollars for the damages wrought on our college campuses when the frustration level of students has reached the breaking point. They have asked only that their education be brought into the twentieth century. Instead, we have maintained a system conceived in the nineteenth century and perpetuated by the reluctance of society to change. (Kennard, 1977, p. v)

Hackney (1981, p. 53) asks several relevant questions: "How is it that the school's well-intended effort can turn the school/home relationships into an adversary relationship? Why do some parents resist the school's advice? Why do some gifted children simply not respond to the school's special programs?"

Sanborn (1979, p. 398) suggests considering three generalizations when schools are working with parents of gifted children:

1. There are often very strong differences of opinions among parents and children concerning desirability of courses of action to take in response to giftedness or talent.
2. Parents are more likely to take action on suggestions made by the school when these suggestions are highly specific and instructions are clear.
3. Parents are likely to take action on school suggestions which are clearly predicated on specific knowledge of their child.

The school can be a valuable resource to parents who want their child to have the best education possible. Parents of gifted children, on the other hand, have in most cases contributed to their child's giftedness. They know their child better than anyone else does. Parents and schools working together can provide excellence in education for students who are gifted.

Conclusion

In American society, as in other societies, parenthood is generally perceived as an expected, positive, and rewarding part of life. The expectations, however, are that the child born into the family will be healthy, will develop according to normal child development standards, will achieve in school at an average pace, and will behave in a manner consistent with family and societal patterns. If the child does not fit the expected norms, the family is affected in two ways.

First, the family as a unit feels the impact of a child who is different. Even if the difference is a positive one, changes occur in family roles and adaptations in family responsibilities. If the difference is viewed as negative, the status of the entire family may be affected; difficult decisions and commitments may be required.

The second ramification deals with society's reaction to an exceptional child. Parents of exceptional children are sometimes viewed as inferior (or as claiming to be superior) and therefore to be pitied or resented. Although society has provided services for exceptional children, adolescents, and adults, parents frequently find themselves in an intimidating position, left to their own ability to find and bargain for services. The price paid for such services is often the acquisition of a label that further differentiates the exceptional person from the average person.

How do families deal with the discrepancy between expectations and reality? The fact that many families do accept and enjoy their exceptional children proves that patterns of acceptance have been established. The fact that some families are unable to accommodate the exceptional child indicates that the patterns do not always work. Chapter 3 explores concepts of acceptance, rejection, and adjustment.

References

Albert, R. S. (1980). Family positions and the attainment of eminence: A study of special family positions and special family experiences. *Gifted Child Quarterly, 24*(2), 87–95.

Bromwich, R. M. (1981). *Working with parents and infants.* Baltimore: University Park Press.

Chinn, P. C., Drew, C. J., & Logan, D. R. (1979). *Mental retardation.* St. Louis: The C. V. Mosby Co.

Chinn, P. C., Winn, J., & Walters, R. H. (1978). *Two-way talking with parents of special children.* St. Louis: The C. V. Mosby Co.

Ciha, T. E., Harris, R., Hoffman, C., & Potter, M. W. (1979). Parents as identifiers of gifted, ignored but accurate. In L. Baruth & M. Burggraf, (Eds.), *Counseling parents of exceptional children,* 206–209. Guilford, Conn.: Special Learning Corp.

Colangelo, N., & Dettmann, D. F. (1983). A review of research on parents and families of gifted children. *Exceptional Children, 50*(1), 20–27.

Coleman, D. (1982). Parenting the gifted: Is this a job for superparent? *G/C/T 25*(2), 47–50.

Dettman, D. F., & Colangelo, N. (1980). A functional model for counseling parents of gifted students. *Gifted Child Quarterly, 24*(4), 158–161.

Faerstein, L. M. (1981). Stress and coping in families of learning disabled children: A literature review. *Journal of Learning Disabilities, 14*(7), 420–423.

Farber, B. (1975). Family adaptions to severely mentally retarded children. In M. J. Begab & S. A. Richardson (Eds.), *The mentally retarded and society: A social science perspective.* Baltimore: University Park Press.

Farber, B. (1960). Perceptions of crisis and related variables in the impact of a retarded child on the mother. *Journal of Health and Human Behavior, 1*(2), 108–118.

Ferrari, M., Matthews, W. S., & Barabas, G. (1983). The family and the child with epilepsy. *Family Process, 22*(1), 53–59.

Featherstone, H. (1980). *A difference in the family.* New York: Penguin Books.

Fine, M. J., (1977). Facilitating parent-child relationships for creativity. *Gifted Child Quarterly, 21*(4), 487–500.

Fisher, E. (1981). The effect of labelling on gifted children and their families. *Roeper Review, 3,* 49–51.

Gallagher, J. (1975). *Teaching the gifted child* (2nd ed.). Boston: Allyn and Bacon.

Gardner, R. A. (1979). The guilt reactions of children with severe physical disease. In L. Baruth & M. Burggraf (Eds.), *Counseling parents of exceptional children*, 189–197. Guilford, Conn.: Special Learning Corp.

Gath, A. (1977). The impact of an abnormal child upon the parents. *American Journal of Psychiatry, 130,* 405–410.

Glass, J. (1983). Pre-birth attitudes and adjustment to parenthood: When 'Preparing for the Worst' helps. *Family Relations, 32*(3), 377–386.

Haac, L. A. (1984). New help, new hope, for handicapped children. *Developments, 9*(3), 1–6.

Hackney, H. (1981). The gifted child, the family, and the school. *Gifted Child Quarterly, 25*(2), 51–54.

Hanson, R. A., & Reynolds, R. (1980). *Child development.* St. Paul: West Publishing Co.

Hardman, M. L., Drew, C. J., & Egan, M. W. (1984). *Human exceptionality.* Boston: Allyn and Bacon.

Karnes, F. A., & Karnes, M. R. (1982). Parents and schools: Educating gifted and talented children. *Elementary School Journal, 82*(3), 236–248.

Kennard, C. (1977). Forward–by a parent. In J. L. Delp & R. A. Martinson, *A handbook for parents of gifted and talented* (2nd ed.). Ventura, Calif.: Ventura County Superintendent of Schools office.

Kirk, S. A., & Gallagher, J. J. (1983). *Educating exceptional children* (2nd ed.). Boston: Houghton Mifflin.

Kübler-Ross, E. (1970). *On death and dying.* New York: Macmillan.

Lerner, J. W. (1981). *Learning disabilities.* Boston: Houghton Mifflin.

Liversidge, E. B., & Grana, G. M. (1979). A hearing impaired child in the family—the parent's perspective. In L. Baruth & M. Burggraf (Eds.), *Counseling parents of exceptional children.* Guilford, Conn.: Special Learning Corp.

Lyon, H. C. (1982). Our most neglected natural resource. In N. West (Ed.), *Educating exceptional children 82/83*, 219–222. Guilford, Conn.: Dushkin Publishing Group

Lyon, S., & Preis, A. (1983). Working with families of severely handicapped persons. In M. Seligman (Ed.). *The family with a handicapped child*, 203–232. New York: Grune & Stratton.

Maeroff, G. (1980). Smart kids have problems too. In R. A. Hanson & R. Reynolds, *Child development.* St. Paul: West Publishing Co.

McCubbin, H., Cauble, A. E., & Patterson, J. (1982). *Family stress, coping, and social support.* Springfield, Ill.: Charles C Thomas.

Michaelis, C. T. (1980). *Home and school partnerships in exceptional education.* Rockville, Md.: Aspen Systems.

Moore, N. D. (1982). The joys and challenges in raising a gifted child. *G/C/T, 25*(6), 8–11.

Olshanky, S. (1962). Chronic sorrow: A response to having a mentally defective child. *Social Casework, 43*(190), 190–193.

Opirhory, G., & Peters, G. A. (1982). Counseling intervention strategies for families with the less than perfect newborn. *The Personnel and Guidance Journal, 60*(8), 451–455.

Osman, B. B. (1982). *No one to play with.* New York: Random House.

Paul, J. L. (1983). *The exceptional child.* Syracuse, N.Y.: The Syracuse University Press.

Potok, C. (1972). *My name is Asher Lev.* New York: Alfred A. Knopf.

Rice, F. P. (1978). *The adolescent: Development, relationships and culture* (2nd ed.). Boston: Allyn and Bacon.

Robinson, N. M., & Robinson, H.B. (1976). *The mentally retarded child.* New York: McGraw-Hill.

Ross, A. O. (1964). *The exceptional child in the family.* New York: Grune & Stratton.

Sanborn, M. P. (1979). Working with parents. In N. Colangelo & R. T. Zaffrann (Eds.), *New voices in counseling the gifted.* Dubuque, Ia.: Kendall/Hunt.

Schulz, J. B. (1982). A parent views parent participation. *Exceptional Education Quarterly, 3*(2), 17–24.

Seligman, M. (1979). *Strategies for helping parents of exceptional children.* New York: The Free Press.

Solnit, A. J., & Stark, M. H. (1961). Mourning and the birth of a defective child. *Psychoanalytic Study of the Child, 16,* 523–537.

Suran, B. G., & Rizzo, J. V. (1983). *Special children.* Glenview, Ill.: Scott, Foresman.

Trout, M.D. (1983). Birth of a sick or handicapped infant: Impact on the family. *Child Welfare, 62,* 337–348.

Tulkin, S. R., & Kagan, J. (1972). Mother-child interaction in the first year of life. *Child Development, 43*(1), 31–41.

Turnbull, A. P., & Brotherson, J. J. (1984). *Assisting parents in future planning.* Paper presented at the CEC 62nd Annual Conference, Washington, D.C.

Warren, F. (1978). A society that is going to kill your children. In A. P. Turnbull & H. R. Turnbull (Eds.), *Parents speak out,* 177–196. Columbus, Oh.: Charles E. Merrill.

Webster, E. J. (1979). Parent counseling by speech pathologists and audiologists. In L. Baruth & M. Burggraf (Eds.), *Counseling parents of exceptional children.* Guilford, Conn.: Special Learning Corp.

Whitford, E. M., Chapman, J. W., & Boersma, F. J. (1982). Family stability and mothers' perceptions of elementary learning disabled children: Implications for counseling. *Canadian Counsellor, 16*(4), 237–244.

Zuk, G. H. (1962). The cultural dilemma and spiritual crisis of the family with a handicapped child. *Exceptional Children, 28*(8), 405–408.

3

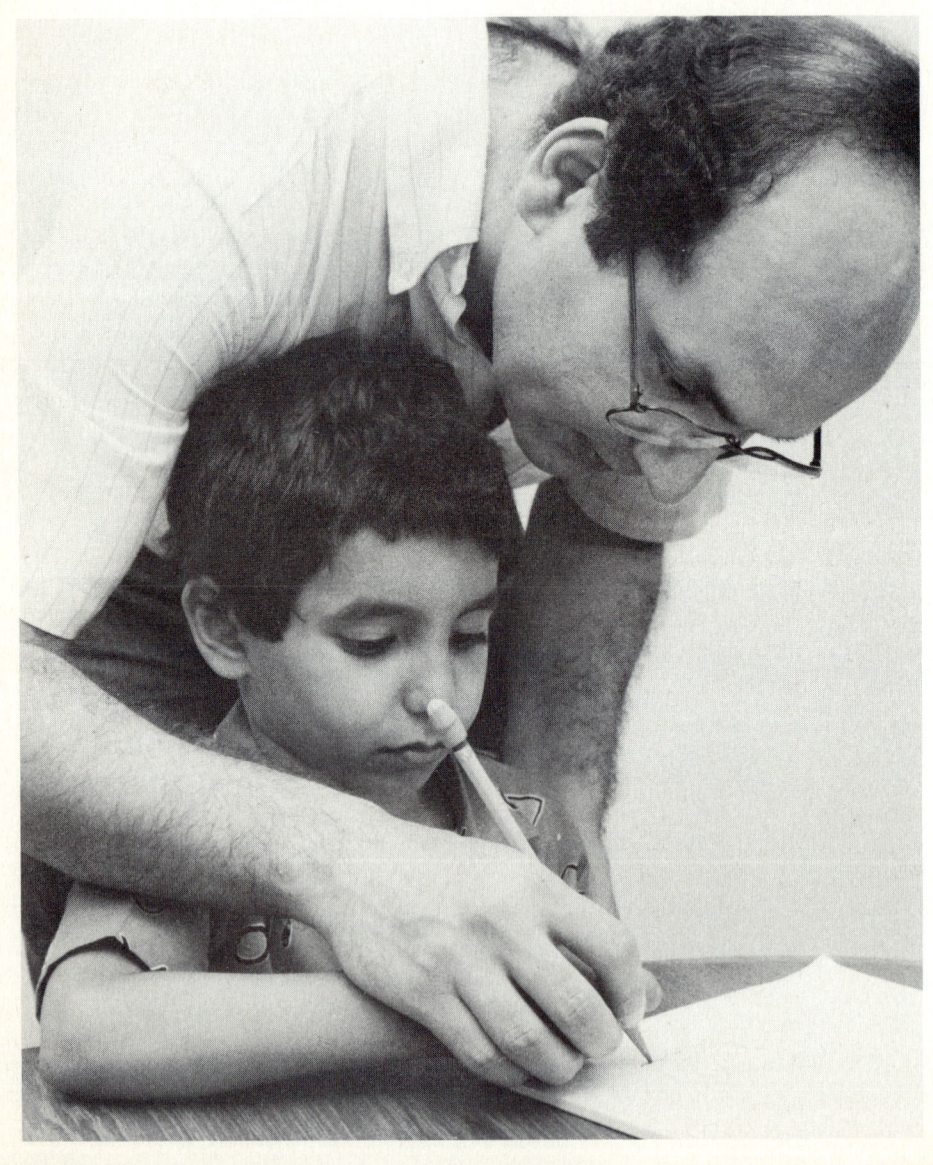

Family Adaptation to Exceptional Children

The relationship established between the family and the exceptional child has a reciprocal effect: a positive relationship fosters optimal development in the child and also helps maintain stability in the family. Since both factors represent desirable goals, the examination of coping patterns and styles of adaptation offers a promising strategy for assistance to parents.

From a social studies perspective, **adaptation** is defined as "Creating means for dealing with functional problems, as a basis for cultural change" (Farber, 1975, p. 247). The cultural change occurs in the larger society, but creating means for dealing with an exceptional child remains the function of the family. The family's ability or inability to adapt is reflected in the development of the handicapped or gifted child and in the integrity of the family.

Adaptation to Handicapped Children

As discussed in Chapter 2, the presence of a handicapped child does influence family stability. Negative effects of various handicaps have been consistently reported.

Effects on the Family

In families of children with spina bifida (a physical disability), the divorce rate has been found to be twice that of controls and the national average (Tew, Payne, & Laurence, 1974). Farber (1968) presents evidence of the adverse effects of the mentally retarded child on marital integration, social activities, job promotion, family roles, and sibling occupational expectations. When a family has a child with a chronic and progressive illness, Holroyd and Guthrie (1979) claim that health, personal relationships, integrity of the family, and finances may become strained and opportunities for personal development may be limited. In a comparison with families of nonhandicapped children, families of handicapped children were found to have less satisfactory marriages, less social support, less religious affiliation, and less psychological well-being (Friedrich & Friedrich, 1981).

Effects on the Child

☐ As families are affected by the presence of handicapped children, so are the children affected by their families' responses (Crnic, Friedrich, & Greenberg, 1983). Fotheringham and Creal (1974) claim that the child's eventual competence is the end result of the interaction of the primary handicap with the physical and social environment.

Jordan (1979) points out the determinate effect the family has on the traits of the child and suggests that the skills a child projects are partially determined by the values and attitudes the family exhibits.

In an investigation of the relationship of the home environment to the social and personal adjustment of moderately retarded children, several factors were delineated. Most important were the harmony and quality of parenting, the degree of available educational and cognitive stimulation, and emotional support and parental approval for learning (Nihira, Mink, & Meyers, 1981).

Davis (1975) reported that a major factor in inadequate child personality adjustment to a physical disability is the impact of poor parental attitudes and reactions to the child's illness. Successful personality adjustment definitely relates to parental understanding, acceptance, and adaptation to the disability.

Farber (1968) points out that major adjustments occur in families with severely handicapped children; Fotheringham and Creal (1974) emphasize the importance of the home environment for mildly handicapped children. Since the family is the major social influence on the child, the home situation and family attitudes may determine the level of competence the child reaches. For mildly handicapped individuals, the home environment may determine whether the person actually becomes disabled.

Although the importance of the family is generally acknowledged, there is a paucity of information concerning adaptation by the family as a system. There is also little attempt to account for individual variations in family adaptation. A model for explaining family adaptation and an examination of adaptation patterns will address these omissions.

Model for Adaptation

☐ Crnic, Friedrich, and Greenberg (1983) propose a model designed to account for individual variations among families in their responses to mentally retarded children. The model integrates concepts from three bodies of research: stress, individual coping, and ecological influences on development and functioning.

This model provides a framework for investigating the adaptation patterns of families of children with various handicapping conditions. Thus:

> Differential family adaptation can be interpreted as a function of the coping resources available to the family, which moderate the impact of perceived stress associated with the presence of a retarded [handicapped] child. In turn, a family's coping resources are mediated by the various ecological systems in which the family interacts. (Crnic, Friedrich, & Greenberg, 1983, p. 136)

Stress There is no question that families of handicapped people experience a great deal of stress. A more relevant question is: Why do some families respond better to the obvious stress than do others? One approach to this question is to identify the sources of stress.

Characteristics of the handicapped child appear to influence the amount of stress the family experiences. In investigating families of mentally retarded children, Farber (1968) reports that initial stress is somewhat sex-linked, with the mother being more affected if the child is a girl, and the father if the child is a boy. Variations have been found in the amount of stress produced by different diagnosis, as in physical disabilities (Holroyd & Guthrie, 1979), Down's syndrome, and childhood autism (Holroyd & McArthur, 1976).

In an investigation of the influence of child characteristics on family stress, Beckman (1983) found the number of care-giving demands to be the variable most highly related to stress. Other characteristics contributing to stress are the presence of behavior problems, the child's temperament, social responsiveness, and rate of developmental gain (Beckman-Bell, 1981). Successful educational intervention and subsequent changes in the child's behavioral characteristics may help reduce the stress the family experiences.

The level of family stress is also a function of the developmental level of the handicapped child. In responding to a questionnaire, parents of mentally retarded children indicated that their sorrow is a periodic phenomenon and that their stress does not decrease with the passage of time. The level of intensity seems to be a function of the particular developmental stage (Wikler, Wasow, & Hatfield, 1981).

Crises may be perceived whenever a discrepancy emerges between what parents expect of a child's development and of parenting as opposed to what actually occurs when raising a handicapped child (Wikler, 1981). Within this framework, developmental crises would occur when the child should begin to walk and to talk, when the child should be starting kindergarten, at the onset of puberty, and at the twenty-first birthday (symbolic of independence from the family). The father of a retarded child relates the impact of such feelings as he and his wife shopped for presents for their daughter's fifth birthday:

> After we left the toy store, Parnel burst into tears. "I don't want to buy those infant toys for her. I want her to go to first grade this year like everyone else."
> "So do I, Parn. So do I," I answered. (Searl, 1978, p. F28)

Mori (1983, p. 29) indicates that parental stress is particularly intense when:

- [ ] the child is born or the parents suspect the presence of a handicapping condition
- [ ] the diagnosis is being made and the handicap is being treated
- [ ] the child is ready to enter a school program
- [ ] the child reaches puberty
- [ ] the child reaches the age of vocational planning
- [ ] the parents grow old and worry that the child may outlive them.

The sources of stress are summarized in viewing the situation of a learning disabled child's family:

> The child's handicaps and slow development; the special arrangements needed for the child's care, training, and companionship; the disappointments and the lost dreams—all combine to create pressures that tend to disrupt the family equilibrium. (Margalit, 1982, p. 594)

Despite the difficulties apparent in families of handicapped children and adults, some families do not appear to be affected greatly. People differ considerably in their reactions to similar conditions (Pearlin, Lieberman, Menaghan, & Mullan, 1981). These differences are the results of how people respond to life problems: the resources, actions, and perceptions they mobilize as they seek to minimize stress.

Coping Resources Parents' coping strategies are highly individualized. Their reactions to stress are conditioned by their previous experience in dealing with stress in general, the nature of the stress, the reactions of other people, and the availability of community support (Fotheringham & Creal, 1974). Several methods of coping have been observed.

First, some parents deal with their handicapped child by altering their expectations. Once the handicap is recognized and accepted as a reality, many parents learn to appreciate the advances their child makes, without reference to normal developmental scales. Progress becomes a happy event rather than the periodic sorrow previously referred to.

Second, parents may cope with the stress of a handicapped child by seeking to ameliorate the problems presented. For example, it is not unusual for parents to engage a speech therapist to stimulate verbal behavior of a very young handicapped child. Good educational programs may provide positive suggestions and reinforcement for parents who are working to raise their child's performance level.

Third, some parents cope with the problem by identifying with it, becoming knowledgeable about the condition and, in many cases, entering related professions. The following account, communicated to the author, describes a mother's development in this direction:

Our family lives in the West Indies which is an ideal place to live and raise a family, but ten years ago, we found one major drawback: no one had heard of specific learning disabilities. (A few people had heard of dyslexia, but the current theory was: "that is not a problem until the child is eight years old."). My youngest, five-year-old daughter, Laura, was not learning the way other children learned those very important subjects that are part of a school curriculum. No one in Jamaica could help me, and, consequently, I had to take her to Miami to discover if she really was as lazy as the teacher thought, or if there was another reason.

When it was discovered that Laura's inability to learn had a name, "Specific Learning Disabilities," I breathed a sigh of relief. "Now that her problem had been diagnosed," I thought, "Someone can do something about it." What I didn't realize was that the person to do "something about it" would be me.

I couldn't find anyone who was willing to teach an almost-six year old and after a month of frustration, I called the psychologist in tears. "You will have to learn how to teach her yourself," said Dr. Carner. I flew up to Miami and picked up an armful of books, games and other assorted supplies which the psychologist picked out, and for the next few years, taught myself and Laura.

Dr. Carner and I organized a "book brigade" between Miami and Jamaica. As soon as I had read one set, he would say, "I think you should know about this aspect of L.D." and send me more articles, text books or whatever was needed to make me more knowledgeable in this particular field. We had books flying back and forth from Miami to Kingston, and I'm sure the customs' officers wondered about the strange packages that arrived for me!

Laura and I were lucky in another way. She went to a Catholic school where the headmistress, Sister Mary, was extremely interested in Laura's problem. She let me keep Laura out of school in the mornings so that I could tutor her, and then take her back to school so that she could play with her friends during recess breaks. After a while, she let me set up a small corner in the school library where I was allowed to tutor Laura and other children who exhibited similar learning problems.

I think that the hardest part was convincing well-wishers that Laura did indeed have L.D. I was constantly told, "Everyone is different and she is young. Why don't you just leave her alone and let her grow out of it?" Laura was obviously bright, so the consensus of opinion was that she was lazy or that her eyes had not recovered from an operation for strabismus, and that in time, she would learn to read as well as the other children. I must admit, I was fed up to my teeth with people who "meant well!"

My main objective was to maintain an ordinary life style for everyone at home. I tried to limit all of the problems that come with L.D. to school hours, but of course, that didn't work. I was told over and over that I was making a neurotic out of my child, and that I was over-reacting. Fortunately, by this time, I could see some progress, and so told everyone that I did know what I was doing, and to please leave me alone.

News travels quickly in a small country like Jamaica and I started receiving letters and phone calls from worried parents who knew that their children had problems and didn't know what to do. This led to the formation of "The Jamaican Association for Children with Learning Disabilities," and a year later, the opening of "The Learning Centre" which provides diagnostic and tutoring services. At time of writing, the Centre has a full complement of administration and teaching staff . . . a far cry from just "me and two Peace Corps workers!"

Family life obviously changed, but I think, in the long term, for the better. My three other daughters have developed a caring attitude towards other people, and I feel that it was because they played an active role in helping Laura. They spent hours playing games to help improve Laura's sequential memory and her motor coordination. When Laura did something "right," we all felt proud of "what we did."

Probably my life has been most affected. I become very angry when I see how sheer carelessness or plain stupidity can hurt a child, and so, I am now enrolled as a full time student at a major university with the ultimate goal of receiving a doctorate. Perhaps, when I get those letters after my name, I will be able to make more people understand that having a child with L.D. doesn't mean that one has a problem child; it just means that one's child happens to have a problem.   (B. Matalon, personal communication, January 26, 1983)

The fields of psychology, special education, social work, nursing and other helping professions have many members who are parents or siblings of handicapped people.

Other coping strategies are more negative in their effect on the child and the family. One mechanism used as a coping strategy is withdrawal—from friends, relatives, professional workers, or from activities that involve the handicapped child (Drew, Logan, & Hardman, 1984). By withdrawing, parents can construct a protective barrier between themselves and inquiring, although interested, outsiders. Isolation protects the family from curious and sometimes rude encounters, but it also separates them from support systems and positive development.

Overprotection can be seen as a strategy in which the parents isolate the child from demands and situations that require risk-taking by the child (Fotheringham & Creal, 1974). Overprotection has been cited as a common posture among parents of handicapped children that frequently presents a barrier to the development of the child and the stability of the family. The child's overprotection can be demonstrated in the amount of attention given beyond that received by the siblings and/or beyond the needs determined by the handicap (Poznanski, 1973). Families of children with learning disabilities have been characterized by overprotection, rigidity, lack of conflict resolution, overindulgence, denial, and projection (Faerstein, 1981; Perosa & Perosa, 1981). Such defences deprive the child of the opportunity for growth and development. Wright (1960, pp. 305–306), in discussing parents of physically handicapped children, identifies behavior patterns that have been ascribed to overprotective parents:

1. They are highly child-centered; they are eager to sacrifice themselves (and the rest of the family) for the "good" of one particular child.

2. They are continually helping the child, even when he is fully capable and willing to help himself; they bathe, dress, and undress him; they feed him.

3. Their discipline is inconsistent. There are occasions when they meticulously adhere to regulations and mete out punishment for the slightest infringement; at other times, they are overindulgent and lax.

4. They are dictatorial and arbitrary; they make decisions which involve the child without considering his wishes. Among overprotective parents, those who are acceptant give lavish toys and tell the child how to play with them; those who are rejectant withhold gifts and privileges or withdraw them on the slightest pretext.

5. They hover over him; they offer suggestions; the rejectant parents nag and criticize; the acceptant parents call attention to the child's every activity and bestow more praise than is deserved.

6. They protect him from every imaginable discomfort or difficulty, the acceptant parents because they cannot bear to see the child suffer; the rejectant parents because their anxiety serves to disguise their rejection of him.

7. They restrict his play, the acceptant parents because they fear he may get hurt; the rejectant ones because by their restriction they frustrate and punish him.

8. They deny him opportunities for growing up; they thwart his curiosity; the acceptant parents because they want to keep him a baby; the rejectant parents because they do not want to take the trouble to teach him.

9. They do not understand his capabilities and limitations; they set goals which are too high for him, or they are content with goals which are too low.

10. They monopolize his time; they sleep with him; they allow him few friends of his own choosing; they take him to parties and call for him; they persuade him to stay at home with them.

In the extreme, parents may become so overprotective of their child that they will not agree to services that are available. Parents will, in some instances, exaggerate the child's need for them, ultimately becoming more dependent on the child than the child is on them.

Some coping strategies are clearly more productive than others. Various resources have been identified as critical in helping families cope in a positive way. Wikler (1981) points to community acceptance, a strong extended family network, a supportive marital partner, close friends and relatives, and nonjudgmental professionals as mediating factors. Additional resources cited are parental health, energy, and morale; problem-solving skills; utilitarian resources, including socioeconomic status and income; and general and specific beliefs, including self-confidence and religious faith (Folkman, Schaefer, & Lazarus, 1979). Friedrich (1979) found that the mother's report of marital satisfaction had the greatest bearing on her ability to cope with her handicapped child. In general, the greater the individual or family resources, the less stress the family will experience and the greater the ability to cope internally (Levinson, 1976).

Despite the predictability of coping strength, many families cope well with very limited resources. The director of a day-care program for severely handicapped children describes such a family:

Tina will be six years old in December. She is a beautiful child with honey-colored hair that falls below her waist, and her hair ribbons match her frilly dresses. She cannot see or voluntarily move. She has cerebral palsy and epilepsy and is fed through a tube into her small intestine.

Her skin is perfect, and she has never had the pressure sores commonly seen in children who cannot change their position. Her mother gets up several times each night to move her. Tina responds to her mother's voice with open eyes and a smile.

Her family lives in a very comfortable and attractive log home, that, as her mother puts it, "was bought one door at a time" from thirteen years of saving.

Tina has been in specialized day care from March to October for the last three years. During the winter months, her family goes to Florida to work in the orange groves. There are no special services for Tina in the small town. The hospital where she was born and is treated is nearly a hundred miles away. Tina's father keeps her on the evenings her mother goes out for necessary shopping.

When surgery was performed to insert the feeding tube, the hospital staff was amazed that Tina's mother insisted on doing the first feeding. She also changes the tube every month. Tina is kept on an oxygen enricher at night, and sometimes must be suctioned with an electric machine to help clear her airways so she can breathe. Her mother does all these "routine" procedures, and has on many occasions revived Tina when she has stopped breathing. She questions Tina's doctors and insists on having medical terminology explained to her. She has trained the day care staff to feed Tina and to suction her when necessary.

The family does not have medical insurance, nor do they receive Medicaid or Supplemental Security Income for Tina. Tina and her two older brothers who are in school are always neat and clean, and are well provided for on a small family income.

Besides taking such special care of Tina, her mother is a model parent and wife, raises a vegetable garden and a yard full of flowers, cans and freezes food from the garden, attends church and P.T.A., visits the sick, works part-time, and sends thank-you cards to Tina's caregivers at the center.

This mother is full of appreciation for the goodness in her life, and she never questions why Tina has so many special needs. She continues to meet each new challenge with love, energy, and an undaunted faith. (J. Spencer, personal communication, May 16, 1984)

Family Ecology Family ecology can be viewed through the concept of "social embeddedness" (Powell, 1979, p. 2), in which the child is seen as embedded in a family system that in turn is enmeshed in society. As stated in the previous two chapters, interaction between these interconnected systems greatly influences the child's development and the family's adaptation. Bronfenbrenner (1984, p. 5) stresses the importance of the family's relationship to other ecological systems:

☐ In order to develop normally—intellectually, physically, socially, emotionally, and morally—a child requires progressively more complex joint

activity with one or more adults who have an *irrational* emotional relationship with the child [parent].
- In order to develop normally . . . the child needs to engage in progressively more complex joint activity with someone who does *not* have an irrational relationship with that child [teacher].
- The developmental potential of these systems, whether rational or irrational, depends on the extent of which third parties are present who support the activities of those actually engaged in interaction with the child.
- A child requires public policies and practices that provide opportunity, status, example, encouragement, stability, and above all, time for parenthood, primarily by parents, but also by all adults in the society. And unless you have those external supports, the internal systems can't work.

The ecological systems within which the family functions and with which it interacts include the home, the school, the neighborhood, places of work, and social networks. The ecological model is discussed in Chapter 5; social networks as part of the ecological system must be considered as factors in the adaptation process.

A family social network consists of family members' relations with friends, neighbors, co-workers, and other acquaintances who interact with a family member concerning an emotional or material issue (Powell, 1979). Membership does not include siblings and other people who live in the household.

Cochran and Brassard (1979) identify three ways in which the parents' social network is effective:

Access to emotional and material assistance. Network helping patterns deal with child care, personal distress, information about jobs and housing, and leisure time.

Provision of child-rearing controls. Friends, relatives, and neighbors encourage or discourage particular patterns of parent-child interactions and actually shape mothering styles.

Availability of role models. Parents may adopt or modify child-rearing practices as a consequence of watching the behavior of network members.

In these outside relationships, parents perceive acceptance or rejection of their child and themselves and receive assistance, encouragement, and criticism for their coping strategies (Fotheringham & Creal, 1974). These outside sources also furnish information and direct parents toward services for their handicapped child.

The quality and availability of services and parent-professional relationships also contribute to the level of family adaptation. Community and personal resources are important factors in understanding families of handicapped people. Examination of adaptation patterns increases that understanding.

Patterns of Adaptation

☐ The parent of a retarded child (Searl, 1978, p. F27) decries the professional concept of parents' stages and ultimate acceptance:

> Most parents, I believe, never fully resolve the complexity of feelings about their child's retardation. They don't "adjust to" or "accept" that fact, at least not in the way psychology books describe it.

Nevertheless, families do adapt to their handicapped children and the children's unique situations. The process is evidenced in three patterns: rejection, acceptance, and adjustment.

Rejection *Parental rejection* can be defined as "the persistent and unrelieved holding of unrealistic negative values of the child to the extent that the whole behavior of the parent towards that child is colored unrealistically by this negative tone" (Gallagher, 1956, pp. 273–274). Parental rejection can be expressed subtly and indirectly due to parental fears of social disapproval or can be more overtly manifested through general negligence or even by direct punishment and attack on the child (Hurley, 1965). Rejected children must deal with disturbed family relationships and emotional insecurity in addition to adjusting to themselves and their handicaps (Lerner, 1981).

In an analysis of child-rearing attitudes of mothers of retarded, emotionally disturbed, and normal children, Ricci (1970) found the most rejecting attitudes to be displayed by mothers of retarded children and the least rejecting attitudes shown by mothers of normal children. Isn't this a finding to be expected? Most, if not all, parents experience feelings of rejection toward their normal children at some time. They reject their attitudes, their behavior, and their personality changes. Handicapped children have, as a rule, more objectionable attributes than normal children have. The normal, expected parental rejection is thus intensified. A number of reasons exist for parents' rejection of their handicapped children. Several are cited in the following paragraphs.

The Parents View the Child as a Physical and Psychological Extension of Themselves   Since the child is a combination of the positive and negative characteristics of the parents, if something is seen as good about the child, it is a reflection of the good in one or both parents. Conversely, if something is seen as bad or wrong with the child, it is a reflection of the same trait in one or both of the parents (Ryckman & Henderson, 1970). A handicapped child represents a blow to the ego—a blow so severe that the child may be rejected to protect the parents' ego.

Parents Are Repulsed by the Abnormal Appearance of the Child   Children with birth defects such as cleft palate and lip may be rejected because they are physically unattractive. Poznanski (1973) suggests that many children with birth defects are not organically retarded but may function that way because of massive rejection by parents during the formative period. With a child who is obviously, visibly handicapped, parents may feel uncomfortable in public. The parent of a physically handicapped child expresses the hazards of being seen in public:

> Let's face it folks. . . . It's a real jungle out there. Yes, my fellow parents, I'm speaking about going out into public places. The grocery store, the bank, McDonald's, the neighborhood park, the beach, and the shopping mall. They all seemed so innocent and routine prior to the birth of a handicapped child. But now, the same places loom around us like fierce giants with a thousand staring eyes and whispering inaudible judgements from every corner. It can be one of the worst experiences encountered by the parent of the handicapped child. (Cushing, 1982, p. 1)

For some parents, rejection and isolation are easier than explanations and stares.

Serious Behavior Problems Contribute to Parental Stress and Rejection Such problems as aggressive behavior, stereotypic behavior patterns, and tantrums are great sources of stress to parents, both as they attempt to handle problems in the home and as they take the child to public places (Beckman-Bell, 1981). Fortunately, many of these behaviors can be changed, resulting in more accepting parental attitudes.

Parents Receive Ambiguous Information from Professionals In referring to marital problems observed in parents of learning disabled children, Faerstein (1981) states that because they are uncertain about the diagnosis of their child, many parents fluctuate between being overprotective and rejecting the child. The lack of consistency leads to family discord and may focus on the child as the scapegoat, the source and cause of all family problems.

Other reasons for rejecting a handicapped child include family pressure, family and career status, and emotional instability. Rejection can be expressed in four general ways:

1. *Strong underexpectations of achievement.* The child is considered worthless and incapable of any useful function. Ultimately, the child feels worthless and acts as if he is worthless.
2. *Setting unrealistic goals.* Some parents set goals that are impossible for the child to reach. When the child fails, they feel their negative feelings and attitudes toward the child are justified.
3. *Escape.* This reaction results in leaving the child or placing the child at a great distance from the parents.
4. *Reaction formation.* Parents who cannot accept their negative feelings present the opposite attitude to the world. Thus the parent who would like to leave or lose her child becomes possessive and overprotective to deny the negative feelings. (Gallagher, 1956, p. 274)

In some cases, parental rejection remains constant. In other instances, it fluctuates, depending on characteristics of the child and family situations. Frequently, rejection is part of the parental growth process, finally leading to acceptance of the child.

Acceptance The father of a mentally retarded child outlines three stages in the growth of a parent. At the first stage, the parent is concerned almost wholly with himself and the effect that having a handicapped child has on him. During the second stage, the parent thinks less of himself and more about the handicapped child, seeking services and resources for the child's benefit. In the final stage, acceptance, the parent is able to see more clearly and to think more rationally, to be concerned about other children and to work for their benefit (Boyd, 1969).

Parental development and reactions are not universal, nor do they occur with the same intensity or duration (Begab, 1969). Previously well-adjusted parents are usually capable of enduring the initial pain of awareness that they have a handicapped child and do, immediately or eventually, accept their child.

In attempting to define ***acceptance,*** Robinson and Robinson (1976, p. 420) state:

> It usually seems to involve a warm respect for the child as he is, appreciation of his assets, tolerance for his shortcomings, and active pleasure in relating to him.

Although acceptance is difficult to define, its presence or absence is readily discernible. Acceptance is felt in a home that is relatively free from tension, in a family in which people are comfortable with each other. Two indexes of acceptance have been identified: the degree to which the mother functions in her usual manner, continuing her association with friends, and the degree to which both parents meet the needs of their normal children as well as those of the handicapped child (Huber, 1979). Teachers can determine acceptance of a handicapped child when the parents:

1. are willing to attend parent-teacher conferences
2. are able to discuss the child's shortcomings with relative ease
3. can abandon overprotective or unduly harsh behavioral patterns toward their child
4. are able to collaborate with the teacher to make realistic short- and long-term plans
5. become involved in advocacy functions and parent groups but not at the expense of interaction with the child
6. pursue own interests unrelated to child, again not to the exclusion of the child
7. can discipline appropriately without undue guilt feelings. (Seligman, 1979), p. 60)

Accepting a handicapped person requires acknowledging the strengths and abilities of that person; it also implies accepting the person's limitations (Buscaglia, 1975). The family can facilitate the acceptance process by allowing and encouraging the handicapped child to work through the phases of personal identity and to develop a positive self-concept (D'Alonzo & Lazar, 1983).

Acceptance requires the concern and effort of the entire family. Buscaglia (1975, p. 130) projects the following ideas to help each family member fulfill a vital role:

- Family feeling regarding each member will vary and can have a monumental effect upon the entire family. If these feelings are internalized they can lead to guilt, anxiety and impotence. On the other hand, if some kind of forum is created in the home for expressing feelings without fear of censure or rejection, it can result in new, creative relationships and more positive solutions for all.
- Developing a well-integrated and functioning family is not exclusively the responsibility of any one person but the duty of each family member.
- Maturity and independence for each person in the family will occur only if each is allowed to seek for himself his own person while being assured of the continual love and support of the entire family, no matter where the search may lead.
- The family should strive to create the type of atmosphere where the only obstacles for growth are self-imposed and where the resultant joy and pain, success or failure, hope or despair can be shared with equal acceptance.
- To grieve temporarily for something of value which is lost is a normal human response. To grieve forever for something which cannot be regained is emotional illness and can prevent the family from experiencing the many gratifications which living life in the "now" can afford.
- To live together in peace, joy and love, each person in the family will need to have a mutual feeling of respect and regard. This recognition of others will require some limitations, some discipline, some giving and some taking, for the benefit of all. The rewards lay in a feeling of security, group support and a more vast repertoire of behavioral alternatives.
- Acceptance of other family members is achieved only through allowing them the dignity of personal strengths and limitations, always recognizing the limitless potentials, not for being what we desire them to be, but for their being what they are.

In addition to accepting their handicapped child, parents need to accept themselves as good parents and to gain confidence in their own abilities to raise a handicapped child. Sometimes it takes a great deal of experience for parents to accept themselves as knowledgeable people. In describing her experiences with professionals, the mother of a retarded child wrote:

The thought began to develop that I knew more about some things than the professionals did. I began to gain confidence in the knowledge I had gained as a *parent*. Years later, I am still convinced that I have learned more from my own children than from any other resource. (Schulz, 1978, p. 33)

It is also helpful if people can be assured of their worth as parents by people they consider to be authorities (Hart, 1970). The confidence and accompanying acceptance are described by parents of a hearing-impaired child:

There seems to be a turning point for mothers when they have overcome the initial heartache and confusion, when they understand deafness and language in terms of their own child, and when they feel competent and knowledgeable in working with, loving, and managing their child. (Liversidge & Grana, 1979, p. 161)

Acceptance involves choices. Some families cannot accommodate handicapped children at home. The severity of the handicap, the resources of the family, and the welfare of the child must all be considered in determining appropriate placement of the child. In a letter to the author, the mother of an autistic child portrays this viewpoint.

When my autistic son was small, it seemed unthinkable he would ever live apart from us. This beautiful boy—who never spoke to us, never understood us, never even looked at us—was our special child and we would care for him forever. We read everything we could find about autism and worked very hard to help him. The birth of his two normal brothers made us more aware of Doug's delays so we redoubled our efforts, worked even harder with him at home, demanded and got better classroom education. There was nothing we wouldn't do, we left no stone unturned. We never stopped trying, never stopped hoping that something would work for Doug. We thought we understood that autism is forever, but in our hearts we wanted him well.

The price of all the attention and work on Doug was high—and all too common. We gave too little attention to each other and suddenly—it seemed— I was a divorced woman with three sons, starting a new life in another state. Within two years I was physically and emotionally exhausted and the unthinkable became thinkable. Doug had to live somewhere else. This was more than a family crisis. It was the crisis of my soul. I had always thought as he got older, it would get easier—that I'd get more accepting. To send him—whom I loved so dearly—away, violated every definition and model of Mother I'd ever know. In my head I knew what had to be done. In my heart I felt a wretched failure. Night after night I dreamed he was dying.

Local agencies added to the nightmare. Unaware or unconcerned with my anguish, they made it clear they didn't want to help and thought I was irresponsible. I'm not sure I would have survived at all but for the caring and support of my dearest friend. She helped me to see that letting Doug go was not an act of rejection and failure, but rather one of love. I loved him and myself enough to let go of traditional models and simply do what was best for both of us. Almost immediately I found a fine foster home where Doug is loved, cared for and disciplined by people who are devoted to handicapped children.

Letting go of Doug was the hardest thing I've ever done, but this story has a happy ending. Shortly after he went to live with his foster family I went to visit. I walked right past Doug. I didn't recognize the serene quiet child watching television. The tantrums, sleeplessness and destructive behavior that I thought signaled his coming adolescence were really signs of his stress and distress. He needed the change as badly as I did! Now more than a year later he is still serene, content and at home with his foster family.

My solution isn't right for everyone. There are many courageous parents who want to continue to care for their handicapped child at home. But it also takes courage to let a child go. Acceptance can take many forms. (P. Stalley, personal communication, December 9, 1983)

Another mother points out that parents may never reach some absolute state of acceptance, but they are likely to experience positive feelings in a step-by-step movement in that direction (Featherstone, 1980). Blacher (1984) stresses the importance of recognizing that there is not an abrupt ending to the stages of parental reactions but rather a lifelong need to make continual adjustments and readjustments to the handicapped person.

Adjustment The stage of adjustment is marked by parental ability to meet the crises of personal frustration and conflict in a realistic way, much as they meet other challenges and stresses in their lives (Canino & Reeve, 1980). For many parents, the nature of the adjustments required in raising a handicapped child are emotional, social, and temporal.

In examining families of psychotic children, Marcus (1977) cites adequacy of self-concept as a vulnerable area for parents in their emotional adjustment. Mothers, in particular, frequently lose their own identities and fail to see beyond the child's needs. First-time parents, in particular, have doubts about themselves as adequate parents.

Fathers may have more difficulty than mothers in adjusting emotionally. Characteristically, they have had fewer opportunities to provide direct care for the child, which provides concrete evidence of their loving concern. Relatively few opportunities for counterbalancing the sense of loss and frustration are included in the father's role (Cummings, 1976). When the perspectives and attitudes of mothers and fathers differ, marital discord may occur.

Coping with emotional strains requires resourcefulness and resiliency. In many cases, the resultant adjustments lead to personal growth (Marcus, 1977). Despite the stress and sorrow, many parents see caring for a handicapped child as an ennobling experience for themselves and for other children (Hart, 1970)

Because of the demands of intensive child care, parents may experience social isolation. Adjustments to societal prejudices heighten feelings of uncertainty, fear, avoidance, and frustration. On the other hand, they may refuse to accept an inferior position and fight the society that imposes it (Buscaglia, 1975).

Perhaps the greatest adjustments are those concerning time. In investigations of family problems, time demands, physical demands, and money problems are often indicated as important (Dunlap & Hollinsworth, 1977). For severely handicapped children, the daily time demands are astounding. For moderately and mildly handicapped children, parents spend an inordinate amount of time on self-help tasks and academic coaching.

The most dramatic temporal adjustment is the realization that parenthood is forever. Parents of handicapped children and adults continue to be responsible for the care and behavior of their offspring long after other parents have relinquished responsibility.

A study of the effects on parents of raising a physically handicapped child failed to categorize the parents as either well or poorly adjusted (Tavormina, Boll, Dunn, Luscomb, & Taylor, 1981). Instead, the group was classified as "an essentially normal group with special problems and with special needs for support and interventions geared to help them deal with the extra stresses they must face" (p. 130). Adequacy of adjustment is probably related to internal supports, access to normal social activities, opportunities for the development of personal identities beyond the parenting role, attitudes of acceptance and hopefulness, and the development of appropriate expectations (Marcus, 1977).

A realistic process of adjustment is described by Featherstone (1980, p. 5), whose initial reaction to her handicapped child, Jody, was presented in Chapter 2.

> When Caitlin was born, fat and healthy, in the fall of 1974, I felt as though I had turned a corner. Jody's problems became an element in my life, rather than the dominant motif. With a thriving infant in the house, our family felt healthy again. Like the baby herself, we began to demand more out of life. Keeping pace with her, we grew. Bad times still came and went, but not all crises centered on Jody. Emotionally we were returning to the mainstream, although we still faced special problems. We were knitting Jody, and our new identities as mother, father, and sisters of a severely handicapped child, into the fabric of an ongoing life.

Although it has been pointed out that adjustment to a handicapped child involves the entire family, the patterns of adaptation presented in the previous sections have focused on parental response. Siblings and extended family members warrant special attention as they deal with unique stresses and make specific contributions to the family's adaptation.

Sibling Relationships

☐ Attention to the concerns of siblings of handicapped people is relatively new; problems faced by siblings are as old as those faced by their parents. A woman now in her eighties recalls her feelings:

I was born in September, 1899. My older sister Mildred was born in February, 1895. I first became aware at age seven that Mildred was different when I heard children in the school yard laughing at her. It was then I realized that she was different in appearance. She was sloppy in her dress and not well coordinated so that she did not run and play as other children did. But she was my sister and once I struck out at one of those who laughed at her. I did not understand my own feelings about Mildred. I was embarrassed for her and ashamed of her. Yet I seldom was angry with her and was constantly protecting her from those who would laugh at her.

Mildred was taken out of school in about the fifth grade when I caught up to her. I noticed that when we had company in our home, Mildred did not join in conversation with the adults. She sought out the children and enjoyed their company. She liked to play games with them—checkers and card games like Old Maid. The children always welcomed her and they had fun together. Then I saw the children outgrow her and move on to other pleasures which did not include her.

My mother kept her at home for the rest of my mother's life. She ran errands at mother's direction, but really was given no responsibility in the family. The other children all grew up, left home and married. After mother's death at 83, Mildred came to live in my home. She continued much as she had in the past, doing some grocery shopping, mending, embroidering and helping with household chores. I lost my temper only once during this time and that was when, during my absence, Mildred chipped the enamel on my new stove and denied knowing how it happened. When I railed at her, she was hurt. She wept and went to her room. I was stricken with remorse and went to her and apologized. She forgave me readily.

When my husband was called to active duty during the Korean conflict it was necessary to put Mildred, now 57, into a retirement home. There she blossomed. As one of the youngest residents, she took on responsibilities such as going to the nearby stores to buy small articles for other residents, delivering their mail and running the bingo games. When she came to visit me she talked constantly about the Home, and kept wondering how the residents were getting along.

Looking back I recall that as a child I knew of only one other odd child. I realize that this was because such children were kept at home and, to some degree, hidden. I also realize now that had Mildred been born in a different generation she probably would have worked at some simple job. She might even have married.

Growing up and living with Mildred was a good influence on me. It made me more tolerant of people who are different. Knowing my feelings of resentment when people laughed at my sister, I would never laugh at anyone who was different. (M. Trembath, personal communication, March 7, 1985)

The same feelings are shared by siblings of handicapped people today—feelings of embarrassment, guilt, and responsibility. These feelings can be understood better by examining the attitudes usually expressed by siblings and by exploring the effects of living with a handicapped brother or sister.

Sibling Attitudes Although they are bothered by the jeers and taunts of their friends, young children are closer to their families than to their friends. They are, therefore, able to defend their handicapped sibling and remain loyal. Embarrassment becomes an acute problem when the nonhandicapped sibling reaches the teen years (Wentworth, 1974). Peer approval is very important at this age; being different or having a family member who is obviously different can be painful. Explanations are difficult; many young people avoid confrontation by not bringing friends home and by not accompanying the family on public excursions.

Guilt is as real to siblings as it is to parents. All of the reactions mentioned, in retrospect, could lead to strong feelings of guilt. In addition, siblings may feel guilty because *they* are not handicapped. When the handicapped child is institutionalized, guilt may be expressed in a different way:

> I was glad when Lillian went away to school, but I didn't think it was right to be glad. Soon I realized that Mom and Dad were glad, although also sad, that Lillian was away at school and I knew it wasn't wrong of me to feel that way.   (Shillingburg, 1982, p. 24)

The same child expressed fear:

> I was also frightened, because it seemed to me that Lillian was being sent away because she was bad. I was afraid that if I was bad I might be sent away too. (Shillingburg, 1982, p. 24)

Younger siblings may also fear that they will become disabled; young people and adults may fear that they will become parents of a handicapped child (Marion, 1981). Finally, they fear the future—for themselves and for their handicapped sibling:

> My parents tell me that things are better than they used to be. But I worry about what is going to happen to John when my parents are not alive anymore. I wish I knew more about what is wrong with him. But my parents never told me. Once I asked and they said that was the way he was born. ("Jerry Got Lost in the Shuffle," 1982, p. 49)

Resentment seems to be the most pervasive negative attitude of siblings. Seligman (1983, p. 164) identifies eight factors determining the degree of resentment harbored or expressed:

1. The extent to which a sibling is held responsible for a handicapped brother or sister.
2. The extent to which a handicapped sibling takes advantage of (manipulates) a normal brother or sister.
3. The extent to which the handicapped sibling restricts one's social life or is considered a source of embarrassment.

4. The extent to which a handicapped sibling requires time and attention from the parents.
5. The extent to which the family's financial resources are drained by services for the handicapped child.
6. The number of siblings.
7. The sex of the siblings.
8. The overall accommodation parents have made to their special circumstances.

The dependency of the handicapped child frequently demands time and attention from parents that leaves other children in the family feeling neglected. Parents may begin to rearrange the family life and resources to meet the needs of the handicapped child; they may give little attention to more capable and independent siblings (Suran & Rizzo, 1983). Robinson and Robinson (1976) describe a mother of four who devoted most of her time to her mentally retarded daughter. In her old age the mother stated that she had given the child everything she could. Another daughter added, "And we gave her our mother" (p. 431).

A deep resentment is expressed by a young woman who is now in college:

> I was always a bright child—a 4.0 student and the best pianist around. I was philosophical and extremely morality conscious. I was also somewhat overindulged, and loved very much by my parents. I had it all, or so it seemed.
>
> Yet, I was paranoid and self-conscious—extremely insecure and unhappy a lot. And I had a sister who received unconditional love, while I was criticized and occasionally even rejected, I felt. How *could* I relate to this "creature" as I saw her? She could not understand or contribute *anything*, except nuisance and heartache!
>
> Family interaction was verbally hostile at times, yet Carolyn never received an angry word. She was the helpless one, so she was spared.
>
> Carolyn began to practice an excruciatingly high-pitched, loud squeal whenever she was really joyful (whenever I played the piano!), angry, or having bad seizures (which increased over the years). I usually answered those screams with my own. Hers were unbearable!
>
> And she never was potty-trained. So there was constant diaper-changing and messes. I never was asked to change her diaper or watch after her more than 5–10 minutes. And I only fed her a few times. I did not want to acknowledge her, and I was not asked to much, since my parents wanted to make my life as normal as possible. But my rejection of my sister did hurt them.
>
> Even though my sister began staying 5 days a week at Western Carolina Center for the handicapped when I was in junior high, she was home on weekends, and Mom's heart broke every Sunday when she had to take her back, though the center *is* one of the best in the country. Mom never got to go to church, and Saturdays became an emotional time, especially when Mom broke her hip and my sister began coming home only on Saturdays. Saturdays were sister-centered, and, emotionally, anything could happen!

Add to these conditions the fact that our house had to remain child-proofed throughout the years. When friends came, Carolyn would scoot to them or to me and pull or bite us; every one in the house had to be quiet during her afternoon sleep hours and bedtime hours . . . and on it goes!

Suffice it to say, I felt different, and I *was* different. My family was abnormal, and I felt abnormal. I did my best to avoid my sister and push her away when she came near. And that is what I did, for most of our life together. (K. McLain, personal communication, March 25, 1985)

Effect on Siblings The effect of a handicapped child on the development of siblings has not been fully determined. In an investigation of eighty-three college-age siblings of retarded children, Grossman (1972) revealed the following data, as condensed by Seligman (1983, pp. 148–149):

1. A number of subjects appeared to have benefited from the experience of growing up with a handicapped sibling. These students appeared to be more tolerant about prejudice and its consequences and more certain about their own futures and about personal and vocational goals than comparable young adults who had not had such experiences.

2. There were clear indications that some normal siblings were harmed by the experience; they showed bitter resentment of their family's situation, guilt about the rage they felt at their parents and at the retarded sibling and fear that they themselves might be defective.

3. Families tended to exempt their sons from the demanding duty of caring for their retarded sibling, whereas daughters were more actively involved in their brother's or sister's care.

4. The strongest single factor affecting the normal sibling's acceptance of his retarded brother or sister was parental feelings and reactions, especially those of the mother.

5. Upper-income families, because of their resources, had more opportunity to relieve their normal children of the burdensome care of the handicapped child, but not without some negative yet manageable consequences, e.g., guilt feelings.

6. Lower-income families experienced more hardship as a consequence of the retarded child, especially as the young normal women were expected to assume a major share of responsibility for their handicapped siblings. Young women from larger families fared better, probably because they had normal sisters and brothers who shared responsibility.

Additional research is conflicting. A study of siblings of children with spina bifida documented an incidence of maladjustment four times that of the normal control children (Davis, 1975). An investigation of siblings of children with Down's Syndrome and cleft lip/palate revealed the contrasting data: there was no greater degree of maladjustment than in the control group of siblings of normal children (Gath, 1972). Another research project indicated that the teenagers interviewed were not adversely affected by a retarded sibling (Graliker, Fishler, & Koch, 1962). Both of these positive studies, however, referred to *young* handicapped siblings, which reflects a variable in sibling reaction.

Trevino (1979) identifies four variables that interact to cause conflict: (1) number of normal siblings, (2) age of siblings, (3) gender, and (4) parental reaction to the handicap. Thus, prospects for the siblings appear to be the worst for families in which "(1) there are only two siblings, a normal and a handicapped child, (2) the normal sibling is close in age to or younger than the handicapped sibling, or is the oldest female child, (3) the normal and handicapped child are the same sex, or (4) the parents are unable to accept the handicap" (p. 489).

Grossman (1972, p. 176) summarized her findings on the effect of a retarded child on college-aged siblings:

> We found a surprising number of brothers and sisters of retarded children who appeared to us to have benefited in some way from the experiences of growing up with a handicapped sibling. These students seemed to us more tolerant, more compassionate, more aware of prejudice and its consequences; sometimes more focused, both occupationally and personally, than comparable young adults without such experiences. We also found many students who seemed damaged: students who were bitterly resentful of the family's situation, guilty about their rage at their parents and at the retarded sibling, fearful that they themselves

☐ *Many adults have benefited from the experience of growing up with a handicapped sibling.*

might be defective or tainted; sometimes truly deprived of the time and resources they needed to develop because every support the family had to give was used in the care of the handicapped child.

Needs of Siblings   Siblings may experience extreme anguish as they attempt to deal with their feelings of rejection. McLain (1985), quoted previously, continues to struggle as she strives toward accepting her handicapped sister:

> The time of reckoning came one weekend when I went home. I had asked to be humbled beyond my own self, and God granted that desire. I felt I *must* accept my sister and show her love, or I would carry guilt and angry disobedience to God for the rest of my life, hindering my ability to love other people.
>
> The scene was the kitchen, where my fifteen-year-old sister sat in her high chair, and my mom and good friend stood looking on with tender, hurting hearts. I rubbed Carolyn's arm and told her I loved her and wanted her to forgive me.
>
> She could not understand my words, but she could understand my attention and loving tone. And she would not accept them! She whined, frowned, and seizured, and my heart broke all the more—so she *had* been aware of and hurt by my rejection over the years, and she now was confused by my love.
>
> I felt as the prodigal son must have felt when he came home, broken, to the mercy of his father. He knew he deserved no love in return, yet the father loved him still. Even as my sister cried out, she finally responded to me in her way of forgiveness, with the unconditional love *she* had never had to learn: she reached for me.
>
> I have never hated my sister again. I have had relapses in my giving of affection and attention to her, since unconditional love comes through me only when I am trusting in God, and I have moved away from Him several times since then. But I have not been angry or cruel. And I have cried many times late at night, remembering the cruelty of my rejection, feeling the pain my mom has gone through, and feeling the pains of my sister's situation.
>
> Even the last time I went home, I saw that Carolyn had grown up in some ways; she no longer has the appearance of a child, rather, a teen-ager. So now there is the new struggle of learning how to relate to a baby who looks like a young woman. Again, God is helping me.   (K. McLain, personal communication, March 25, 1985)

The attitude of the parents toward the handicapped child are usually reflected in the attitudes of the siblings. In addition to providing an appropriate model of adjustment, parents should be aware of the distinct needs of siblings of handicapped children.

Siblings of handicapped children need an explanation: one they can understand and can relay to their friends. They need information about the handicap, about its effect on the child and implications for the sibling. Responses to such questions as, How did it happen? Can I catch it? Will my children have it? should be answered with honesty and age-appropriate terminology. They need understanding from their teachers and awareness that they are not responsible for inappropriate behavior of their handicapped sibling in school.

Frequently, siblings of handicapped people need counseling. Sibling support groups can be particularly helpful in acquiring information and coping skills. Members are able to share concerns and solutions to problem situations with other siblings (Chinitz, 1981). A Sibling Information Network has been established to disseminate information and facilitate communication about and among brothers and sisters of handicapped people.

Sibling adjustment is as complicated and conflicting as parental adjustment. The insight gained in the process is evident in the reflections of a sister, as communicated to the author:

> I am the youngest child and the only girl in my family. I was born about eighteen months after my brother, Billy. He and I learned to walk and began to talk at about the same time, as if we were twins. He has Down's Syndrome, and I do not remember being unaware that he is retarded; the only family experience I have contains a handicapped person.
>
> My earliest awarenesses of Billy's difference were stimulated by other people's reactions to him, and I learned to construct my own attitudes and actions. I remember trying to explain why my brother was special, witnessing stares and stifled giggles, and being jealous because he stole my place as the family baby.
>
> I find myself not knowing what to say when describing my family to new acquaintances. I wonder whether I should volunteer that my youngest brother is retarded or whether I should describe him (as I would my other brothers) in terms of where he lives and what he does for a living; neither solution seems open-minded. And once we tell someone about Billy, people often suggest that because we have a retarded family member we must be wonderful and patient people, or that we are blessed (or burdened) by God. This kind of prejudicial statement, based on our "distinction," is one of the most difficult things to address; often the intention is kind but I imagine it is the same sort of comment received by other types of minorities.
>
> The most painful reminders of Billy's handicap have come to us in times of celebration. I don't think any of us has taken for granted the "normal" life conquests of learning to read and to drive, graduating, finding suitable jobs, getting married and having children. At every event, Billy has wondered if it would ever happen for him. The times we have all struggled for our independence were hard on us and on our parents. For my retarded brother, whose need and desire for independence equal ours, the problem has been compounded by one major question: to what degree is he capable of being independent? Billy and my parents have spent years refining the details of his maintaining his household and holding a job.
>
> When I lived in Europe for two years, I developed an empathetic understanding of Billy. I learned how it felt to be unable to read signs to find my own way, to have no independent transportation, to lack the concept of what my money was worth; most of all, I experienced the isolation of not understanding

others and of expressing myself inadequately. I associated all of these problems with the daily frustrations my brother faces.

His capacity for adapting himself to social situations has caused us not to notice sometimes when we leave him out of involved family problems or secrets. He may feel left out when we all laugh at a joke he doesn't understand—but he laughs along. In church, he listens to the words and looks at the hymnal, and you barely notice that his words lag part of a beat behind. But the accomplishments Billy has made in spite of his handicap do challenge us to fulfill our own potentials; he reminds us not to take our own talents for granted. He and my parents have had to search for creative solutions to problems which didn't have immediate or common answers, and in these ways I believe his handicap has affected us in a positive way.

Some aspects of my brother's handicap cause us unrest for ourselves. My sisters-in-law and I wondered if we were more likely than other women to have a retarded baby. My parents have had to consider how Billy will be cared for when they die; and my brothers and I have had to consider that the responsibility will be ours.

I am sure that having a retarded brother has affected my family in many more subtle and devastating ways than I have related. We do feel special for having him in our family, but I will never think it is lucky that he was born retarded. We don't love my brother because he is handicapped, but because he is a good person who usually does his best, and because he's ours. (M. S. deWit, personal communication, May 3, 1984)

Extended Family Relationships

☐ Close relatives and in-laws of the family may be important parts of the resource network and thus contribute to the family's ability to adapt to their handicapped child. Seligman (1979, p. 71) emphasizes the importance of understanding the extended family.

> Professionals have not taken seriously the potential benefit emanating from extended family members, an added dimension in their arsenal. Teachers, in assessing the family's circumstances, should take other family members into account as they contribute or detract from healthy family relations. . . .

Many families of handicapped children feel that they could not have handled the care and expense involved without the help of extended family members. They usually are referring to the grandparents, who have had, in most cases, their own adjustment problems.

Parents hurt when their children hurt. Grandparents experience the grief, the shock, and the pain felt by their children who have a handicapped child. In addition, their understanding may be hampered by a lack of accurate information and previous misconceptions. At any rate, the joy of having a grandchild is limited when that child is not normal.

It is important that grandparents receive the same information and support that are so vital to the parents. Pieper (1976) suggests that grandparents be encouraged to participate in parents' groups focused on understanding children with disabilities.

In addition, grandparents and other relatives need support from their friends as they go through periods of adjustment (Turnbull, 1983). Sometimes they are strong and able to support and encourage the parents; sometimes the reverse is true. Some grandparents may never accept the child and/or the handicap; most of them do, however. Michaelis (1981) reported her parents' adjustment: "The news of a mentally retarded grandchild was a shock, but they learned to love Jim because they love me" (p. 19).

Other extended family members may be affected in a similar way. Among those particularly vulnerable to adjustment difficulties are people who marry siblings of handicapped people. The siblings have had an opportunity to grow with and understand their handicapped brother or sister. Their marriage partners do not share this experience.

Brothers- and sisters-in-law are expected to embrace the families of their spouses. Difficult, at best, the situation is overwhelming if one family member is handicapped. The initial shock and ultimate acceptance are described by the sister-in-law of a mentally retarded person:

☐ *Extended family members can be important parts of a family's resource network.*

I had been seeing Tom on a very casual basis for a short period of time. One afternoon, he invited me to go home with him. "We'll fly kites and you can maybe stay for dinner." I accepted. I knew he had brothers and a sister, but I was totally unprepared for meeting Billy. We walked in the door, and there was Billy, sitting on the sofa watching television and eating his afternoon snack. "Hi, Bill," said Tom. "Hi, Tom," said Billy. "This is Michelle, Billy," said Tom. "Hey," said Billy, without looking away from the television. I think I said "Hey" back, but I really don't remember. Tom had never mentioned the fact that one of his brothers was retarded. I had never been introduced to a handicapped person before. I was hoping the shock didn't show. I tried to be nonchalant, unaffected, normal.

It took several years for me to develop my own acceptance of Billy. Loving him came much sooner. I still don't always understand him.

Now, Tom and I and our two children live next door to Billy. His wails float across our yards as he sings along with his stereo tape player. He is a happy man—living in his own place, going to work every day at a very respectable job, watching soap operas and Benny Hill. I am frequently surprised by the complexities within this simple man.

My children have been raised so close to Billy, with him nearly from birth. Their reactions are only those towards a loved family member. They respond to him emotionally—from the heart—not intellectually. He is their uncle, their friend and neighbor. The three of them dance together to popular rock and roll, or sometimes play Space Invaders. My eight-year-old only recently observed a difference in Billy. His response has been to congratulate and compliment Billy on correct pronunciation. Viewing this for me was tender—bittersweet. (M. Mazzucco, personal communication, February 5, 1984)

Adapting to a handicapped child is a lifelong process, involving each member of the nuclear and the extended family. Adaptation is also required of the community in making provisions for handicapped children and of professionals who work with the families, the children, and the community.

Adaptation to Gifted Children

After examining the anxieties and adjustments experienced by families of handicapped children, it is difficult to imagine that families of intellectually gifted children have similar problems. Yet, this exceptional condition does present potential problems to the families and to the child who is gifted (Ross, 1972).

Parents need help in raising their atypical, gifted children. They do not have standard societal models to direct their interaction with their children (Malone, 1975). In addition, they are aware of the tremendous potential their children have—potential that requires family support in order to develop fully. Some parents handle this challenge with equanimity; others have difficulty adapting to the exceptional needs of their child (Lester & Anderson,

1981). The two areas that present the greatest amount of stress in the family are parental attitudes and sibling relationships.

Parental Attitudes

☐ Inconsistent parental attitudes toward discipline, as well as ignorance and lack of concern for the emotional and social development of their gifted children are crucial factors contributing to emotional and educational problems (Zorman, 1982). High intellectual ability, by itself, does not compensate for lack of parental support and understanding.

Some parents have difficulty in accepting their gifted children and in letting them develop according to their interests (Bridges, 1973). Parents who are seemingly unaware of their child's giftedness may be insecure about their own social or educational level and may feel incompetent at parenting a gifted child (Lester & Anderson, 1981).

On the other hand, some parents are overconcerned with their child's potential and may expect perfection in all areas of the child's life. Such parents may focus all their attention on the gifted child, neglecting other members of the family and creating a stressful, competitive family environment.

Parents may feel threatened by the special abilities of their gifted child, particularly if they are not unusually bright themselves. In such situations, the children may become manipulative and play one parent against the other. Some parents view gifted children as more trouble than other children (Colangelo & Dettmann, 1983).

Sibling Relationships

☐ Ballering and Koch (1984), in an investigation of forty-nine families, found that giftedness has a greater effect on sibling relationships than on parent-child relationships. Bridges (1973) cautions parents against showing a preference for the gifted child and thereby alienating other children in the family. Another problem may arise when the gifted child participates in special school programs not available to other children in the family (Peterson, 1977).

Parents have a difficult job meeting the needs of the gifted child without neglecting other family members. Each child should feel accepted and valuable; each should be comfortable in finding a unique role in the family. Parents of gifted children frequently need counseling in discipline, developing strengths, guiding sensitivity, and understanding family interaction. Ross (1972, p. 160) expresses the magnitude of the problem:

> Helping parents accept their child's difference and supporting them to accommodate family life and sibling relations to the presence of a gifted youngster can be as difficult a task as helping other parents adjust to having a defective child and it requires no less time and effort.

Conclusion

The presence of an exceptional child in the family affects every member of the family. The family, as a system comprised of individuals, adapts to the changes and demands imposed by the exceptional child. Whether the adaptation results in acceptance or rejection of the child, adjustments are required.

The success of a family's adjustment depends on the perceived crisis and the family's practice in dealing with crises; the family's coping resources; and the total ecological framework within which the family operates. In general, stable and resourceful families are able to withstand the effects of an exceptional child. In some cases, the child has a positive effect on parents and siblings, motivating them personally and professionally.

It is important to recognize that families and individuals respond in unique ways to life events. Adjustment to an exceptional child is one such event. Although research offers avenues for predicting the responses of families, exceptions always exist.

Teachers, in particular, should be cognizant of the stresses and demands placed on parents and siblings of exceptional children and young people:

> If educators are serious about the new roles they are asking parents to play, it is crucial to acknowledge the impact that the child may be having on the parents . . . and recognize the unique problems families must face as they attempt to cope. . . . (Beckman-Bell, 1981, p. 51)

The adjustments necessary to meet the needs of the family and the exceptional child are facilitated by a positive parent-teacher relationship. The relationship is an acknowledgement of reciprocal needs and roles: parents and professional frequently work together in the area of family adaptation; they also share responsibilities in the educational process. The parent role in special education is presented in Chapter 4.

References

Ballering, L. D., & Koch, A. (1984). Family relations when a child is gifted. *Gifted Child Quarterly, 28*(3), 140–143.

Beckman, P. J. (1983). Influence of selected child characteristics on stress in families of handicapped infants. *American Journal of Mental Deficiency, 88*(2), 150–56.

Beckman-Bell, P. (1981). Child-related stress in families of handicapped children. *Topics in Early Childhood Special Education, 1*(3), 45–54.

Begab, M. J. (1969). Casework for the mentally retarded—casework with parents. In W. Wolfensberger & R. A. Kurtz (Eds.), *Management of the family of the mentally retarded,* 74–75. Chicago: Parkinson Division, Follett Educational Corp.

Blacher, J. (1984). Sequential stages of parental adjustment to the birth of a child with handicaps: Fact or artifact? *Mental Retardation, 22*(2), 55–68.

Boyd, D. (1969). The three stages in the growth of a parent of a mentally retarded child. In W. Wolfensberger & R. A. Kurtz (Eds.), *Management of the family of the mentally retarded*, 126–129. Chicago: Parkinson Divison, Follett Educational Corp.

Bridges, S. (1973). *Problems of the gifted child*. New York: Crane, Russab & Company.

Bronfenbrenner, U. (1984). Families and education in the U.S. and other countries. *The University of Michigan School of Education Innovator, 16*(1), 1–6.

Buscaglia, L. (1975). *The disabled and their parents*. Thorofare, N.J.: Charles B. Slack.

Canino, F. J., & Reeve, R. E. (1980). General issues in working with parents of handicapped children. In R. R. Abidin (Ed.), *Parent education and intervention handbook*. Springfield, Ill.: Charles C Thomas.

Chinitz, S. P. (1981). A sibling group for brothers and sisters of handicapped children. *Children Today, 10*(6), 21–33.

Cochran, M. M., & Brassard, J. A. (1979). Child development and personal social networks. *Child Development, 50*(3), 601–616.

Colangelo, N., & Dettmann, D. F. (1983). A review of research on parents and families of gifted children. *Exceptional Children, 50*(1), 20–27.

Crnic, K. A., Friedrich, W. N., & Greenberg, M. T. (1983). Adaptation of families with mentally retarded children: A model of stress, coping, and family ecology. *American Journal of Mental Deficiency, 88*(2), 125–138.

Cummings, S. T. (1976). The impact of the child's deficiency on the father: A study of fathers of mentally retarded and of chronically ill children. *American Journal of Orthopsychiatry, 46*(2), 246–255.

Cushing, P. J. (1982). It's a jungle out there. *Special Edition, 2*(3), 1.

D'Alonzo, B. J., & Lazar, A. L. (1983). The severely multiply handicapped child within the family unit. *Journal for Special Educators, 19*(2), 55–63.

Davis, R. E. (1975). Family of physically disabled child. *New York State Journal of Medicine*, 1039–1041.

Drew, C. J., Logan, D. R., & Hardman, M. D. (1984). *Mental retardation* (3rd ed.). St. Louis: Times/Mirror/Mosby.

Dunlap, W. R., & Hollinsworth, J. S. (1977). How does a handicapped child effect the family? Implications for practitioners. *The Family Coordinator, 27*(3), 286–293.

Faerstein, L. M. (1981). Stress and coping in families of learning disabled children: A literature review. *Journal of Learning Disabilities, 14*(7), 420–423.

Farber, B. (1975). Family adaptations to severely mentally retarded children. In M. J. Begab & S. A. Richardson (Eds.), *The mentally retarded and society: A social science perspective*. Baltimore: University Park Press.

Farber, B. (1968). *Mental retardation: Its social context and social consequences*. Boston: Houghton Mifflin.

Featherstone, H. (1980). *A difference in the family*. New York: Penguin Books.

Folkman, S., Schaefer, C., & Lazarus, R. S. (1979). Cognitive processes as mediators of stress and coping. In V. Hamilton & D. M. Warburton (Eds.), *Human stress and cognition*. New York: John Wiley.

Fotheringham, J. B., & Creal, D. (1974). Handicapped children and handicapped families. *International Review of Education, 20*(3), 355–373.

Friedrich, W. N. (1979). Predictors of the coping behavior of mothers of handicapped children. *Journal of Consulting and Clinical Psychology, 47*(6), 1140–1141.

Friedrich, W. N., & Friedrich, W. L. (1981). Psychosocial assets of parents of handicapped and nonhandicapped children. *American Journal of Mental Deficiency, 85*(5), 551–553.

Gallagher, J. J. (1956). Rejecting parents? *Exceptional Children, 22*(7), 273–276.

Gath, A. (1972). The mental health of siblings of congenitally abnormal children. *Journal of Child Psychology and Psychiatry and Allied Disciplines, 13*(3), 211–218.

Graliker, B. V., Fishler, K., & Koch, R. (1962). Teenage reaction to a mentally retarded sibling. *American Journal of Mental Deficiency, 66*(6), 838–843.

Grossman, F. K. (1972). *Brothers and sisters of retarded children.* Syracuse, N.Y.: Syracuse University Press.

Hart, N. W. (1970). Frequently expressed feelings and reactions of parents toward their retarded children. In N. R. Bernstein (Ed.), *Diminished People.* Boston: Little, Brown.

Holroyd, J., & Guthrie, D. (1979). Stress in families of children with neuromuscular disease. *Journal of Clinical Psychology, 35*(4), 734–739.

Holroyd, J., & McArthur, D. (1976). Mental retardation and stress on the parents: A contrast between Down's Syndrome and childhood autism. *American Journal of Mental Deficiency, 80*(4), 431–436.

Huber, C. H. (1979). Parents of the handicapped child: Facilitating acceptance through group counseling. *Personnel and Guidance Journal, 57*(5), 267–269.

Hurley, J. R. (1965). Parental acceptance-rejection and children's intelligence. *Merrill-Palmer Quarterly, 11,* 19–31.

Jerry got lost in the shuffle. (1982). *The Exceptional Parent, 12*(4), 45–51.

Jordan, T. E. (1979). Physical disability in children and family adjustment. In L. Baruth & M. Burggraf (Eds.), *Counseling parents of exceptional children.* Guilford, Conn.: Special Learning Corp.

Lerner, J. W. (1981). *Learning disabilities.* Boston: Houghton Mifflin.

Lester, C. F., & Anderson, R. S. (1981). Counseling with families of gifted children: The school counselor's role. *The School Counselor, 29*(4), 147–151.

Levinson, R. M. (1976). Family crisis and adaptation: Coping with a mentally retarded child. *Dissertation Abstracts International, A36*(102), 8336A–8337A.

Liversidge, E. B., & Grana, G. M. (1979). A hearing impaired child in the family. In L. Baruth & M. Burggraf (Eds.), *Counseling parents of exceptional children,* 159–166. Guilford, Conn.: Special Learning Corp.

Malone, C. E. (1975). Education for parents of the gifted. *Gifted Child Quarterly, 19*(3), 223–225.

Marcus, L. M. (1977). Patterns of coping in families of psychotic children. *American Journal of Orthopsychiatry, 47*(3). 388–389.

Margalit, M. (1982). Learning disabled children and their families: Strategies of extension and adaptation of family therapy. *Journal of Learning Disabilities, 15*(10), 594–595.

Marion, R. L. (1981). *Educators, parents and exceptional children.* Rockville, Md.: Aspen Systems Corp.

Michaelis, C. (1981). The family makes the difference, *The Exceptional Parent, II*(3), 40–43.

Mori, A. A. (1983). *Families of children with special needs*. Rockville, Md.: Aspen Systems Corp.

Nihira, K., Mink, I. T., & Meyers, C. E. (1981). Relationship between home environment and school adjustment of TMR children. *American Journal of Mental Deficiency, 86*(1), 8–15.

Pearlin, L. I., Lieberman, M. A., Menaghan, E. G., & Mullan, J. T. (1981). The stress process. *Journal of Health and Social Behavior, 22*(Dec.), 337–356.

Perosa, L. M., & Perosa, S. L. (1981). The school counselor's use of structural family therapy with learning-disabled students, *The School Counselor, 29*(2), 152–155.

Peterson, D. (1977). The heterogenously gifted family. *The Gifted Child Quarterly, 21*(3), 396–408.

Pieper, E. (1976). Grandparents can help. *The Exceptional Parent, 6*(2), 7–10.

Powell, D. R. (1979). Family-environment relations and early childrearing: The role of social networks and neighborhoods. *Journal of Research and Development in Education, 13*(1), 1–11.

Poznanski, E. O. (1973). Emotional issues in raising handicapped children. *Rehabilitation Literature, 34*(11), 322–326.

Ricci, C. S. (1970). Analysis of child-rearing attitudes of mothers of retarded, emotionally disturbed, and normal children. *American Journal of Mental Deficiency, 74*(6), 756–761.

Robinson, N. M., & Robinson, H. B. (1976). *The mentally retarded child*. New York: McGraw-Hill.

Ross, A. O. (1972). *The exceptional child in the family*. New York: Grune & Stratton.

Ryckman, D. B., & Henderson, R. A. (1970). The meaning of a retarded child for his parents: A focus for counselors. In M. Schreiber (Ed.), *Social work and mental retardation*, 96–103. New York: John Day Co.

Schulz, J. B. (1978). The parent-professional conflict. In A. P. Turnbull & H. R. Turnbull (Eds.), *Parents speak out*. Columbus, Oh.: Charles E. Merrill.

Searl, S. J. (1978). Stages of parent reaction. *The Exceptional Parent, 8*(2), F27–29.

Seligman, M. (1983). Siblings of handicapped persons. In M. Seligman (Ed.), *The family with a handicapped child*. New York: Grune & Stratton.

Seligman, M. (1979). *Strategies for helping parents of exceptional children*. New York: The Free Press.

Shillingburg, D. H. (1982). Sometimes it's hard to love. *Boy's Life, 72*(12), 24–25.

Suran, B. G., & Rizzo, J. V. (1983). *Special children* (2nd ed.). Glenview, Ill.: Scott, Foresman.

Tavormina, J. B., Boll, T. J., Dunn, N. J., Luscomb, R. L., & Taylor, J. R. (1981). Psycho-social effects on parents of raising a physically handicapped child. *Journal of Abnormal Child Psychology, 9*(1), 121–131.

Tew, B. J., Payne, H., & Lawrence, K. M. (1974). Must a family with a handicapped child be a handicapped family? *Developmental Medicine and Child Neurology, 16*, 95–98.

Trevino, F. (1979). Siblings of handicapped children: Identifying those at risk. *Social Casework, 60*(8), 488–493.

Turnbull, A. P. (1983). Growing with a handicapped child in the family and community: A parent's perspective. In J. L. Paul, (Ed.), *The exceptional child*. Syracuse, N.Y.: Syracuse University Press.

Wentworth, E. H. (1974). *Listen to your heart: A message to parents of handicapped children.* Boston: Houghton Mifflin.

Wikler, L. (1981). Chronic stresses of families of mentally retarded children. *Family Relations, 30*(2), 281–288.

Wikler, L., Wasow, M., & Hatfield, E. (1981). Chronic sorrow revisited: Parent vs. professional depiction of the adjustment of parents of mentally retarded children. *American Journal of Orthopsychiatry, 51*(1), 63–70.

Wright, B. (1960). *Physical disability—a psychological approach.* New York: Harper & Row.

Zorman, R (1982). Parents do make a difference. *Roeper Review, 5*(2), 41–43.

4

The Parents' Role in Special Education

Background of Parent Involvement

☐ ☐ Regardless of the level of acceptance and the positive or negative effect on their lives, families of exceptional children and young people have problems and responsibilities not felt by other families. Although the problems and responsibilities are similar in nature to those of all families, they differ in severity and duration. A handicapped child, for example, may be handicapped for a lifetime, requiring special services and care from parents and community agencies. A gifted child presents a different life situation but still needs an unusual commitment from the parents. In trying to meet these responsibilities, parents of exceptional children have progressed from providers of care to recipients of services and finally to participants in the educational process.

Parents as Providers

☐ Although a number of community agencies are involved with handicapped and gifted people, education has been the primary agency to focus on the needs of this population. In the United States, special education was developed around the middle of the twentieth century, primarily aimed at providing services for mildly mentally retarded children.

Even with the advent of special education, a number of parents of exceptional children found that their youngsters were excluded from school. In many schools, admission policy required that children be ambulatory, verbal, toilet trained, and functional at a specified mental age level. Thus, many parents became providers of their childrens' education. Classes for trainable mentally retarded children, in particular, began to appear in churches and community service buildings. These classes were frequently taught, and always financed, by parents.

More severely handicapped children were institutionalized at state or family expense or were kept at home. As late as 1968, the statement was made that "for the severely retarded trainable child in the community, the major portion of activities generally centers in the home" (Farber, 1968, p. 249). Parents who kept their children at home received little help from social agencies and no help from educational agencies. Education was viewed as academic in nature, and severely handicapped children were not expected to learn. Parents or institutional staff members met their physical needs, with the emphasis on protection from harm rather than on education. This treatment reflected the attitudes of society.

Societal attitudes were also reflected in philosophies toward educating gifted and talented children. Education for exceptionally bright children was viewed as elitism and therefore undemocratic. Concerned parents provided additional stimulation, financed private schools, or worked with their children to the best of their abilities. For all groups of exceptional children, parents were the first providers of special education.

Parents as Recipients

Events leading to and following Word War II had a tremendous influence on attitudes toward exceptional people and the extension of educational services. Group and individual testing, used with service men for purposes of ability grouping, became acceptable practices and generalized to the school situation. As wounded men returned to their communities, disabilities became more visible, the problems of families were recognizable, and rehabilitation became a national responsibility. Acceptance and education of handicapped children began to follow.

During the same period, scientific advances made by the Russians pointed out deficiencies in the education of gifted children, particularly in the areas of math and science. Education of bright and talented children became a national concern.

In 1960, the White House Conference on Children and Youth projected the goal "to promote opportunities for children and youth to realize their full potential for a creative life in freedom and dignity" (President's Committee on Mental Retardation, 1977, p. 30). A recommendation of the conference was to strengthen the U.S. Office of Education, with an emphasis on programs of special education.

In the area of mental retardation, the Kennedy administration led a massive national effort toward education. In addition, parents' demands for equal educational opportunities for their retarded children were being felt by local school boards and in state legislatures.

The President's Committee on Mental Retardation (1977, p. 21) described the situation:

> In 1950, the parents and their retarded children were still stigmatized. Public institutions were intolerable, but still with long waiting lists. Special classes in the

schools, where they existed, were ill-conceived, poorly taught, and sharply restrictive. Private schools were for the wealthy. Doctors spoke of incurability and recommended placing the child in an institution. Psychologists measured I.Q. and gave little help. Social workers knew little of the problems of retardation in the family.

Response at the national level led to federally funded programs of teacher education and special services for children. Special classes became the preferred type of educational services for handicapped students. The role of the parents became that of recipient.

Parents of exceptional children, for the most part, have been expected to be passive concerning the education of their children (Fanning, 1977). If the special classes were filled, their children were put on a waiting list. Placement decisions were made by school personnel based on tests administered without parental knowledge or consent. Curriculum choices, evaluation procedures, and reporting techniques were determined by teachers. As recipients of services, parents were led to feel fortunate that their children had places in the public schools.

Parents as Participants

Kirk and Gallagher (1979) refer to the roles parents have served as scapegoats, program organizers and participants, political activists, and partners. Participation grew as more information was gained regarding the role that parents can play in the early development of disadvantaged children. Programs of the 1960s, aimed at providing compensatory services and developing early childhood programs, also stimulated research related to interaction of families and children. These investigations demonstrated that parental involvement does make a positive difference in children's education (Mandell & Fiscus, 1981).

Parents of exceptional children have become active participants in their children's education. Although there are varying degrees of involvement (discussed later in this chapter), the general feeling seems to be that:

> when parents are involved in a more active way in the day-to-day educational activities of their children, communication between the parents and school personnel becomes more open, thus helping both the teacher and the parent to be more effective. (Dembrowsky, 1983, p. 25)

During the last decade, national attention has been focused on the importance of parents as part of the educational team. Turnbull (1983, pp. 19–20) lists reasons contributing to the recognition of this importance:

1. The experimental evidence that parents can positively influence the development of their children through teaching them at home.
2. The encouraging results of early intervention in ameliorating the developmental deficits associated with actual and "at-risk" handicaps.

3. The success of parents in bringing litigation to establish the educational right of their children.
4. The resulting federal legislation, PL 94–142 (Education for All Handicapped Children Act), which sets forth clear standards for parent involvement in the educational process.

Some parents will continue to be providers, some recipients, and some participants. Most people consider active parent participation to be the ideal. The rights of exceptional people and the role of their parents became clearly defined through parent advocacy and legislative action.

Parent Advocacy

Advocacy can be defined as a process of representing the interests of other people in an effort to insure that their rights are protected. In regard to parents of exceptional children, the advocacy role requires that parents represent the interests of their child and insure that the school system provides an appropriate education for the child (Turnbull & Leonard, 1981).

It is an American conviction that children grow up to be more effective citizens if the ultimate responsibility for their welfare remains with their parents (Boggs, 1969). Montessori (1972, p. 215) declared the focus of this responsibility:

> Parents should be concerned with the great social question of the day, the struggle to gain a recognition of the rights of childhood in the world.

Child advocacy has been described as a growing social movement that speaks to the need to provide more effective services and also the need to protect the child against services that favor the interest of the system at the expense of the child (Paul, 1977). Parents are partial to their children and should be partisans for them (Boggs, 1969).

Advocacy is "a developing methodology for making our child-rearing and special child-serving institutions and practices at least partially accountable to the child" (Paul, 1977, p. 9). Only parents can guarantee the programs and services to which their children are entitled. To be effective, parents must be concerned, knowledgeable, and active.

Parent advocacy has been a strong force in bringing about legislative action for handicapped and gifted children and adolescents. This force has been a result of parental concern, parental pressure, and parent groups.

Parental Concern

In the late sixties and early seventies, parents began to realize that exceptional students were being denied the opportunity to fulfill their potential abilities.

Fanning (1977) perceived lack of access to the "system" as the largest stumbling block to an equal education.

Parents felt the stigma placed on their handicapped children by a school system patterned on "regular or general" education for the so-called normal and another separate system for the so-called abnormal (Corrigan, 1980). Another concern emerged from the growing practice, for economic reasons, of setting up self-contained special classes, often removed from regular classes. Too often, these classes became dumping grounds for children with behavior problems and a place to segregate ethnic or racial minorities (Sarason & Doris, 1978).

Parents and educators were becoming disenchanted with the widespread practice of attaching negative labels to children, frequently without justification. Emerging literature supported the claim by many parents that special education was inferior to regular education.

Parents of severely handicapped children expressed the most direct, forceful, and effective concerns. These children had been denied any access to public education. Their parents were forceful and courageous in seeking appropriate educational services for them.

Parental Pressure

☐ The beginning of parental pressure is expressed in the report of the President's Committee on Mental Retardation (1977): "As the fires of World War II burned out, a smouldering volcano of outraged parenthood erupted, and the mountainside of public opinion moved" (p. 1). By the fifties, legislators and policymakers were turning to parents for advice on planning programs for handicapped children. Interest in serving the handicapped population increased dramatically during the Kennedy administration. In a message to Congress in 1963, President Kennedy called for a "bold new approach" to the care of mentally retarded people (National Association for Retarded Citizens, 1977). The presence of a handicapped individual in the president's family strengthened the parental influence at the national, as well as local, level.

At this time, parents and other advocates of handicapped people increased their pressure on public agencies to provide needed services. This pressure was made effective through the organization of parent groups.

Parent Groups

☐ Following World War II, many groups organized for the welfare of handicapped people. Most of these groups were organized by parents and gained strength from the personal involvement and concern of their founders and members. Cain (1976) reports the existence of local parent groups before the 1930s, although the major thrust came in the 1940s and 1950s with the organization of such national groups as the National Association for Retarded Children (now the National Association for Retarded Citizens) and the United Cerebral Palsy Association.

The effect of parent organization was to provide a source of mutual aid and comfort, a second base from which to act in securing better services for their own children, and a catalytic agent to bring about broad social change in dealing with a human problem (President's Committee on Mental Retardation, 1977). Concerns for handicapped individuals led parent groups to organize formally. The first efforts were to provide educational programs through private schools, and the next step was to sponsor legislation to make special education programs a function of the public schools. Other projects included sheltered workshops, vocational training centers, diagnostic facilities, parent education services, preschool and postschool facilities, guardianship plans, community centers, research, professional training, and medical services (Cain, 1976).

The majority of activities related to advocacy and litigation were initiated by parent groups (Blackhurst & Berdine, 1981). Professional organizations such as the Council for Exceptional Children (CEC) and the American Association on Mental Deficiency (AAMD) joined parent activists to form powerful

☐ *Parent groups provide parents with a source of mutual aid and comfort, a means of securing better services for their children, and a catalytic agent to bring about change.*

advocacy groups. Results of the group work prompted parents of children with other handicaps to organize. In 1963, the Association for Children with Learning Disabilities (ACLD) became active and, with the help of professional organizations, was instrumental in bringing about the passage of the Learning Disability Act of 1969 (Haring, 1982).

Organized parents' groups for gifted children were formed at a later time and have not exerted the same influence as those concerned with handicapped children (Kirk & Gallagher, 1983). The national interest in educating gifted students sparked in the fifties became overshadowed in the sixties by public concern for the disadvantaged and by attempts to provide equal opportunity to all individuals. Gifted programs seemed antithetical to this movement (Silverman, 1982). The public was much more receptive to the concerns expressed by parents of handicapped children. Many parents of gifted children and adolescents feel that these youngsters have been neglected and that the public has failed to provide for their education in any significant way.

> For years we have steadily improved the educational opportunities for the mentally, physically, and emotionally handicapped and should continue to do so. But at the same time, we should recognize the exceptional needs of the gifted as well and realize that neglect can produce mental and emotional problems for this group, too. (Delp & Martinson, 1977, p. 25)

Parents of gifted children often become concerned about their children's education and find it helpful to form advocacy groups for purposes similar to those discovered by parents of handicapped children: to talk about similar problems, to develop strategies in dealing with the schools, and to press for legislature to help their own children and others (Hall & Skinner, 1980).

The dynamic effects of parental activism were demonstrated in 1971, when the Commonwealth of Pennsylvania entered into a consent agreement with the Pennsylvania Association for Retarded Children (PARC). This agreement, the result of a class action suit filed by parents, provided a free and appropriate public education for all mentally retarded children in the state. The next year, in a suit filed against the Washington, D.C. Board of Education (*Mills v. Board of Education,* 1972), a decree was issued that affirmed the right of all handicapped children to a publicly supported education. Subsequently, cases were brought against other school districts over the issues of placement and labeling, techniques of psychological diagnosis, and the role of parents in the process of public education (Haring, 1982).

Following the *PARC* and *Mills* cases, legislators and advocates for handicapped people pressed for federal laws that would specify the responsibilities of public schools and the rights of handicapped people. The most significant pieces of legislation designed to accomplish these goals were Section 504 of the Rehabilitation Act of 1973 and Public Law 94–142, the Education for All Handicapped Children Act, passed in 1975.

Legislative Action

In addition to parental pressure and advocacy, a number of social factors led to legislation for handicapped people. During the sixties, all elements of inhumanity were being challenged, as described by Paul and Porter (1981, p. 14):

> War, bigotry, racism, and human exploitation in all forms were torn from the dark and damp underside of institutional policies and practices, from the courts to the corridors of institutions for the handicapped. These injustices were dragged out into the heat and light of fresh analysis under old lamps—justice, civil liberty, fairness, decency, right to life, right to work, freedom, and the right to dignity.

The 1954 Supreme Court decision to desegregate public schools provided a legal basis for equal protection of all children, including the handicapped. Section 504 of the Rehabilitation Act of 1973 was established to eliminate discrimination against handicapped people in all governmental and private institutions that receive federal assistance, including schools. Public Law 94–142 established the rights of handicapped children and youth in preschool, elementary, and secondary programs to a free appropriate public education (Turnbull & Turnbull, 1982). Corrigan (1978, p. 18) expresses the magnitude of this law:

> The Education for All Handicapped Children Act, Public Law 94–142, received a clear mandate in the Congress of the United States. It was passed 404–7 in the House of Representatives and 87–7 in the Senate. This Act is the most important piece of educational legislation in the history of this country.

Public Law 94–142 is unique in advancing the concept that parents should be involved in decisions about their children's education. A stated purpose of the law is to assure that the rights of handicapped children and their parents are protected (Turnbull & Turnbull, 1982).

The following are mandated or provided for in the law:

- All children with special needs must be provided a free appropriate public education. (The law specifies ages between 3 and 21; exceptions may be made if states do not provide services to nonhandicapped children in this age range.)
- Special needs children must receive this education at no cost to their parents.
- Each child must receive an education designed to meet the child's own needs.
- Parents must be allowed to participate in educational decisions affecting their children.
- The child must be evaluated with tests or instruments which do not discriminate because of his/her special needs.

- ☐ Parents may see all of the education records for their child. The parents must give permission for school records to be shared with anyone not involved in the education of the child.
- ☐ Each child with special needs should be placed in a program as much like the regular class as possible. Some children with special needs may be able to stay in the regular class with special education resources, but others may need a special class or a special school.
- ☐ Children will normally be served within the public school system. Sometimes it may be necessary for the school system to place a child in a private school, another school system, or some other approved program in order to meet the child's needs.
- ☐ Parents may object to the evaluation, placement recommendation or the provision of a free appropriate public education for the child through a due process hearing. (Division for Exceptional Children, North Carolina Department of Public Instruction, 1982, p. 1)

In identifying the role of parents in the education of their handicapped children and adolescents, it is necessary to examine and understand all facets of the law. Of particular importance are regulations concerning parent consent and notice, confidentiality of information, rights of due process, and parent participation in the individualized education program (IEP).

Parent Consent and Notice

- ☐ The school district must notify the parents in writing before it proposes or refuses to make a change regarding the identification, evaluation, or placement of handicapped students. The parents must understand the evaluation and placement procedures and be informed about records that are to be released. Parental consent is given voluntarily and may be withdrawn at any time.

Confidentiality of Information

- ☐ The confidentiality provision guarantees parental control of records. No one who is not involved in the child's education may have access to a handicapped child's records without written permission of the parent. Parents may review any or all of the child's records and may request interpretation or amendment of the records.

Due Process

- ☐ Due process entitles both parents and professionals to fair procedures in the identification, evaluation, and placement of handicapped students. When conflicting opinions exist on these issues, a due process hearing may be initiated by parents or school personnel. The due process requirements constitute a system of checks and balances regarding decisions made by parents and professionals (Schulz & Turnbull, 1984).

Parent Participation in the IEP

☐ An individualized education program, or IEP, must be developed for each student identified as handicapped and in need of special education. The components of the IEP are specified in the law. Each IEP must include the following:

1. A documentation of the student's current level of educational performance.
2. Annual goals or the attainments expected by the end of the school year.
3. Short-term objectives, stated in instructional terms, which are the intermediate steps leading to the mastery of annual goals.
4. Documentation of the particular special education and related services which will be provided to the child.
5. An indication of the extent of time a child will participate in the regular education program.
6. Projected dates for initiating services and the anticipated duration of services.
7. Evaluation procedures and schedules for determining mastery of short-term objectives at least on an annual basis. (Turnbull, Strickland, & Brantley, 1982, p. 5)

Participating members are also designated and include:

1. A representative of the public agency, other than the student's teacher, who has qualifications to provide or supervise the provision of special education.
2. The child's teacher.
3. One or both of the child's parents.
4. The child when appropriate.
5. Other individuals at the request of the parents or public agency.
6. For handicapped children evaluated for the first time, either a member of the evaluation team must be present at the meeting or another individual at the meeting (representative of the public agency, or the child's teacher) must be knowledgeable about the evaluation procedures used with the child and familiar with the results. (Turnbull, Strickland, & Brantley 1982, p. 6)

Parent participation in decision making is an important part of the IEP meeting. Parents must be notified of the purpose, time, and location of the meeting. Unless there is documentation that parents were contacted, meetings cannot be held without them. The clarification of IEP requirements issued by the U.S. Office of Special Education emphasizes the parents' role:

The IEP meeting serves as a communication vehicle between parents and school personnel, and enables them as equal participants to jointly decide what the child's needs are, what services will be provided to meet those needs, and what the anticipated outcomes will be. (Federal Register, 1981, p. 5462)

Parent participation in the development and implementation of the IEP can be the realization of a dream frequently expressed by educators: the opportunity to work with parents in planning for their children. As working members of the multidisciplinary team, parents have the opportunity and the responsibility to fulfill that dream. Parent input is valuable in the areas of evaluation, defining goals and objectives, implementing instruction, and monitoring progress of the student.

Evaluation Parents are to be included in the diagnostic evaluation as soon as a problem is suspected. School personnel should begin by inviting parents to school to explain the suspected problem and the school's plan of action (Strenecky, McLoughlin, & Edge, 1979).

Providing information is a major role parents play in the evaluation process. Indeed, this is their chief (and sometimes only) role as perceived by a number of professional members of the team (Lusthaus, Lusthaus, & Gibbs, 1981). Morgan (1981, pp. 69–70) identifies four types of information for

☐ *Parent input is valuable and necessary to the successful development and implementation of the IEP.*

parents to compile in notebook form for use in the identification and referral process:

1. Informal behavior observations. This will include parental observations as well as those of any professionals in contact with the parents. Frequently, children behave and/or react very differently at home than they do at school. A parent's observations are important and should be recorded. They could be meaningful and well worth sharing at a later date.

2. Formal assessment. These observations are available to parents from the child's school as well as from doctors. Any medical, educational, or psychological test results should be entered into the notebook. Any questions about these reports should be listed, including terms used and the person who conducted the assessments. The answers should be noted so that they may be referred to at a later time.

3. Significant discrepancies. Sometimes there is a difference between what a test says a child can do or what a parent knows a child can do and what the child is actually achieving. These discrepancies should be noted for subsequent discussion.

4. Intervention attempts to date. Any attempts that have been made to address the child's problem should be noted. The relative effectiveness of the intervention efforts should also be logged.

In addition to contributing information to the evaluation of the child, the parents should share in decisions determining appropriate placement for the student.

The National Association for Retarded Citizens (1977, p. 7) has developed a checklist for parents to use in evaluating the identification, referral, and placement process the school uses:

1. Does the school require the parent's consent prior to the evaluation?
2. Are the members of the evaluation team trained in the administration of evaluation tests?
3. Are the members of the evaluation team certified by the state?
4. Is the child tested for physical, mental and social abilities in the evaluation process?
5. Do the parents have free access to all of the information gathered in the evaluation process?
6. Does the school explain to the parents the meaning of the test results in terms that they can understand?
7. Following assessment, are parents advised of the placement options available to the child?

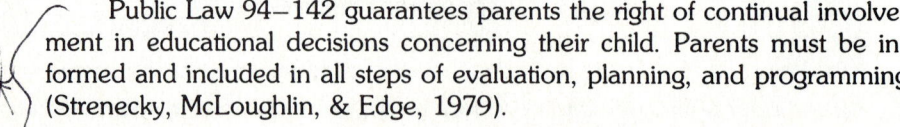
Public Law 94–142 guarantees parents the right of continual involvement in educational decisions concerning their child. Parents must be informed and included in all steps of evaluation, planning, and programming (Strenecky, McLoughlin, & Edge, 1979).

Goals and Objectives Parents, as well as teachers, have expectations of their children on short-term and long-term bases. The IEP conference provides a format for all participants to pool their information and knowledge in proposing realistic goals and objectives. Teachers may be more aware of the academic potential of the child, but the parents have goals derived from family values and cultural expectations.

Parents should consider program elements in addition to academic components. If they believe their child can benefit from a vocational program, for example, it should be considered in IEP development (Crawford, 1978).

Fanning (1977) suggests that the instructional objectives can form the basis or vehicle for a continuing dialogue between parents and the school. They can be used to keep parents informed about the success or failure of the child in designated areas of development and to indicate the need for evaluating the appropriateness of the goals.

Implementing Instruction In testifying before Congress before the enactment of PL 94–142, Senator Harrison Williams stated:

> One of the greatest benefits that can come to the handicapped child is to have the parents brought into the conferences, because the education of the child continues after the school doors close and the child is at home. This is one of the reasons the idea of the mandatory conference was developed, to make sure the parent is part of the education of the child. (Congressional Record, 1975, p. 19489)

Not only do parents play a vital role in advocating for their children's right to an education and in securing appropriate services, but they also play an important role in carrying out instruction specified in the IEP (Morgan, 1981).

Obviously, some parents are better qualified than others to be teachers of their children. Parents are teachers, however, and are present at the most teachable moments. A number of factors affect the amount and quality of teaching that takes place in the home. Some parents do not have the cooperation, time, energy, or resources that promote optimal learning (Schulz, 1982). Other parents will want to become directly involved in their child's learning, particularly if they have had input into the goals and objectives. Interest in implementing the instruction at home not only facilitates learning for the child but also creates a direct and continual communication between the school and the home. Table 4.1 illustrates how parents can extend and reinforce skills specified in the IEP (D'Zamko & Raiser, 1981).

Programs implemented at home are likely to be successful if they are easily managed, integrated into the routine of the home, modeled clearly during a training session, suggested by a parent, and reinforced by the school staff (Porcella, 1980).

TABLE 4.1 Home Activities to Extend and Reinforce IEP Skills

Skill	Activity	Item
Form constancy	Child will find the word "soup" as many time as he can.	Campbell's Soup label
Initial blends	Child will find as many initial blends as he can.	Pringle's Potato Chip can
Long vowel generalization	Child will find and say as many long vowel words as he can.	Tide box
Compound words	Child will find as many compound words as he can.	Mr. Goodbar
Syllabication	Child will divide the following words into syllables: artificial flavor, vitamin, directions, contents, information.	Kool-Aid
Plural nouns	Child will find as many plural words as he can.	Nabisco Shredded Wheat
Vocabulary	Child will find the following words and tell what they mean: essential, natural, nutrition, fortified, analysis.	Froot Loops
Finding facts	Child will recall facts from "Marshmallow Treats" recipe.	Rice Krispies
Comprehension	Child will compare 4 sets of directions and tell how they are different.	Mug-O-Lunch

Source: D'Zamko, Mary and Raiser, Lynne, IEP Development and Implementation: Systematic Parent-Teacher Collaboration. *Teaching Exceptional Children, 13* (3) 1981, p. 123. Copyright (1981) by The Council for Exceptional Children. Reprinted with permission.

Monitoring Progress

If parents have participated in making decisions about the education of their child, they will be aware of the progress being made and, if they are involved in implementing instruction, will be contributing to that progress. The IEP contains an evaluation statement related to each objective. This statement can be used to determine effectiveness of strategies used at home as well as those used at school.

As indicated in responses to a questionnaire presented to 116 parents of exceptional students, more parents would like to be involved in determining how and when their children's progress is to be evaluated (Soffer, 1982). The reason for this desire for increased participation can be attributed to a national movement toward accountability and to the fact that parents want their children to learn.

Ultimately, the parental role defined in PL 94–142 provides for accountability and monitoring to insure that each handicapped child is receiving an appropriate education. The U.S. Office of Special Education, in examining the impact of PL 94–142 on handicapped children and their families, noted:

> progress in inclusion of handicapped children in public education programs; in assuring handicapped children fair, comprehensive evaluations; in provision of a greater range of program and placement options than has been available historically; and in likelihood that handicapped children will be at least administratively—though sometimes not socially and instructionally—integrated with their nonhandicapped peers. (Halpern, 1982, p. 271)

It also noted the difficulties inherent in the necessary realignment of roles and responsibilities among special educators, regular educators, and parents.

Although roles are not yet clearly defined, benefits to children have increased through parent participation. Shevin (1983) expresses concern that the chief focus of parental involvement has become that of signing appropriate forms on the appropriate date. This focus could divert parents and professionals away from the basic purpose of parental input: to allow parents to function effectively as decision makers for their children.

Education of Gifted Children

Gifted children are not included under the provisions of PL 94–142 and remain without meaningful assistance from federal sources. In 1980, for example, the amount spent by the federal government on programs for gifted students was less than 1 percent of that spent on handicapped students (Kirk & Gallagher, 1983).

In 1977, representatives of the Council for Exceptional Children (CEC) called on Congress to realize that the education of gifted and talented children should become a federal priority (Zettel & Ballard, 1978). CEC had also adopted a policy statement that stated:

> special educators should vigorously support programs for the gifted as consistent with their concept of the need for special assistance for all exceptional children. (Zettel & Ballard, 1978, p. 262)

A 1972 federal study referred to as the Marland Report revealed that approximately two million children had been identified as gifted, only a few of whom were being served. For the first time in history, the federal government officially recognized the gifted and talented and established the Office of Gifted and Talented (Silverman, 1982). The national study set goals for education of gifted students but made no efforts toward implementation.

The official federal policy toward gifted and talented students recommends, but does not mandate, special educational services. The primary responsibility for developing and implementing special services for gifted students lies with local and state educational agencies; the national role remains one of technical assistance (Ysseldyke & Algozzine, 1984).

At the present time, thirty states categorize gifted children as exceptional either in statute or state department of education regulations to support the provision of programs (Wolf & Stephens, 1982). Many state programs have the same provisions for referral, evaluation, and IEP development as those provided under PL 94–142 for students who are handicapped.

The lack of federally mandated provisions for the education of gifted children may be due in part to misconceptions about the children and their parents (Callahan & Kauffman, 1982). Many people believe that gifted children can be adequately educated without benefit of special programs or parent involvement. Some people assume that the parents of these students are also gifted and thus can provide appropriate resources for them. This may be true in some cases, but it cannot be assumed as the rule.

Parents play an integral role in the identification of gifted children; parents are often better able to identify giftedness than are teachers, especially in the primary grades (Silverman, 1982). Parents also play an important part in program planning. Kanigher (1977, p. vi) stresses the importance of parent involvement and declares:

> The parent of the gifted child has a very special opportunity to broaden the learning horizons of the child who is a potential leader of our country; a future scientist; an award-winning writer; or one of many accomplished and notable figures.

The special needs of gifted children should be recognized and granted the same urgency as the needs of handicapped children. The same rights should be accorded to parents of gifted children as to parents of handicapped children: the right to share in the decisions made concerning the education of their children. Parent and professional groups are advocating for these rights; perhaps they will soon be recognized on a national level.

Levels of Participation

The rights of parents to participate in the education of their handicapped children are firmly established in the provisions of PL 94–142. Moreover, the parental role is viewed as that of an active participant in making decisions, plans, and evaluations regarding appropriate educational strategies. However, current research efforts reveal that a large discrepancy appears to exist between the promise of parental participation and the practice of parental participation (Dickson & DiPaola, 1980).

In addition to the legal justification, it is assumed that the child will make greater progress if the home and school are in agreement. Therefore, cooperative planning between parents and professionals is in the student's best interest. At the least, parents have the right to approve or disapprove their child's IEP. At the most, they may be actively involved in planning their child's school program and implementing that program at home (Porcella, 1980). The levels of involvement can be described as active participation, passive participation, and nonparticipation.

Active Participation

Yoshida and Gottlieb (1977) conceptualize active participation as a sequential process in which members generate alternatives, evaluate those alternatives, and finally select a solution. Thus, parents would suggest placements for the child and, perhaps, appropriate instructional strategies. They might evaluate the proposed placement and programs by questioning their suitability for the student and, finally, help select the placement and program.

Ongoing active participation requires a serious commitment from parents and from the professionals who work with them. However, this type of parental involvement offers several positive effects:

1. The parent is in a position to provide continuity to the child's program.
2. The parent has access to extensive information concerning resources and alternatives for the child.
3. Parental participation ensures that the goals selected are realistic and feasible, as well as appropriate.
4. Parental participation ensures that there is on the planning team one person—the parent—acting as the child's advocate who does not have concurrent and potentially conflicting responsibilities to the care-providing institutions. (Shevin, 1983, p. 19)

Some parents are not able or willing to make the commitment required for active participation. Also, some professionals are not willing to share their own power and expertise with parents who may not be perceived as capable decision-makers.

Soffer (1982) suggests that some parents are dissatisfied with limited participation. Since parental dissatisfaction can be counterproductive to a positive school-home relationship, it would be helpful for persons working with parents in IEP meetings and other settings to know in which, if any, areas they wish to have more active participation.

Passive Participation

☐ Several studies indicate that parents' attendance at IEP meetings is good (Goldstein, Strickland, Turnbull, & Curry, 1980; Scanlon, Arick, & Phelps, 1981). In fact, the two consistent participants at all observed IEP conferences were the resource teacher and the parent (usually the mother). However, although the parents do attend, their role may involve minimal influence. It must not be assumed, therefore, that the mere presence of the parent at the IEP meeting constitutes involvement (Goldstein, Strickland, Turnbull, & Curry, 1980).

A survey of professionals indicated two areas of involvement they considered appropriate for parents: presenting information relevant to the case and gathering information relevant to the case (Yoshida, Fenton, Kaufman, & Maxwell, 1978). Subsequently, parents were questioned about their perceptions of involvement in school decision-making (Lusthaus, Lusthaus, & Gibbs, 1981). The results indicated that parents most often fulfill the role of giving and receiving information. They also indicated that this is the role they want to have.

Passive participation can be viewed as informed consent in which the parent has two choices: to consent or temporarily to freeze the process by refusing consent to the IEP proposed by the professional team (Shevin, 1983). Even when the presence of parents may be considered important to the IEP meeting, their contribution and influence may be considered low (Gilliam & Coleman, 1981).

Parent participation can be seen as falling along a continuum from passive recipient and provider of information to an active partner in the educational process (Cervone & O'Leary, 1982).

Nonparticipation

☐ Some parents may not participate in the decisions concerning their handicapped children. Cultural and language barriers, difficult family situations, and time constraints may prohibit involvement. In addition, parents may not want to be involved and are willing and eager for the school to assume responsibility for their child's education. The individuality of parents is stressed by Turnbull and Turnbull (1982, p. 116), who present the following thesis:

> Parents are a heterogeneous rather than a homogeneous group. They have different degrees of capability, time, energy, and interest in being education decision makers. The assumptions underlying parent involvement are based more on what some advocates and policy makers think parents ought to be and do rather than on universally held parent preferences for involvement. Expecting all parents to be equal participants in decision making is setting up many—if not most—parents to fail and many educators to be disillusioned by parents who do not fulfill this awesome and sometimes unwelcome responsibility.

Even though some parents may choose noninvolvement, professionals may encourage them to participate. Marion (1981) points out that "teachers not only must learn to work with parents who want to be allies but . . . also must deal with those who might want to abdicate all responsibility and involvement in the teacher-parent relationship" (p. 31).

Conclusion

Although active parent participation has been mandated, the individual capabilities, needs, and desires of parents have not been considered in determining the level of participation that is appropriate or expected. In defining the role of parents in the IEP process, Morgan (1982, p. 38) offers the following three suggestions:

> 1. Parents of handicapped children should be involved in the IEP process as much as they want to be and as much as they can be. Parents should not turn away from their basic responsibility of ensuring their child's health, safety, and welfare. Some parents may need to become more involved in their child's education than they would prefer in order to achieve these goals, and training and technical assistance ought to be available to these parents.
>
> 2. Schools should begin to deal with parents programmatically rather than legalistically. That is, the "one wrong step and I'll end up in court" mentality that has guided many schools' dealings with parents over the last five years should be replaced with an approach that recognizes that parents of handicapped children are a heterogeneous group and conveys the idea that the school encourages, but does not demand, parent involvement.
>
> 3. Although data supporting parental involvement and participation are lacking, it should not be automatically assumed that parental participation in the IEP process is a policy failure or an example of an unwarranted and unwelcome intrusion of federal government into the affairs of local boards of education.

Successful parental participation in the education of exceptional children and adolescents depends on recognizing individuality, establishing a positive parent-professional relationship, and providing training for parents and teachers who need and want it.

Individuality of Parents

☐ In delineating parents' role in educating exceptional students, the individuality of parents must be considered. As Turnbull and Turnbull (1982) state, "Rather than mandating that all parents be equal participants with the school personnel to make decisions jointly, public policy should tolerate a range of parent involvement choices and options, matched to the needs and interests of the parents" (p. 120).

If professional educators are willing to accommodate individual differences and preferences of parents, activities can be structured accordingly. Table 4.2 depicts an example of a framework for varying parent involvement.

Parent-Professional Relationships

☐ Parent participation requires development of a parent-professional relationship built on mutual respect, understanding, and cooperation (Schulz, 1982). This relationship is still at an early stage of development and demands a great deal of consideration for optimal growth. Before a partnership can genuinely

TABLE 4.2 Parent Involvement Continuum

	Reporting Progress	Special Events	Parent Education	Parents Teaching
Parents as Passive Participants	Good News Notes 60 Second Phone Calls Star of the Week Newsletter	Open House Audiovisual Presentations Potluck Supper Father's/Mother's/Sibling's Day Spring Fling End-of-the-Year Picnic The Gym Show	Welcoming Committee Parent Bulletin Board Information on Home and Weekend Activities Information on Community Resources Lending Library (Book, Toy, Record) Classroom Observations Workshops on Topics of Interest to Parents A Course for Parents Parent-to-Parent Meetings	Make and Take Workshop Teachable Moments Home Worksheets Parents Teaching the Classroom Parent Objective in the IEP
Parents as Active Participants	Call-In Times Parent-Teacher Conferences Home-School Notebooks			
	(Parent Leaders)	(Parent Leaders)	(Parent Leaders)	(Parent Leaders)

Parents as Passive Participants ↑ Parents as Active Participants

Source: Barbara Tucker Cervone and Kathleen O'Leary, A conceptual framework for parent involvement. *Educational Leadership,* 1982. 40(2) p. 49 Reprinted with permission of the Association for Supervision and Curriculum Development. Copyright © 1982 by the Association for Supervision and Curriculum Development. All rights reserved.

exist, "both the parent and the professional must attempt to understand the other's point of view, special moral concerns, and culturally determined priorities for the child. Both must relate to each other as adults who possess complementary expertise and responsibility for the child" (Gliedman & Roth, 1980, p. 145). The challenge and the promise of this relationship are discussed in Chapter 5.

Training Programs

☐ Many school districts have initiated training programs for parents who wish to become active participants in their childrens' education. McKinney and Hocutt (1982) found the chief barrier to active parent participation was parents' lack of knowledge base to facilitate their interaction with school personnel. They also found that schools were no more prepared than parents to engage in full consultation about students. The findings of this study suggest key features of training programs:

- ☐ evidence of the benefits of parent involvement for children, parents and programs;
- ☐ consultation and communication strategies to enhance the reciprocal productivity of parent-teacher interaction;
- ☐ techniques for defining desirable roles for individual parents and for facilitating their assumption of these roles;
- ☐ procedures for clearly communicating the rights and responsibilities of parents and school personnel; and
- ☐ alternative organizational strategies for reducing potential barriers to effective parent involvement. (McKinney & Hocutt, 1982, p. 72)

The parent role has grown dramatically during the past decade. It is a dynamic role, changing to meet the needs of the child, the family, the school, and the time. It is a role to be reckoned with, to be examined, and to be nurtured.

References

Blackhurst, A. E., & Berdine, W. H. (1981). Basic concepts of special education. In A. E. Blackhurst & W. H. Berdine (Eds.), *An introduction to special education*, 2–51. Boston: Little, Brown & Co.

Boggs, E. M. (1969). Pointers for parents. In W. Wolfensberger & R. A. Kurtz (Eds.), *Management of the family of the mentally retarded*. Chicago: Parkinson Division, Follett Educational Corp.

Cain, L. F. (1976). Parent groups: Their role in a better life for the handicapped. *Exceptional Children, 42*(8), 432–437.

Callahan, C. M., & Kauffman, J. M. (1982). Involving gifted children's parents: Federal law is silent, but its assumptions apply. *Exceptional Education Quarterly, 3*(2), 50–55.

Cervone, B. T., & O'Leary, K. (1982). A conceptual framework for parent involvement. *Educational Leadership, 40*(2), 48–49.

Congressional Record, Senate Report No. 94–168. Washington, D.C., June 2, 1975.

Corrigan, D. C. (1980). Political and moral contexts that produced P.L. 94–142. In H. J. Burbach (Ed.), *Mainstreaming*. Dubuque, Ia.: Kendal/Hunt.

Corrigan, D. C. (1978). Public law 94–142. A matter of human rights; A call for change in schools and colleges of education. In J. K. Grosenick & M. C. Reynolds (Eds.), *Teacher education: Renegotiating roles for mainstreaming*. Reston, Va.: The Council for Exceptional Children.

Crawford, D. (1978). Parent involvement in instructional planning. *Focus on Exceptional Children, 10*(7), 1–5.

Delp, J. L., & Martinson, R. A. (1977). *A handbook for parents of gifted and talented*, 2nd ed. Ventura, Calif.: Ventura County Superintendent of Schools Office.

Dembrowsky, C. (1983). Parent involvement: A key to student success. *PTA Today, 8*(6), 25–27.

Dickson, R. L., & DiPaola, T. (1980). Parents' perceptions of participation in developing the individualized education program. IEP Implementation Project. Providence: Rhode Island College.

Division for Exceptional Children, North Carolina Department of Public Instruction. (1982). *Handbook on parent rights*. Raleigh, N.C.

D'Zamko, M., & Raiser, L. (1981). IEP development and implementation: Systematic parent-teacher collaboration. *Teaching Exceptional Children, 13*(3), 122–124.

Fanning, P. (1977). The new relationship between parents and schools. *Focus on Exceptional Children, 9*(5), 1–10.

Farber, B. (1968). *Mental retardation: Its social context and social consequences*. Boston: Houghton Mifflin.

Federal Register. (1981). Washington, D.C.: U.S. Government Printing Office, January 19.

Gilliam, J. E., & Coleman, M. C. (1981). Who influences committee decisions? *Exceptional Children, 47*(8), 642–644.

Gliedman, J., & Roth, W. (1980). *The unexpected minority*. New York: Harcourt Brace Jovanovich.

Goldstein, S., Strickland, B., Turnbull, A. P., & Curry, L. (1980). An observational analysis of the IEP conference. *Exceptional Children, 46*(4), 278–286.

Hall, E. G., & Skinner, N. (1980). *Somewhere to turn: Strategies for parents of the gifted and talented*. New York: Teachers College Press.

Halpern, R. (1982). Impact of P.L. 94–142 on the handicapped child and family: Institutional response. *Exceptional Children, 49*(3), 270–273.

Haring, N. G. (1982). *Behavior of exceptional children*. Columbus, Oh.: Charles E. Merrill.

Kanigher, H. (1977). *Everyday enrichment for gifted children at home and school*. Los Angeles: Ventura County Superintendent of Schools.

Kirk, S. A., & Gallagher, J. J. (1983). *Educating exceptional children* (4th ed.). Boston: Houghton Mifflin.

Kirk, S. A., & Gallagher, J. J. (1979). *Educating exceptional children* (3rd ed.). Boston: Houghton Mifflin.

Lusthaus, C. S., Lusthaus, E. W., & Gibbs, H. (1981). Parent's role in the decision process. *Exceptional Children, 48*(3), 256–257.

Mandell, C. J., & Fiscus, E. (1981). *Understanding exceptional people.* St. Paul: West Publishing Co.

Marion, R. L. (1981). *Educators, parents and exceptional children.* Rockville, Md.: Aspen.

McKinney, J. D., & Hocutt, A. M. (1982). Public school involvement of parents of learning-disabled children and average achievers. *Exceptional Education Quarterly, 3*(2), 64–73.

Montessori, M. (1972). *The secret of childhood.* New York: Ballantine Books.

Morgan, D. P. (1982). Parent participation in the IEP process: Does it enhance appropriate education? *Exceptional Education Quarterly, 3*(2), 33–40.

Morgan, D. P. (1981). *A primer on individualized education programs for exceptional children.* Reston, Va.: The Foundation for Exceptional Children.

National Association for Retarded Citizens. (1977). *Classroom programming: What should be taught?* Arlington, Tex.: NARC Research and Demonstration Institute.

Paul, J. L. (1977). The need for advocacy. In J. L. Paul, G. R. Neufeld, & J. W. Pelosi (Eds.), *Child advocacy within the system.* Syracuse, N.Y.: Syracuse University Press.

Paul, J. L. & Porter, P. B. (1981). Parents of handicapped children. In J. L. Paul (Ed.), *Understanding and working with parents of children with special needs.* New York: Holt, Rinehart & Winston.

Porcella, A. (1980). Increasing parent involvement. *Educating and Training of the Mentally Retarded, 15*(2), 155–157.

President's Committee on Mental Retardation. (1977). *MR 76 Mental retardation: Past and present.* Washington, D.C.: U.S. Government Printing Office.

Sarason, S., & Doris, J. (1978). Mainstreaming: Dilemmas, opposition, opportunities. In M. C. Reynolds (Ed.), *Futures of education for exceptional students: Emerging structures.* Minneapolis: National Support Systems Project.

Scanlon, C. A., Arick, J., & Phelps, N. (1981). Participation in the development of the IEP: Parents' perspective. *Exceptional Children, 47*(5), 373–374.

Schulz, J. B., & Turnbull, A. P. (1984). *Mainstreaming handicapped students* (2nd ed.). Boston: Allyn & Bacon.

Schulz, J. B. (1982). A parent views parent participation. *Exceptional Education Quarterly, 3*(2), 17–24.

Shevin, M. (1983). Meaningful parental involvement in long-range educational planning for disabled children. *Education and Training of the Mentally Retarded, 18*(1), 17–21.

Silverman, L. K. (1982). The gifted and talented. In E. L. Meyen (Ed.), *Exceptional children and youth.* Denver: Love Publishing Co.

Soffer, R. M. (1982). IEP decisions in which parents desire greater particpation. *Education and Training of the Mentally Retarded, 17*(1), 67–70.

Strenecky, B. J., McLoughlin, J. A., & Edge, D. (1979). Parent involvement: A consumer perspective—in the schools. *Education and Training of the Mentally Retarded, 14*(1), 54–56.

Turnbull, A. P. (1983). Parent-professional Interactions. In M. E. Snell (Ed.), *Systematic instruction of the moderately and severely handicapped*, 18–43. Columbus, Oh.: Charles E. Merrill.

Turnbull, A. P., & Leonard, J. (1981). Parent involvement in special education: Emerging advocacy roles, *School Psychology Review, 10*(1), 38–44.

Turnbull, A. P., Strickland, B., & Brantley, J. C. (1982). *Developing and implementing individualized education programs*. Columbus, Oh.: Charles E. Merrill.

Turnbull, A. P., & Turnbull, H. R. (1982). Parent involvement in the education of handicapped children: A critique. *Mental Retardation, 20*(3), 115–122.

Turnbull, H., & Turnbull, A. P. (1982). Public policy and handicapped citizens. In N. G. Haring (Ed.), *Exceptional children and youth,* (3rd ed.). Columbus, Oh.: Charles E. Merrill.

Wolf, J. S., & Stephens, I. M. (1982). *Effective skills in parent/teacher conferencing: The parents' perspective*. Columbus: Ohio State University, National Center for Educational Materials and Media for the Handicapped.

Yoshida, R. K., Fenton, K. S., Kaufman, M. J., & Maxwell, J. P. (1978). Parental involvement in the special education pupil planning process: The school's perspective. *Exceptional Children, 44*(7), 531–534.

Yoshida, R. K., & Gottlieb, J. (1977). A model of parental participation in the pupil planning process. *Mental Retardation, 15*(3), 17–20.

Ysseldyke, J. E., & Algozzine, B. (1984). *Introduction to special education*. Boston: Houghton Mifflin.

Zettel, J. J., & Ballard, J. (1978). A need for increased federal effort for the gifted and talented. *Exceptional Children, 44*(4), 261–267.

5

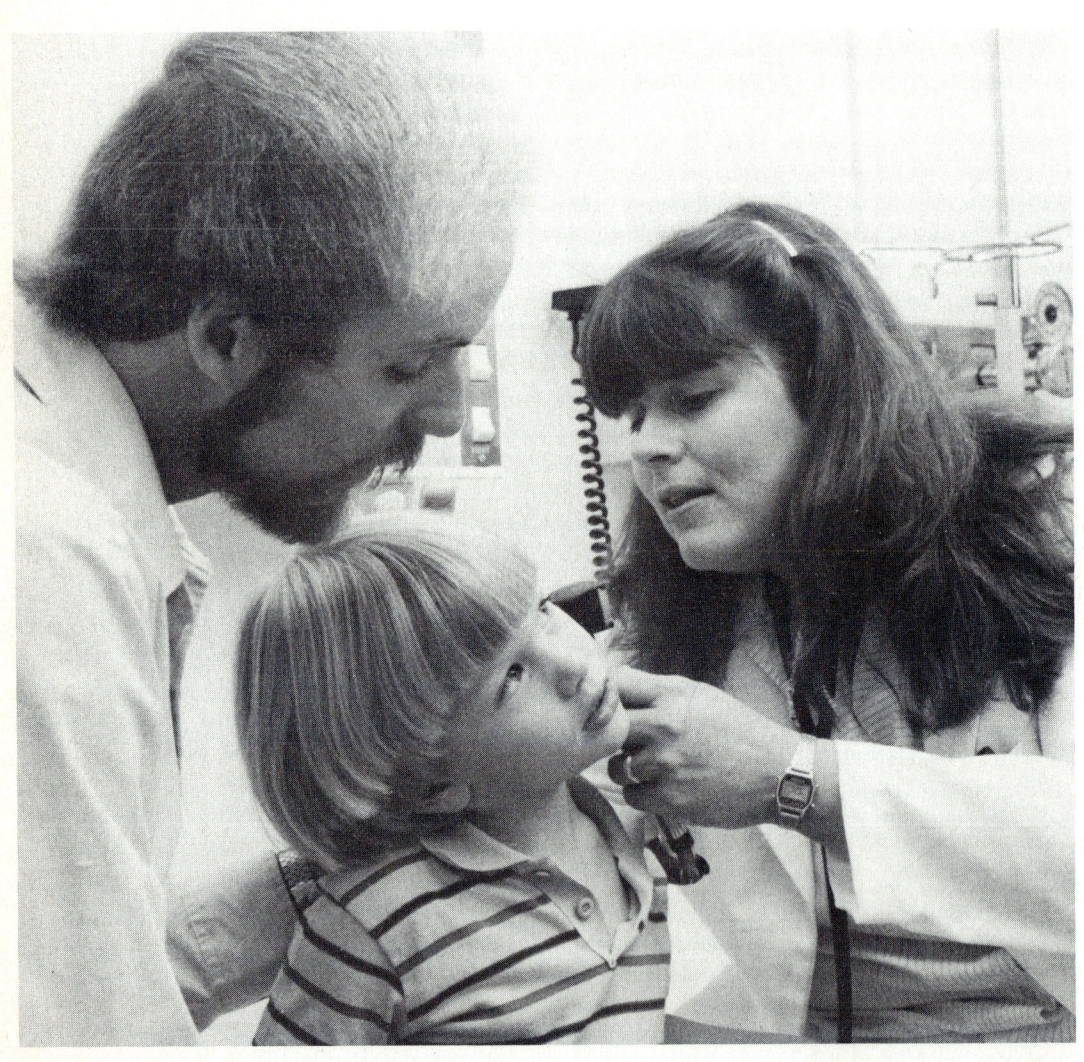

The Parent-Professional Relationship

Because of the legal mandate concerning parent participation, educators are gradually acknowledging parents as members of the professional team. However, central elements of PL 94–142, such as service in the least restrictive environment and parent involvement in evaluation and decision making, have not influenced the medical, mental health, social welfare, and other service systems. Families experience discrepancies in their role and in their child's treatment from service system to service system (Halpern, 1982). Other professionals, influenced by tradition and practice, do not recognize parents as partners or as equals.

Parents of children who are gifted and of children who are mildly handicapped will encounter more professionals than will other parents as their children are evaluated by psychologists and educators for entrance into special programs. Parents of children with moderate to severe handicaps will have become involved with numerous professionals before the child enters school.

The family of a normal child will occasionally visit with a physician; the family of a seriously handicapped child, however, may become involved with an entirely new world of social workers; speech, occupational and physical therapists; nurses; special educators; medical specialists; and many other professionals. During a time the parents are struggling with crucial decisions and family stress, they may also experience professional contacts that are cursory, brusque, and ego-damaging (Fox, 1979).

Handicapped children and their parents are vulnerable because of the limitations of the handicap, the stereotypes society places them in, and the dependence on others for services. According to Gliedman and Roth (1980, p. 141),

> Nowhere is this vulnerability greater than in the child's relationships with those who provide him with specialized medical, educational, and other services. In countless ways, large and small, many professionals define the child exclusively in terms of his handicap and teach him to identify his true self with the image contained in the handicapped role. Yet the child and his parents desperately need many kinds of help that only experts can provide.

A natural antipathy seems to exist between the giver of services and the recipient. Some parents feel demeaned by needing and seeking help (Sonnenschein, 1981); some parents demand it. Negative attitudes of parents contribute to stress professionals experience, as well as the other way around. Dealing with parents has been cited as a major factor in creating stress for educators and as a deterrent to job satisfaction (Pagel & Price, 1980; Smith & Cline, 1980).

Parent-professional cooperation is essential to the welfare and progress of the exceptional child. Before the collaboration can be improved, however, the traditional relationship needs to be investigated, areas of conflict examined, and parent-professional models evaluated.

Areas of Conflict

Parents claim that professionals who work with their children are negative, unavailable, and condescending. At the same time, professionals contend that parents avoid them and are hostile and uncooperative. Even though the objections are similar, the perspectives are not.

Parents' Perspective

In a frequently quoted passage, Gorham (1975, p. 521) stated the position of parents of handicapped children:

> . . . I am clearly one of the lost generation of parents of handicapped children. We are parents who are either intimidated by professionals or angry with them, or both; parents who are unreasonably awed by them; parents who intuitively know that *we* know our children better than the experts of any discipline and yet we persistently assume that the professionals know best; parents who carry so much attitudinal and emotional baggage around with us that we are unable to engage in any real dialogue with professionals—teachers, principals, physicians, or psychologists—about our children.

Roos (1978), a parent and a professional in the field of mental health, has identified ways in which he feels professionals have mishandled parents of handicapped children and adults. He refers to professional ignorance of the handicapping condition, professional hopelessness, referring for unnecessary services, withholding information, ignoring parents' suggestions, using professional jargon, assuming wisdom to make decisions for other people, and treating parents as patients. It is clear that the parent-professional relationship is not only an inadequate one; it is also an adversarial one. Professional attitudes contributing to this poor relationship include negative stereotyping of parents, blaming parents for the child's problems, furnishing inadequate information, and exhibiting nonaccepting attitudes toward parents.

Negative Stereotyping   At a conference on exceptional children, the author attended a workshop designed to help professionals work with parents of preschool handicapped children. The descriptors used to identify the parents were such words as *inadequacy, helplessness, hopelessness, confusion, low self-esteem,* and *lack of attachment.* In a page of descriptors, there was not a single positive statement to describe parents of handicapped children. The inference was that parents had little to offer to a relationship with professional people.

Professionals are quick to label parents as a result of misinterpretation of their behavior. Parents who disagree with a diagnosis are labeled *denying;* those who refuse a certain treatment are *resistant;* and those who are convinced that something is wrong with their child are *anxious* (Sonnenschein, 1981).

Professional training does not eliminate stereotypic thinking. Seligman and Seligman (1980) note that a major contributor to prejudicial thinking is the professional literature, especially early literature related to disabled children and their parents.

Blaming Parents   In referring to a day treatment program for psychotic children, Critchey and Berlin (1981) state that professionals tend to see the parents as adversaries who have caused the child's problems. Even if the cause is not attributed to the parents, secondary conditions (e.g., overprotection and rejection) may be. A very uncomplimentary term, *parentalplegia,* has been suggested for this secondary condition (Murray & Cornell, 1981).

Blame may be extended to program or treatment objectives, where failure of the child to progress is attributed to parents' failure to implement the objectives. Many professionals do not consider that the objectives may not have been appropriate or even that the parent's time was limited.

Lack of Information   Gorham (1975) claims that "the more specialized the diagnostician is, the less concerned he is to give information to the parents and the less willing he is to deal with the parents' situation and feelings" (p. 522). When information is given, it may be cloaked in professional jargon or terms unfamiliar to the parents.

Frequently, professionals are not well informed themselves about specific handicapping conditions. This lack of knowledge may lead to giving the parents misinformation, in turn contributing to unrealistic expectations or to depression. The reluctance to say "I don't know" is common among professionals and may prevent the professional from consulting a more knowledgeable associate.

Nonacceptance of Parents   Perhaps the most demeaning and devastating trait of professional people is the tendency to deny the parents' expertise and knowledge about their own child. Parents report that professionals do not take them seriously and do not consider their impressions useful (Sonnenschein, 1981). Even as professionals themselves, Gallagher and Gallagher (1985) found that "One of the disturbing aspects of dealing with professionals is that when one is playing the role of parent, one is automatically stripped of any knowledge or expertise" (p. 236).

Parents certainly know a great deal about their children. In describing her mother's role with her handicapped sister, Ackerman (1985) recognizes that the mother was the expert. She alone knew the whole story of her handicapped child, whereas professionals had their own specific areas of expertise.

Often, the only parents who have easy exchanges with professionals are those with professional standing of their own in a childhood specialty. Gliedman and Roth (1980, p. 145) comment on the fallacy of this practice:

> A more striking abuse of our culture's concept of the expert cannot be imagined: to be taken seriously, the parents' claim to expertise about their own child must be backed by a socially recognized formal credential that "proves" that they are experts about children in general.

☐ *A dynamic, evolving relationship exists between families and schools — a relationship frequently involving conflict.*

The expectations parents have of professionals are thwarted when professionals do not consider the opinions and perceptions of parents to be worthwhile. Professionals would profit from the following advice:

> Be accepting of parents as equal partners. Even the most limited parents have information and insight into strengths, weaknesses, and potentialities in their children. . . . A professional's job is to find ways, not excuses, to get parents to participate as equals in the planning process and to feel comfortable enough to use their information. (DeWert & Helsel, 1985, p. 105)

Parents of exceptional children and adults who are also professional people have helped develop a common understanding. A physician who discovered that his newborn daughter had Down's Syndrome expressed the agony of his dual role:

> The next five minutes were among the most difficult I have ever spent. I not only confronted "surviving what the doctor has just told you," but I was the pediatrician on the scene. (Durham, 1983, p. 27)

Patterson (1983) suggests that all parents are professionals—professional parents. As the constant in their child's world, they can form a bridge between the professionals and gain confidence in their own status as experts.

Professionals' Perspective

☐ Professionals do not have a monopoly on negative attitudes. Turnbull (1983) asserts that "Sometimes parents are unforgiving and do not realize the difficult position of the professional" (p. 19).

In describing the early history of parent associations, Cain (1976) describes the relationship with professionals as adversarial in nature. Parents lacked confidence in the professionals and jealously guarded their own control within the organization, frequently placing the professional in an advisory role.

Professionals who work with handicapped children and their families have been almost as verbal as parents in enumerating problem areas. The barriers to a positive relationship as perceived by professionals include parents' dependency, unrealistic expectations, antagonism toward professional people, and role conflict.

Dependency Some parents, having found professionals in whom they have confidence, become unduly dependent on their services. Such parents may infringe on the time and energy of the professionals working with their child and actually abuse the relationship.

Parents who call the physician too frequently or take an undue amount of the teacher's time endanger their relationship and that of the professional with the child. Parents must remember that, unlike themselves, professional workers have a number of children to consider.

Unrealistic Expectations Because of their inability to accept their child's handicap, or the degree of the handicapping condition, parents may expect unrealistically dramatic results from professional intervention. Failure of the professional to produce the expected results leads to disappointment and resentment (Golin & Ducanis, 1981).

Parents of gifted children are often dissatisfied with their children's progress. One mother claimed that her child could read on her own at home, but that she was not even doing all of the alphabet at school. As described by a young teacher, "They have a rather arrogant attitude and in some cases think frequently what I do is wrong" (Cruickshank & Callahan, 1983, p. 255).

Other parents, feeling that the professional is pushing too hard, do not cooperate with the program or treatment suggested. A subtle undermining process can occur, which suggests that the program, and therefore the professional, has failed.

Parents may also expect professionals to perform tasks that are unrealistic in their nature and scope. The following note, sent by a mother to the teacher in a preschool program, illustrates the demand for care beyond a teacher's domain:

> Daisey's congested. Keep her under a humidifier. Let her throw up. She needs to get that out.

Parents who have unrealistic expectations about their exceptional children become defensive if their views are threatened (Hart, 1970). When professional people attempt to alter their illusions, parents react by withdrawing or by rejecting the professional opinion.

Antagonism Hostility toward professionals may stem from the parents' fear that they will be blamed for the child's problem; it may be based on jealousy of the professional's relationship with their child. Sometimes, the parents' difficulty in relating to professionals reflects their own negative attitude toward the child. The rejecting or abusive parent may be defensive and hostile, fearing that the professional may discover the abuse (Golin & Ducanis, 1981).

Frequently, parents will not accept the diagnosis of the professional and are antagonistic toward the person who makes it. The professionals' intentions are misunderstood, and nothing they do will please the parents.

Such interactions are extremely frustrating to professionals who are acting in the best interests of the child. The attending quandary is expressed by a speech/language pathologist:

> It is a difficult task for professionals to present information concerning a child that differs from parents' expectations. This is especially true when the objectives we

have set for a child are somewhat less than those envisioned by the parents. Thinking as parents ourselves, it is all too easy to predict a child's future in terms of our goals rather than in terms of his/her capabilities or preferences. This is not to say that parents are categorically manipulative—just heir to the universal hope that, regardless of circumstances, our children will somehow manage to do well. As professionals, we hope to be objective in setting goals for our clients, yet there is the danger of turning objectivity into a roadblock that refuses passage to a child who may, after all, exceed our expectations. The dilemma, then, is to present a realistic picture that remains open ended. The hope is that parents will use our information to come to an understanding of their child's capabilities and provide an environment in which the child can maximize his/her potential with support and guidance that takes individual differences into account. In reality, there are many variations of the ideal.

I recall an instance in which parents brought a pre-school Down's Syndrome child to our office requesting weekly therapy in our clinic. An assessment of the child's skills revealed a developmental level significantly below the chronological age and only a few signs of emerging pre-language skills. The child was enrolled in a day care setting. Further investigation revealed that this day care placement was the most appropriate available in the area. In our professional judgment, this child would benefit most from a program designed to aid in the development of the emerging skills we had observed. The most promising context for generating such skills was the already existent everyday environment (school, home) and not in the context we could offer in our clinic.

In the post-evaluation conference with the attending parent we explained our intent to co-ordinate a step-by-step program for the child that would be integrated into the school/home settings. We also explained our intent to provide close follow-up with more formal intervention at the earliest sign of appropriate skills in more natural environments. Our proposals were met with a barrage of complaints that all anyone ever did was to "evaluate my child," and that "NOBODY WILL DO ANYTHING." All attempts to explain our intent of providing the best intervention we could, met with the same conclusion from the parents—it wasn't enough!

At this point, it would be easy to view these parents in a rather negative light. As I wrestled with the situation, I saw problems for all of us that needed resolution, some of which were beyond the scope of my role. To say to them, "I understand," seemed so inadequate—and, in a sense, just plain untrue. I have known some frustrating moments in raising my child, but it seemed meaningless to compare these to what such parents experience day by day. I desired, however, for them to see that we did care about their child, and that we would do our best given our abilities and available options. A satisfactory resolution has been elusive, but the experience has reminded me once again that in every professional-client relationship there is a truly complex mix of factors that may exert influence on the final success of an interaction. The best results probably occur when we transcend the obvious so that the client is to us more than "a case" and we are to the client more than "a solution." (L. Bowers, personal communication, December 5, 1984)

Role Conflict Interpretation of the difference between the professional role and the parental role may be unclear. From the perspective of the professional, more services for the child or more effort expended on the child is better (Foster, Berger, & McLean, 1981). Parents may not perceive their role as participants in delivering such services and therefore may reject the program.

On the other hand, the parent may interpret the professional role as didactic and domineering. Clarification of the roles in each parent-professional interaction is essential to a good working relationship.

In every handicap speciality, it is essential that parents and professionals actively work together on the child's behalf (Gliedman & Roth, 1980). Cooperation is essential for medical and educational reasons; collaboration is necessary because parents are as vulnerable to irrationality and to confusions of their self-interest with the child's interest as is the professional. Each can serve as a check on the shortcomings and limitations of the other.

The program supervisor of a Developmental Evaluation Center expressed potential outcomes of a positive relationship:

> While doing an early intervention program for handicapped and at-risk infants, a 13-month-old developmentally delayed boy was referred to me by the local health department. His mother was known in the community as a "noncompliant" person because of her failure to keep appointments and her lack of cooperation in following through on the recommendations made by various service agencies and professionals.
>
> A social service worker brought mother and son to the first session to ensure they would show up at least once for the program. The mother's demeanor was somewhat hostile and both she and her child wore ill-fitting clothes and looked as if they had not washed in weeks. She was initially given a chance to observe other mothers and children in the program while we talked about her child. Programmatic goals and expectations were explained to her, including the main objective to teach parents to be the primary trainers or teachers for their child. She would be expected to bring her child to the program twice a week and work with him for an hour. During the hour, she and I would assess her son's developmental skills and plan together activities that would stimulate developmental progress. Her "assignment" was to continue the activities at home and to adapt them to fit her child's needs. Time beyond the hour's work session was social time which she could spend with other mothers and staff members. After hearing all of this, I wasn't sure she would return.
>
> Surprisingly enough, she did return and her attendance became very regular. Her activity adaptions for her child weren't always what I'd hoped for, but at times they were quite creative. The most striking changes over the course of the program weren't so much in the area of the child's developmental progress as in the mother's attitude. She began to take an interest in her appearance and that of her child. She seemed to be more agreeable, particularly in talking with other mothers, and made constructive suggestions about the program. The result of the changes in her was reflected in her child's behavior. He smiled more, began to make some developmental gains, and in general seemed happier.
>
> After the completion of the program, I continued to help the mother in working with her son. Over time, my assistance was less and less necessary as she became more skillful at meeting his needs and accessing other services.

Even though I have encountered a number of parents who have been easier to work with, my experience with this mother has served as a reminder to me of the importance of involving parents in programs for their children. Certainly the positive changes that occurred in the mother as she gained confidence in her abilities were of benefit to the child, both developmentally and emotionally. (J. Minor, personal communication, January 28, 1985)

Parent-Professional Models

Because of the variety of conditions, problems, and needs evidenced by exceptional children and young people, a number of professions are concerned with special education. Members of those professions, like parents of exceptional people, are individuals who have unique strengths, weaknesses, needs, and points of view. There is, therefore, a variety of approaches to serving this population.

Each professional group serving exceptional children and adults, as well as their parents, approach the task from the perspective of that profession. How different professionals approach parents is determined by (1) their assumptions about parents and about parental needs at that time; (2) the background, training, and experience from which the professionals have built a rationale for working with parents; and (3) the goals professionals set for parents and for themselves in their interactions (Webster, 1976). Several professional models serve exceptional people and their parents: clinical, counseling, educational, and ecological.

The Clinical Model

The oldest and most pervasive model for parent-professional interaction is the clinical model. This model is used by social workers, therapists, psychologists, and physicians. Also referred to as the medical model, it clearly distinguishes between the provider of services and the recipient of services. The handicapped child, and therefore the parent, is viewed as a patient whose treatment will be determined solely by professionals.

In a comprehensive clinical setting, for example, the child may be evaluated by a team of professional people, who then form a diagnosis and plan of intervention. The parents are expected to comply with the recommendations and to assume the strategy of passive acceptance.

Schwartz (1970) defines the parents' tasks within this strategy as discovery of (1) the professional's expectations; (2) what the professional considers the appropriate means of action; and (3) the conditions under which these means are to be used. Professionals are assumed to be experts and therefore have the responsibility for diagnosing and treating the problems and for guiding parents toward the best solution of the family problems involved. The parents' responsibilities are to cooperate with the professionals and to carry out their recommendations.

At the conclusion of the comprehensive clinical evaluation, the parents are usually summoned by the social worker, who interprets the diagnosis to the parents, also informing them that the results may only be seen by other professionals. This process has several negative effects: the parents feel that a great deal is being said and done behind their backs; decisions are made without parental input, carrying the possibility that they will not be implemented; and the parent is placed in the position of a patient (Wright, 1960).

Medical and other health-related professionals have a profound impact on families of handicapped children. Physicians are usually the first professionals to diagnose a handicapping condition, particularly if the condition is severe. They are also the first to make referrals for institutionalization, further diagnosis, or treatment. Yet, many professionals, including physicians, are not adequately prepared to interact well with parents.

A study of medical students in child psychiatry indicated that the involvement with parents in the training program is minimal (Wyatt, Bass, Powell, & Lim, 1983). The conclusion was made that "the training of primary care physicians and child psychiatrists must begin during medical school with a comprehensive exposure to child psychiatry, child development, and the problems and views of parents" (p. 140).

Other observations in a day treatment program for psychotic children indicated the therapist's adverse perception of parents (Critchey & Berlin, 1981). The most effective means to counteract this bias was found in sustained interactions with parents, allowing the staff to see the parents as "troubled and terribly hurt human beings" (p. 150).

A major dilemma arises for physicians because although they might be the first to diagnose a handicapping condition, they may find the necessary interventions are not medical. Thus, a close relationship between medical and educational service providers is needed (Adams, 1982).

The physician and other clinically oriented professionals can have significant influence on the development of special education programs and related services. The physician's influence can help substantiate:

1. the nature of child's handicapping condition
2. implementation of one or more of the special therapies requiring medical confirmation
3. eligibility for specialized equipment or training devices
4. qualifying a child for financing from private foundations, i.e., muscular dystrophy, cystic fibrosis, cerebral palsy, etc.
5. admittance into residential center programs for evaluation and/or placement and
6. the need for medication to improve the child's condition for learning. (Sommers, 1982, p. 38)

Gliedman and Roth (1980) decry the clinical model, stating that parents should oversee and orchestrate the services that professionals provide for their children. Certainly, parents need to take an active role in encouraging physicians and teachers to cooperate in planning for their children. The team approach, which combines parents, educators, physicians, and other clinicians, must be used to insure optimal development of the exceptional child and adult.

The Counseling Model

☐ Until recently, counselors in agency and school settings have not devoted a significant amount of interest and involvement to providing services for exceptional students and their families. After the passage of PL 94–142, the American Personnel and Guidance Association began to focus sustained attention on the law's implications for agency and school counseling (Hohenshil & Humes, 1979).

Parent and family counseling and consultation are important aspects of comprehensive services for exceptional children. Neely (1982) identifies the role of the counselor as (1) information giving, (2) parent training, (3) coordination, and (4) counseling. The extent of services depends on the family's needs and the counselor's skills. Services may range from providing information about legal rights and available services to in-depth individual and group counseling.

Information Giving Counselors are frequently in the position to provide assessment information. The counselors may be the professionals whose job it is to tell parents that their child is gifted, learning disabled, or mentally retarded. In such cases, they are expected to interpret test results and to make referrals if necessary. Such information can be startling to parents, and it requires skill and compassion to be nonthreatening.

The counselor can dispense knowledge of legal rights and responsibilities as well as availability of resources the exceptional child needs. Knowing that the counselor is aware of the resources that provide relevant services can relieve the parent's anxiety and help establish immediate trust (Prescott & Hulnick, 1979).

Parent Training Counselors have the skills to help parents develop techniques of observation, evaluating progress, teaching and managing skill development, and providing assistance to other parents. Role-playing and psychodrama of effective parent-child interaction, of interviews with service providers, and of decision making have been effectively included in parent-training and counseling groups (Neely, 1982).

Counselors who found it difficult to convince parents to come to school experienced success with evening or weekend workshops featuring speakers dealing with topics of concern to the parents (Flugman, Goldman, & Katz, 1979). Other communication has been established through newsletters including items written by teachers, counselors, and students.

Coordination Counselors frequently coordinate the services needed for an exceptional child, bringing together the team necessary to provide them. To accomplish this task, the counselor needs to be in touch with a number of community agencies and to have a working relationship with them.

In many schools, the counselor arranges the IEP meetings and notifies the participants. The counselor's involvement in the IEP itself is likely to be in the categories of participation, development, and monitoring (Hohenshil & Humes, 1979).

The school counselor is in a unique position to serve exceptional children and their families (Perosa & Perosa, 1981). As the focal point of contact among parents, teachers, and community specialists, the counselor can integrate a holistic picture of the child's situation.

Counseling Counseling parents of exceptional children presents an opportunity for the counselor to determine the attitudes, feelings, reactions, and concerns of the parents so support can be given to maximize parental coping (Fairfield, 1983). Individual and group counseling has helped parents accept their child's exceptionality and reorganize family roles as necessary. Huber (1979) finds that parent counseling may be more beneficial in some situations than direct therapy or remediation with the child.

A new area of counseling being developed is working with siblings of exceptional children. One counseling group for siblings developed into a vehicle for children to learn about significant family members, to discover that their own feelings were not unique, and to foster the view of themselves as informed and valued individuals (Chinitz, 1981).

In the strict sense, every professional person who interacts with parents and children becomes a counselor (McWilliams, 1976). Successful counseling can be carried out in a variety of ways by a variety of people.

In all settings, emphasis should be placed on the interactive nature of counseling. Counseling is an endeavor that people engage in together (Webster, 1976). Because no two people view the world in exactly the same way, counselors and parents frequently disagree. Counselors, therefore, can experience the satisfaction of discussing, expanding, and sharpening their perceptions through interactions with parents.

The Educational Model

☐ Lightfoot (1978) expresses the irony that although families and schools are engaged in a complementary sociocultural task, they find themselves in conflict with one another. Sociologists have been concerned with describing the role of parents within families, but they have neglected the dynamic, evolving relationships between families and schools. They have not given careful attention to the perspectives of parents who are trying to negotiate the complexities of the school system.

For some time, educators have been aware of the important role parents play in insuring the continuity of behavioral and academic programs in the home (Abramson, Willson, Yoshida, & Hagerty, 1983). However, the routine inclusion of parents for the purpose of educational programming is a recent phenomenon, originating in the mandates of PL 94–142 (see Chapter 4).

Even with the legal requirement for parent participation, many parents have learned that a minimum contact with their children's schools is best (Feldman, Byalick, & Rosedale, 1975) and that educational personnel look unfavorably on parental involvement in program planning (Abramson, Willson, Yoshida, & Hagerty, 1983).

Teachers have also become familiar with parental attitudes and behaviors that appear to block collaboration. Kraft and Snell (1980) refer to the **blame-oriented parent** who consistently pinpoints inadequacies in the school; the **invisible parent** who does not respond to teacher efforts to establish communication; the **supercooperative parent**, who abuses the teacher's time; and the **pseudoexpert parent** who has read enough about behavior and learning problems to have formulated a total educational strategy. When these parental behaviors evoke stress in teachers, the teachers may respond with parallel patterns of blame, avoidance, overcompliance, or expertise.

For the educational model to work, the school must recognize the importance of the parents' role, establish common ground between parent and teacher, and adopt professional advocacy for parents. From this supportive base, the parents' need to blame, avoid, or denigrate the school is greatly diminished (Kraft & Snell, 1980).

Importance of Parents' Role Acceptance appears to be growing for the positive contributions parents can make to their children's education. In addition to the rationale Chapter 4 presents, educators now recognize that daily living, vocational, and leisure-time skills are critical for handicapped children to function in the many environments they will encounter (Heward, Dardig, & Rossett, 1979). Parents are a necessary resource for the expansion of special education services into the home and community.

Parents of gifted children are essential for providing experiences, resources, and stimulation needed for the optimal development of their children. A challenge is being advanced to administrators and teachers of programs for gifted children to "stop ignoring parents and start providing them with relevant information" (Mathews, 1981, p. 207).

Parents know when something is wrong with their child (Stevens, 1980). They know how their children approach new tasks, how much curiosity and determination they have, and how they handle failure. Parents are important as providers of information, as collaborators in decision making, and in the extension of educational programs.

Establishment of Common Ground Riggs (1980) admonishes parents of gifted children, "Listen carefully to your child's teacher because your child in school may not be the one you know at home" (p. 3). By the same token, the goals established by the school may not be the same as those established by the family.

Parents and school systems each have a planning cycle for students with special needs (Anderson, Chitwood, & Hayden, 1982). Understanding the two cycles and how they work can help establish common ground.

As indicated in Figure 5.1, parents begin with awareness that a problem exists. As they gather information to help them understand their child, they come to accept that special education is needed. They are ready for planning to begin, hopefully resulting in special programming.

The school system has a different set of constraints, illustrated in Figure 5.2. The school is required to wait until referrals and evaluations are made before the child is declared eligible for special services. The placement decisions, formulation of the IEP, and instructional planning must be dealt with in the school's time frame. Parents need an explanation for the delay and assurance that a solution will be found.

FIGURE 5.1 Parent's Cycle

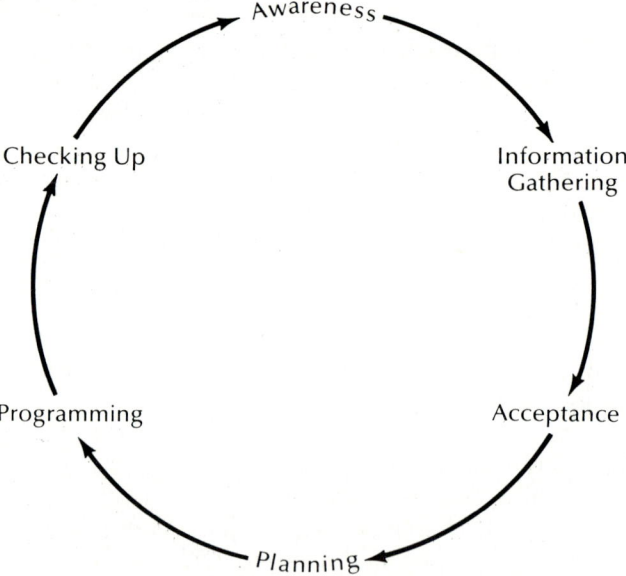

Source: From NEGOTIATING THE SPECIAL EDUCATION MAZE. By Winifred Anderson, Stephen Chitwood and Deidre Hayden © 1982, by LINC Resources, Inc. Reprinted by permission of the publisher, Prentice-Hall, Inc., Englewood Cliffs, New Jersey.

FIGURE 5.2 The School System's Cycle

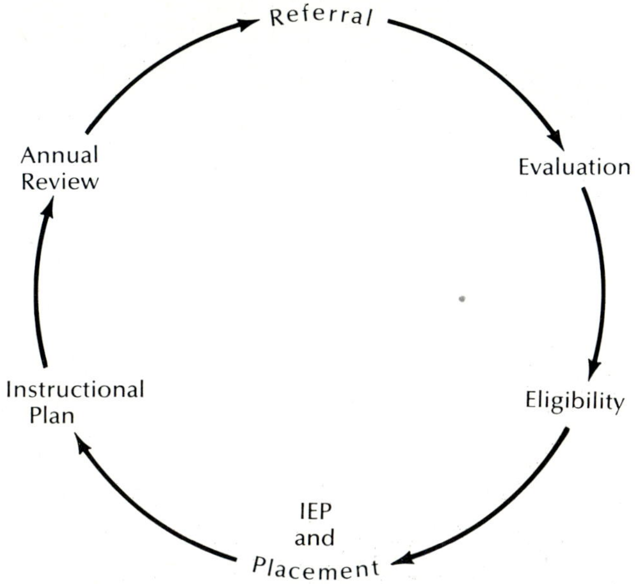

Referral → Evaluation → Eligibility → IEP and Placement → Instructional Plan → Annual Review → (Referral)

Source: From NEGOTIATING THE SPECIAL EDUCATION MAZE. By Winifred Anderson, Stephen Chitwood and Deidre Hayden © 1982 by LINC Resources, Inc. Reprinted by permission of the publisher, Prentice-Hall, Inc., Englewood Cliffs, New Jersey.

If parents do not find a satisfactory solution to their child's problem, the following five steps are suggested:

1. Identify the problem.
2. Know your school system, especially the administrative structure.
3. Know your rights as parents of a handicapped child, and know how to use the special education laws to help solve problems.
4. Try to solve problems at the lowest level in the most informal way possible.
5. If informal efforts fail, then be prepared to take more formal action. (Henley & Spicknall, 1983, p. 8)

Parents and teachers share the frustration of finding a workable solution for exceptional children. They share the common goal of providing appropriate services for exceptional children.

Parents need to lobby for participation in their children's education. They also need to "hold out their hands to good teachers, reforging a broken link in the chain of authority that children desperately need in a confused society" (Westin, 1981, p. 147).

In reconsidering the teacher-parent relationship, special educators are seen as advocates for parents. Educators have as much responsibility to parents as to their exceptional children.

Parental Advocacy When professionals do not advocate for parents, parental rights are abused. Common forms of abuse occur when:

1. Parents are easily intimidated. Schools, clinics and other such environments may be cold and impersonal.
2. Parents are commonly abused in verbal interactions that take place with professionals.
3. Parents are also abused nonverbally. Professionals may not establish eye contact, may confer with parents in distracting and unconducive settings, and may generally indicate lack of consideration and respect for parental involvement.
4. Parental rights are violated when they receive inadequate information about services for their children.
5. Parents are most blatantly abused by professionals who ignore their rights and violate due-process procedures. (McLoughlin, McLoughlin, & Stewart, 1979, p. 53)

Advocating for parents means interceding on their behalf. Kraft and Snell (1980) suggest three ways in which teachers can advocate for parents: (1) interacting with other professionals in the absence of the parent to promote a better understanding; (2) interacting with the parent and the exceptional child in a constructive way; and (3) interacting with other professionals with the parents included, insuring that their rights are protected.

Psychologists play a crucial role in advocacy for parents (Turnbull & Leonard, 1981). In an IEP conference, for example, the school psychologist may direct questions to the parent, clarify questions and disagreements, explain test results and the availability of specialized services, and actively reinforce parents for their contributions.

Ultimately, parents must become advocates for themselves. Parent training programs should focus on the skills of self-advocacy and should help parents learn how they can work as partners with their school system. The partnership between parents and professionals can be successful and enduring only if parents are recognized as full status members in the decision making processes affecting their children's future.

The education model has been the forerunner in recognizing the legal and moral rights of exceptional students and their parents. Increased efforts on the parts of parents and all school personnel will make the collaboration a reality.

The Ecological Model

As defined by Bronfenbrenner (1977, p. 514), the ecology of human development refers to:

> the scientific study of the progressive, mutual accommodation, throughout the life span, between a growing human organism and the changing immediate

> environments in which it lives, as this process is affected by relations obtaining within and between these immediate settings, as well as the larger social contexts, both formal and informal, in which the settings are embedded. . . . The *ecological environment* is conceived topologically as a nested arrangement of structures, each contained within the next.

Ecology is the study of the interrelationships between an organism and its environment. As it applies to education, it is the study of the reciprocal relationship between the child or group and others in the environment (Shea, 1978). Interventions are directed at making the interactions between children and their environments more compatible.

Ecological interventions can be classified into three areas. The first is intervention in natural community settings; the second is intervention in public school settings; and the third intervention is within a residential setting (Paul & Epanchin, 1982).

The ecological model operates from the assumption that the child is an inseparable part of a small social system; of an ecological unit made up of the child, his family, his school, his neighborhood and community (Hobbs, 1966). Programs serving young normal children, gifted children, and disturbed children demonstrate the efficacy of the ecological approach.

Early Childrearing Current interest in parental influences on child behavior and development is accompanied by a concern for the social and economic conditions in which families carry out their childrearing functions (Powell, 1979). The family is viewed as an "open, adaptive system whose exchanges with the environment (a) provide emotional and material support for the family's childrearing functions, and (b) socialize the family into certain childrearing beliefs, practices and family-child relationships" (p. 1).

Family-environmental interaction is the basis of an experimental early intervention project (the Child and Family Neighborhood Program, directed by the Merrill-Palmer Institute). A major aim of the program is to improve the ways families use social networks and neighborhood resources to support childrearing functions.

As Powell (1979) describes, the program works with parents of children aged six months to three years. It facilitates the development of a psychological sense of community, coordinates more effective use of medical and human services, and enhances informal neighborhood mutual aid patterns.

Gifted Children Many programs for gifted children have focused on the ecological view that children reach their greatest potential as they interact with the total environment. The Cullowhee Experience, for example, focuses on a summer program in which students explore the mountain terrain, become acquainted with mountain people and their culture, and develop scientific and musical skills related to the region (The Cullowhee Experience, 1985).

In a broader context, development of gifted children occurs first and foremost with the family and later with the school and the community, including various community agencies. In an effort to strengthen the entire system, a program was designed to focus on three major interrelated systems: the gifted second- to ninth-grade children identified in the community; the parents of these children; and the school personnel in the community. Each system is dealt with on three levels of treatment: by the structural design of the program; by addressing psychological needs with the help of a psychologist; and by addressing social needs with the aid of a social activities coordinator (Zorman, 1982).

Disturbed Children   When a child has been identified as emotionally disturbed, social agencies, physicians, and the clergy, in additon to the family and community, may be part of the picture. Programs serving these children are frequently based on an ecological model.

Project Re-Ed is a program for the reeducation of emotionally disturbed children. It has developed strategies to involve the home, neighborhood, school, agency, and community in dealing with children's problems. The Re-Ed model uses new patterns for the use and development of personnel. A liason teacher is responsible for maintaining communication with the child's regular school; the social worker reaches out to the family, to community agencies, and to individuals. The goal is to make the system work, not to "adjust something inside the head of the child" (Hobbs, 1966, p. 1109). Figure 5.3 illustrates the Project Re-Ed System.

The ecological model depends on community acceptance, more efficient use of community facilities, increased educational options, and recognition that the school does not own education (Paul & Epanchin, 1982). It also depends on the acceptance of parents as essential components of the professional team.

Webster (1976) refers to the early view of parents as analogous to a football team's taxi squad: these players were allowed to dress out, they were informed of all the plays, and they could view the action, but they did not participate in team decisions and planning. As professionals have enlarged their field of vision, they have come to realize that parents are the core of a child's team; professionals are the helpers.

Professionals in all fields have become aware of the human needs of parents of exceptional children and adults. Parents are increasingly aware of their need for professional help in many discipline areas. In developing a working, positive relationship between parents and professionals, two questions surface: What are the expectations of parents and professionals? What are critical factors in establishing a positive relationship?

Expectations

□ □   Based on the roles they have been taught to play, parents and professionals expect certain responses to their overtures, problems, and suggestions. The

FIGURE 5.3 Project Re-Ed

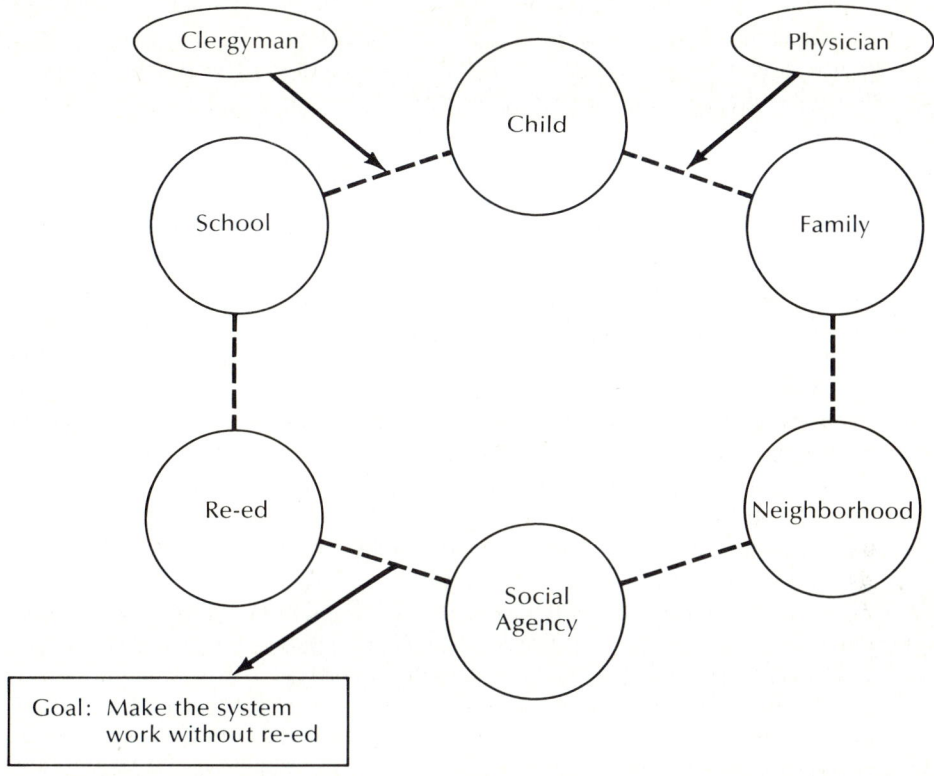

Source: (Modified from Hobbs, 1966.) H. R. Reinert, *Children in Conflict*, Second Edition, © 1980, p. 112. Copyright © Merrill Publishing Company, Columbus, OH. Reprinted by permission of Merrill Publishing Co.

expectations expressed can be helpful in developing a positive relationship.

Professional Expectations

☐ As discussed previously, professional people have views and expectations that vary according to particular disciplines. In general, however, professionals expect cooperation, participation, and trust in professional judgment.

Cooperation Professionals have cited working with uncooperative parents as a major source of teacher dissatisfaction (Pagel & Price, 1980). Teachers and other professionals expect parents to cooperate and to follow through with programs that have been established. These expectations may be thwarted when the parent appears to be disinterested or overprotective.

Participation Berger (1981) has described five levels of participation: (1) parents who avoid schools at all times, (2) parents who need encouragement to come to school, (3) parents who readily respond when invited, (4) parents who are comfortable about coming to school and enjoy some involvement in the educational process, and (5) parents who are overactive and enjoy their power and influence within the school. Parents of exceptional students fall along the same continuum, but professionals expect them to be active participants.

Frequently, parents' nonattendance at meetings is interpreted as disinterest (Heron & Harris, 1982). This viewpoint can lead to resentment of the parents and the child and ultimately may compromise the student's therapeutic or educational program.

Parents' passivity or nonattendance at meetings may stem from a variety of causes. Lack of provisions for child care or inability to leave work may prevent their attendance. Their unwillingness to participate or their discomfort in taking an active role may arise from anxiety, uncertainty about what is expected of them, or from their own expectation that their input will not affect decisions being made about their child (Losen & Losen, 1985).

Trust By definition, professionals are experts in their fields. As experts, they expect parents to trust in their judgment as they diagnose, treat, and plan for exceptional children.

Teachers want to maintain control over the curriculum and their role as instructional specialists (Pagel & Price, 1980). Parents who try to dictate their childrens' programs may be viewed as threatening.

Educators, in particular, have been subjected to criticism in all aspects of public scrutiny. Their competency has been questioned, and their professional status jeopardized.

Professionals are no longer automatically trusted by the nature of their credentials. Parents learn to trust professionals who communicate well with them, work well with their exceptional child, and fulfill their own expectations.

Parental Expectations

☐ In a workshop for parents and teachers of severely handicapped children, mothers were asked to share their expectations of professionals in their early encounters. The expectations most frequently expressed were honesty, respect, and empathy. Several mothers expected the professional to "see what I love" and to "like my child." Parents have the right to expect honesty, services, and understanding from the professionals who work with their children.

Honesty Buscaglia (1975) contends that first and foremost, parents need to hear the truth. The truth, however, is not always apparent or reliable. It should be tempered with the awareness by both parents and professionals that room exists for error. The professional person who gives the initial diagnosis should still leave a basis for hope.

Parents expect accurate information about their child and a realistic view of their child's standing in a given situation or class. They need to know the present and future expectations of their exceptional child.

Services Parents expect follow-through from the initial professional diagnosis. They expect delivery of services at every stage of their child's development and their own critical periods.

Parents' expectations of teachers have been well-defined. Teachers are expected to be competent, to motivate students to learn, and to provide for the pupils affective needs (Cruickshank & Callahan, 1983). In a recent poll of the public's attutude toward schools, parents were asked:

> Suppose you could choose your child's teachers. Assuming they had all had about the same experiences and training, what *personal* qualities would you look for? (Gallup, 1983, p. 44)

The qualities named most often were ability to communicate, to understand, to relate; patience; ability to discipline, to be firm and fair; high moral character; friendliness, good personality, sense of humor; dedication to teaching profession, enthusiasm; ability to inspire, motivate students; intelligence; and caring about students.

☐ *Parents and professionals have the right to expect honesty and cooperation from each other.*

Understanding In addition to honesty and services, parents expect empathy and understanding from the professionals they meet. As one parent stated:

> Please do not believe that we want sympathy, particularly the maudlin kind of sympathy which is damaging to the professional person as well as the parent. But we do need the kind of understanding personality which enables the professional person to put himself in the place of the parent. (Murray, 1969, pp. 68–69)

Parents expect an emotional reaction from the professional. This reaction is the beginning of communication.

Establishing a Positive Relationship

A clear need exists for increased cooperation and collaboration between parents and professionals. Gallagher (1981, pp 270–272) projects several future trends in the relationship:

1. Greater professional insight.
   Professionals are becoming more realistic in terms of how their own personal needs may be impacting on the relationship. A healthier relationship will emerge if they adjust to these needs as they ask the parents to adjust to their needs.
2. Stabilization of parent role.
   As more women work outside the home, the role adaptations that this places on the mother and the father will work out in a more established and acceptable form.
3. Legal rights of parents.
   With an established legal base for parents, they are likely to make fewer demands in policymaking and will probably return to intelligent child care and monitoring of professional activities.
4. Coordination.
   There will likely be a recognition that the important coordination operates at the local level and comes into direct contact with the family and its multiple needs.
5. New models.
   As new models of family dynamics emerge, a greater professional understanding of family needs at every developmental stage will evolve.
6. Research needs.
   There are extraordinary gaps in our understanding of family dynamics: the interaction with siblings of the exceptional child, the change in self-image of the parents as a result of their experiences, or even the degree of family disintegration triggered by the handicapped child's birth or continued presence in the family.

The most promising way to improve relationships between parents and professionals is to establish a view of parents as partners (Sonnenschein, 1981). This view will enable professionals to develop new perceptions of parents and will allow parents to revise some of their assumptions about professionals.

Conclusion

Partnerships are formed by people who have common concerns and common goals. They are fostered and developed through communication, mutual understanding, knowledge, and skills.

A positive parent-professional relationship—a partnership—is both necessary and challenging. The necessity has been established; the challenge is expressed by Klein and Schleifer (1980, p. 3):

> The challenge in the 1980s for both parents and professionals will be to find ways to carry out the legislative mandates for collaborative efforts to help children. Legislation alone cannot achieve this process. It is a human, psychological

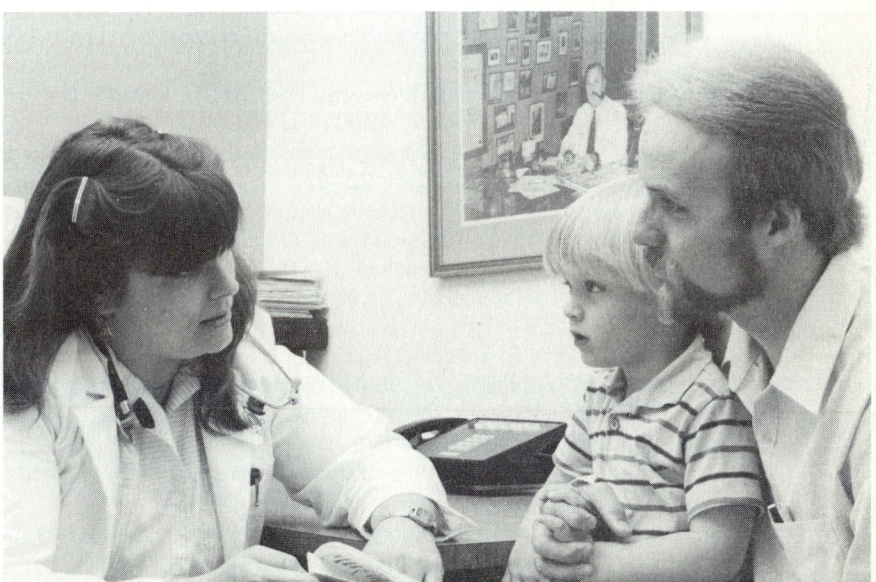

☐ *The most promising way to improve relationships between parents and professional is to establish a view of parents as partners.*

and educational process that must begin with people learning about one another. We must learn to appreciate the perspectives of others, learn to share with one another and learn how to learn from one another.

Empathy and respect are starting points toward meeting the challenge of parent-professional collaboration. The processes of appreciation, sharing, and learning are developed through good communication. This is the focus of Chapter 6.

References

Abramson, M., Willson, V., Yoshida, R. K., & Hagerty, G. (1983). Parents' perceptions of their learning disabled child's educational performance. *Learning Disability Quarterly, 6*(2), 184–194.

Ackerman, J. (1985). Preparing for separation. In H. R. Turnbull & A. P. Turnbull (Eds.), *Parents speak out* (2nd ed.), 149–156. Columbus, Oh.: Charles E. Merrill.

Adams, G. L. (1982). Referral advice given by physicians, *Mental Retardation, 20*(1), 6–20.

Anderson, W., Chitwood, S., & Hayden, D. (1981). *Negotiating the special education maze.* Englewood Cliffs, N.J.: Prentice-Hall.

Berger, E. H. *Parents as partners in education.* St. Louis: C. V. Mosby.

Bronfenbrenner, U. (1977). Toward an experimental ecology of human development. *American Psychologist, 32*(7), 513–531.

Buscaglia, L. (1975). *The disabled and their parents.* Thorofare, N.J.: Charles B. Slack.

Cain, L. F. (1976). Parent groups: Their role in a better life for the handicapped. *Exceptional Children, 42*(8), 432–437.

Chinitz, S. P. (1981). A sibling group for brothers and sisters of handicapped children. *Children Today, 10*(6), 21–23.

Critchey, D., & Berlin, I. (1981). Parent participation in milieu treatment of young psychotic children. *American Journal of Orthopsychiatry, 51*(1), 149–155.

Cruickshank, D. R., & Callahan, R. (1983). The other side of the desk; Stages and problems of teacher development. *The Elementary School Journal, 83*(3), 251–258.

The Cullowhee Experience. (1985). Cullowhee, N.C.: Western Carolina University.

DeWert, M., & Helsel, E. (1985). The Helsel family today. In H. R. Turnbull, & A. P. Turnbull (Eds.), *Parents speak out* (2nd ed.), 101–106. Columbus, Oh.: Charles E. Merrill.

Durham, G. H. (1983). What if you are the doctor? *The Exceptional Parent, 13*(5), 27–28.

Fairfield, B. (1983). Parents coping with genetically handicapped children: Use of early recollections. *Exceptional Children, 49*(5), 411–415.

Feldman, M. A., Byalick, R., & Rosedale, M. P. (1975). Parents and professionals: A partnership in special education. *Exceptional Children, 41*(8), 551-554.

Flugman, B., Goldman, L., & Katz, D. (1979). Training counselors for special education. *Personnel and Guidance Journal, 58*(4), 284–287.

Foster, M., Berger, M., & McLean, M. (1981). Rethinking a good idea: A reassessment of parent involvement. *Topics in Early Childhood Special Education, 1*(3), 55–65.

Fox, D. C. (1979). Shoe on the other foot: Parents teach professionals. *Education Unlimited, 1*(5), 36–37.

Gallagher, J. J. (1981). Future of special education. In J. L. Paul (Ed.), *Understanding and working with parents of children with special needs.* New York: Holt, Rinehart & Winston.

Gallagher, J. J., & Gallagher, G. G. (1985). Family adaptation to a handicapped child and assorted professionals. In H. R. Turnbull & A. P. Turnbull (Eds.), *Parents speak out* (2nd ed.), 233–242. Columbus, Oh.: Charles E. Merrill.

Gallup, G. H. (1983). The 15th annual Gallup poll of the public's attitudes toward the public schools. *Phi Delta Kappan, 65*(1), 33–47.

Gliedman, J., & Roth, W. (1980). *The unexpected minority.* New York: Harcourt Brace Jovanovich.

Golin, A. K., & Ducanis, A. J. (1981). *The interdisciplinary team.* Rockville, Md.: Aspen System.

Gorham, K. A. (1975). A lost generation of parents. *Exceptional Children, 41*(8), 521–525.

Halpern, R. (1982). Impact of PL 94–142 on the handicapped child and family: Institutional responses. *Exceptional Children, 49*(3), 270–273.

Hart, N. W. (1970). Frequently expressed feelings and reactions of parents toward their retarded children. In N. R. Bernstein (Ed.), *Diminished people.* Boston: Little, Brown.

Henley, C., & Spicknall, H. (1983). Solving school-related problems. *PTA Today, 8*(6), 8–10.

Heron, T. E., & Harris, K. G. (1982). *The educational consultant.* Boston: Allyn and Bacon.

Heward, W. L., Dardig, J. C., & Rossett, A. (1979). *Working with parents of handicapped children.* Columbus, Oh.: Charles E. Merrill.

Hobbs, N. (1966). Helping disturbed children. Psychological and ecological strategies. *American Psychologist, 21*(12), 1105–1115.

Hohenshil, T. H., & Humes, C. W. (1979). Roles of counseling in ensuring the rights of the handicapped. *The Personnel and Guidance Journal, 58*(4), 221–227.

Huber, C. H. (1979). Parents of the handicapped child: Facilitating acceptance through group counseling. *Personnel and Guidance Journal, 57*(5), 267–269.

Klein, S. D., & Schleifer, J. J. (1980). The challenge for the 80's: Parent-professional collaboration. *The Exceptional Parent, 10*(1), 2–3.

Kraft, S. P., & Snell, M. A. (1980). Parent-teacher conflict: Coping with parental stress. *The Pointer, 24*(2), 29–37.

Lightfoot, S. L. (1978). *Worlds apart.* New York: Basic Books.

Losen, S. M., & Losen, J. G. (1985). *The special education team.* Boston: Allyn and Bacon.

Mathews, F. N. (1981). Effective communication with parents of the gifted and talented: Some suggestions for improvement. *Journal for the Education of the Gifted, 4*(3), 270–210.

McLoughlin, J. A., McLoughlin, R., & Stewart, W. (1979). Advocacy for parents of the handicapped: A professional responsibility and challenge. *Learning Disability Quarterly, 2*(3), 51–57.

McWilliams, B. J. (1976). Various aspects of parent counseling. In E. J. Webster (Ed.), *Professional approaches with parents of handicapped children.* Springfield, Ill.: Charles C Thomas.

Murray, D. G. (1969). Needs of parents of mentally retarded children. In W. Wolfensberger & R. A. Kurtz (Eds.), *Management of the family of the mentally retarded*, 68–70. Chicago: Parkinson Division, Follett Educational Corp.

Murray, J. N., & Cornell, C. J. (1981). Parentalplegia. *Psychology in the Schools, 18*(2), 201–207.

Neely, M. A. (1982). *Counseling and guidance practices with special education students.* Homewood, Ill.: The Dorsey Press.

Pagel, S., & Price, J. (1980). Strategies to alleviate teacher stress. *Pointer, 24*(2), 45–53.

Patterson, M. (1983). Being a professional parent. *The Exceptional Parent, 13*(4), 22–29.

Paul, J. L., & Epanchin, B. C. (1982). *Emotional disturbance in children.* Columbus, Oh.: Charles E. Merrill.

Perosa, L. M., & Perosa, S. L. (1981). The school counselor's use of structural family therapy with learning-disabled students. *The School Counselor, 29*(2), 152–155.

Powell, D. R. (1979). Family-environment relations and early childrearing: The role of social networks and neighborhoods. *Journal of Research and Development in Education, 13*(1), 1–11.

Prescott, M. R., & Hulnick, H. R. (1979). Counseling parents of handicapped children: An empathic approach. *The Personnel and Guidance Journal, 58*(4), 263–270.

Reinhart, H. R. (1976). *Children in conflict.* St. Louis: C. V. Mosby.

Riggs, G. G. (1980). To parents . . . (with love). *G/C/T, 12* (March–April), 3–4.

Roos, P. (1978). Parents of mentally retarded children—misunderstood and mistreated. In A. P. Turnbull & H. R. Turnbull (Eds.), *Parents speak out*, 13–27. Columbus, Oh.: Charles E. Merrill.

Schwartz, C. G. (1970). Strategies and tactics of mothers of mentally retarded children for dealing with the medical care system. In N. R. Bernstein (Ed.), *Diminished people.* Boston: Little, Brown.

Seligman, M., & Seligman, P. A. (1980). The professional's dilemma: Learning to work with parents. *The Exceptional Parent, 10*(5), 511–512.

Shea, T. M. (1978). *Teaching children and youth with behavior disorders.* St. Louis: C. V. Mosby.

Smith, J., & Cline, D. (1980). Quality programs. *The Pointer, 24*(2), 80–87.

Sommers, P. A. (1982). What parents should know about a doctor's influence on the education of their special child. *The Pointer, 27*(1), 37–40.

Sonnenschein, P. (1981). Parents and professionals: An uneasy relationship. *Teaching Exceptional Children, 14*(2), 62–65.

Stevens, S. H. (1980). *The learning-disabled child: Ways that parents can help.* Winston-Salem, N.C.: John F. Blair.

Turnbull, A. P. (1983). Parent-professional interactions. In M. E. Snell (Ed.), *Systematic instruction of the moderately and severely handicapped.* Columbus, Oh.: Charles E. Merrill.

Turnbull, A. P., & Leonard, J. (1981). Parent involvement in special education: Emerging advocacy roles. *School Psychology Review, 10*(1), 37–44.

Webster, E. J. (1976). *Professional approaches with parents of handicapped children.* Springfield, Ill.: Charles C Thomas.

Westin, J. E. (1981). *The coming parent revolution.* Chicago: Rand McNally.

Wright, B. (1960). *Physical disability—a psychological approach.* New York: Harper & Row.

Wyatt, G. E., Bas, B. A., Powell, G. J., & Lim, P. (1983). Parents' and medical student therapists' perceptions of child mental health services: A teaching program in prevention and early intervention. *Child Psychiatry and Human Development, 13*(3), 139–152.

Zorman, R. (1982). Parents do make a difference. *Roeper Review, 5*(2), 41–43.

Part II
The Parent-Professional Partnership

THE GIRL

I blame her for everything that touches ground,
the girl who throws books and scissors
and screams for no reason
except language will not work for her.
She pulled a fistful of my hair.
She broke my glasses. My back hurts
from lifting her into her wheelchair or desk.

At the school this morning
day was lit with green fog and I half hoped
air on the move would take me ten thousand miles.
I hoped I could teach her something,
the girl who never controlled one thing in her life
but controls me.
                I slam the door of my own house.

Leaves curl on the forest floor like wrens.
My mind must collect itself.
I screamed for no reason
and have come to sit on a stone. At sundown
mountains are purple with rage
and birds are falling from a sourwood tree,
red bird, red bird, yellow one—
I am going to sit here till someone tells me different,
afraid everything is going to fall,
berries from dogwood, hickory nuts,
every leaf on every tree, and rain.

From *Night Student*, (1985, State Street Press).
Used by permission of the author, Nancy Simpson

6

Parent-School Communication

The early history of education in America reflects a close relationship among schools, the community, and the home. The growth of educational systems and the complexity of resulting issues have destroyed the intimacy of the home-school ties that once existed (Gordon, 1976). Confusion about the role of the school, changes in the family, and cultural pluralism have contributed to the division. These and other factors present a challenge to reestablish the bond between home and school.

Parents and schools are striving toward a new kind of relationship to help children learn—a partnership acknowledging more fully the need for schools to share educational decision-making with parents (Losen & Diament, 1978). The participation mandated for parents of exceptional children is desirable for parents of all children. However, public education may go through a period of confusion until educators and parents at all levels learn how to deal with each other equitably (Losen & Losen, 1985).

Teachers of exceptional students are urged to communicate with the interdisciplinary team, with other teachers, and with parents. However, communication skills, like parenting skills, are largely left to chance. It is important to examine modes of communication, the communication process, and the factors contributing to effective and ineffective communication. It is equally important to realize that the communication process must be encouraged and taught at all levels.

Modes of Communication

Although communication is usually considered to be a verbal process, in recent years investigators have become increasingly aware that messages are sent and received in many ways. McGough (1974) reports message impact as 7 percent verbal (choice of words), 38 percent vocal (tone), and 55 percent body language. In the total communication process, verbal and nonverbal modes warrant consideration.

Verbal Communication

☐ The basic verbal communication skills are reading, writing, and speaking. Verbal communication requires a sufficient vocabulary to express one's ideas and the use of mutually understood terms.

Communication of ideas, thoughts, and feelings by language has always been a goal of formal education. Many educators who have been through the educational system assume that the language patterns parents use are the same as those the school system uses (Michaelis, 1980). Such a commonality cannot be taken for granted.

It is important to know what type of language is used in the home. An unusual dialect or a foreign language may prevent communication, as illustrated in the following personal account:

> As a kindergarten teacher, I was concerned about Leon's poor language development. I knew that his father, who was in the army, was overseas. I began sending notes to his mother to arrange for a conference and to plan language development activities for him. My notes went unanswered, and I began to feel angry. As a last resort, I went home with Leon one day. I met his mother and found that she was German and that although she spoke some English, she could not read it. Of course my notes meant nothing to her.

School personnel also need to be aware of the language difficulties minority parents encounter. Marion (1981, p. 227) emphasizes the importance of this recognition:

> Clearly understood language, communicated between equals and in lay terms, will do much to alleviate minority parents' insecurity and anxiety. It will enhance the teachers' stature in the eyes of the parents. Better yet, it will ensure the parents' continued cooperation and consumerism in educational planning.

Whether the message is written or spoken, the accompanying nonverbal communication is equally important in the total process.

Nonverbal Communication

☐ More feelings, intentions, and emotions are probably communicated in nonverbal behavior than in all verbal ways (McGough, 1974). Nonverbal communication refers to eye, facial, and head movements, and entire body postures. It can be defined as "the exchange of information through nonlinguistic signs" (Harrison, 1974, p. 25).

Nonverbal communication serves several functions. It relays messages, augments verbal communication, contradicts verbal communication, and replaces verbal communication (Chinn, Winn, & Walters, 1978).

Replacing Verbal Communication An obvious use of nonverbal language is sign language, used by many hard-of-hearing and deaf people to replace verbal communication. American sign language has enjoyed a recent revival, and many people consider it beautiful as well as useful. A visual-gestural language, its grammar takes advantage of (1) the ability of the human eye to detect small differences in movement and (2) the ability of the human body to produce these different movements, often simultaneously (Baker & Padden, 1978).

Sign language is also used to augment and stimulate the verbal language of mentally retarded children. In some cases, children develop their own unique modes of nonverbal communication, as experienced by the author:

> I became aware of this powerful communication when, as a graduate student in special education, I accompanied a class to a facility for handicapped children. One of our class members, Bobby, was a Viet Nam veteran who had lost his hands and had hooks attached to his arms. As we greeted the children one boy, who was described as noncommunicative, took Bobby's hook in his hand, looked up at him and said, "Aww. . . ." It was one of the clearest messages I have ever encountered.

Relaying Messages Molandro and Barker (1983) suggest that nonverbal communication is "the process of individuals transmitting nonverbal cues that have the potential to stimulate meaning in the minds of other individuals" (p. 9).

Facial expressions readily relay messages of friendliness, surprise, and fear. Sometimes, the expression actually contradicts the verbal message being sent, so that the receiver is confused by a mixed message. Individuals may be adept at masking their facial expressions, so the receiver must be a skilled interpreter in order to decipher the intended message.

Body movement adds meaning through the hands, agreement with a nod of the head, and interest through body posture. Listening, in particular, is aided or thwarted by body language.

Maintenance of eye contact indicates interest and also encourages the speaker to continue. Atwater (1981, p. 22) emphasizes the importance of positive body language in listening:

> Since most of our communicating is nonverbal, positive body language expresses our desire to listen. Sitting toward the front of your chair and leaning forward with an animated expression is a way of saying "I'm all ears." On the other hand, slouching down in your chair expresses a casual, disinterested attitude. Standing with folded arms goes along with a defensive attitude, and putting hands on your hips shows a defiant attitude. When listeners show little or no body movement, especially without eye contact, a speaker may wonder if the listener is "still there." Speakers usually prefer listeners with responsive body language, though an overly fidgety listener may distract the speaker. There is also a tendency for listeners unconsciously to mimic the speaker's posture and ges-

tures, as if to say "I'm with you." Other matters, like sitting or standing too close or too far away may also enhance or interfere with our verbal communication.

In interacting with each other, parents and professionals should be aware of the power of nonverbal communication and learn to use and interpret it in facilitating understanding. Nonverbal communication is important because of its role in the total communication process, the quantity of information it relays in any particular situation, and its widespread use in daily living (Knapp, 1980).

The Communication Process

In defining communication, Swap, Clark, and Knox (1980) state that "effective communication takes place when each person obtains a clear understanding of the other's message, takes time to consider the significance of the message, and gives the sender a response" (p. 53). Such an exchange should result in respect for the other person's experience and frame of reference.

Talking and exchanging information are common occurrences; the actual process of communicating with another individual happens much less frequently (Simpson, 1982). Effective communication requires mutual acceptance, attentiveness, trust, and an open atmosphere.

Although parents and educators have expressed the need and desire to communicate more effectively, this goal has not been reached in many schools. Barriers to communication have been present throughout the years in the parent-educator relationship.

Barriers to Communication

In addition to the problems previously revealed in the parent-professional relationship, school-related problems may interfere with communication. Marion (1981, p. 223) identifies the bases of anxiety parents frequently feel in school encounters:

1. Their own school experiences.
2. The apprehension of learning that their child is not performing satisfactorily in school.
3. The fear of being blamed by the teacher for much of their child's problems.
4. Previous contacts with schools that proved to be embarrassing.

Parents' School Experience Most parents face the school system with reactions held over from their own school days (Michaelis, 1980). Memories of authoritarian teachers, strict administrators, and drab surroundings influence their attitudes toward the school.

If their child has been identified as handicapped, parents may face emotions that are totally negative. The special class, in their experience, could have been an isolated, segregated part of the school—an area to be avoided. It is possible that parents themselves were members of groups that, in their school days, were ostracized.

Sometimes, parents have had previous negative encounters with school personnel. Such experiences might have concerned their children or might have occurred when the parents were students. They may be tired of hearing about what a failure their child is, what a failure they are as parents, or what a failure they were as children (Idol-Maestras, 1983).

Parents of gifted children have, in many cases, been frustrated because there have been no programs designed to meet their children's needs (O'Neill, 1978). In other cases, parents are reluctant to admit that their children are gifted and assume that schools will automatically take care of them or that the children will get along by themselves (Tuttle, 1980).

Child's Performance When parents are asked to come to school, frequently it is to deal with the school's contention that their child is not performing adequately, either academically or behaviorally (Feldman, Byalick, & Rosedale, 1975). The first contact about a problem can have a profound effect on the parents. Thus parents may interpret a routine call home as signifying something has gone wrong (Losen & Diament, 1978).

The parents' apprehension may be heightened by their own unacknowledged feeling that a problem exists. If this is a beginning awareness, the parents may not be ready to face the problem publicly. In this case, the school and the teacher can become the scapegoats. It is important that school personnel understand and be sensitive to the parents' difficulties.

If parents have had positive experiences in prior encounters with the school, they will view the initial contact as a problem-solving opportunity. If their previous experiences have not been satisfactory, they will be reluctant to hear about the problem and to deal with it.

Fear of Blame When communication is initiated in a crisis situation, the typical reaction is to seek someone to blame. If parents feel they will be blamed for their child's problem, a communication barrier immediately exists. This feeling is intensified if the approach to the problem is stated as the parents' responsibility. The mother of a high school student related her experience in dealing with insensitive school personnel. Faced by the school principal, the psychologist, and the teacher, she was informed, "Your son is impossible. What are you going to do about it?"

On the other hand, the parent whose child is encountering difficulties can produce many convenient scapegoats, such as an absent father, the child next door, or last year's teacher (Moeller, 1971). Blame sessions are unproductive and time-consuming. Parents and teachers can overcome this tendency if they put aside their own concerns and focus on the well-being of the child.

Embarrassing Contacts Some parents have had years of ego-shattering encounters with school personnel. A parent could be embarrassed by the child's label, by not understanding evaluation procedures, by unfamiliarity with educational terms, or by seemingly irrelevant factors. For example, a parent who feels poorly dressed, uneducated, or unfamiliar with school protocol is at a great disadvantage.

Parents who have expressed hostility in previous contacts are likely to be embarrassed in succeeding ones. If they have grown in acceptance and perception of their child's difficulties, they need to be reassurred that future communication can be positive and productive.

Overcoming Barriers

> In working with people there is no escaping the fact that differences exist among us. . . . Consequently, we must learn how to recognize and manage our differences if we hope to be successful. . . . Our differences result naturally from our individuality. Each of us brings to an encounter with others our own experiences, our way of perceiving the world and other people, and our own expectations and assumptions. The important thing to recognize is that differences are natural, should be expected, and are a source of creativity as well as potential disruption of our relationships. (National Association for Retarded Children, 1967, p. 17)

Parents and teachers should recognize and respect differences in experience, background, and values. Such differences, if they are not acknowledged, can lead to disagreement about roles, objectives, and methods in the educational process.

If conflict exists, direct confrontation of the problem is an effective approach. When an honest effort is made to resolve differences, a more relevant and appropriate education for the child is achieved (National Association for Retarded Citizens, 1977).

Effective communication requires sufficient time to share ideas, to listen, and to respond. Parent-teacher transactions are frequently brief and often unexpected. Such interactions are usually causes for alarm, eliciting a frightened "What's wrong?" from the parent (Swap, Clark, & Knox, 1980). Teachers should use strategies to initiate early, frequent, and positive interaction between the school and the home.

The exchange of understandable terms eliminates a strong barrier to communication. Teachers should lessen or clarify educational jargon and disclose all relevant information.

Communication cannot be developed until barriers are removed. Acknowledgment of individual differences, mutual respect, and resolution of conflicts will provide the foundation on which to build communication.

Establishing Positive Communication

Figure 6.1 illustrates the process of communication. This model presents four stages at which a breakdown might occur before the listener responds to the speaker. The first stage of the communication process involves listening, observing, and interpreting what the speaker is saying. The second stage of the model involves control of one's emotional and attitudinal responses. During the third stage of communication, the receiver decides what to say, and, at the fourth stage, how to communicate the response (Chalfant & Pysh, 1981).

The sender of a message must be able to transmit information in a way that will motivate another person to attend and respond. The success of this effort is directly related to the sender's communication skills and attitudes (Simpson, 1982). Receivers of messages must also be alert to the message's content and sensitive to its emotional implications. Effective communication depends on the development of positive attitudes and professional skills.

Attitude

Atwater (1981) claims that when it comes to communication, attitude is even more important than technique. The three attitudes essential to communication are acceptance, self-acceptance, and empathy.

FIGURE 6.1 The Communication Process

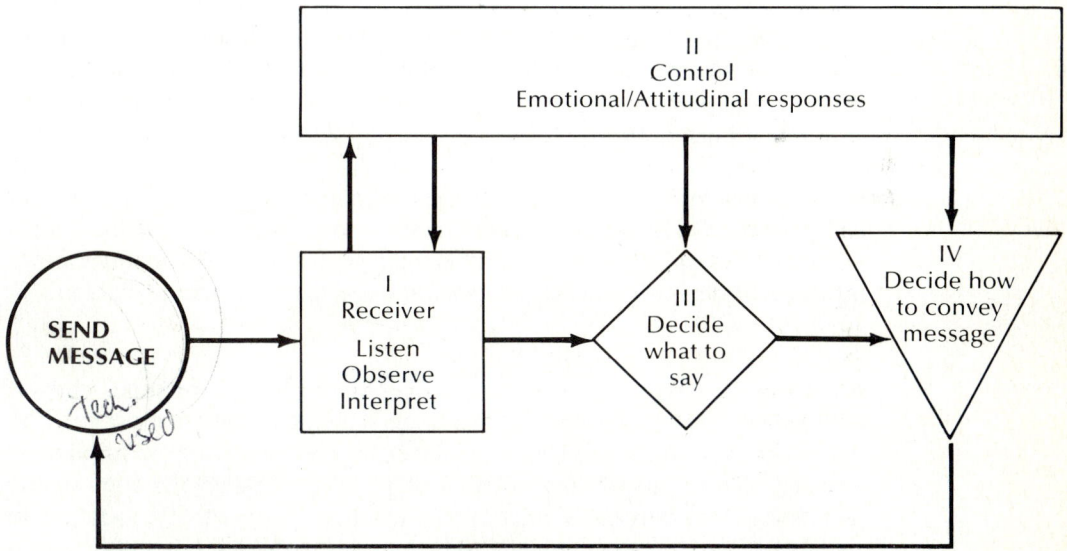

Source: J. C. Chalfant and M. V. D. Pysh (1981). *Talking with parents: Communication skills for educators* (Leader's Manual). New Rochelle, N. Y.: Pathescope Educational Media, Inc.

Acceptance Acceptance is a basic attitude of positive regard toward another person. The heart of acceptance is a nonjudgmental attitude—acknowledging another's right to feel, think, and act as an individual (Atwater, 1981).

Professionals should thus accept parents as they are. They should not criticize parental values and attitudes that conflict with their own.

When attitudes are positive, people who are communicating remain open and receptive despite the differences between them. With negative attitudes, people become closed, unduly critical, and nonaccepting of others.

Many parents of exceptional children have experienced prejudice and nonacceptance. Handicapped children have often been ostracized, stared at, or not called on in class. Gifted children have received similar treatment and know the feeling of not being accepted. Through their children, parents have experienced this rejection.

It is vital that parents and teachers model acceptance and understanding of others. Parents and professionals should remember that each group needs to be accepted: parents as the first teachers of their children, and school personnel as those who share concern and responsibility for the students they teach.

Self-acceptance The more people come to terms with themselves, the more fully they can accept other people. Parents who are secure in their own capabilities are more accepting of the teacher's efforts. The same is true of teachers; as they become skilled and confident in teaching exceptional children, they more readily accept their unique qualities and those of the students' parents.

Feelings of self-esteem, or a positive sense of regard for oneself, are essential to the success of teaching. If low self-esteem is present, initial hardship with a task convinces the teacher or the parent that failure will follow and prevents the investment of time and energy necessary to master the task (Klein & Schleifer, 1980).

Parents' becoming involved in their child's education may at first question their own abilities to convey their cares, hopes, and opinions about their child's interests and needs. As they become knowledgeable about the educational process and skillful in presenting their views to school personnel, negative feelings diminish and self-acceptance develops (Anderson, Chitwood, & Hayden, 1982).

Empathy Empathy is the awareness of another's feelings of anger, sorrow, or joy and the communication of that understanding to the other person. The explanation of "walking in another's shoes" is a misleading conception of empathy. It is not possible for another person to experience the anguish and uncertainty that parents of exceptional children have felt. It is possible to understand and to care, however. As expressed earlier by the author:

> while I have been offended as a parent, I have also been rebuffed as a teacher. I have found that many parents think that no one else knows their problems, no

one else has experienced their heartaches, no one else understands. In conferences the parents of my students would frequently say, "But you don't know what we go through." While I could empathize on one level as a parent, I also was angered as a teacher because in many cases the teacher spends more time with the child than the parent does. (Schulz, 1985, p. 7)

Parents of handicapped children appreciate professionals who accept their child, conveying neither pity nor denial of the disability (Cansler & Martin, 1974). Parents of gifted students also appreciate teachers who realize that raising very bright children is not an easy task and that they also need help and empathy.

Pierce (1972) defines communication as a process of adjusting understandings and attitudes. Certainly, the attitudes of the people involved can greatly influence the quality of communication.

Skill

Obviously, the sender of a message must have basic communication skills that enable the message to be expressed. The more skill the sender possesses, the greater is the likelihood the message will be received and interpreted accurately. The ability to organize and present one's thoughts accurately is a skill that can be developed through instruction and experience.

Because professionals are frequently initiators and therefore leaders of conversations, they tend to be good senders of messages. If parents are to be actively involved in the educational process, professionals also need to focus on the skills of listening, responding, and interacting.

Listening The basis for most of the difficulties resulting from poor communication lies in the inability of individuals to listen effectively. Effective listening requires effort and skill; it is hard work (Gargiulo, 1985).

Most interested and concerned people have listening postures ranging from a passive, attending manner to one of becoming actively involved in the messages of others (Kroth, 1975). These various postures can be placed into a listening paradigm (see Figure 6.2).

As Kroth (1975) conceptualizes, people may move from one quadrant to another, depending on the situation. However, most people tend to fall into one of the following categories:

> *Quadrant A—Passive Listener.* The passive listener is supportive, encouraging the parent to talk. Nonverbal signs of acceptance promote confidentiality and trust.
>
> *Quadrant B—Active Listener.* An active listener is involved with helping other people identify and clarify their problems. Feelings expressed are fed back to the parent; complex statements may be reverbalized with "I hear you saying . . ." to test perceptions.

FIGURE 6.2 A Listening Paradigm

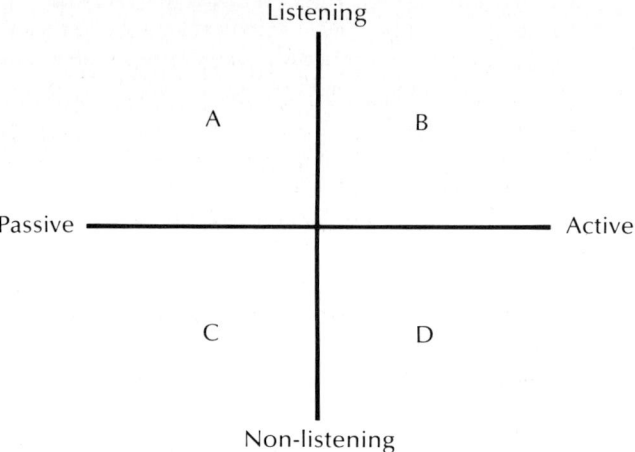

Source: Roger L. Kroth, *Communicating with parents of exceptional children.* (1975) Denver: Love Publishing Co., p. 29.

Quadrant C—Passive Non-listener. The passive non-listener seems to hear what is said, but is not involved in listening to the emotional content of the message. Thus the listener can repeat the message, but may miss the underlying intent.

Quadrant D—Active Non-listeners. The active non-listener is not particularly interested in what the other person has to say. In parent-teacher communication efforts of this nature, little is accomplished because they are not taking the time to listen to each other. Some non-listeners react to the incidentals of the message, never allowing the theme to be unfolded. (Kroth, 1975, pp. 28–35)

Although individual styles may differ, many people consider active listening to be the most productive form. Adler (1983) claims that the most prevalent mistake people make about listening is to regard it as passively receiving rather than as actively participating. An active, participating listener pays attention, thinks along with what is being said, and looks beyond the words for meanings and messsages in all levels of information and emotion (Dean, 1985).

In the parent-professional interaction, participatory listening is particularly important but frequently neglected. As parents report:

> Again and again we have heard the plea from parents that the diagnostician respect the occupation of parenting, that he not only listen to the parent but *hear* what he or she says. (Gorham, Des Jardins, Page, Pettis, & Scheiber, 1975, p. 163)

Listening presupposes that people want to listen, that they pay attention, and that they share responsibility with the speaker (Atwater, 1981). Although most people are inefficient listeners, they can improve their listening skills. The following suggestions may help:

1. Listen. Show interest. Give the person speaking your full attention. This doesn't mean just being silent. There are ways you can actively show the speaker that you are really listening. Look at the person speaking to show that he has your attention. Respond to what the other person has said. Ask questions to check that you really understand; paraphrase. Avoid interrupting. Let the other person finish speaking while you listen for details instead of just waiting to get your point across.

2. Be open-minded. This means being flexible and willing to change your ideas. Don't assume you have all the information and facts you need. The other person may know something you don't.

3. Avoid getting angry just because the other person's ideas are not in agreement with yours.

4. Find out *why* another person holds opinions and how he came to believe certain ideas.

5. Show that you are sympathetic by recognizing the other person's feelings and concerns.

☐ *According to Kroth (1975), most people tend to fall into different categories of listeners: the passive listener, the active listener, the passive nonlistener, and the active nonlistener. Which category does this father fit?*

6. Check to be sure you understand the language used.

7. Check to be sure everyone involved in the situation is clear on agreements made. (Brownstone & Dye, 1973, p. 32)

As Figure 6.1 depicts, the first stage of the communication process involves listening, observing and interpreting. In parent-teacher communication, Chalfant and Pysh (1981, pp. 9–11) outline this stage as follows:

A. Listen:
Passive Listening
—No verbal response, but maintain direct eye contact
—Hold body in an attitude of attention
—React to what is being said with appropriate facial expression
Active Listening
—Verbally respond to acknowledge what is being said
—Assure speaker you are listening
—Assure speaker you are trying to understand
B. Observe:
—How parent conveys message
—What parent is telling you with postures and gestures
—Note facial expressions, voice tone and inflections
C. Interpret:
To help form an accurate interpretation, ask yourself:
—Have I given the parent a chance to talk?
—Am I certain I have listened for and understood the parents' point of view?
—Are the various pieces of information I have gathered consistent?
—Does the parents' verbal message match the nonverbal behavior?
—What has the parent failed to say or avoided saying?
—Have I drawn hasty or incorrect conclusions?
—Do I need more information?

The second stage requires a response to the person who sends the message.

Responding Teachers need to respond accurately and empathetically to parents. Certain conditions help insure the success of this process:

1. Teacher responses should be as nonauthoritative as possible.
2. Teachers should be truly accepting, empathetic, and responsive without giving the impression they are making value judgments.
3. Teachers should ask open-ended questions, i.e., those that encourage further discussion rather than close off additional inquiries.
4. Teachers should be considerate of parents' vulnerability to the child's problem.
5. Teachers should accord parents of all economic, racial, and ethnic groups the same respect and rights as they work together for the welfare of the child. (Marion, 1981, p. 227)

Responsiveness is encouraged by stating the purpose of the conversation. Parents are frequently asked to give information without being given a reason; this practice creates distrust and makes the listeners suspicious.

Parents' questions should be responded to with honesty and clarity. They need and deserve accurate feedback. It is important to find out, directly or indirectly, what parents expect from their child's teacher. It is equally important for the teacher to let them know what is expected of them and of their child.

Conversation should be between two responsible individuals with the aim being mutual understanding. Brownstone and Dye (1973, p. 31) have established helpful guidelines for the speaker:

1. Stick to the subject. Be specific, not vague.
2. Be aware that your tone of voice and manner (e.g., facial expression, posture, gestures) communicate as much as do your words.
3. Don't let discussions break down into nagging, arguing, or repetitious criticism. Be calm; show common courtesy and patience. Use a diplomatic approach.
4. Don't monopolize the conversation.
5. Show respect for the other person's feelings and dignity. Avoid rudeness, name-calling, and insinuations so that the other person doesn't have to avoid conversation and be forced to just defend himself.
6. Don't assume you're making yourself clear. Check to be sure that real communication is occurring by asking if the other person understands or by asking him to repeat what you said.
7. Don't demand or be a dictator in your style of speaking or in giving your standards. However, be honest and direct about your ideas, your feelings, and about what you expect and plan to do. Let the other person know why you hold a certain idea.
8. Give your point of view as information, not as "law" or as the only good idea. Remember that right and wrong vary with opinion and that it's necessary to consider the other person's point of view.
9. Avoid focusing on the negative aspects of the situation. Focus on giving and getting information in order to solve a problem.
10. Don't attack the other person, attack the problem.

As parents and professionals become responsive, they move from a passive to an active relationship. They begin to interact.

Interacting A cursory examination of the communication model presented in Figure 6.1 results in a feeling that the process begins with the sender of a message and ends with the responder. A closer look reveals that communication is a continuous, interactive process.

Figure 6.3 depicts a clear representation of the interactive aspect of communication. As Chinn, Winn, and Walters (1978) explain, in typical human communication the person who is the source is also the receiver of the message, and the receiver a source (or sender). Through this process, roles are constantly changing and messages are sent congruently.

When people are comfortable with each other, they are free to interact, to exchange information, and to understand each other on intellectual and on affective levels. Clear communication is a meeting of minds, not just an exchange of words.

Nirenberg (1963) suggests five human characteristics that interfere with a meeting of minds: (1) resistance to change, (2) the urge to think one's own thoughts rather than listen, (3) wishful hearing, (4) unwarranted assumptions, and (5) habitual secretiveness. These tendencies can be related to experiences with parents of exceptional children.

Resistance to Change People cling to certain ways of thinking, feeling, and acting—not because they have always done it that way but because it serves some purpose for them.

> Jeff has cerebral palsy, with severe mental retardation. When a class for severely handicapped children was established in his county, school personnel called on his parents to advise them of the available services. Jeff's father visited the class; his mother would not go. She continues to keep him at home, treating him like a baby. School representatives are no longer welcome in the home.

Thinking One's Own Thoughts To hold another person's attention, the conversation has to matter more than anything else on that person's mind.

> Mr. Lewis took time off from his job to respond to the teacher's note about Kim's reading achievement. Kim's mother was unable to leave a sick child; Mr. Lewis was worried about both of them. Between missing work and wondering about the welfare of his family, Mr. Lewis found it difficult to be concerned about Kim's test score.

FIGURE 6.3 Two-Way Talking is a Continuous Two-Way Process

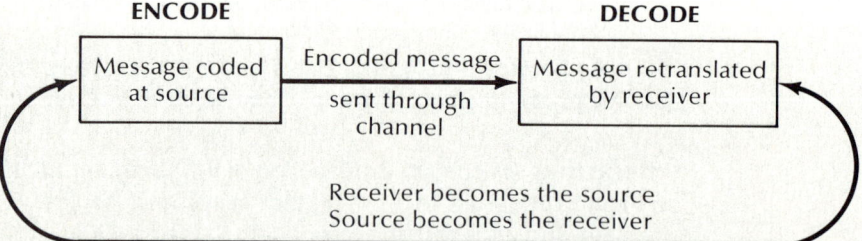

Source: Philip C. Chinn, Joyce Winn and Robert H. Walters (1978) *Two-way talking with parents of special children.* Saint Louis: The C. V. Mosby Company, p. 60.

Wishful Hearing The wishful listener gives an angry or a cheerful tone to a neutral voice, supplies words that were never meant to be there, and gives meaning that originates only in the listener's mind.

> Scott is an excellent student in math. His teacher related this information to Scott's mother, who received it enthusiastically and interpreted it as meaning that Scott would qualify for the academically gifted program. When his other academic grades did not meet program criteria, Scott's mother was irate, declaring that the teacher had misinformed her.

Unwarranted Assumptions A speaker should not make assumptions about what the other person knows. On the other hand, one cannot assume that the listener lacks knowledge.

> My good friend and I attended a conference concerned with educating severely handicapped children. Both of us were there as college professors in special education and as parents of retarded children. As we listened intently to one of the major speakers, we heard him say, "This book would be valuable to parents of retarded children, since it is written on an eighth-grade reading level." (Schulz, 1985, p. 6)

Habitual Secretiveness Many people conceal thoughts and feelings; they feel safe because any revelation seems dangerous. Communication requires going beyond the question to give all the information the other person wants. It also means sharing oneself.

> As a teacher, Nancy had been reluctant to admit that her own son had emotional problems that were disrupting the family as well as the school. In talking with the parent of one of her students, Nancy blurted out, "I do know what you mean; my son is driving me crazy!" The parent and the teacher began talking as friends, helping each other as they shared a common problem.

Everyone communicates. Although not everyone communicates well, everyone can develop effective communication skills. Bolton (1979, p. 12) identifies five sets of basic communication skills required for effective human relationships:

> *Listening skills*: These methods enable a person to really understand what another person is saying. They include new ways of responding so that the other person feels his problems and feelings have been understood. When these methods are used appropriately, the other person often solves his problems without becoming dependent on you.
> *Assertion skills*: These verbal and nonverbal behaviors enable you to maintain respect, satisfy your needs, and defend your rights without dominating, manipulating, abusing, or controlling others.
> *Conflict-resolution skills*: These abilities enable you to deal with the emotional turbulence that typically accompanies conflict—abilities that are likely to foster closer relationships when the strife is over.

Collaborative problem-solving skills: These constitute a way of resolving conflicting needs that satisfies all parties—it is a way of solving problems so they stay solved.

Skill selection: These guidelines enable you to decide what communication skills to use in any situation in which you find yourself.

Parents and school personnel are responsible for meeting the needs of exceptional students. By maintaining effective two-way communication, they can meet those needs in a productive and cooperative manner. In addition to developing positive attitudes and communication skills, the knowledge and use of various strategies can facilitate the home-school partnership.

Strategies

The relationship between parents and teachers is usually the strongest link between the home and the school. The roles of other school personnel are not less important in the partnership but are usually of a shorter duration and of a less direct nature.

The school administrator, for example, sets the tone of acceptance or nonacceptance for the school. The psychologist is critical to parents' understanding of the evaluation procedures. The counselor forms a link between parents and other essential services. These people and other professionals communicate and work with parents in many situations. It is the teacher, however, who is usually responsible for initiating and maintaining a lasting relationship.

Teachers and parents are in constant and intimate contact with students. They should, therefore, be in continuous contact with each other. A sustained relationship requires a basic understanding of each other's motivations and values and a repertoire of techniques to establish an on-going communication system.

Understanding

Many teachers feel that parents of exceptional children are uncaring, uncooperative, and noncommunicative. Other teachers are concerned because the parents deny that a problem exists and refuse to permit the student to receive special services. Still others just do not understand why their efforts to establish communication are not working.

Parents as well as teachers sense the absence of a good rapport. Seligman (1979, p. 115) suggests that the teacher consider the following seven causative factors:

1. You have a strong dislike for the parents' child, who happens to be the most demanding and exasperating youngster you've worked with in years. Your sense of frustration with the child makes it difficult to be open in your relationship with the parents.
2. You sense that there is an adverse reaction to you but you are not sure why.
3. You know that the parents view their child's educational program with considerable skepticism.
4. Either you or the parents are preoccupied with events not related to the conference.
5. You sense that the parents are uncomfortable talking about their handicapped child.
6. You are threatened by the parents because their professional status equals or exceeds yours.
7. You are threatened by the parents because you know they are sophisticated in their child's exceptionality.

Sometimes, understanding the problem can lead to its resolution. For example, if the teacher is aware of a family crisis, efforts may be directed toward establishing contact with an appropriate agency and postponing the school problem for a while. Other conflicts may be resolved by establishing open discussion with the parents.

Parents' motivations for behaving in certain ways may not be immediately apparent. A puzzled teacher related the following incident to the author:

> When Sue enrolled in my home economics class, I soon realized that she was "different." I suspected that she was mentally retarded, but the school records did not reflect any problem except consistently low grades in every subject area. Conversations with other teachers substantiated my suspicions, so I asked the parents to come in for a conference.
>
> It was immediately apparent that both parents were professional, career-oriented people. They adamantly refused to consent to Sue's evaluation, denied that there was a problem, and insisted that she be treated like everyone else.
>
> I was amazed that seemingly intelligent parents could be so blind! Why were they denying such an obvious problem and witholding the help that their child needed? What can I do to help Sue?

Understanding the parents' level of motivation is a starting point in such a situation. Long, Frye, and Long (1985) suggest the use of Maslow's theory of human motivation in helping to explain parental behavior.

As depicted in Figure 6.4, the basic needs of human beings can be arranged in a hierarchy from the lowest to the highest; these needs constitute motives for their behavior. Maslow (1943) claims that the key to the developing human capacities lies in gratifying these needs.

Once a need is met, it no longer functions as a motivator but is replaced by a higher level in the sequence. Thus, parents who are concerned with meeting physiological needs may not be concerned with school problems, which do not have priority in their present hierarchy of needs.

FIGURE 6.4 Depiction of Maslow's Hierarchy of Needs

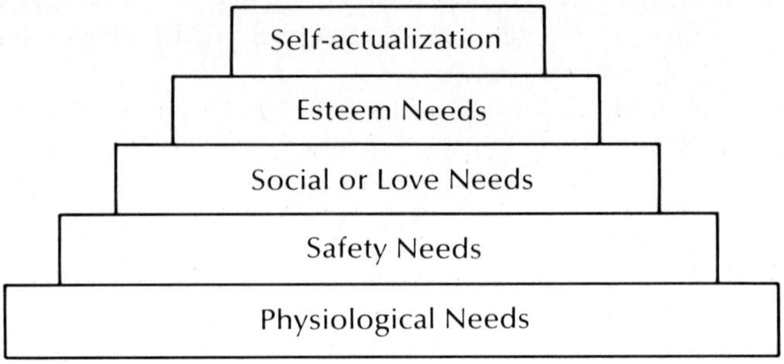

- Self-actualization
- Esteem Needs
- Social or Love Needs
- Safety Needs
- Physiological Needs

On the other hand, parents who have met their physical, safety, and social needs are motivated by esteem needs, which continue to be reflected in their behavior. Being told their child is slow in school represents a blow to their self-esteem and to their perceived esteem in the eyes of the community. Their lack of cooperation may be an attempt to continue to meet their esteem needs by denying their child has a problem (Long, Frye, & Long, 1985). In the previous incident, the behavior of Sue's parents may be explained in this fashion.

Although understanding the problem may not be a solution in itself, it does suggest some approaches. Sue's teacher, for example, can make efforts to individualize her instruction and can continue to involve the parents in nonthreatening activities.

Techniques

☐ Successful school-home communication can be accomplished by reaching out to parents in ways that demonstrate respect, concern for the student, and a sincere desire for cooperation (Magnusson & McCarney, 1980). Techniques designed for this purpose include telephone calls, open-house meetings, newsletters from school, report cards, parent-teacher conferences, and informal visits at the school or in the community.

The overall goal of home-school communication is, of course, to encourage parents and teachers to coordinate their efforts to insure optimal progress of the student. Toward this end, five specific purposes of communication are:

1. Introduction, which incorporates the initial contact
2. Information sharing, including notification for special services
3. Reports on student progress
4. Problem solving
5. Parent involvement in student learning.

Communication techniques are designed to carry out these five objectives.

Introduction The initial contact with parents of a student who may need special help is probably the most important because it sets the stage—positive or negative—for future contacts. The first contact can be made by the parents or by the teacher.

Unexpected calls from parents about their children are among the most difficult for school personnel to handle. If this is the first contact, it usually occurs because the parents are concerned about what they perceive to be a problem. Unless the parents are calling for specific information, they are likely to be hesitant, unsure about the procedure to follow, and uncertain about the magnitude of the problem (Losen & Diament, 1978). When the school makes the initial contact, it is more likely to be a positive one, leading to a reciprocal communication strategy.

The school can open lines of communication by sending an introductory letter to the parents. The five advantages of this early contact are clear:

1. [It] gives the school the opportunity to take the initiative in developing a positive contact
2. Demonstrates an interest in the student and the family
3. Marks the beginning of a personal relationship
4. Provides a stimulus for a reciprocal contact by the parents
5. Guarantees one positive contact.   (Magnusson & McCarney, 1980, p. 24)

☐ *Positive parent-school communication can begin with an introductory letter from the teacher to the parents.*

The form of the letter is not important; the tone is critical. The letter should be warm, sincere, and inviting. Figure 6.5 is an example of an introductory letter. Follow-up letters may contain specific information related to administrative procedures, list of support personnel, and rules and regulations.

Other techniques for meeting parents include open-house meetings, telephone conversations, and specific invitations to visit the class or to assist in some way. The most important consideration is to make the initial contact positive.

Information Sharing Heron and Harris (1982) define **home-school communication** as "a broad range of oral or written messages between parents and teachers for the purpose of exchanging information and providing training to the parents" (p. 114). Telephone calls, notes, newsletters, handbooks, and conferences are used as vehicles for exchanging information.

Although teachers frequently see their role as information givers, parents have a great deal of information about their child that will help the teacher. Michaelis (1980) points out that parents know more than teachers do about their child's developmental history, medical history, social and educational

FIGURE 6.5 A Teacher's Introductory Letter to Parents

```
                                          September 7, 1986

Dear Mr. and Mrs. Adams,

    I am delighted to have Charles in my class this year.
Our goal is to help each student develop to his or her
greatest potential. Toward that end, I make every effort
to individualize our lessons and to make them relevant and
interesting.
    As I get to know Charles better, I would like to talk
with you about specific objectives for him. If you can
think of things about Charles (such as interests or rein-
forcement techniques) that would help me know and work
with him better, I would appreciate your suggestions.
    I will send information to you on a regular basis and
will look forward to meeting you. Please feel free to visit
our class or to contact me.

                                          Sincerely,

                                          Susan Allen

                                          Scott Elementary School
                                          Telephone: 586-2656
```

history, favorite toys and activities, and medication and diet. Knowledge of changes in the family status and in the child's behavior at home also add to the teacher's understanding. In addition, parents may have specific areas of expertise that will enable them to contribute valuable information and knowledge.

Information emanating from the school may be general or specific to the child. General information is exemplified by the newsletter, which keeps parents posted on school activities (see Figure 6.6, p. 166). Newsletters usually inform parents about school programs, special events, lunch menus, and sometimes personal items.

Newsletters from the child's teacher are used to keep parents informed about classroom activities and instructional objectives. Not only does a newsletter answer the question "What did you learn in school?" but it also gives the parents some ideas for follow-up activities at home. Figure 6.7 (p. 167), is a sample of a weekly letter sent home by a kindergarten teacher.

The school may contact parents of exceptional children for the first time when their child is being considered for special services. Parents must be notified of the need for evaluation before the initiation of any assessment procedures. The notification, which can be given in oral form, must also be given in written form and should provide both a rationale for the proposed evaluation and a description of the evaluation instruments to be used. The notification should also contain information relating to the time span anticipated for the beginning and ending of the evaluation, with benefits to the student stipulated. If this is the first contact, the teacher of the child and other persons involved with the referral process should be available to talk with the parents and to answer any questions they may have. If prior communication has been established, the notification procedures will be much smoother than if previous contact has not been made.

Parents of exceptional children must also be apprised of the suggested placement for the student. In addition, parents must be provided advance notice of the IEP conference, including the purpose, time, location, and a statement of individuals who will attend.

Because the parents' involvement is crucial to the implementation of PL 94–142, information sharing includes details relating to the regulations, responsibilities, and time lines required by the law. Because this information is lengthy and complicated, many schools find it helpful to parents and school personnel to develop a handbook of information. The handbook contains, in addition to the above-mentioned regulations, characteristics of various exceptionalities, state definitions and regulations, and suggested approaches to instruction. Such handbooks frequently create a common base of knowledge that enables parents and teachers to talk freely and to share information that will benefit the student.

Student Progress As PL 94–142 mandates, parents' involvement must go beyond attendance at IEP meetings and assume the responsibility of monitor-

FIGURE 6.6 Elementary School Newsletter

Krannert Knews
Krannert Elementary

Special 3rd Grade Edition   January 13, 1985

Important!

There are three different <u>Krannert Knews</u> editions this week. One for kindergarten, one for 1st and 2nd grades, and one for 3rd grade. The reason for this is to explain about the skills continuum for these different grade levels. Be sure to look over each newsletter from those different grade levels if you have a child there. Some information is the same in each newsletter but the <u>REAL IMPORTANT</u> information is different. If you have any questions about the information discussed, please call the school office or contact your child's teacher.

P.T.A.

There will be no PTA meeting this month due to the teacher's planning day that falls on the normal meeting date. Please mark your calendar for the February meeting, Monday, February 20 at 7:30.

YOUTH INSTRUCTIONAL BASKETBALL

6, 7, and 8 year olds - Boys and Girls
Location: Coosa Elementary Gym
When: January 7 - February 18
Saturday mornings 10 a.m.

Youth will learn the basic skills and fundamentals and rules. <u>Everyone participates.</u>

Registration: January 14 last day. enroll at 10 a.m. at Coosa Elementary Gym.

For more information call 291-0766.

Thank You

Thank you for your thoughtfulness in bringing all the food for me at Christmas. It made me happy to know you care about me.

Frances Hull

No SCHOOL For students January 23

Skills Continuum... Things your child must know!

The term "Skills Continuum" has been mentioned in several news letters and at PTA meetings. Our skills continuum list the minimal skills that a child at a particular grade level needs to advance to the next higher grade level. Grades K-2 have an approved list of skills. Grades 3-5 are field testing their skills this year. Next year students in grades 3-5 will have a reporting system similar to the one used in 1st and 2nd grades this year. Required skills as will as grades will be marked. This system allows parents to monitor progress of learned skills as well as see performance grade in a subject area.

If you are interested in how your child is progressing with the skills, contact his/her teacher for a conference.

Source: Krannert Elementary School, Rome, Georgia. Used with permission.

FIGURE 6.7 Teacher Newsletter sent to Parents

October 10, 1986

Dear Parents,

    This week we completed our study of the letter S and our fire safety unit. Among many activities we walked to the fire station, made "Dougie Dalmation Fire Station" dogs, learned about Christopher Columbus, helped animals beginning with S, B, and F find their homes, and in math we worked on numbers one and two.

    Next week we will begin our unit on the five senses and the letter H. Halloween activities and games will begin to sneak their way into our room. I have included some activities on the five senses which you and your child may enjoy doing together.

    Our new contracts have worked out very well. If you notice a special star in the right hand corner of your child's contract, this means that your child remembered to clean up the center after playing in it.

    October 17 is a teacher workday; there will be no school for the children.

    Have a nice week-end!

Sincerely,

Beth Meyer

Source: Courtesy of Beth Hartje Meyer.

ing their child's progress toward the IEP's goals and objectives. Monitoring requires constant and thorough knowledge of what the child is accomplishing in school. Parents who want daily progress reports find that a notebook that goes back and forth with the child enables both the teacher and the parents to make comments. Another system successful in some instances is a daily report card (Powell, 1980). Behavioral as well as academic information keeps parents and teachers aware of the progress being made in both settings.

    Although daily reports are not considered necessary in all cases, it is important to keep parents informed of progress on a regular basis. Following the initial contact, regular reports should be made concerning the child's behavior, academic performance, and concerns of the parents as well as the teacher. The rationale for frequent reporting suggests it:

Provides an opportunity for more frequent communication regarding progress
Affords an additional opportunity to reinforce progress
Builds on a positive communication process and encourages interaction
Offers an opportunity for early identification of special needs. (Magnusson & McCarney, 1980)

When students who are having problems in school begin to make progress, the parents need reinforcement as much as the children do. One teacher, who gave such a student an award bearing the title "Key to Success Award," attached a note to the parents that read:

Dear Parents,
    I am very proud of Paul for having done all thirteen daily assignments given so far this six weeks in English. With these assignments I stress following directions and completing the task (two skills that are important throughout life), and I feel sure that you, too, are proud of your child for doing such a fine job. (Barbara Schulz, 1985)

The note, in addition to the award, informed the parents of the skill activity their son was engaged in. It also made the son feel good.

Traditional modes of reporting can be more effective when they are personalized. One teacher, for example, wrote a note on the final report card

☐ *Telephone calls are a useful technique in promoting positive and open parent-school communication.*

of a gifted student, "One day when John's work is in some art gallery, I will be able to boast that I taught him in second grade."

Parents are entitled to know what their children are learning. Such information also enables them to plan activities that complement the work done in school. Many states are now sending reports based on instructional objectives. An example of such a report is in Figure 6.8 (pp. 170–171).

This report reflects the work of an academically gifted child and informs the parents of precise skills he has acquired. Such information gives the parents direction for goal setting and for activities to be carried out at home. A letter from the teacher contained a follow-up to this kind of formal report at another grade level.

> Parents,
> Some students are having trouble with the multiplication tables. We have been working with them in class (and will continue to do so) but we have now moved on to division. As you know, you cannot divide without first knowing the multiplication facts. Also, objective number thirteen on the fourth grade report cards states that to be promoted to fifth grade, your child must "Know all the basic multiplication facts through 9's." We have gone through the 8's and will be doing 9's next week. Your child has passed these tables: 3,5,2,4.
> He still must pass these to go on to fifth grade: 6,7,8,9.
> Please sign _____ .
>
> (Barbara Schulz, 1985)

This procedure informs the parents of their child's progress and actively involves them in the educational process.

Problem Solving Bolton (1979) identifies three kinds of conflict: a conflict of emotions, values conflicts, and a conflict of needs. After the values issues have been sorted out and the emotional components resolved, important issues often need to be dealt with and problems solved. Because such issues and problems are usually discussed in a conference setting, techniques for solving problems are discussed in the next chapter.

Parent Involvement Although there are occasions when a one-way information-giving system may be appropriate (newsletters, notes, and bulletins), the most effective system in dealing with issues relative to educational services for children is the two-way information system that requires full participation of parents and teachers (Evans & Needle, 1981). The rationale for parent involvement is presented in Chapter 4; techniques for ensuring their involvement are relevant to the topic of parent-teacher communication.

Many parents who want to be involved with their children's education state that they would like to have more direction from teachers. By the same token, many teachers who believe in parent involvement do not know how to bring it about. According to a survey conducted by the National Institute of

FIGURE 6.8 Georgia Criterion-Referenced Test, Parent Report

GRADE 2   PARENT REPORT   DATE OF TESTING SPRING 1983

SCHOOL: Krannert Elementary   6575052   2122853 0022

A MESSAGE TO THE PARENTS OF: John R.

Your child's school recently tested second graders with reading and/or mathematics achievement tests developed by the State Board of Education. The objectives tested were selected by teachers and other educators throughout Georgia as being very important skills for all children in the state to learn. This is your copy of your child's test results. Your child's teacher has a more detailed report to help in looking at your child's strengths and weaknesses.

READING John achieved 25 of 25 objectives.
The 25 reading objectives tested are grouped into three (3) skill areas. The following is a description of the skill areas and what is included in them:

1. Word Attack Skills. These skills involve the student's ability to change printed words into words that are recognized as if he or she had heard them spoken. *In this skill area, your child:*

Did well with consonants and consonant blends, digraphs.
Did well with sounds of vowels.
Did well on sight words and contractions.
Did well on plural forms and prefixes, suffixes.

2. Reading Comprehension. These skills involve a student's ability to understand a printed message. In comprehension, the student recognizes words and gives them meaning both individually and together. The meaning or central theme can be literal (exactly as stated in the words) or implied (indirectly stated, such as interpreting the writer's opinions, seeing the cause and effect relationships, and identifying the sequence of events). *In this skill area, your child:*

Did well seeing words as language units representing meaning.
Did well on opposites and multiple meanings of words.
Did well using context clues to find meaning.
Did well on stated main idea, details, sequence, cause-effect.
Did well on non-stated main idea, sequence, cause-effect.
Did well on distinguishing between fact and opinion.

3. Study Skills. These skills involve the student's ability to locate information from sources such as books, newspapers, magazines, and libraries including following oral and written directions. *In this skill area, your child:*

Did well classifying words by objects and ideas.
Did well in alphabetization.
Did well using table of contents to find information.
Did well with punctuation and capitalization.
Did well following directions.

FIGURE 6.8 (continued)

MATHEMATICS   John achieved 20 of 20 objectives.
The 20 mathematics objectives tested are grouped into six (6) skill areas. The following is a description of the skill areas and what is included in them.

1. Sets, Numbers and Numeration. This skill area involves the student's ability to determine which numbers to use to tell how much and how many, including both whole numbers and fractions. *In this skill area, your child:*

Did well recognizing sets and in simple counting.
Did well recognizing place value, number-name correspondence.
Did well with ordinal numbers, regions and sets.

2. Operations, Property and Number Theory. This skill area involves the student's ability to determine when to add, subtract, multiply, and divide to solve problems. This area also involves understanding of odd and even numbers. *In this skill area, your child:*

Did well adding and subtracting, seeing relation between them.
Did well with multiplication.
Did well with properties of 0 & 1, commutative, associative.
Did well interpreting math symbols.
Did well solving word problems.

3. Relations and Functions. This skill area involves comparing things and using the right words to describe comparisons. *In this skill area, your child:*

Did well identifying order, least, greatest of numbers.
Did well using a number line.
Did well with tables and sequence of numbers.

4. Geometry. This skill area involves recognizing shapes when they are in different positions or when they are made larger or smaller. *In this skill area, your child:*

Did well with open and closed curves and figures.
Did well with recognizing and naming geometric figures.
Did well sorting figures by shape, size, reflections, etc.

5. Measurement. This skill area involves measuring length, weight, and capacity, telling time and solving simple money problems. *In this skill area, your child:*

Did well comparing objects as larger, smaller, least, greatest.
Did well recognizing coins and the value of combinations.
Did well estimating measures using familiar units.

6. Probability and Statistics. This skill involves counting or measuring to get information and reading simple graphs. The concept of chance is also covered. *In this skill area, your child:*

Did well collecting and reading data from charts, graphs.

Source: Floyd County Schools, Rome, Georgia.

Education (1985, p. 2), teachers who actively and successfully promote parent participation frequently use the following nine methods:

1. Ask the parents to read aloud to the child or listen to him/her read. This is a technique used most often by many teachers.
2. Ask the parents to sign a child's homework. Besides involving the parents, this also keeps them informed of their child's progress.
3. Encourage parents to drill students on math and spelling. This practice helps children strengthen basic skills.
4. Suggest the parents help the child with workbook and homework lessons.
5. Encourage parents to ask the child to discuss his/her school day activities.
6. Suggest things at home that parents can use to teach their children. For example, a simple activity might be alphabetizing books or spices on a shelf at home. A more complex activity might be using kitchen supplies for specific science experiments.
7. Send home suggestions for game or group activities related to the child's schoolwork that can be played by parents and child.
8. Invite parents to the classroom to watch how the child is taught. This helps the parents see how the teacher teaches and may give parents ideas on what they can do at home with their children.
9. Encourage parents to take their children to the library regularly and frequently.

Teachers need to develop a plan for involving parents, and they must communicate that plan to the parents. The National Education Association (Tuttle, 1980) further suggests to parents of gifted children that they contact other parents and share concerns and ideas. Such communication not only helps each feel less alone, but also provides resources for the children, including contact with other gifted children of similar interests. Parent involvement has also been suggested as a solution to meet the needs of gifted children in situations lacking special teachers or funds (O'Neill, 1978).

Communication is the greatest single factor affecting a person's relationship with other people. Knowing how to respond to parents in normal and critical situations can make the difference between parents who are receptive to school involvement and parents who are not. Parents and teachers who openly communicate with each other are likely to strengthen their relationships through continued positive interactions (Beale & Beers, 1982).

Conclusion

The home-school relationship is generally recognized as critical to optimal development of the student, but this relationship does not occur incidentally. Many barriers to communication exist between parents and school personnel.

This is particularly true for parents of exceptional children, who may have experienced negative encounters with the school. Yet, it is critical that these parents be invited to participate in their children's education; the school, the parents, and the child benefit from the cooperation that can occur.

The requirements of PL 94–142 have promoted a home-school relationship that has become the goal of educators and parents. For a positive relationship to occur, parents and teachers need to develop attitudes and skills that will promote communication. A number of strategies have been devised to facilitate communication and to promote cooperation. The most successful techniques actively involve parents in the instructional process.

The communication technique that has become most popular for creating teacher-parent interaction is the conference. As a culmination of effective communication, the conference is discussed in Chapter 7.

References

Adler, M. M. (1983). *How to speak, how to listen.* New York: Macmillan.
Anderson, W., Chitwood, S., & Hayden, D. (1982). *Negotiating the special education maze.* Englewood Cliffs, N.J.: Prentice-Hall.
Atwater, E. (1981). *I hear you.* Englewood Cliffs, N.J.: Prentice-Hall.
Baker, C., & Padden, C. (1978). *American sign language.* Silver Springs, Md.: T. J. Publishers.
Beale, A., & Beers, C. S. (1982). What do you say to parents after you've said hello? *Teaching Exceptional Children, 15*(1), 34–38.
Birney, D. (1981). Consulting with administrators: The consultee centered approach. In J. C. Conoley (Ed.), *Consultation in schools*, 101–131. New York: Academic Press.
Bolton, R. (1979). *People skills.* Englewood Cliffs, N.J.: Prentice-Hall.
Brownstone, J. E., & Dye, C. J. (1973). *Communication workshop for parents of adolescents.* (Leader's Guide). Champaign, Ill.: Research Press.
Cansler, D. P., & Martin, G. H. (1974). *Working with families, a manual for developmental centers.* Reston, Va.: Council for Exceptional Children.
Chalfant, J. C., & Pysh, M. V. D. (1981). *Talking with parents: Communication skills for educators.* (Leader's Manual). New Rochelle, N.Y.: Pathescope Educational Media, Inc.
Chinn, P. C., Winn, J., & Walters, R. H. (1978). *Two-way talking with parents of special children.* St. Louis: C. V. Mosby.
Dean, W. S. (1985). Stop, listen . . . and profit. *PACE*/Piedmont Airlines, *11*(4), 81–84.
Evans, J., & Needle, N. A. (1981). Talking it over: How parents and school professionals can work together. *Education Unlimited, 3*(4), 49–50.
Feldman, M. A., Byalick, R., & Rosedale, M. P. (1975). Parents and professionals: A partnership in special education. *Exceptional Children, 41*(8), 551–554.

Gargiulo, R. M. (1985). *Working with parents of exceptional children.* Boston: Houghton Mifflin Co.

Gordon, I. J. (1976). Toward a home-school partnership program. In I. J. Gordon & W. F. Breivogel (Eds.), *Building effective home-school relationships*, 1–20. Boston: Allyn and Bacon.

Gorham, K. A., Des Jardins, C., Page, R., Pettis, E., & Scheiber, B. (1975). Effect on parents. In N. Hobbs (Ed.), *Issues in the classsification of children,* Vol. 2, 154–188. San Francisco: Josey-Bass.

Harrison, R. P. (1974) *Beyond words.* Englewood Cliffs, N.J.: Prentice-Hall.

Heron, T. E., & Harris, K. C. (1982). *The educational consultant.* Boston: Allyn & Bacon.

Idol-Maestas, L. (1983). *Special educator's consultation handbook.* Rockville, Md.: Aspen Systems.

Klein, S. D., & Schleifer, M. J. (1980). Parent-professional collaboration: A continuing problem in self-esteem. *The Exceptional Parent, 10*(5), 51–52.

Knapp, M. L. (1980). *Essentials of nonverbal communication.* New York: Holt, Rinehart & Winston.

Kroth, R. L. (1975). *Communicating with parents of exceptional children.* Denver: Love Publishing.

Long, J. D., Frye, V. H., & Long, E. W. (1985). *Making it till Friday.* Princeton, N.J.: Princeton Book Co.

Losen, S. M., & Diament, B. (1978). *Parent conferences in the schools.* Boston: Allyn & Bacon.

Losen, S. M., & Losen, J. G. (1985). *The special education team.* Boston: Allyn & Bacon.

Magnusson, F. J., & McCarney, S. B. (1980). School-home communication. *Pointer, 25*(1), 23–27.

Marion, R. L. (1981). *Educators, parents and exceptional children.* Rockville, Md.: Aspen Corp.

Maslow, A. H. (1943). A theory of human motivation. *Psychological Review, 1,* 370–396.

McGough, E. (1974). *Your silent language.* New York: William Morrow.

Michaelis, C. T. (1980). *Home and school partnerships in exceptional education.* Rockville, Md.: Aspen Systems.

Moeller, G. B. (1971). The parent-student-teacher triangle. *Today's Education, 60*(4), 40–41.

Molandro, L. A., & Barker, L. L. (1983). *Nonverbal communication.* Reading, Ma.: Addison-Wesley.

National Association for Retarded Children. (1967). *Organizational development workshop trainers manual.* New York: National Association for Retarded Children.

National Association for Retarded Citizens. (1977). *The partnership: How to make it work.* Arlington, Tex.: NARC Research and Demonstration Institute.

National Institute of Education. (1985). *Research in Brief* (Feb.)

Nirenberg, J. S. (1963). *Getting through to people.* Englewood Cliffs, N.J.: Prentice-Hall.

O'Neill, K. K. (1978). Parent involvement: A key to the education of gifted children. *The Gifted Child Quarterly, 22*(2), 235–242.

Pierce, J. R. (1972). Communication. *Scientific American, 227*(3), 31–41.

Powell, T. H. (1980). Improving home-school communication: Sharing daily reports. *The Exceptional Parent, 10*(5), 524–526.

Schulz, J. B. (1985). The parent-professional conflict. In H. R. Turnbull & A. P. Turnbull (Eds.), *Parents speak out*, 3–9. Columbus, Oh.: Charles E. Merrill.

Seligman, M. (1979). *Strategies for helping parents of exceptional children.* New York: The Free Press.

Simpson, R. L. (1982). *Conferencing parents of exceptional children.* Rockville, Md.: Aspen Systems.

Swap, S. M., Clark, J., & Knox, L. (1980). A process of discovery. *The Pointer, 25*(1), 53–57.

Tuttle, F. B. (1980). *Gifted and talented children.* West Haven, Conn.: National Education Association.

7

Parent-Teacher Conferences

Communication is the key to good home-school relationships. In earlier times, parents and teachers interacted within the community, establishing relationships that facilitated communication. In today's larger and more complicated society, parents and teachers may never see each other outside of the school setting. Communication, therefore, must be structured and promoted. The formal conference has replaced informal contacts as a means of communication between parents and teachers.

Although parents are full participants in the parent-teacher conference, the primary responsibility for the success of the conference lies with the teacher. Successful conferences do not occur accidentally; they require purpose, planning, and structure. Canady and Seyfarth (1979, pp. 10–11) outline four outcomes important to a successful parent-teacher conference:

1. A conference has been successful when the parents depart with a positive attitude toward the school and a willingness to continue to work cooperatively with the school staff. Although some issues may remain unsettled and some questions unanswered, if parents have committed themselves to a continuing dialogue, the conference has succeeded.

2. A conference has been successful when the parent and the teacher leave the conference trusting one another more than before. This outcome is related to the first outcome but goes beyond it. Parents may be willing to continue to talk, although the level of trust has not changed. Trust is related to questions of control. We trust those whom we believe will allow us the freedom to be ourselves and who will not seek to dictate or control our behavior.

3. A conference has been successful when the parent and the teacher leave the conference knowing more about the child than before. The teacher may have learned about health problems that contribute to difficulties in learning; about special interests that can be used to motivate a child; or about fears that interfere with and inhibit the child's capacity to learn from new experiences. Parents may have learned that a child's coping style at school is radically different from that with which the parents are familiar; that habits of self-criticism are so ingrained that they interfere with learning; or that difficulties in making and keeping friends have eased and that the child is now a popular, accepted person among peers.

Whether good or bad, happy or sad, information of this kind is invaluable to parents and teachers seeking to help a child to achieve up to his potential and to make school a satisfying experience.

4. A conference has been successful when the parent and the teacher leave with a better understanding of what each other is trying to do. If the teacher succeeds in explaining to parents what he or she is trying to accomplish and the means employed to do it, and if parents make clear to the teacher their aspirations and hopes for their child, a firm basis for future cooperation has been established.

A valuable medium for developing communication, the parent-teacher conference requires dedicated work and a significant time commitment. A successful conference is based on clearly defined purposes and careful structure. Some special situations also challenge the teacher.

Conference Purposes

The **conference** can be defined as "an individualized, personalized meeting between two or three significant persons in the child's life with the purpose of accelerating his or her growth" (Kroth & Simpson, 1977, p. 2). This broad goal is brought about through the creation of a bond between teacher and parents that invites an open and positive exchange of information and encourages an alliance of home and school. To meet this general goal, Roberds-Baxter (1984) emphasizes the process of the parent conference through the "parent connection model" (p. 55).

The parent connection model is based on techniques that enable teachers to feel confident and at ease while leading the meeting and that encourage parents to feel wanted and necessary to the procedure. The model in Figure 7.1 suggests that educators engage in behaviors clustered into three categories: structure, teacher well-being, and parent comfort. Behaviors listed in the first category, *structure*, free teachers from concern about content detail and allow them to concentrate on interpersonal dynamics. Behaviors listed in the second category, *teacher well-being*, enable teachers to enter a meeting feeling calm, confident, and attentive. The third category, *parent comfort*, lists strategies that encourage psychological comfort in the parents (Roberds-Baxter, 1984).

If the conference is parent-initiated, the teacher must be alert to the real purpose for the meeting. Sometimes parents have a hidden message, particularly if a problem exists. At other times, the teacher may not listen to what the parent is saying. The following account of a conference experienced by the author illustrates this point:

A gifted student, Mary was usually well-motivated and interested in all her courses. I was concerned, therefore, when she lost all interest in her French

FIGURE 7.1 The Parent Connection: A Flow Chart of Activities

	Structure	Teacher Well-Being	Parent Comfort
Before the conference		Practice relaxation and visualization.	
			Make positive contact.
	Gather family information. Decide time constraints. Decide location.		
			Send personal messages home.
		Review delicate issues. Set personal goals.	
			Check presentation for jargon and technical terms.
	Prepare objectives. Prepare agenda. Prepare environment.		
		Center	
During the conference	Present agenda and objectives. Keep to time constraints.	Be straight with your feelings and thoughts.	Provide get-acquainted time. Listen actively. Use facilitating questions.
	Mention 7 minutes to end of meeting.		Remember the grief issue.
After the conference	Record notes.		
		Reward yourself.	
			Continue positive contact.

Source: Roberds-Baxter, Sharon (1984). The parent connection: Enhancing the affective component of parent conferences. *Teaching Exceptional Children. 17* (1), p. 55. Copyright (1984) by the Council for Exceptional Children. Reprinted with permission.

class. I asked for a conference with her teacher to discuss the change in attitude. I told him that I wondered about her sudden lack of interest in a subject that had previously been so exciting for her. He immediately pulled out his grade book, stating, "As you can see, Mary is making good grades in French."

"You don't understand: I don't care about her grades; I'm interested in her attitude."

"But she's doing well; her grades are excellent."

"What about her sudden lack of interest? Can you give me any explanation for that?"

"Well, Mary needs to understand that learning is not always fun."

Frustrated over our lack of communication, I understood why Mary was dissatisfied.

It must be remembered that the primary goal of the parent-teacher conference is to establish positive communication between the home and the school. Parents and teachers should set more specific goals and objectives before the conference. In general, the purposes of parent-teacher conferences fall into one or more of four categories:

1. To give information.
2. To get information.
3. To plan for the student, as in IEP conferences.
4. To solve problems.

Giving Information

☐ A parent conference should be a goal-directed meeting, providing for the exchange of information between teacher and parent so that educational programming can be enhanced (Heron & Harris, 1982). Sometimes, the conference is used in lieu of other forms of reporting progress. In certain ungraded situations and in unique programs, parent-teacher conferences have been successful as a reporting system; in other instances, parents and teachers have not been fully satisfied. A teacher who had just completed such a conference gave an example:

> Jon's mother and I had a delightful conference. I showed her samples of his work, explained his rank in the class, pointed out areas in which he excelled and areas in which he needed more work. I also explained to her that we were not using grades in this class and that the purpose of this conference was to report on Jon's progress and to answer any questions that she might have. In conclusion, I asked if everything was clear. The mother responded, "Yes, but if you *were* going to give Jon a grade, what would it be?"

In addition to information concerning student progress (discussed in Chapter 6), there is a great deal of information that parents of exceptional students need to be given. Teachers need to communicate what the child is learning and to provide evidence of learning; to explain what special education is; and to insure that parents are familiar with the philosophy, goals, and procedures of the special education system.

The information parents must receive under the requirements of PL 94–142 is very specific. The due process provisions require that parents be fully informed about and consent to important decisions related to the special education of their children; that parents be given the opportunity to participate in the decision-making process; and, if parents disagree with what is proposed, procedures for resolving conflicts are guaranteed. Parents must be notified of their right to examine their child's school records, to request an independent evaluation, and to initiate a due process hearing (Agard & Barry, 1982). Although such notification is to be written, using conferences to supplement the written notice and consent provides an ideal way to share information about the proposed action and parents' rights. In this way, parents are provided with all the necessary information and given full opportunity to participate and ask questions. Specifically, the notice to parents must contain:

> A description of the proposed or refused action.
> An explanation for the proposed or refused action.
> A description of each evaluation procedure, test, record or report used as a basis for the proposed or refused action.
> A full explanation of all the procedural safeguards available to parents and children. These are:
> > opportunity to examine records
> > independent educational evaluation
> > prior notice of evaluation and reevaluation
> > written consent to preplacement evaluation
> > prior notice of program/placement change
> > written consent to initial placement
> > impartial due process hearing and appeal
> > fair and nondiscriminatory evaluation
> > placement in the least restrictive environment
> > confidentiality of records. (Agard & Barry, 1982, p. 3)

In informing parents of evaluation procedures and results, schools do not routinely inform parents of their child's IQ score, although parents do have the right to this information. Teachers and administrators are encouraged to emphasize the child's potential range of behaviors rather than merely report the IQ score. Many psychologists now write their reports with the parents as readers in mind. Thus, written and verbal reports might contain the following information:

1. Levels of performance in academic subjects,
2. Length of attention span,
3. Performance on memory tasks (e.g., child can remember a series of no more than two sequential directives),
4. Learning strengths (e.g., conscientious approach to work tasks, expressive language related to sports and general information),
5. Learning weaknesses (e.g., reasoning skills, generalization, comprehension of written material),
6. Response to various types and schedules of reinforcement. (Turnbull, Strickland, & Brantley, 1982, p. 95)

The parent conference is a useful format for providing information to parents. In addition to the verbal presentation of evaluative data, samples of the student's work and checklists of academic and social behavior may be shared.

A further advantage to the conference as a supplement to written notice of evaluation results is clear if the evaluation produces negative or unexpected information. At this time, alternatives may be presented and explored, and all issues related to the evaluation may be discussed.

An important outcome of the evaluation process is determining the child's eligibility for special education services and, if the student is handicapped, the handicap designation. Parents need to be told what the handicap designation is, what it means, and how it was determined. If parents are to assume their role as full participants, they must be well informed about all aspects of their child's evaluation and placement.

Getting Information

☐ Teachers can assume a pedagogical role during the conference in which they only give information without hearing what the parent has to say. However, they can receive valuable information by listening objectively to the parent's words, observing carefully the parent's actions, and reflecting accurately on the parent's emotions during the conference (Rabbitt, 1978).

Parents need to provide information about their child's health problems, about what their child likes or does not like to do, what hobbies or sports the child is most interested in, and what is discussed in the home (National Education Association, 1977). Teachers need to know about the success or failure of suggestions they have made and to hear suggestions parents have to offer.

Parents of exceptional children need to provide information concerning the child's educational, medical, and developmental history; the child's behavior and habits at home; the child's social relationships; the child's personal interests and nonacademic skills; and the parents' and child's perceptions of the problem. Parents also need to inform school personnel about how they would like to be involved in the planning process and to let them know about any special knowledge or skill they possess.

Many parents are ready and eager to give information freely; others feel ill at ease in the school setting and are reluctant to open up immediately (Rabbitt, 1978). Questions about their child, other children in the family, and positive statements about their child will frequently put them at ease and encourage them to speak more openly. When parents are encouraged to give information, conferences result in the acquisition of valuable data about the child and relevant past experiences.

Planning

☐ Information sharing, assessment, and evaluation should result in the formation of plans that will give direction for implementation of remedial or developmental strategies. The ultimate goal of planning is the improved education of the student.

The process of planning requires a team effort; the team must apply experience, skills, and knowledge to the data collected in order to chart an educational course for the student. Areas of strength as well as areas of deficiency must be considered, resulting in both short- and long-range objectives. Figure 7.2 illustrates the process.

This graphic presentation demonstrates the continuing nature of assessment and planning. The team develops the necessary interventions and instructional recommendations based on the objectives. The educational plan results in specific educational intervention strategies for achieving the objectives (Johnson, 1974). From a practical point of view, parents of all children

FIGURE 7.2 Planning Process

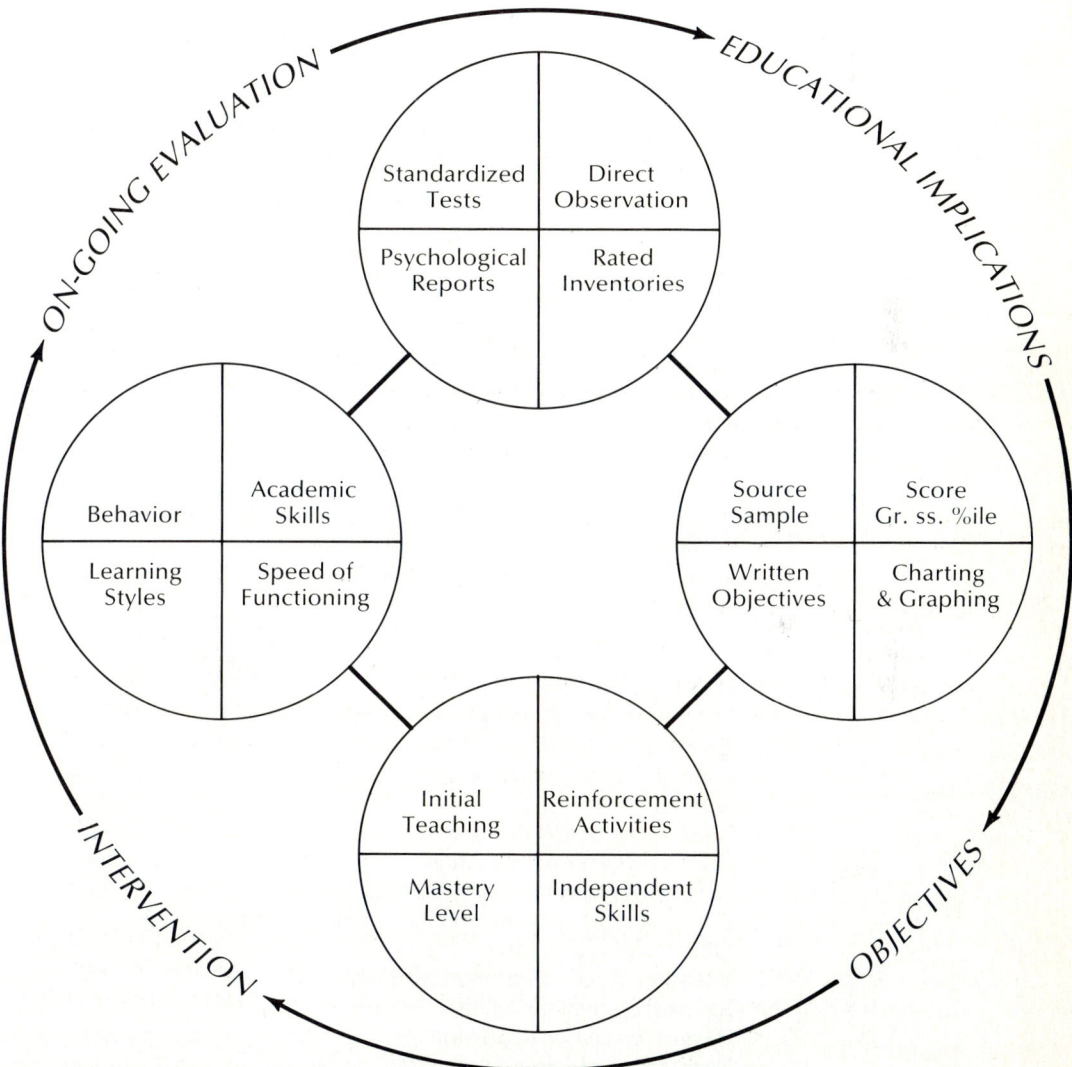

Source: Johnson, Steven B. (1974). *A process for educational planning.* Castro Valley, Calif.: Castro Valley Unified School District, p. 4.

should be involved in the process; from a legal point of view, parents of handicapped children must be involved. As discussed in Chapter 4, there are different levels of parental involvement. However, school personnel must provide the opportunity for parents to assist in the planning process through the development of the IEP.

Although federal law does not require services for gifted students, many school systems, under state law, do provide such programs. In states in which gifted students are included in programs for exceptional children, parent involvement is mandated.

Based on the assessment data and on the goals and objectives contained in the IEP, a final decision regarding an appropriate placement for the student can be made. Deciding what is appropriate for the particular child involves complex questions of judgment and calls for a full and open exchange of information between parents and school personnel. Agard and Barry (1982, p. 17) suggest the following agenda outline for a program planning conference:

1. Welcome
    a. Appreciation for parents' attendance
    b. Introduction of staff
2. Orientation
    a. Meeting agenda
    b. Solicitation of parents' questions and comments
3. Evaluation Results
    a. Summary and interpretation of results
    b. Parent reactions
    c. Confidentiality of child's school records
    d. Student's eligibility for special education
    e. Discussion of handicapping condition
4. IEP Development
    a. Purpose and general content of IEP
    b. Current levels of performance
    c. Goals and objectives
    d. Criteria for determining whether goals and objectives are met
    e. Special education and related services to be provided
    f. Starting date and duration of services
5. Placement
    a. Relationship of IEP to placement
    b. Placement proposed by school
    c. Alternative placements considered but rejected
    d. LRE [least restrictive environment] and mainstreaming
    e. Time in the regular class
    f. Invitation to parents to visit placement
    g. Reminder of parents' rights
    h. Parents' responses to placement
    i. Presentation of request for consent

j. If parents consent:
   Practical details on entering placement
   Ways to discuss placement with student
   Supporting activities parents can do with child at home
k. If parents are reluctant to grant consent:
   Reasons for their reservations
   Possible compromises
   Alternative placements that parents might visit
6. Conclusion
   a. Review of information discussed and action to be taken
   b. Invitation of additional questions
   c. Name of school contact person
   d. Tentative date for next contact

Because there is no one standard procedure for conducting IEP meetings, formats vary among school systems. However, certain components of IEP conferences should be considered in all cases. The six essential components are:

Preconference preparation—advanced planning on the part of participants to insure that necessary information is gathered, the meeting is scheduled at a convenient time, and special concerns to be discussed are identified;

Initial conference proceedings—creating an atmosphere for open communication and a plan for decision making;

Interpretation of evaluation results—reporting formal and informal evaluation information as a basis for establishing the student's current levels of performance and the subject areas to be covered in the IEP;

Development of goals, objectives, and evaluation methods—specifying the skills and concepts appropriate to the needs of the handicapped student and the methods to be used to evaluate the student's progress;

Decision of special education placement and related services—specifying the particular classroom placement for the student, the percentage of time in the regular class, the nature and extent of related services, the dates for initiating services, and the anticipated duration of services; and

Conclusion of the meeting—synthesizing decisions that have been made and outlining future actions, such as communication with parents and timelines for reviewing and revising the IEP. (Schulz & Turnbull, 1984, pp. 92–93)

The successful IEP conference is the result of team planning. In contrast to open-ended parent-teacher conferences, the IEP conference has a distinct purpose: to develop the best educational plan for the exceptional student. For this purpose to be realized, educators must be able to organize a setting for involving parents and professionals in meaningful planning (Swick, Flake-Hobson, & Raymond 1980). Suggestions for structuring conferences are discussed in a later portion of this chapter.

Solving Problems

☐ As indicated in Chapter 6, the first communication between parents and teachers may occur because a problem exists. Although not an ideal beginning, problem solving can result in the establishment of positive relationships. Before a discussion of problem-solving strategies through conferencing it may be helpful to review common techniques used to solve problems. Bolton (1979) identifies five alternatives: denial, avoidance, capitulation, domination, and collaborative problem-solving.

Denial Some conflicts are so threatening to people that they deny the existence of a problem. When parents face problems concerning their children, they may pretend everything is all right and refuse to discuss the matter. As noted in several instances in other chapters (5 and 6), such denial results in lack of educational services for the child. One teacher described a difficult situation caused by the parent's denial of a problem:

> Frankie transferred from another school where she had been served in a learning disabilities class. In order to continue services, the parent had to give permis-

☐ *Cooperative problem-solving between parents and the school can result in establishing a positive, constructive relationship.*

sion for the child to be placed in the learning disabilities class in our school. Several attempts were made for the parent to attend a school based committee meeting; we received no reply. A home visit was made by the learning disability and speech teachers; the mother refused to sign the placement forms and said she would send the forms with the child the next day. Enraged by the visit, the mother called the principal and requested to see him. The next morning a conference was held with the mother, the principal, the classroom teacher, guidance counselor, speech therapist, special education teacher and the school psychologist. The school personnel explained the child's needs and described the program that they suggested for her. The mother still refused to let Frankie receive services, saying that her child was smart and didn't need to go to any type of special class.

Avoidance People can be aware of problems but do everything possible to avoid facing them. Parents of exceptional students may present an attitude of cooperation and friendliness while suppressing their reluctance to face a problem. Continued avoidance leads to denial and all its negative effects.

Capitulation Parents who feel inadequate in an educational setting tend to give in to suggestions they feel are inappropriate. Even though the outcome appears to be agreeable, such parents may harbor resentment that the teacher controlled the decision process.

Domination Domination results in imposing one's own solution on another person. Although it would be expected that aggressive people rely on domination during conflict, it has also been found that many primarily submissive people, when in a position of authority, are likely to impose their solutions on others (Bolton, 1979). This fact may be particularly true of teachers, who feel they have more knowledge and experience in educating children than do the children's parents. Although some parents seem to expect teachers to be the problem solvers, they may harbor additional resentment and be reluctant to accept the solution. When the authoritarian approach is consistently used to solve problems, the interpersonal relationship may be seriously damaged.

Compromise Defined as "a settlement of differences in which each side makes concessions" (Morris, 1981, p. 274), compromise can be useful. However, since each party settles for less than total needs, it is not a strategy that can be used successfully on a consistent basis.

Collaborative Problem Solving In collaborative problem solving, people join together to find a solution acceptable to both. When it is possible to use this technique, it is usually preferred, because no one loses, capitulates, or dominates. As demonstrated in the team approach, collaborative problem solving is generally advocated in dealing with problems that occur with children within the school setting or in a home-school conflict.

As in all forms of communication, attitudes and skills are essential to the successful use of collaborative problem-solving techniques. Certain basic attitudes must be present during interactions between teachers and parents:

1. You must want to hear, and have the time to hear, what the parent has to say. If you don't, say so.
2. You must want to be helpful with the parent's problem at that time. Otherwise, wait until you do.
3. You must be able to accept the parent's feelings, whatever they may be or however different they are from yours. To accept his feelings does not mean that you must accept them as your own, but simply that you allow him to feel as he does. It is a way of saying, "I can be me, and you can be you."
4. You must believe in the parent's ability to find solutions to his own problems. This requires the teacher to give up decision making power over the parent's life. (Lichter, 1976, pp. 71–72)

Collaborative problem solving requires the use of listening skills, assertion skills, and the collaborative problem-solving method. The process involves six steps:

1. *Define* the problem in terms of *needs*, not solutions.
2. *Brainstorm* possible solutions.
3. *Select* the solution(s) that will best meet both parties' needs and *check possible consequences.*
4. *Plan* who will do what, where, and by when.
5. *Implement* the plan.
6. *Evaluate* the problem-solving process and, at a later date, how well the solution turned out. (Bolton, 1979, p. 240)

Defining the problem is a point of frequent breakdown in problem solving. This breakdown occurs because problems are defined too broadly, or too simplistically, or because insufficient information is used (Birney, 1981).

Many terms teachers use are so global that they do not define the problem. For example, *hyperactive* may be used to describe a child who squirms in his seat during the math lesson or one who runs about the classroom during the entire day. Such terms as *gifted, retarded,* or *disturbed* are not particularly descriptive of the behaviors of the child. The problem should be reduced to behaviors that can be observed and measured.

Kroth (1975) emphasizes the importance of establishing ownership of the problem. The problem may lie with the student, with the parents, and/or with the teacher. Once it is understood where the problem lies, it is obvious who will have the major responsibility for its solution. Gordon (1970) suggests that only those individuals directly involved in a particular problem should be involved in its solution.

Defining the problem in terms of needs requires "asserting one's own needs, listening reflectively until you understand the other person's needs, and then stating both sets of needs in a one-sentence-long summary of the problem" (Bolton, 1979, p. 243). This first step of the problem-solving method is time consuming; it usually takes about half the time required for the whole process. However, it is worth the effort to have a clearly defined, objectively stated problem.

Brainstorming involves generating alternative solutions to the problems that are identified. The concept of brainstorming recognizes that there is more than one solution to any problem and that a number of ideas may be suggested before a selection is made. In clarifying alternatives, it is important to look at relevant information, discover and examine all alternative solutions, and explore the possible results of each alternative.

Selecting the best possible solution involves looking at the various alternatives and selecting one that appears to be the most viable. All options should be explored and everyone's feelings expressed. The list of solutions should be reviewed and unacceptable options excluded. The discussion will usually lead to a consensus on a favored solution. If no agreement emerges, it may help to go back to the brainstorming step and generate more solutions (Lowe, 1980).

Based on the alternative chosen, a plan of action is developed. The plan should clearly explain what the student will do, what the teacher will do, and what the parents will do. If a home program is agreed on, observation charts and data should be developed and clarified. If a school program is to be implemented, methods of reporting should be discussed. If there is a contractual agreement with the student, parents and teachers need to be informed of all its requirements and contingencies.

Implementation is facilitated by the collaborative problem-solving method. If each participant has been involved in the problem-solving process, and if the needs of all participants have been met, there is a strong likelihood that the plan will be implemented. If it is not, another conference should be called and accountability required.

Evaluation can occur at the end of the conference to determine the degree of satisfaction felt by all participants. It should also occur after the plan has been in action for a while to explore the efficacy of the strategies and to explore new alternatives, if necessary. Lowe (1980) suggests three conferences for the problem-solving process. The first conference would identify the problem, the second would prescribe a plan, and the third would evaluate the results.

Collaborative problem-solving provides a means for meeting both the parents' and educators' needs while serving the best interests of the child. To be effective, it requires an atmosphere of constructive openness. Such openness uses confrontation as an essential part of the negotiation process. Confrontation, however, must be accompanied by other problem-solving tools and communication facilitators (Simpson, 1982).

When teachers meet with parents to discuss problems a student is having, positive aspects of the student's progress should be discussed along with the problems. If the teacher initiates the conference, it should begin on a positive note. If it is parent-initiated, the teacher must assume a listening posture until the problem is revealed.

Structuring the Conference

Regardless of the purpose of the parent-teacher conference, the structure is important to its success. Although the conference may last no more than twenty or thirty minutes, during that time impressions are made that will facilitate or impede the development of trust between teacher and parents for a long time (Canady & Seyfarth, 1979). Parents and teachers need to be aware of the importance of planning, conducting, and evaluating the conference. The structure also involves teachers in postconference activities.

Planning the Conference

The parent-teacher conference can be a highly workable method of improving the student's learning opportunities and opening lines for continued communication between parents and school personnel. And yet, both parents and teachers often fear the conference, and sometimes the actual experience is traumatic (Rabbitt, 1978). As the parent of a learning-disabled child stated, "I really began to dread parent-teacher conferences during the first and second grade" (Gargiulo, 1985, p. 106). The parent of a mentally retarded child expressed a much stronger reaction:

> I have as much or more education as the professionals attending the meeting. I am middle class as they are and I certainly know my way around the public school system because I have been a resident of the city for 27 years.
> But I still feel cowed when I go to the conference. I often feel that what I am being given is charity. I feel guilty because my child is sometimes very disturbing in school and I feel that I am a bad parent. I get nervous, angry, defensive, aggressive and apologetic. (Markel & Greenbaum, 1981, p. 17)

In many cases, parents and teachers find themselves participants in conferences for which they have had no training, experience, or preparation. Advance planning and careful preparation are the first steps in ensuring that the conference is pleasant for all participants and that it achieves its purpose (Price & Marsh, 1985). Even though planning for the conference is generally considered the responsibility of the educator, preparing for the conference is vital for parents as well as for teachers.

Parent Planning When parents were asked to read a long list of feelings and to check the ones they experienced during a meeting with school personnel, the words they most often checked included:

inadequate	confused
exhausted	tentative
hopeful	worried
fearful	anxious
challenged	intimidated

For the most part, these feelings tend to inhibit communication and to restrict participation (Anderson, Chitwood, & Hayden, 1982).

One obvious factor accounting for the lack of parent involvement in special education programs for their children is that parents have not been prepared to participate (Schuck, 1979). This lack of preparation includes conference planning and participation.

Parents should prepare for the conference by knowing what to expect and should follow up with action afterward. The National Education Association (n.d., n.p.) offers suggestions to help parents prepare for the conference:

> Decide what you want to ask the teacher. Discuss the forthcoming conference with your child to see if there is anything she/he would like you to talk about with the teacher. Check with your spouse and decide which aspects of your child's schoolwork are puzzling or worrying you.
>
> Determine what you can tell the teacher about your child. The teacher sees only one side of your child. There may be things you know about the child that could help the teacher better understand her or him.
>
> Get a babysitter if you have young children. Don't bring either the schoolchild (unless specifically requested) or younger brothers or sisters to the conference.
>
> Be on time. Write down the time of your appointment and arrive promptly. The teacher may have other appointments after yours.

Information gained before the meeting will help prepare parents for more intelligent participation. A parents' information checklist for planning meetings would be helpful. Information concerning the meeting would include:

> Who has been invited to attend? Does this list include any nonschool personnel you would like invited?
> What is the agenda?
> What decisions need to be made?

Information concerning the child would include:

> Have you seen relevant documents concerning your child's education? (e.g., child's records, educational goals, psychological reports, reading tests, etc.) Have you written down the following information about your child (for your own clarification)?
> a. Your concerns, opinions, and questions about his education.
> b. Your expectations about his learning and development.
> c. Your expectations about what the school can offer him. (Lusthaus & Lusthaus, 1979, p. R3)

When parents first learn their child is exceptional, it would help them and school personnel if they began keeping good records. Copies of evaluations, dates and results of professional visits, questions asked and answers received about services, and other pertinent information contribute to the data the school gathers and also puts the parents in a position of equality.

Parents need a thorough knowledge of their rights before attending school conferences. In addition to rights granted to parents by federal and state laws, parents have the right to:

> know about available services or facilities before making decisions;
> help plan the best program for their child;
> ask for and receive explanations from professionals;
> act as child advocate;
> refuse requests or pressures without feeling guilty, selfish or ignorant;
> express opinions and be heard with the same respect and consideration afforded others;
> make the ultimate decision regarding the child's placement within the limits of the law. (Markel & Greenbaum, 1981, p. 18)

Acquiring the necessary knowledge and developing assertiveness where participation is concerned are critical needs for many parents of exceptional children. These and other skills are included in parent education programs, discussed in Chapter 9.

The parents' energy during conferences should be directed toward planning for their child. If planning before the conference is thorough, parents may be more efficient during the conference and be in a better position to contribute to the decision-making process.

Anderson, Chitwood, and Hayden (1982, p. 8) have good advice for parents:

> The more knowledge you have of the educational planning process and of the people who participate in that process, the more comfortable you will become in your role as advocate for your child. As you gain skills in presenting your view of your child to the school people, negative feelings like inadequacy and incompetence will diminish, allowing you to be a more effective partner in the educational planning process.

Teacher Planning Teachers sometimes feel overwhelmed and perhaps frightened at the idea of conducting individual parent conferences. Frequently, they have not had professional preparation in the skills of conducting conferences and other techniques of home-school communication. Even if they have the ability to conduct the conference, they may neglect pre-planning activities. The result could be lack of parent attendance and/or a conference that does not accomplish the purpose for which it was intended.

Price & Marsh (1985, p. 275) suggest eight simple preparatory steps that, when completed before the conference, can greatly facilitate the meeting. These steps include:

1. Selecting the site for the conference.
2. Sending adequate advance notice to all participants, including time, location, date, purpose, and length of conference.
3. Studying the school file of the student.
4. Taking note of previous teachers' comments, pertinent test data, relevant health data, and other factors.
5. Developing a clear understanding of the purpose of the conference.
6. Listing any information specifically to be included, such as anecdotes, test scores, and comments.
7. Having work samples available if they would contribute to the conference.
8. Listing positive aspects of the student's performance and behavior to prevent a totally negative focus.

The three planning events that appear to be most important are (1) inviting the parents, (2) scheduling the conference, and (3) arranging the setting.

☐ *Arranging the classroom setting is one of the most important planning steps in preparing for a parent-teacher conference.*

Parents should be invited to conferences well in advance, so they have adequate time to change other commitments. If parents do not respond to an invitation, a phone call lets them know that the teacher is really interested and may encourage parents who are threatened by the idea of the conference. A phone call also enables the teacher to respond to questions about the nature of the conference (Fredericks, Harrington, Hill, Hunter, Loesch, Pasztor, & Simms, 1983).

If written notices are sent, several follow-up techniques appear to increase parent attentance and participation. In attempting to determine the effectiveness of intervention strategies on parent participation in IEP conferences, Goldstein and Turnbull (1982) investigated two techniques. One strategy involved sending parents questions before the IEP conference with a follow-up telephone call; the second strategy involved having the school counselor present as a parent advocate. Although there was no significant difference in parental involvement in the IEP conference between the parents in the control group and the parents who had been sent questions, there was significantly more parental involvement in the conference attended by a parent advocate. A significantly larger proportion of fathers who received questions attended conferences.

Wolf and Troup (1980) compared procedures in which (1) school personnel sent notices inviting parents to IEP conferences home with students and (2) parents were sent a letter in the mail, inviting them to the IEP meeting. Follow-up handwritten notes were sent to parents who did not respond, and telephone calls made to those who did not respond to the second note. Twenty-two percent of parents who received the conventional letter participated in the IEP meeting, whereas 58 percent of the parents who were sent follow-up notes participated. The two studies indicated that the method of notification influenced who attended and the follow-up procedures resulted in more parent involvement.

Scheduling may be the most critical factor in planning for parent-teacher conferences. Traditionally, conferences are scheduled during the school day or shortly after school. Many parents cannot attend meetings at these times. Kroth (1980) reports that in the Houston Public Schools, only about 7 percent of the children came from a family with a working father and a mother who stayed home. More than 70 percent of the children had working parent(s), and more than 50 percent of the children will have lived with a single parent by the age of fifteen. In situations like these, to hold conferences during the school day means that parents will either have to take time from work or not attend. Evening meetings may be poorly attended because parents are tired, they may be doing household chores, or they may prefer to spend the time with their children. Educators are challenged to design appropriate strategies for interaction.

In an age of the single parent and two-career families, it is important to accommodate people who work. Conferences can be scheduled early in the morning, during a lunch hour, or late in the afternoon (Fredericks et al., 1983).

In one county, teachers set aside two teacher workdays for conferences with parents. Instead of being at the school during the regularly scheduled time, teachers schedule conferences from noon to eight o'clock in the evenings on these days. This particular school system has noted a dramatic increase in parent attendance and positive attitude with the new scheduling.

Parents and teachers are busy people. Professionals need to provide sufficient flexibility to accommodate the needs of parents, both fathers and mothers. At the same time, parents should appreciate the problem of scheduling a number of conferences at mutually satisfactory times (Klein, 1979).

The conference setting can create a positive or a negative orientation to the meeting. Everything involved in the process, from availability of parking outside the school to the arrangement of furniture in the conference room, can convey a feeling of equality or inequality to the parents and other people (Klein, 1979).

For parents not familiar with the school, a map could be included with the invitation. It may be advisable to have someone available at the school entrance to direct parents to the appropriate room, particularly on a specified conference day.

Kroth and Simpson (1977) claim that "the total environment speaks and therefore influences the interaction between two people" (p. 71). They suggest considerations to keep in mind to guarantee privacy (p. 73):

1. Arrange beforehand for an appropriate private room for the interview.

2. Make arrangements so that you will not be interrupted by outside influences such as phone calls, knocks on the door, etc.

3. Arrange for all materials to be available before the interview starts.

4. Develop alternatives to putting "DO NOT DISTURB" signs on the door of the office, since this can actually increase the anxiety of the parents. It is better to ask for the cooperation of the staff than to communicate with signs.

Make the parents feel that they have your undivided attention. The most direct method of doing this is to allow the parents the use of all of their appointment time without interruption.

If interruptions do occur, it is best to show the parent that you understand these distractions are disturbing and that you can empathize with the difficulty that the circumstances provide.

The setting for the meeting, the furnishings within the room, and the arrangement of the furniture all convey meaning. A parent recently described an arrangement that caused her considerable stress:

I sat on one side of the table, and the special education teacher, the psychologist, the principal and the guidance counselor sat on the other side. I felt like I was one against a team; I didn't have a chance!

Discussions held around a table or in a circle are much less threatening than those conducted from opposite sides of a desk. The conference area should be as comfortable as possible. If the classroom is used, adult-sized chairs should be provided, rather than expecting parents to sit in student chairs. The sizes of chairs, the seating arrangement, and the use of desks and tables can create feelings of inequality if they are not carefully prearranged. Conference seating should promote comfort, facilitate eye contact, and permit recognition of participants as adults and equals (Davis & Davis, 1981).

Conducting the Conference

☐ Although the parents are participants in the conference, the teacher is the manager. Managerial responsibilities include locating a meeting room, starting and ending the meeting on time, keeping the discussion on track, insuring that participants understand the purpose of the conference, and clarifying agreements (Canady & Seyfarth, 1979).

Because the conference takes place in the school, the teacher is also the host. Therefore, the success or failure of the conference is, for the most part, contingent on the skill and empathy with which the teacher conducts it. One of the most critical aspects of the conference is the beginning. As a guest in the school, the parent should be welcomed and made to feel comfortable. The teacher and other school personnel should view the conference from the parent's point of view.

Greeting parents at the door helps establish a warm, inviting relationship. Parents should be greeted as any guest would be greeted—with respect, a handshake, a smile, and a welcoming statement.

One mother recently described her apprehension in approaching the initial conference concerning her junior-high son. A former teacher herself, she was nevertheless concerned that she might hear negative reports. The teacher greeted her with the statement, "I'm so glad to see you; Sean is doing so well in my class!" The mother was immediately relieved, and entered the conference with positive expectations.

It may be difficult to make a positive statement about the student's academic progress, particularly if the student is experiencing learning problems. It may be necessary to refer to the child's leadership qualities on the playground, grooming, willingness to try, and even good attendance record. Some positive statement can be made about every student.

It usually takes about five minutes to establish rapport with parents in the initial conference. They may wish to look around the room, to inspect any aspects of their child's work that may be available, and to become familiar with the environment.

Stevens (1984) asserts that parents must be treated gently. They may anticipate blame of some sort or fear they will meet resistance instead of cooperation. Until teachers demonstrate otherwise, parents think of them as adversaries. A beginning responsibility is expressing confidence in the parents' ability as members of the educational team.

As teachers initiate and conduct conferences, they should bear in mind the essentials of good communication (see Chapter 6). Good eye contact is essential and assures parents of the teacher's continued interest and attention. Body language is an important component to what the teacher is communicating and also in reading the parents' attitudes, emotions, and reactions. In choosing appropriate clothing for the conferences, teachers should dress as professional people, and consider the life style of the parents they will greet.

Formal conferences, such as the IEP conference, follow procedures established by legal requirements and official school protocol. If a number of professional people are present, they should be sure to include the parents as full participants from the beginning.

The progress of the conference will be expedited if adequate preparation has been made. If an agenda has been prepared and distributed to all attendants of the meeting, the conference should proceed on schedule. Figure 7.3 presents an example of an appropriate agenda. As professionals make progress reports, they should give parents checklists of skills being discussed and provide opportunities for parental input on the child's progress at home.

The smaller, less formal conference also requires clear structure and management. Because of the increased intimacy, parents may be more expressive in an informal meeting. If discussion is encouraged and appreciated, it may be difficult to keep the conference on a business-like basis. Teachers need to develop skills for bringing the conversation back and keeping it on target. Even in an informal conference, a conference outline limits the discussion to pertinent content. If the conversation strays, professionals can tactfully remind parents of the conference's purpose.

Parent-teacher conferences should be conducted in a relaxed manner. Price and Marsh (1985, p. 276) offer six suggestions for achieving a relaxed atmosphere:

> a. Begin with a friendly comment and some informal conversation about a neutral topic. Avoid jumping immediately into the problem since participants need time to overcome initial anxiety.
>
> b. Handle the conference in a straightforward manner, explaining the purpose and asking for parent input.
>
> c. Listen carefully to the parents. Parents will recognize sincere interest and willingness to listen and will participate more openly as a result.
>
> d. Consider whether or not it is necessary to take notes during the conference, weighing the advantages of an immediate record of certain information against the possibility of making the parents uncomfortable.
>
> e. If notes are taken, reassure the parents that it is being done merely to ensure the accuracy of important information. Read the notes back to the parents to ensure clarity and to relieve any concerns the notetaking might have fostered.
>
> f. Follow the outline or format planned prior to the conference to avoid losing sight of the purpose of the conference. A format for conducting the conference should include opening remarks; introduction of all participants, with an expla-

FIGURE 7.3 Agenda for Parent Conference

Child's Name _____
Date _____
Place _____ Room _____
From _____ to _____ (time)
Team Leader _____
Discussion Leader _____

I. Introduction.
   Purpose of the meeting
   Introduction of those present, including a statement of how each worked with child
II. Review materials.
   Content of referral form
   Reading of any previous Individual Education Programs
III. Report on evaluations.
   Formal evaluations made
   Information evaluations
   Progress made by the child since last conference
IV. Parents make statement of the child's progress.
V. Complete the developmental checklist for the child.
VI. Discuss needs as shown by the checklist.
VII. Decide which are priority needs.
VIII. Write goal statements for these needs.
IX. List related services needed for the child.
X. Discuss appropriate setting to deliver needed educational services.
XI. Sign forms, if agreement—set another meeting time if necessary.

Meeting will adjourn at _____ .

Source: Michaelis, C. T. *Home and school partnerships in exceptional education.* Reprinted with permission of Aspen Publishers, Inc., copyright 1980.

nation of the role of each; a statement of the purpose of the meeting; communication of specific information; an opportunity for input from parents and other participants; and finally, a summary of what has been disclosed and recommendations for follow-up activities.

In all conferences, it is important for professionals to communicate and demonstrate support to the parents. Listening and relating to parents with understanding is supportive; finding helpful ways within the interview to respond to parental feelings is supportive; and sometimes parents need to be supported in accepting their child. Giving parents specific suggestions on helping their children is also supportive. The strategies suggested will vary with the needs of the child and the abilities of the parents. Suggestions can include tutoring strategies or general activities that could be carried out in any home.

Ending the conference is not difficult if a time limit has been communicated in advance. The time limit should be clearly established in the note or telephone conversation used to schedule the conference. It is also wise to mention it at the beginning of the meeting and to set a pace that will allow discussion of intended matters within the time allotted (Stevens, 1984). If the material has not been covered or if the parents have additional concerns, another conference should be scheduled.

There are many lists of suggestions for successful parent-teacher conferences. Thornburg (1980, pp. 53–54) suggests fourteen particularly helpful guidelines for conducting effective conferences:

1. Establish good rapport. Be a good listener and absorb the feelings of the parents.
2. Be a friend. Meet parents in a nonauthoritarian way.
3. Sympathize and empathize. See the child from the parents' view.
4. Help parents feel good about themselves and their child.
5. Use language that parents understand. Avoid jargon.
6. Don't interrogate parents. They will respond more openly if the teacher does not put them on the defensive.
7. Respond to parents differently, remembering that their personalities and problems are different.
8. Discuss, don't argue. The teacher's role in a conference is that of a reference person, not a judge. If parents need help with a problem or have not considered other methods of dealing with it, suggest new ways.
9. Let parents know that you are interested in their child as an individual, including good points and those that could be improved upon.
10. Don't compare one child with another.
11. Don't take notes—this is distracting and hinders ease of discussion.
12. Don't criticize. That is fatal to a relationship.
13. Be careful in getting too personal. If a home situation has been affecting the child's behavior at school, report the behavior and ask if the parents have any ideas about the cause. But don't pressure them.
14. Close on a positive note. And invite the parents for a follow-up session, if desirable. Also, invite them to visit your classroom.

Evaluating the Conference

☐ Conferences are learning opportunities for parents and for teachers. At the conclusion of the meeting, some time should be scheduled for evaluation and for indications of the success or failure of the conference. Five questions to use in evaluating the conference are:

1. Did the conference run smoothly? If it proceeded on schedule and if the agenda was covered, it probably meant the conference was well planned.
2. Were the purposes of the conference fulfilled? If not, perhaps the time frame was too short or another conference is needed. If the goals were met, the time was appropriate and the purpose was communicated to the participants.
3. Did the parents participate fully? If they did not, the terms and language used may need to be expanded or communicated more fully. On the other hand, the parents may participate more during ensuing conferences if this one was successful.
4. Were parents and professionals comfortable with each other? If they appeared to be ill at ease, the structure of the conference should be examined and participants in the conference contacted about their perceptions of the atmosphere.

☐ *At the conclusion of a parent-teacher conference, the teacher should take time to evaluate the meeting and to determine the factors that caused its success or failure.*

5. Did the conference end on a positive note? If so, the likelihood is that communication lines are open.

In reflecting on the conference, teachers and parents may feel that their conferencing skills need improvement. Even though improvement will come with experience, additional training may be indicated. If this is the case, teachers and parents should express their needs as part of on-going and new programs within their schools and communities.

Postconference Activities

☐ The conference is a beginning to parent-teacher communication. The follow-up is thus critical to establishing continuous home-school relationships. Activities should be designed to foster communication, to reinforce parent participation, and to improve the student's education.

One of the first postconference activities is to finalize the IEP form. When the final form is sent to the parents, a personal note may be included to thank them for their interest and their contributions to the conference (Swick, Flake-Hobson, & Raymond, 1980). A parent feedback form may also be included, to be returned to the teacher or brought to the next conference.

Five additional conference follow-up activities could include the following:

1. Filing the conference format plan along with accompanying notes, comments, and materials.

2. Preparing a conference summary to be sent to parents as an official conference report. The summary would include such information as names of conference participants; the purpose of the conference; relevant information communicated; information gained or modified as a result of the conference; and outcomes or follow-up activities and responsibilities assigned.

3. Identifying any additional tasks resulting from the conference, such as testing, communicating with mainstream teachers, securing special materials, and planning special instructional sequences.

4. Establishing timelines for completing the follow-up tasks, if any were identified as a result of the conference.

5. Completing any actions required by due process procedures or school policies. (Price & Marsh, 1985, p. 277)

Follow-up conferences are usually devoted to planning and arranging supplementary instructional assistance or support services. The parents' cooperation and active involvement should be sought with regard to the need for ongoing support services (Losen & Losen, 1985).

Special Situations

☐ ☐ Although the purposes and structure of parent-teacher conferences can be defined in general terms, parents and teachers are unique individuals who function, react, and interact in unique ways. In conferencing with parents of exceptional students, teachers must be aware of the differences manifested in background, educational level, value system, intelligence, and responsibility. Two of the finest arts of conferencing are the abilities to perceive these differences and to relate to others in a nonjudgmental way. Even though it is impossible to anticipate the many variances in parental attributes, several groups in general do warrant special consideration. These groups are minority parents, single parents, parents of gifted students, intellectually limited parents, and difficult parents.

Minority Parents

☐ No cultural, ethnic, or racial group is immune to social problems. However, Simpson (1982, p. 42) points out that the educational conferencer must be aware that issues related to minority status may commonly require attention. He cites the following examples:

> minority groups have experienced more than their share of social and economic problems; . . . minority children have been overly represented in educational programs for exceptional children; . . . and discriminatory and otherwise biased assessment procedures have long represented significant concerns for minority children experiencing school-related problems. Just as significantly, educational conferencers must be sensitive to the communication-related issues that must be dealt with when interacting with minority parents and families of exceptional children.

Minority parent involvement with schools in general has not always been pleasant; experiences with special education have been even less satisfying. As detailed in Chapters 3 and 4, the resulting cultural and legal issues have constituted major forces in the promotion and implementation of PL 94–142.

Minority parents' history in dealing with schools may foster an unwillingness to accept decisions to place their children in special education programs or to become involved in IEP decisions. Marion (1981, p. 219) describes as two-fold the teacher's task in seeking to involve minority parents:

1. When the child needs special education and the parents in all probability still are relating to the old stereotypes. The special educators must work with minority parents to change the stereotype and help them develop the best educational plan for the child.
2. When the minority child already is enrolled in special education. The pres-

ence of the reluctant parents is needed to draw up the IEP and their participation in and their understanding of the process is essential.

Family characteristics have been blamed for the educational failures that plague disproportionate numbers of children from Hispanic and black families (Henderson, 1982). Other characteristics, such as education, intelligence, and socioeconomic level, have altered this generality in recent years. The sensitive teacher will want to know more about parents than their minority status. Marion (1979, p. 14) presents a model for parent participation that accommodates parents at all levels (see Figure 7.4). This model, which allows minority parents to interact maximally in and contribute to the IEP process has the following six features. It:

1. Designates responsibility for parent contact, thus eliminating confusion in the minds of minority parents and professionals.
2. Records the numbers and kinds of parent contact, placing the accountability upon the educator and assuring that one is exhausting all means to involve the parent.
3. Makes provision for cultural differences, so that the professional is led to understand why minority parents may be defensive or non-communicative about school affairs, while allowing lines of communication to stay open.
4. Provides for different modes of communication, emphasizing that the educator should develop some understanding of dialectal and language difference and communicate in layman's terms.
5. Stresses the personal attention factor—making the minority person feel like "somebody."
6. Supports parents through changing teacher roles, as advocate, ombudsman, or information exchanger.

Many parents from minority racial, ethnic, or religious backgrounds are sensitive to the possibility that evaluation and placement procedures may place their children at a disadvantage. Because minority children have been mislabeled or inappropriately placed in the past, school personnel must be alert to ensure that such stereotyping and mislabeling do not occur.

Parents who are known to have difficulty with communication should be encouraged to have a third party present at the conference. A third party may help the parents realize the true intent of the school personnel and may serve as a sounding board later on to help them review the proceedings (Losen & Losen, 1985).

Single Parents

☐ Many children live in a society of divorced parents, remarried parents, single parents, unwed parents, and families in which parents work outside the home.

FIGURE 7.4 Parent Participation Model*

	Procedure	Person Responsible	Documentation
Step 1	Contact parents	Classroom teacher or principal	A copy of written communication; log of contacts
Step 2	Refer to Local Support Team (LST)**	Classroom teacher or principal	Form
Step 3	Schedule LST to discuss child's educational needs	LST coordinator with teacher consultation	
Step 4	Invite parents to LST meeting	LST coordinator with teacher consultation	Form
Step 5	LST Meeting	Team members	
Step 6	Summarize meeting in writing; send copy to parents	LST coordinator or designated team member	Form
Step 7	Carry out recommendations of LST	Designated team member	Existing or modified parent permission forms as appropriate
Step 8	Review recommendations and new data; requires return to Step 3 if data do not indicate that special education is needed	Team members	
Step 9	Refer to Admission, Review and Dismissal (ARD)***	Designated team member	Form
Step 10	Continued parent contact (phone, written, home visits, parent groups)	Designated team member	Teacher records

*Adapted from Austin (Texas) School District
**Local Support Team—Site team that meets to discuss possible special education placement for the child
***Admission, Review, & Dismissal—Committee that places, reviews or dismisses students from special education

Source: Parent Participation Model. Marion, Robert L. (1979). Minority parent involvement in the IEP process: A systematic model approach. *Focus on Exceptional Children. 10*(8), p. 6

The necessities of making a living often drain single parents of energy they would otherwise devote to their children; these parents may feel guilty for "neglecting" their children (Croft, 1979).

For the single parent, a conference may be an added burden in what is frequently an already overwhelming daily schedule (Werner, 1980). Demands from the school may arouse feelings of anger, resentment, and helplessness in a parent who is singlehandedly trying to feed, clothe, and care for the family.

Because of time and job pressures, the single parent may have minimal involvement with the school. Interactions, therefore, may center around crisis situations. By its concern and sensitivity to the parent's situation and to the particular crisis at hand, the school can involve the single parent in a positive way.

A recent phenomenon is the participation of fathers in school activities. For years, the tradition was for the mother to accept responsibility for educational matters and to be the participant in parent-teacher conferences. Although some fathers attend conferences with the mothers, many fathers participate alone (Manning, 1984). The father who is unaccustomed to the procedures of parent conferences will benefit from acceptance, understanding, and sensitivity in the meeting. Rather than stereotyping fathers with the strong-man image, teachers should give them objective opportunities to express their concerns without confronting them with a defensive attitude.

Conferencing with single parents starts with an acknowledgement that one out of four households with children is headed by a single parent (*Newsweek*, 1985). Although the number of single parents is increasing, they receive few guiding traditions and little recognition from schools, religious institutions, or government agencies.

All single-parent families are not deprived. Some have adjusted well and may, in fact, be happier than some more traditional families. However, a national study concluded that children with only one parent have significantly more academic and disciplinary problems than their peers (Werner, 1980). It is clear that single parents and the school must work together to solve the students' problems.

Parents of Gifted Students

☐ Gallagher (1985) enumerates three responsibilities of the school to parents of gifted and talented children: "(1) to help the parents understand the child, and his or her own special needs; (2) to interpret the goals of the school program so that parents understand what the school is attempting to accomplish; and (3) to be a friendly ally to parents in the common purpose of helping the young people develop their potential in a secure, stimulating, and rewarding environment" (p. 403). Parents of gifted children have few opportunities to discuss their concerns with other adults. Through the conference, the teacher can provide a friendly listening post, thereby learning a great deal about the parents' concerns.

Parents of gifted children are viewed as central in the intellectual and affective development of their children (Dettmann & Colangelo, 1980). Although these parents are generally presumed to be affluent and well-educated, this is not always the case. Many parents cannot provide for all the needs of their gifted children and young people; ongoing programs are more appropriately housed within the school. A cooperative approach synthesizes the resources of home and school and is rewarding to parents, to teachers, and to students. For such an approach to work, parents and teachers must plan together and assess progress. A well-planned conference is essential to the process.

To maximize the effectiveness of the parent-teacher conference concerning gifted students, Strom (1983) proposes a method for insuring that parents and teachers are prepared and can resolve important issues quickly. He suggests the use of two lists of conference questions—one for parents to ask the teacher, and another for the teacher to ask the parents. The following letter, along with the questionnaire worksheet, is sent to the parents two weeks before the conference. Figure 7.5 presents a copy of questions from the teacher to parents.

```
Dear Parents:

   You will be contacted in a few days to arrange our
parent-teacher conference. Each of us sees your child in
different situations and can gain new awareness of his or
her needs, strengths, and limitations by sharing our
observations. This sharing process may reveal ways in
which we can cooperate to the benefit of your child.
   I have circled some questions that I would like to
discuss with you at our next conference. You will also
find a list of questions that you may wish to discuss with
me. Please read the list and choose several questions that
you would like me to answer. Place the numbers of your
choices on the bottom of this form and return it to me by
next Monday. Feel free to add any questions which you do
not find included in the list. I am looking forward to our
cooperative efforts to make this a productive year for
your child.
                                        Sincerely,
                                        Mrs. Jane Smith
                                        Fourth Grade Teacher
------------------------------------------------
QUESTIONS FROM PARENTS TO TEACHER

   After choosing from the list those questions you would
like me to answer, please circle them and place the numbers
```

of the questions on the lines below. You may keep the list of circled questions for your record.

#_____ #_____ #_____ #_____ #_____

Parent Signature _____

Other Questions _____

_____

(Strom, 1983, p. 287)

FIGURE 7.5 Questions from the Teacher to Parents

1. What types of activities take up your child's leisure time when he or she is alone? With peers? Adults?
2. What activities do you and your child especially enjoy doing together?
3. How does your child act when you identify a mistake or a weakness the child needs to work on?
4. What methods of discipline do you use with your child?
5. What kinds of chores does your child have at home?
6. How does your child handle the chores you assign?
7. What place is available for your child to study without interruption?
8. How do you feel about the homework your child is expected to do?
9. How does your child react to your helping with homework?
10. How often do you and your child read together?
11. How often does your child play and work alone?
12. How do you encourage good behavior at home?
13. What things at school tend to upset your child?
14. What aspects of school does your child consider the most difficult?
15. What television programs do you and your child watch together?
16. What observations can you share about your child's relationship with peers?
17. What does your child do when angry? Upset? Doing well?
18. How much sleep does your child usually get each night?
19. What does your child have to say about his or her progress in school?
20. In what ways is your child not meeting your expectations?
21. In what ways is your child working up to your expectations?
22. In your child's opinion, what would make life at school more interesting?
23. What does your child like most about school?
24. Are there any attitudes you hope your child will be able to change?
25. Is your child able to stick to tasks for a long time?

Parent Signature _____

Teacher Signature _____

Confidential—For Professional Use Only

Source: Strom, Robert D. Expectations for educating the gifted and talented. *The Educational Forum.* 47(3), 1983, p. 288.

With adequate preparation, parents and teachers can decide together what each will do to assist the student. General conference guidelines, presented in preceding sections, help complete the partnership concept and improve communication between teachers and parents of gifted students.

Intellectually Limited Parents

☐ Sometimes it is obvious that parents of handicapped students are, themselves, handicapped in some way. Losen and Losen (1985) refer to such parents as limited in their ability to "articulate, comprehend, or communicate" (p. 129).

The importance of an early, stimulating environment for the maximum development of children has been established. The reverse may also be true: if children have not developed adequately, the problem, in some cases, lies with the parents' inability to provide the appropriate learning milieu. In conferencing with parents who are limited, educators need to develop understanding, compassion, and skill. The following attitude is frequently apparent:

> Professionals often respond to parents with unrecognized intellectual limitations in the same way that parents react to intellectually limited children—with frustration and annoyance. In both cases, it is assumed that the individual's failure to cooperate results from unwillingness to meet expectations, when in fact he or she is unable to do so. (Kaminer, Jedrysek, & Soles, 1981, p. 39)

Failure to identify and communicate with intellectually limited parents can result in some disastrous situations. The author recalls an experience of this nature:

> Katie's mother had signed the forms permitting Katie, who was mildly retarded, to be placed in a resource room. The following year, the same protocol was followed, with the exception that the terms "educable mentally retarded" were used in describing Katie's placement. The day after the forms were sent home for signature, Katie's mother arrived at the school with an attorney. She was irate that the school had identified her child as "retarded" and was seeking legal retribution. Fortunately, all legal procedures had been followed, but in the ensuing discussion it was clear that the early diagnosis and placement had not been explained fully to the mother. It was also clear that special steps would need to be taken in the future to insure that details concerning Katie's education were communicated to her mother.

In a study of mentally retarded parents, it was found that identification of mental retardation improved the understanding of the parents' needs and facilitated the child's program needs (Kaminer, Jedrysek, & Soles, 1981). They devised the following checklist to identify intellectually limited parents:

1. Cannot travel alone on public transportation; always comes to clinic accompanied by another adult

2. Reading and writing problems seen when filling out application:
   a. unable to write
   b. writes minimal factual information only
   c. reads words but with very limited comprehension
3. Erratic appointment keeping (early, late, odd excuses, wrong day)
4. Provides vague or naive information about basic facts
5. Problems managing money
6. Overwhelmed by routine demands
7. Child management difficulty of excessive degree observed or reported
8. Uses covering-up techniques to conceal deficit
9. Central role of a "benefactor"; requires help in areas not expected for an adult
10. Historical information documenting limitation/retardation from:
    a. self-report
    b. family member
    c. social agency (Kaminer, Jedrysec, & Soles, 1981, p. 43)

The same problems exist in identifying and stigmatizing parents as children; professionals must not assume that parents of retarded children are also retarded. However, in instances where these characteristics are demonstrated, it is evident that special help is indicated.

The conference is an ideal vehicle for identifying parents who need help. To insure that legal rights of limited parents are met, the school can appoint a third party to act as a parent advocate. It is the school's responsibility to communicate the procedures, rights and responsibilities delegated to parents by law; the provisions are equal for all parents, regardless of their abilities.

An additional advantage to discovering parents who are intellectually limited is the opportunity for the school to engage in parent education activities. Through conferences, teachers can plan, with parents, strategies for use in the home and can determine whether there are additional training needs. Most parents want to help their children; some need more direction than others.

Difficult Parents Regardless of teachers' efforts in planning a conference, there are times when communication does not take place. Some parents, for a number of reasons, create problem situations that are tremendous challenges and sources of frustration for educators. Such parents can be described as angry, defensive, unstable, aggressive, uncooperative, uncaring, demanding, alcoholic, overprotective, dependent, or even overly helpful.

In recognizing such severe problems as emotional disturbance, alcoholism, and mental retardation, the teacher may need to ask for help from other professionals and agencies. The parent-teacher conference is not a counseling session; it is a vehicle for communication. In dealing with problems of a less serious nature or problems that appear to be temporary, diplomacy and skill can make the situation more manageable.

Seligman (1979) makes a valid point that parents perceived as "problems" by one teacher may not be problems for another. It is extremely important that educators view the situation, rather than the parents, as problematic. In any event, the conference becomes a very difficult one and demands expert handling by the teacher.

In previous chapters, the point has been made that parents of exceptional children have not always had good relationships with professional people. They may also be dealing with their own acceptance/adjustment problems and exhibit anger or defenses inappropriately directed at school personnel. A good starting point in difficult conferences is to understand that the negative feelings may be misdirected and should not be taken personally.

The teacher can provide an outlet for the angry or hostile parent by listening without saying anything. Parents and teachers may need to acknowledge their anger and feelings. However, nothing can be accomplished by open confrontation with an angry parent. A useful response might be a paraphrase and an invitation to convey one's perceptions. Seligman (1979, pp. 157–158) presents the following example:

> Mrs. Koerner, I can certainly sense your feelings of frustration and anger. You seem to be concerned with your daughter's behavior, which seems to have gotten worse since she has been in school. I wonder if you have any thoughts about why her behavior has changed?

When parents are suspicious, defensive, or legalistic, the following eight strategies can be effective:

1. Avoid confrontations at team meetings.

2. Be willing to defer decisions, if necessary, until major conflicts have been resolved.

3. Appeal to reasonableness for the sake of the child when legalisms threaten to overwhelm the team's efforts.

4. Deal directly with the parents' mistrust or hostility. Acknowledge it; discuss it with them; try to deal with the reasons for it.

5. Acknowledge openly that the parents have an intelligent point of view. They usually do! Don't fall into the trap of thinking, and behaving as if, all the expertise resides with the school staff and the parents don't have valuable perspectives and contributions.

6. Make strategic use of independent consultation. Sometimes the corroboration of an outsider will swing the parent over. On the other hand, an outside consultant's disagreement with the team's recommendations may open the team to another perspective.

7. Therefore, when parents ask for recommendations for outside consultants (which, surprisingly, they often may, even if they are suspicious), do not succumb to the temptation to recommend outsiders willing to "play ball" with the school system. Help all outside consultants maintain their independence. Guard the integrity of the consultation procedure.

8. If a parent will agree only to part of a program rather than the complete recommendation, don't take a rigid position. A good start may be all the team can hope for immediately. (Losen & Losen, 1985, p. 116)

These techniques also apply to other parents who appear to be difficult. Regardless of the situation, the teacher is in control of the conference and should always behave professionally. If nothing seems to improve the conference atmosphere, the conference should be ended and another one scheduled.

When parents refuse to act in the best interests of their children, the school has the legal right to intervene through due-process proceedings. For example, if parents refuse to permit placement in special programs for their exceptional child, the school can institute the same processes to which parents are entitled. However, this is a last resort that school systems use infrequently. The reason is obvious: if parents do not cooperate, the program is not likely to be successful for the student. Fortunately, in most cases, schools and parents cooperate in their joint efforts to provide the best possible education for all students.

Conclusion

The parent-teacher conference is the foremost vehicle used in schools to facilitate communication between the home and the school. For parents and teachers who work with exceptional students, it is a vehicle for carrying out the provisions of PL 94–142, which mandate parent involvement in the education of their children.

Three alternatives to the conference are telephone conversations, notes, and group meetings. However, the individual conference, as well as the team conference, provides an atmosphere conducive to sharing information and planning for students. Further, it may be the means to continued, improved communication between the home and the school. As Beale and Beers (1982, p. 35) state:

Parents and teachers who openly communicate with each other are likely to strengthen their relationships through continued positive interactions. Once they have developed such facilitative relationships, parents and teachers can build mutually satisfying partnerships that serve as a foundation for productive parent education and parent involvement.

Educators have a professional and an ethical responsibility to involve parents in the education of their exceptional children. In planning parent involvement and parent education, professionals need a great deal of information about the families with which they are working. Conferences help provide direct and indirect information. Rodriguez (1981) points out that parent conferences provide school personnel with knowledge of language use in the home, expectations and perceptions of the parents, and general home situations.

As a means of promoting information exchange, parent-teacher conferences present a viable tool for assessment of parents' strengths and needs. Additional considerations and techniques for parent assessment are presented in Chapter 8.

References

Agard, J. A., & Barry, S. L. (1982). *First steps to parent notification: A guide for school administrators.* Washington, D.C.: Abt Associates, Inc.

Anderson, W., Chitwood, S., & Hayden, D. (1982). *Negotiating the special education maze.* Englewood Cliffs, N.J.: Prentice-Hall.

Beale, A., & Beers, C. S. (1982). What do you say to parents after you say hello? *Teaching Exceptional Children, 15*(1), 34-38.

Birney, D. (1981). Consulting with administrators: The consultee centered approach. In J. C. Donoley (Ed.), *Consultation in schools.*, 101–131. New York: Academic Press.

Bolton, R. (1979). *People skills.* Englewood Cliffs, N.J.: Prentice-Hall.

Canady, R. L., & Seyfarth, J. T. (1979). *How parent-teacher conferences build partnerships.* Bloomington, Ind.: Phi Delta Kappa Educational Foundation.

Croft, D. J. (1979). *Parents and teachers: A resource book for home, school, and community relations.* Belmont, Calif.: Wadsworth Publishing Company.

Davis, D. H., & Davis, D. M. (1981). Managing parent-teacher conferences. *Today's Education, 70*(2), 46GS–50GS.

Dettmann, D. F., & Colangelo, N. (1980). A functional model for counseling parents of gifted students. *Gifted Child Quarterly, 24*(4), 158–161.

Fredericks, A., Harrington, A., Hill, B., Hunter, M., Loesch, P., Pasztor, J., & Simms, S. R. (1983). How to talk to parents, *Instructor, XCIII*(4), 64–67.

Gallagher, J. J. (1985). *Teaching the gifted child* (3rd ed.). Boston: Allyn and Bacon.

Gargiulo, R. M. (1985). *Working with parents of exceptional children.* Boston: Houghton Mifflin.

Goldstein, S., & Turnbull, A. P. (1982). Strategies to increase parent participation in IEP conferences. *Exceptional Children, 48*(4), 360–361.

Gordon, T. (1970). *Parent effectiveness training.* New York: Peter H. Wyden.

Henderson, R. W. (1982). *Teacher relations with minority students and their families.* Washington, D.C.: The American Association of Colleges for Teacher Education.

Heron, T. E., & Harris, K. C. (1982). *The educational consultant.* Boston: Allyn and Bacon.

Johnson, S. B. (1974). *A process for educational planning.* Castro Valley, Calif.: California Child Services Demonstration Center System.

Kaminer, R., Jedrysek, E., & Soles, B. (1981). Intellectually limited parents. *Developmental and Behavioral Pediatrics, 2*(2), 39–43.

Klein, S. D. (1979). Parent-school conferences. *The Exceptional Parent, 595*(4), E19–E21.

Kroth, R. L. (1980). The mirror model of parental involvement. *Pointer, 25*(1), 18–22.

Kroth, R. L. (1975). *Communicating with parents of exceptional children.* Denver: Love Publishing Co.

Kroth, R. L., & Simpson, R. L. (1977). *Parent conferences as a teaching strategy.* Denver: Love Publishing Company.

Lichter, P. (1976). Communicating with parents: It begins with listening. *Teaching Exceptional Children, 8*(2), 67–71.

Losen, S. M., & Losen, J. G. (1985). *The special education team.* Boston: Allyn and Bacon.

Lowe, J. P. (1980). Solving home problems through parent-teacher conferencing. *Pointer, 25*(1), 28–30.

Lusthaus, C., & Lusthaus, E. (1979). When is a child ready for mainstreaming? *The Exceptional Parent, 9*(5), R2–R5.

Marion, R. (1979). Minority parent involvement in the IEP process: A systematic model approach. *Focus on Exceptional Children, 10*(8), 1–16.

Marion, R. L. (1981). *Educators, parents, and exceptional children.* Rockville, Md.: Aspen Systems.

Markel, G., & Greenbaum, J. (1981). Assertiveness training for parents of disabled children. *The Exceptional Parent, 11*(4), 17–22.

Michaelis, C. T. (1980). *Home and school partnerships in exceptional education.* Rockville, Md.: Aspen Systems.

Morris, W. (1981). Ed., *The American heritage dictionary of the English language.* Boston: Houghton Mifflin.

National Education Association (1977). *Know your teachers.* West Haven, Conn.: National Education Association.

National Education Association (undated pamphlet). *Let's have a conference: You and your child's teacher.* West Haven, Conn.: National Education Association.

Playing both mother and father. (1985). *Newsweek,* July 15 (3) 43–44.

Price, B. J., & Marsh, G. E. (1985). Practical suggestions for planning and conducting parent conferences. *Teaching Exceptional Children, 17*(4), 274–278.

Rabbitt, J. A. (1978). The parent/teacher conference: Trauma or teamwork? *Phi Delta Kappan, 59*(7), 471–472.

Roberds-Baxter, S. (1984). The parent connection: Enhancing the affective component of parent conferences. *Teaching Exceptional Children, 17*(1), 55–58.

Rodriguez, R. F. (1981). The involvement of minority group parents in school. *Teacher Education and Special Education, 4*(4), 40–44.

Schuck, J. (1979). The parent-professional partnership—myth or reality? *Education Unlimited, 1*(4), 26–28.

Schulz, J. B., & Turnbull, A. P. (1984). *Mainstreaming handicapped students.* Boston: Allyn and Bacon.

Seligman, M. (1979). *Strategies for helping parents of exceptional children.* New York: The Free Press.

Simpson, R. L. (1982). *Conferencing parents of exceptional children.* Rockville, Md.: Aspen Systems.

Stevens, S. H. (1984). *Classroom success for the learning disabled.* Winston-Salem, N.C.: John F. Blair.

Strom, R. D. (1983). Expectations for educating the gifted and talented. *The Educational Forum, 47*(3), 279–303.

Swick, K. J., Flake-Hobson, C., & Raymond, G. (1980). The first step—establishing parent-teacher communication in the IEP conference. *Teaching Exceptional Children, 12*(4), 144–145.

Thornburg, K. (1980). Working with parents. *Instructor, 89* (8), 52–58.

Turnbull, A. P., Strickland, B. B., & Brantley, J. C. (1982). *Developing and implementing individualized education programs.* Columbus, Oh.: Charles E. Merrill.

Werner, M. S. (1980). Single parents and adolescent school crisis. *Pointer, 25*(1), 46–50.

Wolf, J. S., & Troup, J. (1980). Strategy for parent involvement: Improving the IEP process. *The Exceptional Parent, 10*(5), 31–32.

8

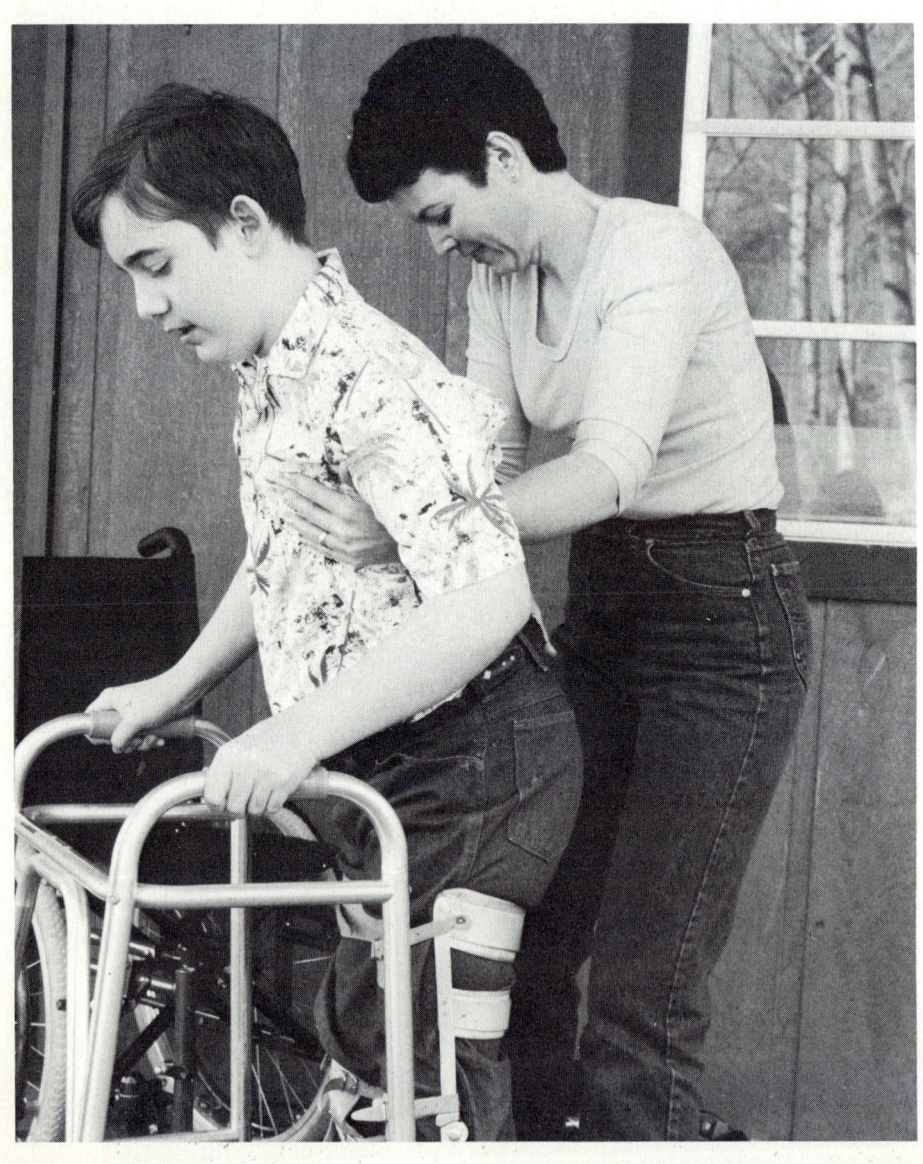

Assessment of Parents' Strengths and Needs

For years, educators have stressed the individuality of each child in the school and have been concerned with meeting the unique needs of each child. Rarely does one encounter the concept of the individuality of parents; programs for parent education are frequently planned as if all parents were the same. The theme of this book is that parents are individuals, too, individuals who have unique strengths as well as unique needs. As Michaelis (1980) states, "Each parent deserves to be known and understood for himself or herself" (p. 72).

The previous seven chapters have emphasized the need for communication between parents and school personnel. One primary outcome of this communication is that teachers get to know the parents of the students with whom they work. Teachers who know parents well develop a sensitivity to individual differences among them.

The informal exchange between parents and teachers creates a base for communication, but it does not constitute a means of determining specific strengths and needs of parents. Programs designed to improve parents' knowledge and skills should emerge from a sound assessment of their abilities and areas of need. To complete the analogy of individuality, teachers would not base a program of instruction for an exceptional child merely on a conversation with that child or on general knowledge of other children and programs. Parent training programs should be planned with equal care. Factors to consider are the individuality of parents, areas of assessment, and assessment techniques and models.

Individuality of Parents

□ □   The observation that parents react in different ways to the accommodation of an exceptional child in the family is explored in Chapter 3. Some of the same factors are present in the diversity of their needs for training. Socioeconomic level, educational level, ethnic background, experience, and the needs of the particular child all enter into the determination of training needs.

In some instances, well-meaning professional people have set out to teach parents skills they already possess. Professionals can no longer assume that parents are unsophisticated about educational processes and parents' rights. The massive increase in research that began in the early 1960s, plus widespread governmental endorsement of the importance of the early years through the funding of such programs as Head Start, have made an explosion of information regarding child development available to parents (Foster, Berger, & McLean, 1981). The result has been a plethora of articles, books, and courses intended to improve parenting skills, particularly with infants and young children.

The coverage of the provisions of PL 94–142 has been equally widespread. In addition, a number of parents were actively involved in promoting the legislation for exceptional children and are, themselves, experts in the field. Many parents, however, are not aware of their rights and responsibilities and desperately need information and skill training.

It is clear that parents of exceptional children represent a divergent group in terms of their knowledge and skills. Their individuality, strengths, and needs are closely related to three major distinctions: the nature of their child's exceptionality, characteristics of the family, and the parents' level of participation in their child's education.

Nature of the Exceptionality

☐ It is a fallacy to assume that the needs of children and of parents are separate. Within a family systems context, the boundaries between services for children and services for families are negligible (Foster, Berger, & McLean, 1981). It follows that the nature and severity of the exceptionality dictates the nature of services the child needs and thus the nature of training and information the parents need. The differences are most obvious in the training needs of parents of handicapped children and those of gifted children.

Parents of Handicapped Children Although parents of handicapped children vary in their personalities, abilities, strengths, and requirements, some needs apply to all families of handicapped children. These six needs are:

1. Emotional understanding and support
2. Information and facts
3. A greater degree of active participation in the planning of habilitation
4. [The ability] to maintain an identity of themselves as parents, as participating members of the community, and as competent individuals within themselves
5. A thorough and dynamic understanding of their role in the habilitation process
6. . . . Present and future expectations of the handicapped child. (Marion, 1981, p. 16)

The critical needs of parents of handicapped children are related to developmental stages of the child and the ability of the family to cope. As Figure 8.1 illustrates, parental needs increase with the age of the child, under conditions producing the most stressful situations.

The mother of a physically handicapped child explains her dilemma:

> I need a lot of help with Eric. We didn't know he had cerebral palsy until he was three years old and we had already lost a lot of time. He's eleven now and he's doing pretty well in school, although his teacher says he's lazy. I don't like to think he's lazy. He needs more physical therapy. I know the law says he's supposed to have it, but it's not there and I don't know what to do about it. If he's not going to get it, I need to know how to work with him myself.
>
> I would like to be able to talk to other parents and I know I'll need help as he gets older. What do you tell him when he wants to drive?
>
> I'm not a teacher; I don't know how hard I should push on his school work or on his dressing himself. Should I use velcro or teach him to button? I wish I knew. (M. Sorrell, personal communication, January 15, 1985)

Neely (1982) makes a distinction in the expressed needs among parents of children with various exceptionalities. He claims that parents of LD children want to know how to manage professionals and developmental aspects of learning disabilities and how to carry out consistent behavior management. Parents of developmentally disabled children want to know how to help their children achieve full and independent lives. Parents of severely handicapped children require unique skills in helping their children achieve developmental tasks. Although these statements are broad generalizations, they have some merit in linking needs to disabilities.

A surprising parental need was expressed by Kershman (1982), who investigated training needs of parents of deaf-blind, multihandicapped children. She found that a greater need for training was expressed by parents of institutionalized children than by those whose children remained in the home. This finding contradicts the assumption often held by school personnel that parents whose children are in residential facilities are not as concerned about

FIGURE 8.1 Parents' Critical Needs

Parents' Needs	*Time of Greatest Need*
Emotional support	At birth or identification of exceptionality
Facts and information	At time of diagnosis of exceptionality
Active involvement in planning	As child approaches school age
Identity as individuals	As child approaches puberty
Reorganization of roles	As child approaches age for vocational/career planning
Expectations for future	As parents age

Increasing Need of Parents ↓   *Advancing Age of Child* ↓

their childrens' education as are parents whose children remain at home. It also demonstrates the need for developing innovative materials and approaches for reaching parents who are geographically separated from their children.

Educators and counselors should be sensitive to the needs of each individual family member, as well as to the overall needs of the family as a unit (Opirhory & Peters, 1982). The mother of a mentally retarded child expresses the need for family help:

> Sharon was diagnosed as Down's Syndrome as a baby. She started school in kindergarten at age five. Now, at nine, she adds two digit numbers, she reads simple books and listens to taped books.
>
> I need all the help I can get. I've never been to school much and know nothing about teaching. I'd love a course where couples could talk and learn to work with their children.
>
> I don't know much about the law. I got upset last week when people were signing a petition to stop the group home that's going up. I need to know what the law is and where we stand in helping handicapped people. Those people need to be looked after; it's our responsibility.
>
> I don't have any gripe where the school is concerned. They have done a great job with Sharon.
>
> As a family we need help. My husband has a bad heart, so we have two handicaps. He doesn't stop to think that Sharon is handicapped; he's real short with her. We all get tired, but she's first in my life. It would be good to have other people to talk to. I wish we could have open discussion with other parents. It's no bed of roses, but we can make it. (J.S. Jones, personal communication, February 2, 1985)

Professionals who want to help parents of handicapped children must consider the nature of children's developmental delays and the significance of the delays in the ongoing conditions of the parents' lives. Parent-run groups, functioning in conjunction with early intervention programs, can be effective sources of support in helping parents address their needs (Eheart & Ciccone, 1982).

Parents of Gifted Children   The needs of parents of gifted children are quite different from the needs of parents of handicapped children. Fine (1977) contends that parents of gifted children are not only vociferous on behalf of their children but as a group are also quite perceptive. Rather than focusing on skill development, the general question parents pose to school personnel is: What can I do to help this child develop his or her potential (Gallagher, 1985)?

In general, parents of gifted children have expressed the need for more counseling and a knowledge of teaching methods (Malone, 1975). These needs are confirmed in a conversation with the mother of a gifted child:

> I would benefit from a constructive rap session—getting together with parents of children who are exceptionally gifted or bright to see if their children have gone

through any of the bizarre behavior we have experienced. I see certain behavior patterns that I would like to compare with other parents. I could use some counseling.

I've read my share of books on parenting. I don't need a course. I would like to have a checklist of things I could do to ensure that my child has been exposed to all areas; I could always use help with methodology. (C. Homolka, personal communication, 1985)

Parents are seeking help in the guidance of their gifted children. They do not have the standard societal models to direct their interaction with their children and to interpret their own parental roles. Parents of gifted children want to insure the best education for their children. Many of them have the capabilities to become involved in the needs of other children and parents as well.

Characteristics of the Family

☐ A number of parent education programs have ignored the differences in parental values and needs among groups of ethnic and socioeconomic diversity. Lack of awareness of the differences has frequently led to conflict in the programs, and planning separate programs for each group has not helped parents adapt to the multiethnic society in which they live (Strom, Griswold, & Slaughter, 1981). If the training needs of all parents of exceptional children are to be met, cultural differences and expectations must be assessed and accommodated in program planning.

In determining the strengths and needs of families of exceptional children, investigators have identified a number of variables. The four variables consistently discussed are socioeconomic level, educational level, ethnic background, and experiences with children.

Socioeconomic Level To assess maternal strengths and needs in child rearing, the Parent as a Teacher Inventory (discussed later in this chapter) was administered to a population representing three socioeconomic levels (Strom, Rees, Slaughter, & Wurster, 1981). The greatest differences among the three groups were found in mothers' feelings regarding control of their children's behavior. Lower-class mothers revealed a desire for greater control over their children's behavior than did upper-class groups. They also had less confidence in themselves as teachers of their children.

In investigating the needs of low-income mothers of developmentally delayed children, Eheart and Ciccone (1982, p. 30) discovered four main topics of concern. They found:

(a) that maternal needs seem to continue to be created or intensified throughout the preschool years of a developmentally delayed child's life,

(b) the severity of a child's developmental delay appears to be a significant variable in relation to maternal needs,
(c) maternal needs may be created primarily when children cause changes in ongoing conditions in their mother's lives, and
(d) safety needs tend to surface when low-income mothers are subjected to changes associated with caring for a developmentally delayed child.

In a study of 456 gifted children, Barbe (1956) found that the majority came from an upper-middle-class economic group. The occupations of the parents varied from professional and managerial groups to laborers. On the whole, gifted students have a better-than-average home life and socioeconomic background. However, giftedness can be found in all populations (Heward & Orlansky, 1984).

As it relates to needs, the family's socioeconomic status is important in terms of resources in the home, access to treatment, and availability of parents' time with their children. As discussed in Chapters 1 and 3, poverty is also associated with stress in the family and thus relates to family interactions and psychological needs.

Educational Level Although education is related to socioeconomic status, it offers an independent clue to a family's motivation and needs. Education influences both what parents want for their children and how they expect the child to achieve that goal. In a longitudinal study of gifted boys and their families, Albert (1980) found the families to be well-educated and to have significantly more formal education than the national norms. A strong correlation was found between parents' educational levels and their children's SAT scores in a study of students who are mathematically gifted. Barbe (1956) supported this idea in stating that the educational level of the parents of gifted children is far above the average. There are, of course, gifted children whose parents are not well-educated.

There is variability in the expressed needs of parents of handicapped children when educational level is considered. Kershman (1982) reports that among parents of deaf-blind children, the least well-educated group of parents expressed a significantly greater need for training in four areas: family roles and interactions; health, care, and maintenance; handicapping conditions; and affective adjustment. These parents expressed a strong need for training and a desire for learning in a wide variety of areas. The most well educated subgroup of parents in this study scored their need for training in the area of curriculum and interaction significantly lower than the other subgroups of parents.

It is important to be aware of parents' educational level in preparing written materials for their response. As Kroth and Otteni (1983) point out, if consent forms, rights explanations, and informational materials are written at a level too difficult for a significant percentage of parents, informed consent and involvement cannot be attained easily.

Ethnic Background Parents of different cultural groups have different goals of parenting and childrearing (Dembo, Sweitzer, & Lauritzen, 1985). A study of parenting attitudes and skills among black, non-Hispanic white, and

Mexican-American mothers revealed significant differences on the Parent as a Teacher Inventory (Strom, Rees, Slaughter, & Wurster, 1981). In general, the non-Hispanic white as compared to black mothers indicated less need to control their children, greater confidence in themselves as teachers, and greater interest and skill in playing with their children.

Many minority group parents feel inadequate and uninformed because they lack the necessary communication skills to express themselves. Negative experiences of their own may prevent their participation in parent education programs (Rodriguez, 1981). To prevent the perpetuation of this insecurity, it is essential that the training needs of minority parents be determined and met. Their unique cultural and linguistic strengths should be evaluated and used in programming.

Experiences with Children The size of the parents' original family, as well as the size of their present family, affect the amount of family and childrearing experience they have had. Parents who have helped raise siblings and who have had successful experiences with other children are more comfortable with their own children.

Parenthood is also much easier with the second child; parents are secure in the roles they have developed. Differences in kinds of stress have been found in the experience of first-time and experienced parents (Dembo, Sweitzer, & Lauritzen, 1985). The degree of experience and confidence also affects the kind and amount of training parents need as well as the training skills they have to share.

Although experience with children who are not exceptional is helpful to parents, they may require skills of a different sort for their exceptional child. For example, they may be well versed in the principles of behavior management but not aware of the necessity to break tasks into small steps for teaching a handicapped child. The challenges presented in the intellectual and creative development of a gifted child could be vastly different from those presented by a less gifted sibling.

Parents who are knowledgeable about normal child development will be at a distinct advantage in raising their exceptional child. Other people with experience in working with exceptional children may be prospective parent trainers.

Other factors, such as sex of the parent, marital status, and parenting style are family characteristics to consider in planning parent education programs. Adequate assessment can pinpoint relevant concerns and help educators plan more effective programs.

Levels of Participation

☐ Just as parents have diversified needs, they also demonstrate varied kinds and levels of participation in educational planning and implementation. As discussed in Chapter 4, school personnel should consider the degrees to which parents want and are able to participate.

The Mirror Model of Parental Involvement (presented in Figure 8.2) represents an attempt to respect the parents' strengths and to acknowledge their needs (Kroth, 1980).

The model is divided into areas of professional service and parental service. Within each area are four levels of participation, designated by the terms *all, most, some,* and *few.* Lower levels of participation need to be firmly established before higher levels of involvement can be expected. For example, all parents might provide information concerning the child's preschool medical and social history; most parents could provide relevant information during the IEP process; some parents might become strong advocates for services for exceptional students; and a few parents might become involved enough to form active parent groups and conduct parenting workshops them-

FIGURE 8.2 Mirror Model of Parent Involvement

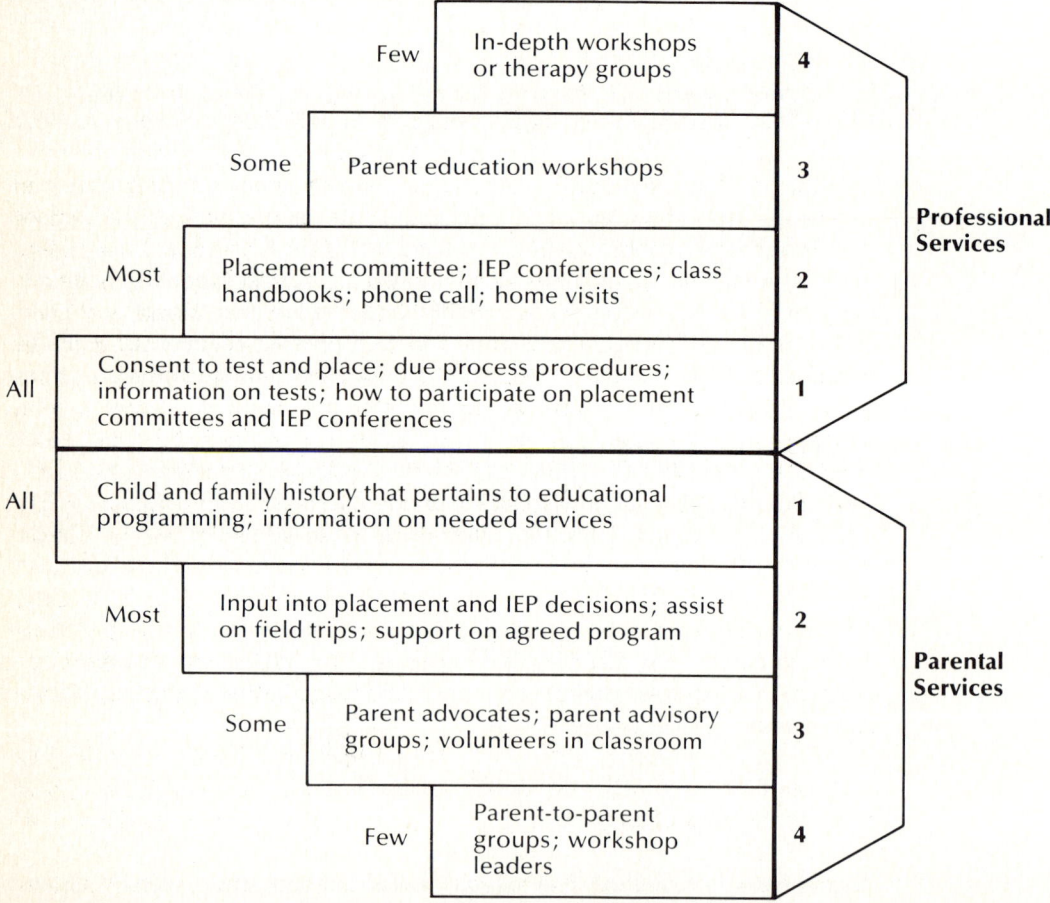

Source: Kroth, Roger L. (1980). The mirror model of parental involvement. *Pointer 25,* (1), 18–22. Used with permission.

selves (Heron & Harris, 1982). This model provides the educator with an excellent perspective on the reciprocal nature of the parent-professional relationship. It also provides direction for planning parental education programs.

The assessment of parent participation is a relatively new concept. In the entire study of parent involvement, it is essential to consider that programs differ not only in whether they involve parents, but also in how they involve them and to what degree (Cone, Delawyer, & Wolfe, 1985). The Parent/Family Involvement Index measures parent participation in twelve different areas:

1. Contact with teacher.
2. Participation in the special education process.
3. Transportation.
4. Observations at school.
5. Educational activities at home.
6. Attending parent education/consultation meetings.
7. Classroom volunteering.
8. Parent-parent contact and support.
9. Involvement with administration.
10. Involvement in fund raising activities.
11. Involvement in advocacy groups.
12. Disseminating information.   (Cone, Delawyer, & Wolfe, 1985, p. 418)

The purposes of the index are to measure overall parent involvement in special education programs and also to assess specific types of involvement for mothers and fathers separately. Field testing of the instrument showed that mothers are more involved than fathers in nearly all areas, including transporting their child to school, conducting educational activities at home, and interacting with the school administration. The top three types of involvement for mothers and fathers were participation in the special education process, contact with teacher, and transportation. Income and education levels of both mothers and fathers were positively correlated with degree of participation, whereas grade level of the child is generally negatively correlated with participation (that is, the higher the grade, the less participation). Overall, teachers did not see parents as highly involved in their child's program (Cone, Delawyer, & Wolfe, 1985).

The level of parental involvement depends on factors related to time, other commitments, educational background, degree of interest, experience, and confidence. The demographic variables most predictive of mothers' involvement are family income level and mother's and father's education levels (Cone, Delawyer, & Wolfe, 1985).

As demonstrated in the Mirror Model of Parent Involvement (Figure 8.2), participation is not necessarily static. As parents learn and have good school experiences, it is hoped they will grow in their ability to participate at higher levels.

Ideally, all parents of exceptional students will become involved in planning for their children. Realistically, there will continue to be parents who, for a variety of reasons, do not participate. The following challenge results:

> The individual differences among parents require individual approaches to training models and strategies and the recognition that all parents will not be interested in training. Parents have the right to refuse training without being criticized. (Turnbull, Strickland, & Goldstein, 1978, p. 414)

Parent involvement programs best serve the community, and exceptional students, when their design reflects the differences found among parents (Kroth & Otteni, 1983).

Areas of Assessment

Most parents of exceptional children want and need help with a number of aspects of their child's development. Understanding their special problems and concerns can form the foundation for a parent-teacher relationship, and a central purpose for continuing the relationship should be to provide parents with effective ways of dealing with those problems (Heward, Dardig & Rossett, 1979). The teacher can share knowledge and skills with parents in an informal, personal way; through class meetings and workshops; or through parent education programs. Regardless of the technique used, careful assessment should be the starting point. Areas of assesssment and programming usually include (1) knowledge of legal rights and advocacy strategies, (2) behavior management techniques, (3) information on child development and care, (4) information about exceptional conditions, (5) instructional skills, and (6) the family environment and interaction.

Knowledge of Legal Rights

If parents are to be full participants in the education of their exceptional children, they must become knowledgeable about the implications of PL 94–142, their rights, and their responsibilities. Although a great deal of information has been disseminated about legal provisions, many parents have not had access to the information or have not fully understood what they have read.

There is some evidence that PL 94–142 and other mandates are most beneficial to families who are well informed, well educated, resourceful, and who insist that the laws protect their children (Sullivan, 1981). In other words, people who need protection most may not be receiving it. The primary need of many families may be to become more aware of what their legal rights are. Parents of children with special needs should be aware of due process procedures, protection in evaluation, least restrictive environment provisions, and confidentiality of information. They need to be aware of the specific rights and how they can exercise the rights with respect to the education of their children.

There are many sources of information for parents. The National Information Center for Handicapped Children and Youth, Closer Look, and other federal agencies have excellent materials readily available to parents and others. In addition, there are a number of projects whose mission is the dissemination of information concerning exceptional children. However, unless parents are informed about the availability of such resources, they cannot take advantage of them. Thus, information about legal matters becomes a primary content area for parent education programs.

Since parents are at such different levels of knowledge about PL 94–142, a pretest can reveal areas of knowledge and need on which to build a program. Several instruments have been designed for this purpose within federally funded projects. One test produced at Utah State University (undated) with funds from the Bureau of Education consists of a booklet (a self-test) with multiple-choice items related to elements of PL 94-142. The thirteen items are very simple and straightforward and would give program planners some idea of the type of information the particular parent needed. Another instrument, developed by the Kentucky Department of Education, is illustrated in Figure 8.3. In addition to pinpointing parents' lack of knowledge

FIGURE 8.3 Parental Knowledge About PL 94–142

What Does Public Law 94–142 Mean for My Child?

Directions: Respond to each item by circling "yes" or "no."

1. Special education means the total school program for my handicapped child.   yes no
2. Special education is to be available for every handicapped child of school-age.   yes no
3. If my child is in kindergarten and needs special education, we will need to pay for this.   yes no
4. If my child is handicapped he/she will automatically be considered for a special class or school.   yes no
5. Each child who will receive special education services must have a written Individualized Education Program.   yes no
6. My child's Individualized Education Program is planned by his/her teacher.   yes no
7. The school must invite me to come to all of the committee meetings where they discuss my child's program.   yes no
8. When I go to a committee meeting, I can listen and offer ideas even though I am not a member of the committee.   yes no
9. The school must have my consent before they can evaluate or place my child in a special program.   yes no
10. If I disagree with the school about my child's program, I will need a lawyer to straighten it out.   yes no
11. Federal money pays for special education, and all my school needs to do is apply for it.   yes no

Source: Knapp, D. (1979). Parent education packet: Parents' and children's rights. Frankfort: Central Kentucky Child Service Demonstration Center, Bureau of Education for Exceptional Children, Kentucky Department of Education.

about PL 94–142, such instruments could be used to identify parents whose knowledge would enable them to teach other parents.

Some parents may need to develop advocacy skills to help them pursue their rights and obtain the services to which they or their children are entitled. Such topics as legal services, family support needs, and therapeutic services may be areas to probe. Apolloni (1984) has developed a conceptual model for explaining successful self-advocacy strategies for use by service recipients and parents. The cycle includes stages of targeting, preparing, influencing, and following-up. For parents who are aware of their rights and for those who become aware through parent involvement programs, the determination of advocacy skills is a practical step.

Parents of gifted students have been staunch promoters of advocacy skills among the members of parent groups. Under the topic of "Friendly Persuasion," Lockhart (1976) urges the progression of decision, awareness, evaluation, exploration, and organization in developing program advocates. Figure 8.4, a simple checklist of skills, is an assessment instrument used in this endeavor.

Some parents may not wish to take a test or respond to a checklist. Their needs in the legal area may be determined through informal discussion or through parent-teacher conferences.

Behavior Management

☐ Programs focusing on behavior management usually have two objectives: (1) to train parents in the theory and application of behavior modification principles and practices and (2) to assist parents in modifying selected target behaviors their children exhibit (Walker & Shea, 1984). Distinguishing between these two areas is an important aspect of program planning. The first general area relates to the needs of many parents as they seek to establish systematic management of their children's behavior. The second area is specific and personal; it will probably be done on an individual basis.

A general measure of knowledge of behavioral principles and their practical application to children and childrearing can be obtained by using *Knowledge of Behavior Principles as Applied to Children*. This instrument consists of fifty multiple-choice items and yields a single summary score (Haffey & Levant, 1984).

If parents are seeking help with a specific behavior problem, they need a definitive type of assessment. The teacher needs the following information:

> The history of the problem
> Specific areas of conflict
> A description of the behavior that makes it receptive to direct observation and measurement
> The identity of the person or persons present when the behavior occurs

FIGURE 8.4 "Talent Pool" Form for Parent Organization

Association for Gifted and Talented Students in Louisiana
_____ Chapter

"Association" means people working together for a common purpose.

Let's pool our talents to accomplish our goal:
Developing to the maximum Louisiana's greatest natural resources—
Gifted and talented children and youth.
Volunteers are needed for committees to obtain a fully functioning organization. Please check the area or areas in which you are willing to serve in the work of the Association for Gifted and Talented Students.

___ Program	___ Bulletin
___ Publicity	___ Library
___ Membership	___ Mimeographing
___ Telephone	___ Offset Facilities
___ Mini-Course Aides	___ Address Envelopes
___ Community Resources	___ Typing
___ Public Affairs	___ Stencil Cutting
___ Budget	___ Office Assistance
___ Finance	___ Federal Funding
___ Scholarships & Awards	___ Newsletter
___ Other	

Signed _____
Street _____
City _____ Zip _____
Telephone _____

Source: Talent Pool Form for Parent Organization. Coffey, K., Ginsberg, G., Lockhart, C., McCartney, D., Nathan, C., and Wood, K. (1976). *Parentspeak*. Ventura, Calif.: Ventura County Superintendent of Schools Office, p. 53.

Reinforcers that appear to maintain the behavior
The roles and responsibilities of the parents and other family members in the child's life
Parental expectations and behavior requirements and the reasonableness of these expectations and requirements
Methods presently used in attempts to change the behavior
Rewards that are available or that can be made available in the home
Observational data on the rate or frequency of the behavior (Walker & Shea, 1984, p. 171).

In both cases, trainers will need to know the parents' present methods of behavior management, the skills they have in recording behavior, and the support available in the home. It is difficult to use objective measurements to obtain this sort of information; observation is more effective.

Blackham and Silberman (1975) have suggested four methods for obtaining data on parent-child interactions and problem areas:

1. Direct observation of the child and other family members in the home.
2. Direct observation of the child and other family members in the school setting.
3. Parental observation of the child's interaction within the family at home and reporting the resultant data to the educator.
4. A personal interview with the parents and child.

Successful behavior management in the home has the potential to make a positive difference in family life. For that reason, it is vital that the proper needs of children and parents be determined and the appropriate goals developed.

Child Development

☐ As indicated (Chapter 4), a great deal of information regarding infant and child development has been made available to the general public through programs initiated in the 1960s. Many parents have availed themselves of the opportunities to learn through this material; however, many other parents remain relatively uneducated about the stages of development and therefore about knowledge of deviance from normal development. Data collected by researchers at the University of Delaware (1983) indicate that child development information prepared for distribution via text form will not reach all parents, particularly the ones who need it the most (i.e., the less educated).

Parents expect to receive assistance in knowledge of child growth and development and their role in fostering positive development. Powell (1981) finds that in a typical assessment procedure, the parents will usually ask, "Is my child doing all right in his growth and development?" (p. 180). Parents need to know that they have the capacity and ability to respond appropriately to the child's needs in developing language, fine motor skills, gross motor skills, and personal-social skills. In order to assess their own abilities, they need the reference provided through adequate understanding of child development.

Educators' knowledge of what parents know about child development is extremely limited. Parent needs assessment should include the parents' actual or expected childrearing practices, their questions about desired practices, and their knowledge about child development and how the knowledge is applied (Harman & Brim, 1980).

In an attempt to learn what parents know about how young children develop, researchers at the University of Delaware (1983) assessed the information mothers have about young children's physical, intellectual, and social-emotional development. The instrument developed for this purpose (Parent Knowledge Scale) is composed of thirty-one items that ask such questions as:

1. When do you think a baby will sleep through the night?
2. When do signs that the baby is ready to be toilet-trained usually begin to appear?
3. When do you expect children to put 2–4 words together to make a sentence? and

4. How long do you think a two-year-old can sit quietly and play or listen to a story? (University of Delaware, 1983, p. 2)

In addition to the importance of knowledge about child development for parental assistance and feedback, it is vital if parents are to participate in identifying children who are handicapped or gifted. It is difficult to identify exceptional characteristics if normal characteristics are not available as referents. A number of checklists are available for parents in every area of exceptionality. Typical is the Developmental Checklist for Young Children available from the Association for Retarded Citizens, presented in Figure 8.5.

Although such checklists do not indicate the parents' knowledge about child development, they are starting points in helping parents learn to observe their child's development and to assist in the professional evaluation process. Training in this area may be an indication of parent education curriculum. Powell (1981, p. 181) expresses the importance of parent training in child development:

> Increased sensitivity and a willingness to listen to parents giving accurate descriptions of their child's behavior are critical. A parent's report or statement that a child is behind, slow, or unusual always merits consideration for developmental assessment and observations.

☐ *Parents need to learn to observe their child's development and to assist in the professional evaluation process.*

FIGURE 8.5 Developmental Checklist for Young Children

This checklist is designed for you to record your child's growth and development. There is space to fill in the age when your child begins each activity.

When you fill in the checklist, remember that each child develops at his or her own pace. The age listed on the chart is when most children usually start the activity.

If your child is not doing one activity at the age listed, there is probably no need to be concerned. However, if you child is late for several activities, you should discuss it with your child's doctor.

(For the child under 2 years old who was born prematurely, subtract the length of prematurity from his or her age. For example, if a 2 month-old baby was born one month early, his or her development should be compared to a 1 month-old-baby.)

		Usual Activities During . . .	
1 Month	Your Child's Age	*2 Months*	Your Child's Age
Able to raise head from surface when lying on tummy	_____	Smiles and coos	_____
		Rolls part way to side when lying on back	_____
Pays attention to someone's face in his or her direct line of vision	_____	Grunts and sighs	_____
Moves arms and legs in energetic manner	_____		
Likes to be held and rocked	_____		
3 Months		*4 Months*	
Eyes follow a moving object	_____	Holds a rattle for an extended period of time	_____
Able to hold head erect	_____	Laughs out loud	_____
Grasps objects when placed in his or her hand	_____	Sits supported for short periods of time	_____
Babbles	_____	Recognizes bottle and familiar faces	_____
5 Months		*6 Months*	
Reaches for and holds objects	_____	Turns over from back to stomach	_____
Stands firmly when held	_____	Turns toward sounds	_____
Stretches out arms to be picked up	_____	Sits with little support (one hand bracing him/her)	_____
Likes to play peek-a-boo	_____	Persistently reaches for objects out of his or her reach	_____
		Listens to own voice	_____
		Crows and squeals	_____
		Reaches for and grasps objects and brings them to mouth	_____
		Holds, sucks, bites cookie or cracker—begins chewing	_____
7 Months		*8 Months*	
Can transfer object from one hand to the other	_____	Can sit steadily for about five minutes	_____
Can sit for a few minutes without support	_____	Crawls (on hands and knees)	_____
Pats and smiles at image in mirror	_____	Grasps things with thumb and first two fingers	_____
Creeps (pulling body with arms and leg kicks)	_____	Likes to be near parents	_____
Is shy at first with strangers	_____		

Usual Activities During . . .

9 Months	Your Child's Age	10 Months	Your Child's Age
Says Ma-ma or Da-da	____	Able to pull self up at side of crib or playpen	____
Responds to name	____	Can drink from a cup when it is held	____
Can stand for a short time holding onto support	____		
Able to hit two objects together on his or her own	____		
Copies sounds	____		

11 Months		12 Months	
Can walk holding onto furniture or sides of crib or playpen	____	Waves bye-bye	____
Can find an object placed under another object	____	Can walk with one hand held	____
		Says two words besides Ma-ma/Da-da	____
		Enjoys some solid foods	____
		Finger feeds self	____
		Likes to have an audience	____

15 Months		18 Months	
Walks by self; stops creeping	____	Can build a tower with 3 blocks	____
Shows wants by pointing and gestures	____	Likes to climb and take things apart	____
Scribbles on paper after shown	____	Can say 6 words	____
Begins using a spoon	____	Tries to put on shoes	____
Cooperates with dressing	____	Drinks from cup held in both hands	____
		Likes to help a parent	____

2 Years		3 Years	
Able to run	____	Can repeat 2 numbers in a row	____
Walks up/down stairs using alternate feet	____	Knows his or her sex	____
Says at least 50 words	____	Dresses self except for buttoning	____
Sometimes uses 2 word sentences	____	Can copy a circle	____
Points to objects in a book	____	Can follow 2 commands of on, under, or behind (i.e., stand on the rug.)	____
		Knows most parts of the body	____
		Jumps lifting both feet off ground	____
		Can build tower with 9 blocks	____

4 Years		5 Years	
Can repeat a simple 6 word sentence	____	Can follow three commands	____
Can wash hands and face without help	____	Can copy a square	____
Can copy a cross	____	Can skip	____
Can stand on one foot	____		
Can catch a tossed ball	____		

Source: Developmental Checklist for Young Children. Arlington, Texas: Association for Retarded Children.

If parents are able to notice aspects of their child's development, to anticipate what the child should do next, and to work toward that goal, their ability to respond appropriately is enhanced.

Exceptional Conditions

☐ Parents who are good observers may recognize signs of exceptional characteristics when their children are young. By the time the children are in school, such parents may have become quite knowledgeable about the origin and manifestations of the particular exceptionality. Other parents may be asking, "What's wrong with my child?" or, when confronted with a label, "How can you tell?" For training purposes, it is necessary to determine how much the parents know and what kind of information they need.

When children are diagnosed in early childhood, it usually means (1) a severe handicap is present or (2) unusual giftedness is apparent. When such obvious exceptionalities are exhibited, parents have probably been in contact with agencies outside the school and have learned a great deal about their child's exceptionality. If the difference is less obvious, school personnel will need to assess the parents' knowledge and to provide the necessary information. Appropriate assessment areas are definitions and characteristics.

Definitions Parents of children who are handicapped and of children who are gifted can be queried formally or informally about their understanding of the federal and state definition of their child's exceptionality. In the area of handicapping conditions, a great deal of information is available for parents and for teachers from the National Information Center for Handicapped Children and Youth (P.O. Box 1492, Washington, D.C. 20013). This office provides information about state agencies, organizations and publications, descriptions of specific disabilities, legal information, information on direct services for children, fact sheets on implications for teaching children with specific handicaps, and descriptions of careers in special education. Similar information can be obtained for parents of gifted children from state and local agencies and from parent organizations.

Characteristics Parent organizations in every area of exceptionality have developed checklists of characteristics that are useful in determining the parents' knowledge as well as in identifying the child's exceptionality. Parent handbooks developed by state and local school agencies are also helpful in assessing and providing information.

Parents of gifted children have been particularly concerned with learning to identify their children's exceptional abilities. Some questions these parents ask are:

Aren't all children gifted?
Are all gifted children the same?

Are children always gifted in everything they do?
What intellectual characteristics do many gifted children seem to share?
What criteria should be used in identifying gifted children?
Is education for the gifted elitist?
What is done in a program for the gifted that makes it different?
What services may I expect from my child's school relative to providing supplemental education for gifted children? (Delisle & Licence, 1980, pp. 37–38)

One way of determining parents' knowledge of gifted and talented children is through the administration of a short test. Figure 8.6 is a true/false test based on the findings of educational research on the gifted. People who are planning parent education programs in all areas of exceptionality can develop similar instruments.

Instructional Skills

☐ Once parents have recognized and accepted the exceptionalities their child exhibits, their next question becomes, "How can I help?" Identifying skills the child needs and the instructional skills of the parents is a logical sequent. Several instruments have been developed to measure the effectiveness of parents as teachers.

The Teaching Skills Inventory (Rosenberg & Robinson, 1985, p. 163), designed to measure parents' teaching skills, reflects five assumptions regarding methods of instruction:

(a) a developmental match should exist between a child's current developmental level and the developmental level of the new expectations being made of him;
(b) the parent should be responsive to the child's interests and moods when interacting with him;
(c) active rather than passive responding should be emphasized;
(d) the language used with the child should be at an appropriate developmental level and should also provide enriched or expanded information; [and]
(e) feedback should be provided that is both positive and corrective.

Research with this instrument indicated that the Teaching Skills Inventory is appropriate for assessment of teaching skills of parents and that teachers can learn to rate the performance of parents with whom they work. In rating the abilities of parents, teachers were able to identify areas in which parents had skill deficits that could be improved with training.

The Parent as a Teacher Inventory (Strom, 1984) is a composite attitude scale revealing how individuals feel about certain aspects of the parent-child interactive system, their standards for assessing the importance of various child behaviors, and their value preferences concerning child behavior. Responses are grouped into subsets related to five areas of parent curriculum:

FIGURE 8.6 Parents of Gifted and Talented Children

True/False Test	
1. If my child does not score 130 or better on an IQ test, she/he is not gifted.	True False
2. Enrolling my child in a program for the gifted/talented is undemocratic.	True False
3. Creative children prefer to have direct instruction.	True False
4. The best way to ensure friendship for your gifted/talented child is to have him/her associate with the same chronologically aged child.	True False
5. When looking at the bell shaped curve, mentally retarded and intellectually gifted have been found to include approximately the same percentage of the total population.	True False
6. There are no states that offer programs for the gifted and talented. States only offer programs for children with handicaps.	True False
7. Gifted/talented children are precocious, physically weak and socially maladjusted.	True False
8. A gifted/talented child will automatically perform up to his/her intellectual potential.	True False
9. Teachers do a better job than parents in spotting gifted/talented children.	True False
10. You are the 34-year-old parent of a gifted 7-year-old. The child is so bright you can not provide for his/her needs.	True False
11. As a parent you should never admit you don't know an answer to your child's question.	True False
12. Gifted/talented children should not have to do household chores.	True False
13. Gifted/talented children require total freedom.	True False
14. A child gifted in mathematics will also be gifted verbally and socially.	True False
15. A child's intellectual growth is least active in development from birth to age four.	True False
16. Gifted/talented students always finish high school.	True False
17. Gifted/talented children rarely learn to read before they enter school.	True False
18. Gifted/talented children learn basic skills more quickly than do other children of the same age.	True False
19. The only way to provide for a gifted/talented child is by acceleration.	True False
20. The best way to teach gifted/talented children is by ability grouping.	True False

Source: Anthony, Margaret (1981). Parents of Gifted and Talented Children, *G/C/T*, Jan/Feb., p. 39. Used with permission.

1. *Creativity*—parents' acceptance of creative functioning in their child and desire to encourage or suppress its development;
2. *Frustration*—parental childrearing frustration and focus of the frustration;
3. *Control*—parental feelings about control and the extent to which parental control of child behavior is deemed necessary;
4. *Play*—Parental understanding of play and its influence on child development; [and]
5. *Teaching-Learning*—parents' perception of their ability to facilitate the teaching-learning process for their child. (Strom, 1984, pp. 1–2)

The rationale for using this instrument in connection with parent education programs is that an individual's emotional and behavioral responses to his or her own parent-child relationship are a combination of present parenting experiences, value-laden expectations, and beliefs regarding child behavior (Strom & Slaughter, 1978). The Parent as a Teacher Inventory has been used for research purposes with parents of exceptional children as well as with parents of other children (Strom, Rees, & Wurster, 1983; Strom, Rees, Slaughter, & Wurster, 1981; and Strom, Rees, Slaughter, & Wurster, 1980).

A comprehensive assessment program was devised to evaluate a behavioral training program for parents of developmentally disabled children (Weitz, 1981). Three pretreatment assessment procedures involved acquisition of a developmental history, administration of a developmental profile, and assessment of the child's language functioning. The final step of the assessment was videotaping the Teaching Behavior Task, a structured interaction designed to permit measurement of parents' proficiency as teachers for their children. Each parent was asked to use any techniques desired to teach one item from skills in the language assessment, one skill to be chosen within the child's ability and the other slightly beyond the child's ability. As each parent worked with the child, the researcher recorded the number of cues being used. The Teaching Behavior Code (Table 8.1) detailed the criteria used to quantify the level of parents' teaching skills. Research data with the Teaching Behavior Code indicated it to be a reliable device for assessing teaching behavior. In spite of difficulties with interobserver reliability and cost of videotaping, this process is valuable in identifying strengths and weaknesses in parent teaching ability (Weitz, 1981).

Family Environment

☐ Although the focus of this chapter is on the assessment of parental needs, another broad area must be addressed in determining the needs of exceptional children and youth and the training needs of their parents. When the family is conceptualized as a system, it is essential to evaluate the environment in which that system operates if predictions are to be made and positive changes effected.

TABLE 8.1 Teaching Behavior Code

1. Discriminative stimulus. Teacher's instructions to the child that impart task-relevant information. Must be clear and discriminable, appropriate to the task, fully specify the target behavior, consistent with previous trial, uninterrupted, and given when child is attending.
2. Prompts need: Need for Usage. Prompt must be used only when needed. If child does not respond within 3 seconds of command or gives incompatible response, prompt should be used.
3. Prompts Quality: Quality of the guidance. If prompt is used, it must be effective.
4. Consequence: Quality of reinforcer or punisher. Consequences must be unambiguous and appropriate.
5. Shaping: Appropriately contingent dispensing of positive consequences. Each correct target response must be reinforced with primary reinforcement. Secondary reinforcement must be used on every correct trial. Secondary reinforcement must accompany the primary. Secondary reinforcement must be used after effectively prompted target behavior. Child must not have access to noncontingent reinforcement during work session.
6. Discrete trials. Each trial must have a discrete intertrial interval of at least 2 seconds after a correct response. The child should be allowed 5 seconds to respond if no target response is made and no prompt used.
7. Recording data. After every trial, teacher records results.
8. Obstruct. If one or more categories are unscorable because teacher and/or student is off camera, score "–".
9. Rule violation. It will be specified on top of coder's sheet whether teacher is to ignore or work through tantrums and other disruptive behavior. Score adherence to that rule.

Source: Weitz, S. E. (1981). A code for assessing teaching skills of developmentally disabled children. *Journal of Autism and Developmental Disorders, 12* (1), p. 18. Used with permission of Plenum Publishing Corporation.

Even though more efforts have been directed toward standardizing tools that assess growth and development of children, concern is increasing for ways to assess the quality and quantity of social, emotional, and cognitive support available in a child's environment (Powell, 1981). Prominent accomplishments in this direction are the Home Observation for Measurement of the Environment (HOME) and the Family Environment Scale (FES).

Home Observation for Measurement of the Environment   Two aspects of the HOME have been developed: one to tap the environmental characteristics of a child from birth to three years and one to measure the changing environment of the child between three and six years of age. Both inventories offer a framework for systematically collecting information about the subtle aspects of a child's environment that can be used for the benefit of the child and his parents. The HOME can be used in the following nine ways:

1. Determining the frequency of contacts between adult caregivers and children
2. Determining that the child is in an environment that is both stimulating and responsive to his needs
3. Helping determine whether the emotional climate is positive or negative in nature

4. Helping determine if there is provision for sensory experiences that are neither understimulating nor overstimulating to the child
5. Helping determine the adequacy of novelty and range of contacts with others
6. Helping identify areas of strengths and weaknesses in a family
7. Planning appropriate guidance for a family
8. Identifying developmental risk before a child is three years of age [and]
9. Planning intervention strategies when weaknesses or deficits are observed. (Powell, 1981, p. 129).

Figure 8.7 reproduces a portion of the HOME.

In research concerning environmental factors in infant development, the HOME has produced some interesting data. Chief findings are that there is a complex pattern of relations between early environmental and early developmental measures (Bradley, Caldwell, & Elardo, 1979) and that correlations between home inventory data and measures of infant development were higher than those typically reported relating infant tests or level of parental education to childhood IQ (Elardo, Bradley, & Caldwell, 1975). HOME Inventory scores obtained during infancy have been found to predict later developmental status in developmentally normal children (Affleck, Allen, McGrade, & McQueeney, 1982). It has also been demonstrated that this instrument can be effective in evaluating environmental influences on handicapped children and their families.

Three categories of variables were examined as correlates of HOME Inventory scores for infants who were identified as developmentally disabled or at high risk for developmental disability (Affleck et al., 1982). The first category was parental mood disturbances associated with adaptation to a developmentally disabled infant; the second category examined was infant characteristics thought to affect parental responsiveness; and the third set of variables was parental perceptions of the infant's temperament. Results of the study suggested that the interactional and perceived temperamental characteristics of the infant associated with HOME Inventory ratings could be viewed as determinants rather than as outcomes of differing practices in the home.

The assessment of home and family variables may also make an important contribution to the early identification of a child's learning disabilities. In a review of literature, Freund, Bradley, and Caldwell (1979) observe in the home environments of learning-disabled children a reaction to, as well as a determinant of, the child's behavior. They recommend that in future home environmental assessment of learning problem families, investigators should compare the transactions between parents and their LD children with the transactions between the same parents and their non-learning-disabled children. They also suggest that subscales of instruments such as the HOME be used to develop profiles of home environments to help predict children's learning disabilities.

Although the HOME was designed for use with preschool children of normal development, it has been used successfully in a five-year longitudinal

FIGURE 8.7 Home Observation for Measurement of the Environment: Birth to Three

Date of interview _____

Child designee _____
  Name   Age   Sex   Ethnicity
Child's birthday _____ Birth order _____
Mother's name _____ Father's name _____
Address _____

Categories	Raw scores	Percentile scores
I. Emotional and verbal responsivity of mother	_____	_____
II. Avoidance of restriction and punishment	_____	_____
III. Organization of physical and temporal environment	_____	_____
IV. Provision of appropriate play materials	_____	_____
V. Maternal involvement with child	_____	_____
VI. Opportunities for variety in daily stimulation	_____	_____
Totals	_____	_____

I. Emotional and verbal responsivity of mother

	Yes	No

1. Mother spontaneously vocalizes to child at least twice during visit (excluding scolding).
2. Mother responds to child's vocalizations with a verbal response.
3. Mother tells child the name of some object during visit or says name of person or object in a "teaching" style.
4. Mother's speech is distinct, clear, and audible.
5. Mother initiates verbal interchanges with observer—asks questions and makes spontaneous comments.
6. Mother expresses ideas freely and easily and uses statements of appropriate length for conversation (e.g., gives more than brief answers).
*7. Mother permits child occasionally to engage in "messy" type of play.
8. Mother spontaneously praises child's qualities or behavior twice during visit.
9. When speaking of or to child, mother's voice conveys positive feeling.
10. Mother caresses or kisses child at least once during visit.
11. Mother shows some positive emotional responses to praise of child offered by visitor.

Subscore ☐ ☐

*Items that may require direct questions.

Source: Powell, M. L. *Assessment and management of developmental changes and problems in children.* St. Louis: C. V. Mosby. From Caldwell, Bettye M.: Home Observation for Measurement of the Environment (birth to three), 1970. Used with permission.

investigation of the effects of educational and residential environments on cognitive and social development of children in various special-education programs (Nihira, Meyers, & Mink, 1983; Nihira, Mink, & Meyers, 1981). The first study examined the nature and degree of the relationship between home environment and the school adjustment of trainable mentally retarded students. The age range of the students was nine to sixteen years. Specific factors of the home environment that were significantly related to the personal and social adjustment of TMR children in school were the harmony and quality of parenting, the degree of available educational and cognitive stimulation, and emotional support and parental approval for learning. These factors were found to be more important than social climate, family values or orientation, and such traditional indices of family background as the mother's education, socioeconomic status, or number of children in the home (Nihira, Mink, & Meyers, 1981). The authors concluded that the preschool version of the HOME Inventory was appropriate for assessing aspects of home environment relevant to school adjustment of older TMR children.

In the second study, Nihira, Meyers, and Mink (1983) examined the reciprocal relationship between the home environment and social competency of TMR adolescents. Assessment of home environment included child-rearing attitudes, educationally relevant stimuli and opportunities available at home, and general psychosocial climate among family members. Measures of social competency included the student's adaptive behavior, psychosocial adjustment, and self-concept. The environmental effects on the adolescents appeared to have broad influence over a wide range of adjustment behavior of adolescents, including self-direction, socialization, antisocial and violent behavior, and self-abusive, autistic behavior. In contrast, the student's effect on the home environment appeared to have more direct and specific consequences. The adjustments of TMR adolescents seemed to influence social and emotional aspects of parenting behavior; showing pride, affection, and warmth toward the child; and encouraging social maturity. The HOME Inventory was used effectively in establishing a general trend of child-environment relationship in the study of mentally retarded children and young people.

The Family Environment Scale In conformity with previously cited research, Fowler (1980) views the relationship between the family's structure and the child's behavior as an interactive system of reciprocal influences. In such an interactive system, the effect of the child's behavior on other people is conceived to have as important an influence on the system's dynamics as the actions of others on the child.

The exact nature of the interdependency between the family social system and individual child functioning has not been adequately determined. One problem has been a lack of reliable instruments to assess family systems (Forman & Forman, 1981).

The Family Environment Scale (FES) uses the concept of *perceived environment,* in which the climate of a setting is defined by the shared perceptions of members of the setting along a number of environmental dimensions (Forman & Forman, 1981). Comprised of ten subscales that measure the social-environmental characteristics of all types of families, the FES assesses three sets of dimensions: the Relationship dimensions, the Personal Growth dimensions, and the System Maintenance dimensions (see Figure 8.8).

The FES can be used to describe or compare the social environments of families, to compare parent and child perceptions, to compare perceptions of mothers and families, to compare actual and preferred family milieus, and to assess and facilitate change in family environments (Moos & Moos, 1981). Through preliminary research, the authors found that previous conceptualizations of family environments were oversimplified, using descriptors of only two parental attitudes: acceptance versus rejection and high versus low control. The resultant typology helps researchers understand how different family environments are linked to different family outcomes (Moos & Moos, 1976).

A shortened version of the FES was used in an attempt to measure family structure directly and to view it in terms of the child's early behavioral

FIGURE 8.8 FES Subscales and Dimension Descriptions

	Relationship Dimensions
1. Cohension	The degree of commitment, help, and support members provide for one another
2. Expressiveness	The extent to which family members are encouraged to act openly and to express their feelings directly
3. Conflict	The amount of openly expressed anger, aggression, and conflict among family members
	Personal Growth Dimensions
4. Independence	The extent to which family members are assertive, are self-sufficient, and make their own decisions
5. Achievement orientation	The extent to which activities (such as school and work) are cast into an achievement-oriented or competitive framework
6. Intellectual-cultural orientation	The degree of interest in political, social, intellectual, and cultural activities
7. Active-recreational orientation	The extent of participation in social and recreational activities
8. Moral-religious emphasis	The degree of emphasis on ethical and religious issues and values
	System Maintenance Dimensions
9. Organization	The degree of importance of clear organization and structure in planning family activities and responsibilities
10. Control	The extent to which set rules and procedures are used to run family life

Source: Moos, R. H. & Moos, B. S. (1981). *Family environment scale manual.* Palo Alto, Calif.: Consulting Psychologists Press, p. 2.

characteristics (Fowler, 1980). Although stable relationships between early structures of behavior and later family environmental structure were found, the order of the relationship was not reflected. Forman and Forman (1981) used the FES to investigate the relationship between family characteristics, conceptualized in terms of a social systems framework, and adolescent personality functioning. The conclusions were that significant variance in child behavior can be attributed to family social system functioning and that child behavior varies with total system functioning more than with separate system factors.

The FES has been used successfully in investigating the relationship between environmental factors and exceptional children. In a study of families of learning disabled children, the FES was used to construct a group profile to identify characteristics of such families and to construct individual profiles to help understand the dynamics of the individual family with a learning-disabled child (Zevon, Fox, & Nash, 1981).

The FES has also been useful in examining the family environments of gifted and creative children. Findings in one study indicated that parents who perceived the family as low in organization were more likely to have children who are creative; in climates that emphasized intellectual and deemphasized religious activities, parents of creative children were less likely to exert a high degree of control on their children; and parents who differed in their perceptions of the characteristics of the family, particularly on control, achievement, and independence, were more likely to have verbally creative children than those who did not differ (Brown, 1979).

An understanding of the family environment and of the interactive variables within the family has strong implications for parent education and involvement. Families who need supportive interventions can be identified and helped before the family is adversely affected by the presence of an exceptional child. In addition, family structure and practices can be altered to foster the child's maximum development.

Techniques discussed in the preceding sections are based on external assessment of parents' training needs as determined by program planners. Table 8.2 presents a compilation of appropriate instruments.

Assessment Techniques and Models

Although most parent education programs have been based on topics selected by the person or group planning the program, the current trend is toward involving the parents more closely in developing the topics. In fact, Dembo, Sweitzer, and Lauritzen (1985) have suggested that because of the great variability in parent characteristics and the problems they report with child-rearing, individually tailored programs may be more effective in producing desired results for a wider range of parents. Techniques used for arriving at parents' interests and concerns may be directed or open-ended.

TABLE 8.2 Parent Assessment Instruments

Author	Title	Date	Description	Source
**Ahr, A. E., & Simons, B.	Parent Readiness Evaluation of Preschoolers (PREP)	1968–69	Designed for use by non-professionals in assessing whether their children are average in readiness. Involves parents in early identification of learning disabilities.	Priority Innovations, Inc.
**Bienvenu, M. J.	Parent-Adolescent Communication Inventory (PACI)	1968–69	Designed to help counselors, educators, and researchers assess parent-teen relations for purposes of individual counseling. Organizes information about the familial communication situation.	Family Life Publications
Caldwell, B. M.	Home Observation for Measurement of the Environment (HOME)	1970	Measure for preschoolers: one version to be used when children are less than three years old; the other for children between three and six. The major function is to identify homes likely to impede or to foster cognitive development.	Caldwell, B. M. *Home Observation for Measurement of the Environment.* Little Rock: University of Arkansas at Little Rock, Center for Child Development and Education.
Cone, J. D.	Parent/Family Involvement Index (PFII)	1985	Objective, 63-item measure of 12 types of parent participation in their child's education program.	Morgantown, W. Va.: Department of Psychology, West Virginia University.
*Cromwell, R. L.	Parental Practices Inventory	1966	Parents describe actual practices they have used in a specific situation. In each of 11 behavioral situations, parents select the best way to handle it.	Cromwell, R. L. (1966) Parent Practice Inventory. Unpublished paper, Vanderbilt University Hospital.
*Drews, E. M., & Teahan, J. E.	Parental Attitude Scale	1957	Thirty items containing an equal number of items assigned to 3 subscales: a dominating scale, a possessive scale, and an ignoring scale.	Drews, E. M., & Teahan, J. E. (1957). Parental attitudes and academic achievement. *Journal of Clinical Psychology, 13,* 328–332.
*Farber, B., & Jenne, W. C.	Scale of Parental Dissatisfaction with Instrumental Behavior	1963	Scale measures parents' estimate of the extent to which the child has behaved to the degree expected by them, and the child's estimate regarding the degree to which the parental expectations have been abided by.	Farber, B., & Jenne, W. C. (1963). Family organization and parent-child communications. *Monographs of the Society for Research in Child Development, 28,* (7).
*Emmerich, W.	Parental Nurturance-Control Attitude Scale	1959	Projective questionnaire consisting of 8 hypothetical situations in which parents are asked how they would deal with their child.	Emmerich, W. (1959). Parental identification in young children. *Genetic Psychology Monographs, 60,* 257–308.

TABLE 8.2 Parent Assessment Instruments (continued)

Author	Title	Date	Description	Source
*Oppenheim, A. N.	Parent Attitude Inventory	1964	Consists of 52 items covering attitudes areas of overprotection (dominant), overprotection (submissive), democracy, autocracy, acceptance, rejection, strict infant training, strictness concerning habits and manners, strictness about sex play, and objectivity.	London, W. C.: London School of Economics, Houghton Street.
*Larson, L.	Questionnaire for Parents of Pre-school Handicapped Children	1954	Ninety-five-item questionnaire with items grouped into 5 classes: socialization, recognition, outside experiences, knowledge, and experience.	Larson, L. (1954). Preschool experiences of physically handicapped children—ages three through six. Unpublished doctoral dissertation, State University of Iowa.
Moos, R. H., & Moos, B. S.	Family Environment Scale	1981	Ten subscales that measure the social-environmental characteristics of all types of families. The subscales assess 3 sets of dimensions: the relationship dimensions, the personal growth dimensions, and the system maintenance dimensions.	Palo Alto, Calif.: Consulting Psychologists Press.
***(n.a.)	***Parent Opinion Inventory (POI)	1976	Parents of school children; attitudes toward elementary and secondary school program.	National Study of School Evaluation
*Porter, B. R.	Porter Parental Acceptance Scale	1954	Forty-five option multiple-choice items designed to measure parental acceptance. Four dimensions of acceptance are involved: parents who respect the feelings of the child, value the child's uniqueness, recognizes and encourages the child's autonomy, and love the child unconditionally.	Provo, Utah: Brigham Young University, 1206 Smith Family Living Center.
*Schaefer, E. S., & Bell, R. Q.	Parental Attitude Research Instrument (PARI)	1958	Twenty-three subscales to evaluate the attitudes of parents toward child rearing. Each subscale is measured by 5 items, yielding a total number of 115 items. Has been found to provide measures of 2 main factors: hostility-rejection and authoritarian-control.	Schaefer, E. S., & Bell, R. Q. (1957). Development of a parental attitude research instrument. Child Development, 29, 339–361.

(continued)

TABLE 8.2 Parent Assessment Instruments (continued)

Author	Title	Date	Description	Source
*Sears, R. R., Maccoby, E. E., & Levin, H.	Parent Interview Schedule	1957	Scales measuring 5 aspects of maternal behavior: disciplinary technique, permissiveness, severity, temperamental qualities (of mother), and positive inculcation (by mother) of more mature behavior (in child).	Evanston, Ill.: Row Peterson.
*Sears, R. R.	Structured Parental Acceptance Scale	1964	A standard set of open-ended questions for the purpose of obtaining parental perceptions regarding some of their child's in-home behavior. Covers attitudes relating to self-care activities and management of the child as applied to a wide range of behaviors.	Sears, R. R., Rau, L., & Albert, R. (1965). *Identification and child rearing*. Stanford, Calif.: Stanford University Press.
Strom, R. D.	Parent as a Teacher (PAAT)	1984	Composite attitude scale revealing how individuals feel about certain aspects of the parent-child interactive system, their standards for assessing the importance of various child behaviors, and their value preferences concerning child behavior.	Bensenville, Ill.: Scholastic Testing Service, Inc.
*Torgoff, I.	Parental Development Timetable	1961	Consists of 48 items, 24 designed to measure along the achievement-inducing dimension and 24 along the independence grating dimension. Respondents give an age at which they think boys and girls should be induced or allowed to undertake a particular activity.	Rochester, Minn.: Oakland University.

*Johnson, O. G., & Bommarito, J. W. (1971). *Tests and measurements in child development; Handbook I*. San Francisco, Calif.: Jossey-Bass.
**Buros, O. K. (Ed.) (1972). *The seventh mental measurements yearbook* Vol. II. Highland Park, N.J.: The Gryphon Press.
***Buros, O. K. (Ed.) (1978). *The eighth mental measurements yearbook* Vol. I. Highland Park, N. J.: The Graphon Press.

Directed Assessment

☐ Appropriate planning for parent education programs should be based on continuous needs assessments. Berger (1981, p. 135) suggests a technique that is sequential and thorough:

1. Conduct a brainstorming session with leaders and members at large. Make certain that the group is representative of the community.
2. Make a list of programs that represent the indicated interests and needs of those in the brainstorming session.
3. Give the list of programs to a trial group. Have them add new ideas and concerns.
4. Construct a needs assessment tool (assessment of needs) for wide distribution.
5. Disseminate the needs assessment questionnaire to adults throughout the school or center community.
6. Choose from the questionnaire those items that received the most requests.
7. Develop a program to meet the needs of the community.

☐ *Because of the unique needs and concerns of each parent, an individually tailored parent education program may be more effective than one general program.*

In the brainstorming session, different ethnic and socioeconomic groups should be represented. To facilitate the session, lists of problem areas recognized by parents previously surveyed can be distributed.

In a nationwide survey, parents were given a list of sixteen parent education topics and asked to identify the topics that most nearly met their needs. The suggested topics were then reported in rank order according to frequency of identification by parents whose oldest child was twelve years of age or younger and parents with children between thirteen and twenty years of age (Gallup, 1977). As an example of the choices made, the following list was compiled from rank-ordered selections of parents whose oldest child was twelve years or younger:

1. What to do about drugs, smoking, and use of alcohol
2. How to help the child set high achievement goals
3. How to develop good work habits
4. How to improve the child's school behavior
5. How to improve the child's thinking and observation abilities
6. How to deal with the child's emotional problems
7. How to increase interest in school and school subjects
8. How to help the child organize his/her homework
9. How to improve parent/child relationships
10. How to use family activities to help the child do better in school
11. How to encourage reading
12. How to help the child get along with other children
13. How to reduce television viewing
14. How to deal with dating problems
15. How to improve health habits. (Gallup, 1977, p. 42)

Parents whose oldest child was thirteen to twenty years old ranked topics as follows:

1. What to do about drugs, smoking, use of alcohol
2. How to help the child choose a career
3. How to help the child set high achievement goals
4. How to develop good work habits
5. How to encourage reading
6. How to increase interest in school and school subjects
7. How to help the child organize his/her homework
8. How to improve parent/child relationships
9. How to improve the child's thinking and observation abilities
10. How to deal with the child's emotional problems
11. How to use family activities to help the child do better in school
12. How to improve the child's school behavior
13. How to reduce television viewing
14. How to help the child get along with other children
15. How to improve health habits
16. How to deal with dating problems. (Gallup, 1977, p. 42)

Parents chose essentially the same concerns for children at both age levels but expressed greater concern for career plans and encouragement of reading for older children.

The Appalachian Educational Laboratory developed a comprehensive needs assessment to determine a parent-education course for television. Parents of children in twenty-six schools in ten states identified six factors: (1) family care, (2) child growth and development, (3) child management, (4) parent-self, (5) treating your child like a person, and (6) baby care (Coan & Gotts, 1975). As an example of a directed assessment instrument, Figure 8.9 presents the Appalachian Educational Laboratory model. Berger (1981) recommends this particular format as a guide to constructing an instrument for local usage.

A parent handbook entitled *Helping Parents Grow* (Bell, 1981) contains a format for self-evaluation. Activities for parents include:

> List the things you believe a "good father" and a "good mother" do.
> What kind of model are you? Make a check if you usually
> Say please and thank you.
> Try new things.
> Express anger or frustration in positive ways.
> Talk about the good you see in others.
> Share feelings and thoughts.
> Eat well and exercise.
> Show affection.
> Encourage even small successes.
> Say "I was wrong" when you were.
> Have a sense of humor. (Bell, 1981, pp. 50–54)

Following the evaluation, activities are suggested to help mothers and fathers become better parents.

Open-ended Assessment

☐ Although directed assessment produces data that are convenient to analyze and use, the structured classification of responses also guarantees that some parental concerns will not be allowed to surface (Strom, 1985).

Open-ended questionnaires can provide specific, detailed information about parental needs and interests. Figure 8.10 (see p. 253) lists sample open-ended questions.

Strom (1985) claims that if parents serve as the only source of perception about their competence, some deficiencies are likely to be overlooked. He suggests the inclusion of teachers who observe the behavior of many children and can detect problems that the parents may overlook. The children's feelings about family interaction should be respected. Strom also suggests consulting publications of experts on various stages of human development in determining the content of a program. He summarizes:

FIGURE 8.9 Learning to Be a Better Parent

Name: _____
My city and state: _____
My children's ages (in years): _____
Name of nearest grade school: _____

What to do: First, read what it says below about each thing you might learn more about. Then decide how much you feel you need or want to learn about that. For example, if you feel you already know all or just about as much as you need to know about "How Children Grow and Develop," then mark the box *Nothing more at all*. However, if you feel you need or want to learn *more* about that, then you may wish to answer *A little more* or *A lot more*. Put a check mark (√) in the box under *A lot more*, *A little more*, or *Nothing more at all* for each question. We are interested in what you feel. You may, of course, feel that you need or want to learn more about some things, and nothing more about others. No one will judge you as a parent, whatever your answers are. If you do not want to answer a question, then leave it blank.

	A Lot More	A Little More	Nothing More at All
A. How children grow and develop			
How much do you feel you need or want to learn more about:			
1. Where you can find out about how children develop.	☐	☐	☐
2. What your child should be able to learn at his age, so as not to "push" your child too much.	☐	☐	☐
3. How children grow into special, one-of-a-kind people.	☐	☐	☐
4. How the world looks and sounds to your child, and how to help him learn about it.	☐	☐	☐
5. How your child's personality is formed.	☐	☐	☐
6. How your child learns to use his body by playing (runs, jumps).	☐	☐	☐
B. Taking better care of your baby			
How much do you feel you need or want to learn more about:			
1. What happens before the baby comes (what to eat; what drugs not to take; how long to wait before having another baby; things that can happen to the baby).	☐	☐	☐
2. How babies learn to talk (what the baby hears; what it learns from what you do and say).	☐	☐	☐
3. Helping the baby feel good (not too warm or cool; enough to eat; food that might upset the baby; giving the baby room to move around).	☐	☐	☐
C. Treating your child like a person			
How much do you feel you need or want to learn more about how to:			
1. Tell what children are doing by watching them.	☐	☐	☐
2. Help your child see and accept his or her own feelings.	☐	☐	☐
3. Show love and care to your child.	☐	☐	☐
4. Talk with your child about his problems and answer his questions.	☐	☐	☐
5. Help your child to behave when he starts to fight.	☐	☐	☐
6. Help your child learn to get along with family and friends.	☐	☐	☐
7. Help your child see why rules are good.	☐	☐	☐

	A Lot More	A Little More	Nothing More at All

D. Taking care of your family
How much do you feel you need or want to learn more about how to:
   1. Pick things for the child's bed and for him to wear (so that they last and are easy to take care of).
   2. Find and take care of a home for your family (how to shop and pay for housing and furniture)
   3. Pick the right foods and take care of them so they will not spoil (fix meals that are good for your family's health).

E. Teaching and training your child
How much do you feel you need or want to learn more about:
   1. What ways of teaching will work best with your child (the way you teach; use of books, TV).
   2. How to control your child by using reward, praise, and correction in a loving way (how to help your child control himself).
   3. How to teach your child to be neat and clean and to show good manners.
   4. How to get your child to go to bed on time (and to rest or take naps).
   5. How to get your child to change from doing one thing to doing something else.
   6. How to plan your child's use of TV (picking TV programs, not watching too much TV).
   7. How to place your chairs, tables, and other things so that your child will have room to play and learn (and keeping some things out of sight so your child will not want them).
   8. How to feed your child; teach him to feed himself; and making eating fun for your child.
   9. How to teach your child to dress and undress.
   10. How to help your child think for himself (choose what he wants to do; make plans).
   11. How to teach your child to tell right from wrong (to be moral).

F. Keeping your family safe and well
How much do you feel you need or want to learn more about:
   1. How to keep your child from getting hurt (and how to give first aid).
   2. How to keep your child well (get shots and have the doctor check your child).
   3. How to know if something is wrong with your child (is not learning; cannot walk well; cannot see or hear well).
   4. How to know when your child is sick (has a fever or says he hurts some place).
   5. How to pick things that are safe to play with.
   6. How to tell if your child is growing right (body size, height, weight).

(continued)

FIGURE 8.9 Learning to Be a Better Parent (continued)

	A Lot More	A Little More	Nothing More at All
G. Taking care of things at home How much do you feel you need or want to learn more about:			
1. Making good use of your time (plan your time for child care, house work, school or job, time for yourself and your friends.)	☐	☐	☐
2. Getting good help with child care (day care, baby sitter, nursery school).	☐	☐	☐
3. How your child deals with the way that your family lives (people in the home, what they do together, how they get along).	☐	☐	☐
4. Finding help for people who don't take care of their children, or who hurt their children.	☐	☐	☐
H. Yourself as a parent How much do you feel you need or want to learn more about:			
1. Your own feelings and habits and how these help or hurt your child care (how they affect your child care).	☐	☐	☐
2. Your need to make your child mind you (how your own needs can affect how your child feels about himself, and your child's learning).	☐	☐	☐
3. Why your child will not mind you and how this bothers you (how to get over being upset).	☐	☐	☐
4. How to be sure that you are doing what is best for your child (or your worries about what other people think).	☐	☐	☐

What to do: Just as before, read what it says about each thing from which you can learn. That is, if you think you would enjoy learning about being a better parent from "reading books," then you may wish to answer *A lot* or *A little*. But if you would *not* enjoy learning from "reading books," then mark the box *Not at all*. You may, of course, think that you would like to learn from some things and not from others. Put a check mark (√) in the box under *A lot, A little* or *Not at all* for each question.

	A Lot	A Little	Not at All
I. How to learn about being a better parent How much would you like to learn about being a better parent from:			
1. Reading books.	☐	☐	☐
2. Talking with parents in group meetings.	☐	☐	☐
3. Watching a special TV series.	☐	☐	☐
4. Seeing movies near my home (at a school).	☐	☐	☐
5. Having a person visit my home and talk with me each week.	☐	☐	☐
6. Seeing slides and hearing a person tell about them.	☐	☐	☐
7. Reading about this in magazines or in small newspapers (4 to 8 pages long).	☐	☐	☐
8. Hearing a special radio series.	☐	☐	☐
9. Listening to records or tapes.	☐	☐	☐
10. Playing games that teach me to be a better parent.	☐	☐	☐

	A Lot	A Little	Not at All

I. How to learn about being a better parent
On TV or radio or in the movies, how much would you like to learn from:
1. A funny show (humor, comedy, jokes). ☐ ☐ ☐
2. A talk show with well-know guests and parents. ☐ ☐ ☐
3. Stores about real people (not humor). ☐ ☐ ☐
4. Special stories done by actors (not humor). ☐ ☐ ☐
5. An M.D. (doctor) or other expert. ☐ ☐ ☐
6. A show that goes into real people's homes. ☐ ☐ ☐

Other ideas
What else do you think you need or want to learn more about in order to be a better parent? Print so that your ideas will be easy to read.

_____
_____
_____

Source: Coan, D. L., & Gotts, E. E. (1976). *Parent education needs: A national assessment study.* Charleston, W. Va.: Appalachia Educational Laboratory, Inc., pp. 75–84. (Eric Document #ED 132–972.) Used with permission.

FIGURE 8.10   Open-Ended Questionnaire

1. The best family time for my child is when we _____
2. I will never forget the time that my child and I _____
3. When I take my child to the store, I am concerned that he/she will _____
4. Other people wonder about how my child will _____
5. I wish people knew the good times my child and I have when we _____
6. I would be embarrassed if people knew how difficult it was to _____ with my child.
7. People think my child is unable to _____ . They would be surprised to know that _____
8. I'm worrying about making a decision about my child's _____
9. Sometimes I think my child will never _____
10. My child is especially difficult around the house when he/she _____
11. My husband (or wife) gets especially upset when our child _____
12. I give my child a hug when he/she _____
13. It is especially difficult around the house when my child _____
14. My child wants _____ and sometimes I just don't have the energy.
15. It is sometimes difficult for our other children to _____ for the child with special needs.
16. The hard thing about having a special child is _____
17. I am so glad that my child likes to _____
18. I wish I knew more about _____

Source: Heward, W. L., Dardig, J.C., & Rossett, A. *Working with parents of handicapped children.* Columbus, Oh.: Charles E. Merrill, p. 240.

> When the separate views of parents, teachers, children and experts are combined, the resulting perspective can be used to identify parental needs and strengths at all levels of child development. (Strom, 1985, p. 162)

Within this philosophy, an open-ended survey with parallel items for parents, teachers, children, and adolescents was developed. The instrument contains an assessment of parent potential and parent concern. Questionnaire items reflecting these areas are:

1. What are some things about being a parent that you find very satisfying at this stage of your child's life?
2. Of all the many things you have to do as a parent, which do you think you do especially well?
3. What do you think you as a parent should be helping your child learn at home?
4. Thinking about your own child, what are some things about childrearing that you find most difficult at this time?
5. What are some things your child does that frustrate you the most?
6. As you observe your child, what problems do you see the youngster having that you could use more information about? (Strom, 1985, pp. 162–163)

The use of open-ended assessment techniques allows more individual in-put from parents, leading to a more individualized program. It also permits the evaluator of the instrument to determine strengths as well as needs of particular parents, therefore offering indications of potential trainers within the program.

The assessment model and appropriate techniques develop as program planners examine the makeup of the groups for whom they are planning. If the program is to meet the needs and tap the strengths of its participants, accurate and appropriate assessment is essential.

Conclusion

In the past, programs for parents of exceptional children and young people have been based on curriculum content chosen for parents by other people. With the growing awareness of the need for parent education, there is also a growing exigency to make parent education more relevant. If programs are going to address parents' needs, careful assessment must be the first step in planning.

The choice of assessment techniques, as well as the choice of program, should be based on a thorough knowledge of the parents and students to be served. Parents of exceptional children are individuals who respond to school personnel and programs in different ways. In assessing their needs and strengths, educators should consider such factors as the age and exceptionality of the child, demographic data about the family, and interaction within the family.

A number of assessment instruments are available to educators. However, a thorough plan of assessment should be instituted and followed throughout the program. Parents' needs are not static; the assessment should reflect individual and family changes. Adequate needs assessment can help educators plan more appropriate programs, which, in turn, will facilitate parents' involvement and success with their children.

References

Affleck, G., Allen, D., McGrade, B. J., & McQueeney, M. (1982). Home environments of developmentally disabled infants as a function of parent and infant characteristics. *American Journal of Mental Deficiency, 86*(5), 445–452.

Albert, R. S. (1980). Exceptionally gifted boys and their parents. *Gifted Child Quarterly, 24*(4), 174–179.

Anthony, M. (1981). Parents of gifted and talented children. *G/C/T, 16*(1), 39.

Apolloni, T. (1984). Self-advocacy: How to be a winner. Washington, D.C. National Information Center for Handicapped Children and Youth.

Barbe, W. B. (1956). A study of the family background of the gifted. *Journal of Educational Psychology, 47*(5), 302–309.

Bell, C. (1981). *Helping parents grow.* Machias, Me.: Washington County Children's Program Outreach Project.

Berger, E. H. (1981). *Parents as partners in education.* St. Louis: C. V. Mosby.

Blackham, G. J., & Silberman, A. (1975). *Modification of child and adolescent behavior* (2nd ed.). Belmont, Calif.: Wadswordth Publishing Co.

Bradley, R. H., Caldwell, B. M., & Elardo, R. (1979). Home environment and cognitive development in the first 2 years: A cross-lagged panel analysis. *Developmental Psychology, 15*(3), 246–250.

Brown, F. F. (1979) The relationship between gifted children's creative thinking abilities and their parents' perceptions of the family environment. *Exceptional Child Resources, 12*(3), 677.

Buros, O. K. (Ed.). (1972). *The seventh mental measurements yearbook.* Vol. II. Highland Park, N.J.: The Gryphon Press.

Buros, O. K. (Ed.). (1978). *The eighth mental measurements yearbook.* Vol. I. Highland Park, N.J.: The Gryphon Press.

Coan, D. L., & Gotts, E. E. (1975). *Parent education needs: A national assessment study.* Charleston, W. Va.: Appalachia Educational Laboratory, P.O. Box 1348.

Coffey, K., Ginsberg, G., Lockhart, C., McCartney, D., Nathan, C., & Wood, K. (1976). *Parentspeak.* Ventura, Calif.: Ventura County Superintendent of Schools Office.

Cone, J. D., Delawyer, D. D., & Wolfe, V. V. (1985). Assessing parent participation: The parent/family involvement index. *Exceptional Children, 51*(5), 417–424.

Delisle, J., & Licence, C. (1980). Questions parents ask. *G/C/T, 15*(3), 36–38.

Dembo, M. H., Sweitzer, M., & Lauritzen, P. (1985). An evaluation of group parent education: Behavioral, PET, and Adlerian programs. *Review of Educational Research, 55*(2), 155–200.

Eheart, B. K., & Ciccone, J. (1982). Special needs of low-income mothers of developmentally delayed children. *American Journal of Mental Deficiency, 87*(1), 26–33.

Elardo, R., Bradley, R., & Caldwell, B. M. (1975). The relation of infants' home environments to mental test performance from six to thirty-six months; A longitudinal analysis. *Child Development, 46*(1), 71–76.

Fine, M. J. (1977). Facilitating parent-child relationships for creativity. *Gifted Child Quarterly, XXI*(4), 487–500.

Forman, S. G., & Forman, B. D. (1981) Family environment and its relation to adolescent personality factors. *Journal of Personality Assessment, 45*(2), 163–167.

Foster, M., Berger, M., & McLean, M. (1981). Rethinking a good idea: A reassessment of parent involvement. *Topics in Early Childhood Special Education, 1*(3), 55–66.

Fowler, P. C. (1980). Family environment and early behavioral development: A structural analysis of dependencies. *Psychological Reports, 47*(2), 611–617.

Freund, J. H., Bradley, R. H., & Caldwell, B. M. (1979). The home environment in the assessment of learning disabilities. *Learning Disability Quarterly, 2*(4), 39–51.

Gallagher, J. J. (1985). *Teaching the gifted child* (3rd ed.). Boston: Allyn and Bacon.

Gallup, G. H. (1977). The ninth annual Gallup Poll of the public's attitudes toward the public schools. *Phi Delta Kappan (Sept.), 33–48.*

Haffey, N. A., & Levant, R. F. (1984). The differential effectiveness of two models of skills training for working class parents. *Family Relations, 33,* 209–216.

Harman, D., & Brim, O. G. (1980). *Learning to be parents.* Beverly Hills, Calif.: Sage.

Heron, T. E., & Harris, K. C. (1982). *The educational consultant.* Boston: Allyn and Bacon.

Heward, W. L., Dardig, J. C., & Rossett, A. (1979). *Working with parents of handicapped children.* Columbus, Oh.: Charles E. Merrill.

Heward, W. L., & Orlansky, M. D. (1984). *Exceptional children* (2nd ed.). Columbus, Oh.: Charles E. Merrill.

Johnson, O. G., & Bommarito, J. W. (1971). *Tests and measurements in child development: Handbook I.* San Francisco: Jossey-Bass.

Kershman, S. M. (1982). The training needs of parents of deaf-blind multihandicapped children. *Education of the Visually Handicapped, XIV*(1), 5–14.

Knapp, D. (1979). *Parent education packet: Parents' and children's rights.* Frankfort: Central Kentucky Child Service Demonstration Center, Bureau of Education for Exceptional Children, Kentucky Department of Education.

Kroth, R. L. (1980). The mirror model of parental involvement. *Pointer, 25*(1), 18–22.

Kroth, R., & Otteni, H. (1983). Parent education programs that work: A model. *Focus on Exceptional Children, 15*(8), 1–16.

Lockhart, C. (1976). In K. Coffey, G. Ginsberg, C. Lockhart, D. McCartney, C. Nathan, & K. Wood, *Parentspeak.* Ventura, Calif.: Ventura County Superintendent of Schools Office.

Malone, C. E. (1975). Education for parents of the gifted. *The Gifted Child Quarterly, 19*(3), 223–225.

Marion, R. L. (1981). *Educators, parents, and exceptional children.* Rockville, Md.: Aspen Systems.

Moos, R. H., & Moos, B. S. (1981). *Family environment scale manual.* Palo Alto, Calif.: Consulting Psychologists Press.

Moos, R. H. & Moos, B. S. (1976). A typology of family social environments. *Family Process, 15,* 357–372.

Neely, M. A. (1982). *Counseling and guidance practices with special education students.* Homewood, Ill.: The Dorsey Press.

Nihira, K., Meyers, C. E., & Mink, I. T. (1983). Reciprocal relationship between home environment and development of TMR adolescents. *American Journal of Mental Deficiency, 88*(2), 139–149.

Nihira, K., Mink, I. T., & Meyers, C. E. (1981). Relationship between home environment and school adjustment of TMR children. *American Journal of Mental Deficiency, 86*(1), 8–15.

Opirhory, G., & Peters, G. A. (1982). Counseling intervention strategies for families with the less than perfect newborn. *The Personnel and Guidance Journal, 60*(8), 451–455.

Powell, M. L. (1981). *Assessment and management of developmental changes and problems in children.* St. Louis: C. V. Mosby.

Rodriguez, R. F. (1981). The involvement of minority group parents in school. *Teacher Education and Special Education, 4*(4), 40–44.

Rosenberg, S. A., & Robinson, C. C. (1985). Enhancement of mothers' interactional skills. *Education and Training of the Mentally Retarded, 20*(2), 163–169.

Strom, R. D. (1985). Developing a curriculum for parent education. *Family Relations, 34*(2), 161–167.

Strom, R. D. (1984). *Parent as a teacher inventory manual.* Bensenville, Ill.: Scholastic Testing Service.

Strom, R., Griswold, D., & Slaughter, H. (1981). Parental background: Does it matter in parent education? *Child Study Journal, 10*(4), 243–260.

Strom, R. D., Rees, R., Slaughter, H., & Wurster, S. (1981). Childrearing expectations of families with atypical children. *American Journal of Orthopsychiatry, 51*(2), 285–296.

Strom, R. D., Rees, R., Slaughter, H., & Wurster, S. (1980). Role expectations of parents of intellectually handicapped children. *Exceptional Children, 47*(2), 144–147.

Strom, R., & Slaughter, H. (1978). Measurement of childrearing expectations using the parent as a teacher inventory. *Journal of Experimental Education, 46*(4), 44–53.

Strom, R. D., Rees, R., & Wurster, S. (1983). Parents as teachers of their exceptional children. *Journal of Instructional Psychology, 10*(2), 139–145.

Sullivan, O. R. (1981). Meeting the needs of low income families with handicapped children. *Journal of the International Association of Pupil Personnel Workers, 25*(1), 26–31.

Turnbull, A. P., Strickland, B., & Goldstein, S. (1978). Training professionals and parents in developing and implementing the IEP. *Education and Training of the Mentally Retarded, 13*(16), 414–423.

Utah State University. (no date). You and one four two! Logan, Utah: Outreach and Development Division, The Exceptional Child Center.

Walker, J. E., & Shea, T. M. (1984). *Behavior management* (3rd ed.). St. Louis: Times Mirror/Mosby.

Weitz, S. E. (1981). A code for assessing teaching skills of parents of developmentally disabled children. *Journal of Autism and Developmental Disorders, 12*(1), 13–24.

University of Delaware (1983). *Research Report.* Newark, Del.: College of Education.

Zevon, M., Fox, R., & Nash, L. (1981). The family environment of the learning disabled child: An objective description. Paper presented at the Annual International Convention of the Council on Exceptional Children, New York, N.Y., April.

9

Parent Education Programs

Parent education programs are the culmination of parent-professional interaction; they are the realization of joint concern for the optimal development of the student. In no other relationship is the parent-professional partnership more evident than in planning and implementing programs designed to meet the needs of parents as well as their children. Professional people are also served in such program development, as they frequently gain support and encouragement as a result of the alliance.

The concept of parent education is not new. The Child Study Association, since its establishment in 1888, has been concerned specifically with parent education (Berger, 1981). Organized parent education began early in the twentieth century to deal with adjustment problems experienced by immigrant families and their children. These programs were followed by neighborhood parent discussion groups and the publication of books, such as that written by Dr. Benjamin Spock, designed to help parents in the proper training of their children (Fine, 1980). Systematic approaches to parent education have grown rapidly during the last two decades.

What has prompted the rapid growth of parent education programs? What are the purposes of such programs? Are they effective? These questions have been asked by many educators and parents as they react to mandated programs. Before investigating specific programs and their effectiveness, it is necessary to understand the rationale for parent education programs in general.

Rationale for Parent Education

☐ ☐ The main emphasis on parent education has been, in part, a result of the changing American family. Working mothers, single-parent families, and fewer extended family members create situations in which parents are insecure in their roles and uncertain about appropriate techniques of parenting.

The recent emphasis on early child development and its importance has also led to a concern for stimulating home environments and capable parents. One approach implies that the school cannot change the child whose home environment has been less than adequate:

> It seems essential to the healthy psychological development of children that their first few years of life be rich in opportunity for consistent and progressively complex interaction with others (usually family members) with whom they have formed deep emotional bonds. If such interaction is interrupted or otherwise interfered with, the child's chances for healthy growth are hindered. Also, there is little hope that the absence of such interaction at early stages of a child's development can be made up by remedial work in an institutional setting. (Bessent & Webb, 1976, p. 99)

Efforts to overcome environmental deficits have been attempted, however, through such compensatory programs as Head Start. Other federally sponsored programs, such as Title I and Right to Read, mandated the participation of parents on advisory councils and in tutoring activities. Many of these programs were designed to incorporate minorities and other target populations into the mainstream by improving perceived educational weaknesses of the parents and the home environment. Based on evidence that the children's achievement is greatly influenced by learning experiences provided in the home, the compensatory education programs sought to improve children's achievement by teaching the parents to improve the home environment.

The rationale for educating parents of young children is based on the premise that the typical context for learning generally occurs in the home through interaction with family members (Rosenberg, Robinson, & Beckman, 1984). It is assumed, then, that greater benefits of intervention will come from programs that actively involve parents in program implementation.

Inherent in the philosophy of parent education is the belief that parents are and should be teachers of their children. Westin (1981, p. 140) strongly states this belief:

> Parents are their children's first and most natural teachers. Every professional teacher I talked with assured me that it is impossible to teach children without the support of the children's parents.

Parent support is essential for all children. For optimal development, it is particularly important for exceptional children. For children who are handicapped, stimulating environments can facilitate the early acquisition of language and other developmental milestones. For gifted children, early recognition and encouragement can make the difference between full and partial development of the childrens' abilities. In both cases, parents frequently need support in dealing with their own feelings as well as in teaching their children. Because the goals and approaches are different in programs for parents of handicapped children and for those of gifted children, they are discussed separately.

Educating Parents of Handicapped Children

Parental support for programs serving handicapped children is, of course, mandated by PL 94–142. In many cases, this support is a vital component to preschool programs for children with special needs. The development of quality programs may depend on parent involvement:

> The one single factor that permits early childhood educators to meet this challenge is the active and intelligent inclusion and involvement of the parents of these exceptional children. (McLoughlin, Kershman, & Netick, 1984, p. 41)

In addition to training parents to teach their children, some programs are based on the idea that parents and other family members need help with their emotions and their attitudes as well as with their skills. Sharing feelings and information with other families is therapeutic for some parents. The Chapel Hill Training-Outreach Project is devoted to a family focus and lists the following nine benefits of such a program:

1. It acknowledges parents' right to be involved.
2. It enables the staff to recognize the child as part of a dynamic unit, the family.
3. It helps facilitate individual programs for the child and parents.
4. It provides for greater continuity and coordination in the child's training.
5. It teaches family members about child development and gives them specific skills.
6. It forms a supportive community for the families of handicapped children.
7. It keeps the center program relevant to the needs of the families and the community.
8. It helps families use and develop other community resources as needed.
9. It builds a base of community knowledge and support for the center program. (Cansler & Martin, n.d., pp. 1–2)

Effective programming is based on the establishment of meaningful goals and the development of an appropriate model.

Program Goals

Parent education refers to a systematic and conceptually based program intended to impart information, awareness, or skills to the participants on aspects of parenting (Fine, 1980). Although the goals and format differ widely, most programs attempt to help parents achieve some of the following goals:

develop greater self-awareness, use effective discipline methods, improve parent-child communication, make family life more enjoyable, and provide information on child development. In addition, programs for parents of handicapped children frequently provide information on PL 94–142, including parents' rights and responsibilities.

Snell and Dunkle (1979, p. 54) have summarized the goals for parent education into three main categories:

> To enable the family members to help themselves (parents as parents).
> To assist the handicapped child (parents as teachers).
> To further the program (parents as advocates).

Parents as Parents One aim of parent education is to strengthen or stabilize the general family climate. Some parents may need help in working toward the establishment of a home in which there is emotional warmth, mutual respect, encouragement, good communication, consistency, and security (Enzer, 1976). While acknowledging that handicapped children need special help, professionals should recognize the needs of the families in which the children live. From a systems approach, assistance to the entire family is essential.

Parents as Teachers In looking at specific goals, Simmons-Martin (1976, p. 75) claims that an early childhood program must provide an opportunity for parents to learn about:

(1) approaches to child-rearing;
(2) ways to use ordinary elements in the child's environment as teaching tools and how to turn everyday experiences into learning experiences;
(3) ways to encourage the children's language growth;
(4) ways to promote social and emotional development; and
(5) ways to find and use various resources in the community.

Programs should aim toward increasing parents' understanding at many levels of developmental learning so they acquire greater competence in dealing with their child.

Goals will change with program focus and parent need. A practical way of examining and establishing goals is found in designating them as immediate, intermediate, and long-range. Figure 9.1 illustrates an example of such goal-setting. An approach of this nature enables parents to deal with daily, urgent needs while developing the ability to foresee future needs and feel competent to handle them.

Parents as Advocates A final goal of parent programs is enlisting the aid of parents in various aspects of programmatic work and/or support (Enzer, 1976). As noted in Chapter 4, parent groups have been extremely effective in

FIGURE 9.1 Three Categories of Goals and Activities

LONG-RANGE GOALS AND ACTIVITIES

Child's maximal achievement of his innate abilities

INTERMEDIATE GOALS AND ACTIVITIES

- Modify the child's environment to minimize those attitudes or behaviors of parents or siblings which could impede the child's opportunity for development.
- Help parents in setting and resetting realistic targets for achievement in their child.
- Assist parents in providing a stimulating home environment for promoting total growth in their child.
- Assist the parents in selecting the type of education which gives the child optimum opportunity for development.

IMMEDIATE GOALS AND ACTIVITIES

- Listen to the parents.
- Deal with the parent's feelings.
- Provide emotional support to the parents.
- Determine the extent of the parents' background knowledge.
- Provide information to the parents in a way that they can understand.
- Help the parents become thoroughly familiar with the facts and implications of their child's problems as they become known.
- Assist the parents to achieve consistently firm, but affectionate, handling of the child in a variety of situations.
- Strengthen the positive aspects of parent-child interaction.
- Help the parents learn to be sensitive to natural and informal situations in everyday life which make language more readily meaningful to the child.
- Teach the parents to be alert to ideal opportunities, not only for the development of communication skills, but also the total, integrated development of the child.
- Provide parents with information about available resources.

Source: Simmons-Martin, A. (1976). Facilitating positive parent-child interactions. In Lillie, D. L. & Trohanis, P. L. (Eds.), *Teaching parents to teach.* New York: Walker and Co., pp. 80–81.

bringing about change for people who are handicapped. As advocates, parents can exert a great deal of influence on program instigation, implementation, and direction. As a parent, Rettberg (1980, p. 41) offers suggestions that parents might consider in developing courses of action:

- ☐ The involvement of both parents is vastly more effective than even the most dedicated single parent member.
- ☐ Don't let dedication to group efforts detract from the most important aspect of your available time—your own son or daughter.
- ☐ Identify those parents who are effective speakers and use them; however, the tasks at hand will require ten times as much routine effort as it will eloquent speeches. Get and keep everyone involved by constant communication.
- ☐ Find and stick like glue to those public officials and organizations that can most effectively support your cause. Let them know that you appreciate their help and reciprocate.
- ☐ Obtain personal commitments for support and don't rely on potential actions committed through secondhand sources.
- ☐ Where at all possible work within the system. Get actively involved in those organizations and committees working for or supporting your cause.
- ☐ Meet deadlines and don't expect things to happen unless you take timely follow-up action.

Objective information available on the effects of parental involvement with young, handicapped children is minimal. The question of whether to encourage the inclusion of families in programs for handicapped children has been answered, for the most part, by the mandates of PL 94–142. The combination of federal mandates and common sense insists that parents play an important role in such programs. The question, therefore, appears not to be whether families should be included, but how they can be involved most effectively (Bricker & Casuso, 1979). A review of program models provides alternatives for selecting an appropriate vehicle.

Models for Educating Parents of Handicapped Children

☐ A number of innovative models have been developed to meet the training needs of parents of handicapped children and young people. These models vary from one-session meetings to ongoing educational plans. Although the programs are presented in many formats, in general they are delivered as workshops, home-based models, school-based models, and parent-trainer models.

Parent Workshops The workshop format has been used extensively to provide information to parents of handicapped children. As an example, the Parent Advocacy Coalition for Education Rights (PACER) was organized to inform parents of their rights and responsibilities under state and federal special education laws (Goldberg & Goldberg, 1979). Originally funded by the state of Minnesota, this project was later extended through funds from the Bureau of Education for the Handicapped at the federal level. Five levels of activity operate through PACER to reach and inform parents: (1) public information and education; (2) workshops for parents of all handicapped children; (3) workshops for specific groups, such as parents of preschool handicapped children or single-disability organizations; (4) advocacy training; and (5) individual advocacy assistance to parents.

Another example is the Advocacy Center for Children's Education and Parent Training (ACCEPT). This program originated in North Carolina as a federally funded parent training project dedicated to training, sharing information, and building coalitions. ACCEPT trains parents in intensive, two-day regional workshops; the parents, in turn, train other people in their own communities. In addition to providing information, ACCEPT teaches parents to be responsible and active advocates in legislative matters and provides current information on state and federal issues through a newsletter funded by a private foundation in the state (ACCEPT, 1984).

The workshop format is useful and practical for providing parents with information of a general nature. It also gives parents the opportunity to relate to a group of people who have common concerns. However, the information level of the participants should be considered in planning the program to insure the interest and understanding of all parents. The workshop format is a good start for parents who wish to become involved at a higher level. However, it does not facilitate the ongoing communication and working relationship between the school and home provided by other models.

Home-based Programs An exemplary program for preschool handicapped children, the Portage Project operates through a regional educational agency serving twenty-three districts in rural Wisconsin. The basic operational premises of the project as they relate to parents are (1) parents care about their children and want them to attain their maximum potential, however great or limited that potential may be; (2) parents can, with instruction, modeling, and reinforcement, learn to be more effective teachers of their own children; (3) the socioeconomic and educational or intellectual levels of the parents do not determine either their willingness to teach their children or the extent of gains the children will attain as a result of parental instruction; (4) the precision-teaching method is the preferred learning model, since feedback is provided daily to parents and weekly to staff, thereby reinforcing both when goals are met (Shearer, 1976).

The Portage Model provides weekly visits by home teachers to families with young handicapped children. The program has demonstrated that a systematic, data-based, individualized parent training program can be implemented by home teachers who are teaching parents to work with their children (Boyd, 1979).

Other projects based on the home-based model are Parent Action in Childhood Education (PACE) and Precise Early Education for Children with Handicaps (PEECH). In both projects, professional teachers visit the homes to train parents to instruct their handicapped children (Shea & Bauer, 1985). The advantages of home-based programs are many:

- ☐ The parent teaches the child in his natural environment. Therefore, they do not have the problem of transferring learning into the home as they would if the child were in a center-based program.
- ☐ This model is totally dependent on parent involvement for success. Since one and a half hours one day per week is not a sufficient amount of time for a child to learn developmental skills from the home teacher, parents must be taught to teach their own child between home visits. Thus, training parents is more than a program adjunct—it is absolutely mandatory.
- ☐ Another major advantage in using the home-based precision teaching model is that the home teacher and the parents have direct access to the child's behavior as it occurs naturally. This situation engenders realistic curriculum goals that will be functional for the child within his unique environment. In fact, the differences in cultures, life styles, and value systems of parents are incorporated into curriculum planning, since the parents determine what and how their child will be taught.

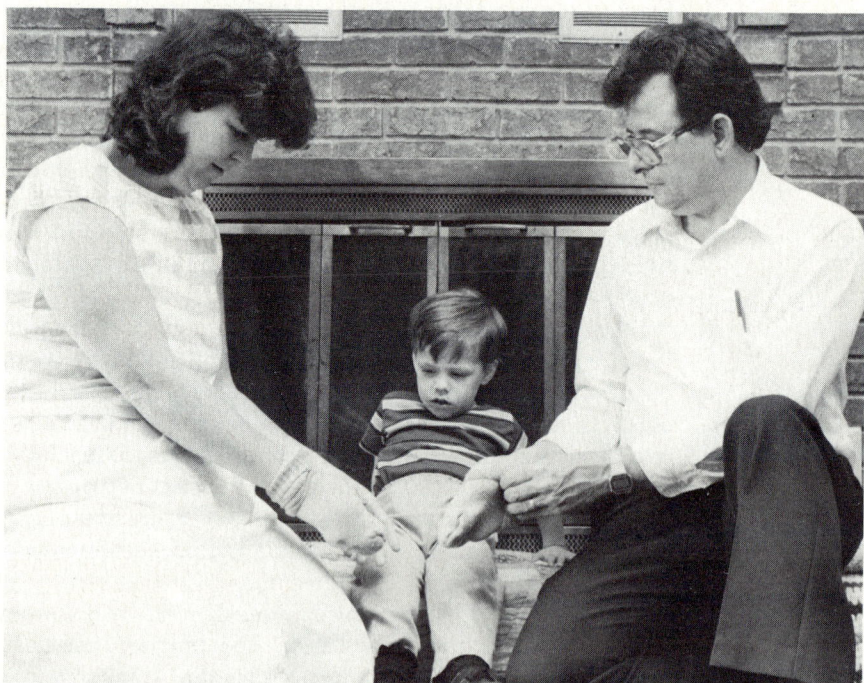

☐ *Some advantages of home-based programs include the benefit of teaching the child in his or her natural environment, increased parent and family involvement, and access to the child's behavior as it occurs naturally.*

- ☐ It is more likely that the skills that the child learns will generalize to other areas and be maintained if the skills have been learned in the child's home environment and taught by the child's natural reinforcing agent—his parents.
- ☐ Father, sibling, and extended family involvement become a realistic and obtainable goal. When instruction occurs in the home there is more opportunity for full family participation in the teaching process.
- ☐ There is access to the full range of the child's behavior: such as temper tantrums, which only occur in the home, or hearing from the parents that their child is crawling into bed with them each night. Much of this behavior could not be targeted for modification within a classroom.
- ☐ Finally, since the home teacher is working on a one-to-one basis with the parents and child, individualization of instructional goals for both is a reality rather than an idealized goal. (Shearer, 1976, pp.133–134)

Home-based remediation programs have also been established to train parents of older handicapped students. The Parent/Child Learning Clinic at the University of Washington has developed a program based on the contention that parents are in the best position to coordinate and to assume the long-term responsibility for remediation of learning disabilities. In this model, the clinic's professional staff members share with the parents findings of a comprehensive evaluation. An intervention program is developed and detailed written instructions are given to the parents. All parents are given general suggestions, and subsequent instructions are based on the student's unique abilities and disabilities. The individualized home program consists of a variety of tasks designed to build specific abilities into the student's repertoire (Townes, Trupin, & Doan, 1979).

A form of home-based program is the current emphasis on teaching parents to help their children achieve in school. One publication designed for this purpose has been disseminated by the National Institute of Education (Weinstein, Wittrock, Underwood, & Schulte, 1983). Parents of all students are instructed in ways to help their children pay attention, to keep them interested in schoolwork, to teach them techniques for learning and remembering, to help them study and take notes, and to improve their ability to take tests.

Home-based programs establish parents as their children's first and continuous teachers. At the preschool, elementary, and secondary levels, such programs involve the parents in the learning process and acknowledge the importance of the home-school relationship.

School-based Models The school-based model includes programs in community preschool, Head Start, day-care, kindergarten, or public school settings. School programs have three advantages: (1) they expand the teacher's available human resources, thus permitting a more personalized and individualized program; (2) they bring about closer and more sustained contact between parents and teachers; and (3) they enable parents to make direct contributions to their children's progress by working in the classroom (Karnes & Lee, 1980).

School- or center-based programs offer some advantages to handicapped children and their families that are not easily obtained in home-based programs (Heward & Orlansky, 1984). Opportunities exist for professionals from many fields, such as medicine, education, physical and occupational therapy, and speech and language pathology, to interact in diagnostic and intervention strategies. In such settings, parents can meet with the interdisciplinary team and raise questions that can be answered immediately. Parents also have opportunities to meet with other parents and to receive the support and empathy so important to many people.

An exemplary program in the Child Development and Mental Retardation Center at the University of Washington provides instructional programs for handicapped children from birth to eighteen years. The school also serves as a demonstration-training facility for university students from many disciplines and for parents who are trained at school to work with their own

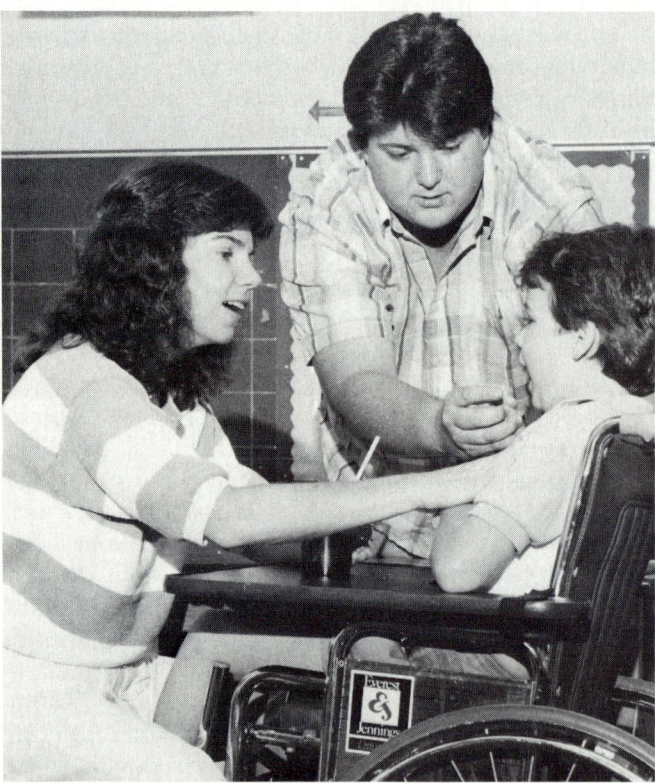

☐ *School-based programs have some advantages over home-based models, including involvement of professionals from many fields, opportunities for parents to meet with the interdisciplinary team, and opportunities for parents to meet and gain support from other parents.*

children at home (Hayden, 1976). In this program, the different types of parent training and involvement depend on the particular program the child is in and on the family's special needs.

Although the training is individualized, some common procedures are used throughout the program. These procedures include initial assessment of child needs, ongoing assessment and systematic observation, daily measurement of student progress, and modification of individual programs when expected progress is not made.

Many school-based remedial programs are aimed at increasing parents' programming knowledge and teaching skills. One program using this model added a component providing additional action-oriented parent training in conjunction with an educational program for their children (Brightman, Ambrose, & Baker, 1980). School-based programs have been designed for parents of severely handicapped children, handicapped infants, emotionally handicapped children, learning disabled children, and multiply-handicapped children.

An extension of the home-based and school-based models results in a home-center or home-school parent training model (Fredricks, Baldwin, & Grove, 1976). Such programs are based on evidence that if parents of children enrolled in a school or center engage in some teaching of that child, the child's learning will be significantly accelerated, as well as response to pressure from parents who want to participate in teaching their child and therefore must be taught how to teach their child. The following encounter that the author experienced illustrates the importance of the home-school emphasis:

> I had been asked to address a group of parents of children in a center for severely handicapped students. The purpose of the meeting was to create some interaction between the parents and the teachers. Following a brief talk, I asked if there were questions, comments, or requests from the audience. One mother responded, "Yes, I would like to request that my child be toilet trained at school." The teacher replied, "But your child is toilet trained!" Clearly, there had been no extension of the school program into the home.

Intervention that carries over from school or center to the home offers many advantages of both the home-based and the school-based models.

Parent-trainer Models Parent training is multiplied and extended when the parents themselves become leaders in educational programs for other parents of handicapped children. A project that recognized parents as a resource early in its inception is the Regional Intervention Program in Nashville, Tennessee. This program was one of the first group of projects funded by the Bureau of Education for the Handicapped under the Handicapped Children's Early Education Program in 1969. It was certainly one of the first in which parents themselves implemented the organization to provide services to their own children (Wiegerink & Parrish, 1976). The project is monitored and evaluated by a committee selected by the parents and consisting of three parents and three consultants. Parents who have received training and who exhibit technical competence become implementers of the program.

Other programs have followed suit, realizing that parents supply a source of personnel not readily available from other sources. In some cases, program graduates receive further training to enable them to be parent leaders. In other cases, parents are trained initially to become advocates and parent group leaders.

One project in California selects parent volunteers from graduates of the parents' course. Criteria for selection are (1) a score of 90 percent or higher on the Behavioral Vignettes Test, (2) successful performance of behavior modification interventions with their own developmentally disabled children, and (3) verbal ability as demonstrated during class discussions (Ball, Coyne, Jarvis, & Pease, 1984). The outcome of the procedure was measured in terms of the following three criteria: (1) cost effectiveness as savings of professional staff's time resulting from an investment in training and supervising parent teaching assistants; (2) by direct observation, the evaluation of changes in training outcome as a function of introducing parent graduates as teaching assistants; and (3) an evaluation of problems and limitations encountered in using parent volunteers. The results strongly supported the continued use of parents as teachers and as teaching assistants in the program.

The Parent Involvement Center in Albuquerque, New Mexico, identifies parents who have the time, strength, and ability to implement parent-to-parent programs and parent groups (Kroth, 1980). A training sequence for becoming a group leader begins with the parent's going through a program as a participant. Next, the parent will act as an assistant to the group leader, learning to use the equipment, offering assistance to parents, and observing the leader. During the third phase, the parent takes the leadership role, assisted by the parent trainer. The parent then moves on to help teachers who would like to implement parent groups in their schools.

Parent-operated groups are based on the idea that attitudinal change results from active involvement, with responsibility resting on the parents' shoulders (Berger, 1981). One program initiated and run by parents is the Pilot Parents Program in Nebraska. One member stated her purpose for becoming part of such a group:

> As parents of special children, we are joining to provide support and information to parents with similar handicapped children. The training session included six programs covering information on available services, established organizations and methods in approaching and helping parents of handicapped-diagnosed children. (*Southwest Lincoln Sun*, 1979, p. 1)

According to their brochure, Pilot Parents offer:

- ☐ Emotional support and understanding.
- ☐ Factual information about developmental disabilities.

- ☐ Factual information about medical services, educational programs, and supportive agencies.
- ☐ Introduction to helpful persons and groups that share their interests and concern.

Parent education groups can be organized with professional leaders or with parent leaders. Parent groups organized and led by lay leaders can be quite effective if the parent is able to develop leadership skills and has such traits as sensitivity to and acceptance of others, flexibility, and an outgoing personality (Berger, 1981). Heward, Dardig, and Rossett (1979, p. 237) suggest questions to ask when determining who can be a group leader:

- ☐ Do parents like to talk to and work with this person?
- ☐ Does this person spend time communicating with parents of exceptional children?
- ☐ Does this person have skills necessary to produce effective group interaction?
- ☐ Will this person choose to invest the necessary time and energy planning, implementing, and evaluating a parent group?
- ☐ Is this person competent in using and teaching behavior management procedures (or whatever the curriculum is to cover)? Can he aid parents in designing and carrying out home programs for their children?
- ☐ Is this person knowledgeable about the skills and limitations of children with special needs?
- ☐ Will this person be able to recognize when he needs additional help or further resources and how to get that help?

Leadership in parent education can be viewed as a continuum that ranges from the lay leader, the nonprofessional with little training, through the professional, a knowledgeable expert trained to expedite group processes, to the professional who lectures as an authority. Figure 9.2 illustrates this continuum. Regardless of the level of involvement, parents are a valuable resource: they are readily available, already engaged in teaching their children, and eager to learn more effective ways to rear their children (Wiegerink & Parrish, 1976).

FIGURE 9.2 Leadership Continuum

Parent leader with no training	Parent leader with leadership training	Parent leader with a structured curriculum	Parent leader with professional support	Professional leader with parent support	Professional teacher

Source: From Berger, E. H. PARENTS AS PARTNERS IN EDUCATION, p. 133. Copyright © 1981. C. V. Mosby, Copyright 1985 Merrill Publishing Company, Columbus, Ohio. Reprinted by permission of Merrill Publishing Company.

Persons interested in looking at specific models for involving parents in programs for handicapped children can obtain information by writing to those program directors. A list of federally funded programs can be obtained from the Office of Special Education. In addition to models of programs for parents of handicapped children, many popular parent education programs can be adapted to apply to parents of handicapped children. These programs include Caring, Communicating and Being Real (Ginott, 1965), Parent Effectiveness Training (PET) (Gordon, 1970), Transactional Analysis (Berne, 1964), Democracy and Adequacy (Dreikurs & Soltz, 1964), and Systematic Training for Effective Parenting (STEP), developed by Dinkmeyer and McKay (1976). Once a program model is adopted, planning can begin.

Planning Programs for Parents

☐ The Mirror Model of Parental Involvement (Figure 8.2) has been extended to reflect the relationship between parents' needs and program planning. Figure 9.3 illustrates the process. In looking at the needs of few, some, most, and all parents, it is clear that design of the parent program should reflect time and commitment directed toward the *all* and *most* levels, with selected involvement at the *few* and *some* levels. The same process can be applied to using the strengths of the parents, related to the activities indicated at different levels (Kroth & Otteni, 1983). Within a large school system, it is possible that all the activities could be taking place at the same time. Use of this information for planning at different levels of parental need has resulted in active participation in the Parent Center in Albuquerque.

An investigation of successful programs has resulted in the delineation of five major dimensions:

> Target population—who should participate in the training?
> Rationale and objectives—why should they participate?
> Procedures—what is the nature of the involvement?
> Delivery system—where does training occur?
> Incentives—how is participation induced? (Snell & Dunkle, 1979)

The target population might be single parents, couples, parents with preschool children, parents with school-age children, or parents with adolescents and might include siblings, grandparents, and other members of the extended family. The greater the involvement, the greater will be the impact on the entire family.

Wyckoff (1980) contends that keeping parent groups fairly homogeneous tends to result in higher levels of success. When such variables as intelligence, reading level, and educational level have been kept fairly constant within a group, the success of the program has been found to be higher. This suggestion is confirmed by Westin (1981), who found that husband-wife

Parent Education Programs

FIGURE 9.3 Mirror Model of Parental Involvement

			WHAT	HOW
Few		4	Therapy—Intensive education and support	Counseling; group therapy
NEEDS				
Some		3	Skill training in management interaction with system, child rearing	Parent education groups; bibliotherapy; parent support groups
Most		2	Knowledge of child's progress, environment, friends; assistance in parent-home programs	Notes home; daily/weekly reporting systems; conferences; phone calls; home visits
All		1	Parents and children's rights; consent to test and place; school policies and procedures; school and class events	Newsletters; handbooks; conferences
All		1	Special knowledge of child's strengths and needs, family characteristics and aspirations	Intake interviews, conferences, questionnaires
Most		2	Short-term assistance with projects at school, projects at home; special knowledge of world of work	Telephoning for PTAs or parent meetings; assistance with meeting arrangements; reinforcing at-home or school work; talking to classes at school
Some		3	Leadership skills, with time, energy, and special knowledge for _____	Serving on parent advisory groups, task forces; classroom volunteers; tutoring; writing newsletters; fund raising
STRENGTHS				
Few		4	Special skills, knowledge, time, energy, and commitment for leadership training to _____	Lead parent groups; work on curriculum committees; develop parent-to-parent programs

Developed by the Parent Center, Albuquerque Public Schools, 1982
  Source: From Kroth, R. & Otteni, H. (1983). Parent education programs that work: A model. *Focus on Exceptional Children 15* (8), p. 6.

teams had more in common with other couples, single parents with other single parents, and so forth, although there are always individuals who fit in anywhere.

Lillie (1976) presents four sequential steps that should be followed in planning an effective parent education program. Figure 9.4 illustrates these four stages: (1) needs of parents, (2) outcome objectives, (3) strategies and activities, and (4) evaluation procedures.

As Chapter 8 emphasizes, parent education programs begin with an assessment of parental and family needs. The information gathered through the various means available enables the program leaders or instigators to develop goals suitable for their particular audience.

Program objectives should be stated in language that makes it possible to determine if they have been successfully reached. Objectives are used as tools for planning; they should be limited to a practical and manageable number.

Activities selected for use in reaching an objective must be consistent with that objective. The questions about needs and objectives, as outlined in Figure 9.5, must be answered before activities can be planned.

Evaluation involves determining whether objectives have been accomplished. Many evaluation techniques are available: standardized testing, criterion-referenced testing, observation and counting frequency of behaviors, and testimonials (Lillie, 1976). Evaluation procedures should be established during the initial planning stage of the project. The importance of determining the program's effectiveness is critical to its continuation and replication. Areas that prove to be ineffective can be changed if they are clearly pinpointed. Figure 9.5 demonstrates how each of the four planning steps can be placed into a clear and detailed plan.

Other considerations in planning programs are the kind and degree of involvement parents want and can manage. The involvement can be direct or indirect. Direct participation includes five activities in which parents are directly involved: identification, assessment, design, implementation, and evaluation. Parents participate indirectly by exerting significant influence on societal groups in favor of programs for handicapped children (McLoughlin,

FIGURE 9.4 Stages in Planning Parent Programs

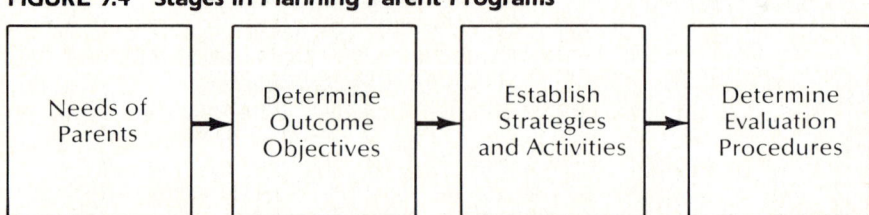

Source: Lillie, D. L. (1976). An overview to parent programs. In Lillie, D. L. & Trohanis, P. L. (Eds.), *Teaching parents to teach.* New York: Walker and Co., p. 11.

FIGURE 9.5 Planning Parent Programs

PROGRAM AREAS	GOALS	OBJECTIVES	ACTIVITIES	EVALUATION
SOCIAL AND EMOTIONAL SUPPORT	What emotional support do parents need?	What changes do I want to occur by the end of the year?	What are the best ways to achieve those objectives?	How successful was I in meeting the objectives?
INFORMATION EXCHANGE	What information do the parents and center staff need from each other?	What information do I want known and by whom at the end of the year?	What are the best ways to provide that information?	How successful was I in meeting the objectives?
PARENT PARTICIPATION	What are the parents' needs to improve their interaction with their children?	What interaction and with what consistency do I want to occur by the end of the year?	What are the best ways to assure that these interactions take place?	How successful was I in meeting the objectives?
PARENT CHILD INTERACTION	What are the parents' and centers' needs for participation?	What participation is to take place by the end of the year?	What are the best ways to achieve the objectives?	How successful was I in meeting the objectives?

Source: Lillie, D. L. (1976). An overview to parent programs. In Lillie, D. L. & Trohanis, P. L. (Eds.), *Teaching parents to teach.* New York: Walker and Co., p. 13.

Kershman, & Netick, 1984). Table 9.1 presents examples of parent involvement and training activities, with professional support.

Planning for parent education programs requires a strong commitment from professional staff members involved. Initial feelings about the worth of parent involvement should be discussed, followed by an articulation of basic assumptions regarding the parents of handicapped children. Once the staff agrees on the assumptions, they can be used as a basis for activities. The most essential assumptions are that the parent is the principal person in the child's educational program and that the school's role is to support the home in helping the handicapped child develop (Karnes & Esry, 1981).

A major step in the planning process is determining the content of the parent education program. Adequate needs assessment can help parent educators deal with important concerns.

Program Content Each program has aims and goals (Dembo, Sweitzer, & Lauritzen, 1985). Are these goals consistent with the parents' own goals? Are they relevant to the family's changing needs? Although it is generally recognized that formal and informal assessment should be used to answer these and other questions, parent education programs are frequently arranged to accommodate the goals perceived by professionals who anticipate the parents' needs. Therefore, programs seem to fall into three predictable content groups: early intervention strategies, behavior modification techniques, and skills training.

Early Intervention Early intervention has been a focus of many programs described in the previous sections. The rationale for working with children at an early age has been discussed, and the concentration of programmatic efforts in this direction cannot be overstated. Fotheringham and Creal (1974, p. 364) emphasize the importance of early education:

> If the community wishes to reduce the numbers who are disabled and alleviate the degree of disability in others, then it is necessary to pay increasing attention to the early preschool period and the major role the family plays in children's development. The preschool period is when the child is developing the most rapidly and is most susceptible to influence. The family's influence is paramount in this period. These points underline the need for early identification of children at a risk of being disabled and providing child and family programs to help stimulate and train the child and support the family in this task.

Parent training can begin when the handicapped child is still a baby; parent trainers can also begin at this early stage. Some parents of Down's Syndrome children remain on call for physicians who have delivered babies with Down's Syndrome and other conditions that are immediately apparent. Frequently, they are able to interact with the parents in an empathetic and meaningful way, helping in their initial adjustment and in the later location of resources and support systems.

TABLE 9.1 Sample Parent Involvement and Training Plan

I. Need	Parent II. Role	III. Professional Support	Action
Social-emotional support	Assessment	Observe PL 94–142 regulations regarding assessment	Interview parents with sensitivity to their feelings about the child's handicap
Social-emotional support	Implementation	Develop programs and materials for parent use	Supply parents with suitable activities to work with their children at home
Exchange of information	Parenting	Develop programs and materials for parent use	Observe parent-child interactions at home and supply feedback to parents
Parental participation	Implementation	Offer necessary training and support	Teach parents behavior management skills
Improvement of parent-child interactions	Parent group member	Offer necessary training and support	Arrange for parent group discussions on child management strategies
Specifics of handicap	Advocate and lobbyist	Maintain and use appropriate communications	Explain handicap in lay language so parents can explain the issues to others
Specifics of handicap	Advocate and lobbyist	Offer necessary training and support	Supply simulation activities of handicaps for parents
Expectations	Programming	Encourage parental role in IEP design	Take parents on visits to classes of older students who have similar handicaps
Expectations	Identification	Assist parents in identifying early signs of disabilities	Prepare handouts with information about charteristics of disabilities
Stages of growth	Assessment	Observe PL 94–142 regulations regarding assessment	Have parents complete a case history as part of the assessment process
Optimal home environment	Implementation	Offer necessary training and support	Use doll house furniture to demonstrate ways to rearrange physical surroundings for the child
Financial expectations	Parent group member	Advocate parental rights	Work with parent groups to obtain tax breaks and other financial assistance
Financial expectations	Assessment	Model positive attitudes	Convince colleagues to offer free clinical services and involve parents
Support agencies and educational services	Resource person and advisor	Incorporate parents in monitoring IEP success	Supply parents with criteria for evaluating services
Special equipment (e.g., hearing aids)	Parent group member	Offer necessary training and support	Have parents from a parent group demonstrate the use of special equipment
Tests, measurement, and evaluation	Assessment	Offer necessary training and support	Teach parents to take observational data, give tests, etc.
Principles of learning	Parenting	Develop programs and materials for parent use	Develop techniques and activities for home use that can benefit siblings and fit into the lifestyle
Multiple conditions	Assessment	Observe PL 94–142 regulations regarding assessment	Inform parents of agencies that offer comprehensive testing for many disabilities

Source: McLoughlin, J. A., Kershman, S. & Netick, A. Parents and teachers of young exceptional children: Meeting training needs. *The Pointer, 28* (3), p. 46. Reprinted with permission of the Helen Dwight Reid Educational Foundation. Published by Heldref Publications, 4000 Albemarle St., N.W., Washington, D.C. 20016. Copyright © 1984.

Families may also need help during the first few months of life in helping their handicapped babies acquire needed skills. Such early intervention may actually serve to prevent secondary physical, emotional, and learning problems that can develop in children with disabilities as they grow older (Connor, 1981). Home visits are particularly helpful in the early developmental period and may assist the entire family in learning to improve their skills in living and working with the handicapped child.

Goals for early intervention programs vary but frequently include two major goals:

1. Family members will gain an understanding of available resources and legal and political issues that affect their child.
2. Family members will gain a working knowledge of educational intervention strategies in relation to their child. (Bricker & Casuso, 1979, p. 115)

Even though the goals are to teach parents specific intervention skills to help them become more effective change agents with their children, it is often necessary to meet other family needs before parents can learn to use educational intervention strategies. These needs may range from dealing with a mother's feeling of overprotectiveness to the family's need for food stamps and financial assistance (Bricker & Casuso, 1979). Providing of social, financial, and emotional support may precede formal parent training but will ultimately produce a family climate in which the child is likely to develop more fully.

Participation in early intervention programs affects families in important ways. Moran (1985) investigated early intervention programs to identify meaningful variables. She found that the type of program intervention was the most significant factor in maternal attitudes toward the child. Contrary to earlier findings, such child-related variables as the type of handicap were not significantly related to mothers' attitudes toward the child. The provision of interaction with other parents was important; providing the context for interaction appeared to be more important than structuring interaction. Mothers who attended support groups were less likely to experience the severe stress reported in other studies, and fathers were affected significantly through the mothers' feeling less stressful.

Although the objective information available on the effects of parental involvement with young handicapped children is minimal (Bronfenbrenner, 1975), increasing evidence indicates that early intervention efforts make a positive difference in the families of handicapped children. Part of that difference may result from improved behavior management of the handicapped child.

Behavioral parent education involves many different kinds of programs, materials, and formats (Dembo, Sweitzer, & Lauritzen, 1985). The concepts taught usually include an overview of basic behavioral principles, the nature and use of social and nonsocial reinforcers, the manner in which children shape the behavior of their parents, observations and recording procedures, and techniques for weakening undesirable behavior and strengthening desirable responses.

Walker and Shea (1984) point out that in the parent training situation the teacher is removed from direct observation of the child's behavior in the home setting; thus, the teacher must rely on the parents' observations and reports. Assessment strategies, therefore, must be implemented to facilitate the parents' selection of a target behavior. Parents' identification of appropriate home reinforcers is also critical, since the reinforcers used in the home setting differ from those available and applicable in the school setting.

Several programs have been used to teach parents techniques in behavior modification. Parents Are Teachers (Becker, 1971) shows parents how to use consequences systematically to teach children what they need to learn. The program consists of ten units with exercises and projects to reinforce the principles presented. Simple and straightforward, the program is based on three assumptions:

- ☐ You can change behaviors in others that need changing.
- ☐ You can help others change your behavior.
- ☐ You can change your child's behavior. (Becker, 1971, p. 9)

Becker's program is concise, easy to understand, and economical. His book is complete with examples, exercises, and forms that can guide the parent in defining behavior and in developing an appropriate response (Wilson, 1979).

Heward, Dardig, and Rossett (1979) present a detailed parent education program designed to strengthen the home-school relationship by providing parents with strategies to change the behaviors of their exceptional children. Topics developed are principles of behavior change, a behavior change process for parents, and behavior management systems for the home. The goal of the program is to examine "how the behavioral approach to teaching can be used to build and maintain parent-professional relationships that will produce the greatest benefits for handicapped children" (p. 8).

The parent training program Walker and Shea (1984) present has two primary objectives: (1) to train parents in the theory and application of behavior modification principles and practices and (2) to assist parents' efforts systematically to modify selected target behaviors their children exhibit. A secondary benefit is the mutual support and understanding derived from the program educator and members of the group. A unique feature of this program is the individual assessment interview with each parent or couple. The objectives of the interview are to determine the parent or parents' needs, interests, and readiness to participate in the program, and to clarify at least one behavior they wish to modify (see Chapter 8). Following this preparation phase is the instructional phase, which lasts for eight weekly sessions; it is devoted to principles and practices in behavior modification. The follow-up phase includes a plan for maintaining periodic contact with the group and individuals to provide assistance and reinforcement.

In addition to providing strategies for direct intervention, parent training in behavior modification techniques can bring about changes in parental perceptions of the family environment (Karoly & Rosenthal, 1977). Evaluation of a behaviorally oriented parent training group indicated that parents who participated would (1) view their home environments as less psychologically noxious, and (2) view their exceptional child as displaying fewer maladaptive behaviors as compared to preprogram levels and to the perceptions of an untrained control group.

An improved home environment was also evidenced in a study of thirteen "Groups for Parents" (Sadler, Seyden, Howe, & Kaminsky, 1976). Family and individual child problem behavior checklists results indicated that there was a decrease in problem behaviors for the child with the problem and also for the rest of the family's children. Such outcome measures demonstrated that the course was successful in teaching parents new ways of altering problem behaviors and thus enhancing the quality of family life.

Behavior modification techniques can also be used in helping parents develop skills to teach their children. Teaching parents to be more successful instructors of their children is a primary goal for parent education programs.

Skills training is the goal of some parent programs. Although Stevens (1980) states that "parents should not ruin their role as parents by trying to be teachers as well" (p. 83), many parents want to get directly involved in the education of their child. As contended in Chapter 4, the most positive and continuous participation parents can experience in their children's education is through involvement in their learning process.

Direct parent involvement in educational programs needs to be well structured and organized. One way of doing this is to train parents through parent-tutor programs; another is through parent education groups (Strenecky, McLoughlin, & Edge, 1979).

Parent-tutor programs require the participation of parents in a thorough, ongoing training program. Elements to be included are child management techniques, record keeping, teaching techniques, and construction of educational materials. The program should also involve working with classroom teachers, during which time teachers and parent tutors can discuss mutual concerns and suggestions for enhancing and facilitating teacher-parent interaction (Strenecky, McLoughlin, & Edge, 1979).

In a comparison of the teaching styles of maternal and remedial teachers with good and poor readers, it was found that teachers and mothers provided considerably different learning environments for their children. They differed in terms of the information they transmitted, the structuring of the tasks, feedback provided, and the amount of independent activity required. Based on the findings, training for parent tutors should involve teaching them principles of reinforcement and task structuring, as well as strategies to transmit information effectively (Steinert, Campbell, & Kiely, 1981).

In a review of programs designed to teach parents to tutor their learning disabled children, Shapero and Forbes (1981) cite a variety of formats used.

These formats include a workshop for teaching parents to use games and activities for academic and perceptual training, individual instruction on procedures designed to help children enjoy reading (using practice, feedback, and modeling procedures), use of token reinforcers to teach children reading skills, training parents to measure oral reading rates and comprehension, use of supplemental teaching activities (such as reading aloud to their children and asking comprehension questions), and training by mailing instructions to parents on how to tutor their children in academic areas. Although the populations, training techniques, methods, and evaluations were varied in the studies reviewed, the overall results suggested that parents can be trained to tutor their children successfully.

Parents can also be trained to teach their children to reach developmental milestones. In a highly individualized program, parents of a Down's Syndrome child were taught to use shaping procedures to teach their child to walk (Angney & Hanley, 1979). A combination of small-group and individual instruction was used to instruct parents to teach their young children self-help skills identified on their IEPs. Videotaped sessions provided immediate feedback to parents and provided them with additional methods of instruction and the use of fewer instructional commands (Sandler, Coren, & Thurman, 1983).

In group training, parents have been instructed in teaching skills through behavioral techniques and through a communication skills approach. Bergan, Neumann, and Karp (1983) investigated the effects of a short behavioral training package on parental application of behavioral techniques during child instruction. Parents were taught to use brief verbal instructional prompts, modeling, positive reinforcement, and physical prompting to teach their children intellectual skills. The resultant training produced differences in child learning in one of the two skills targeted for instruction. The success of this approach has been correlated with parental education, reading ability, and pretraining knowledge of behavioral principles (Clark & Baker, 1982).

In an effort to evaluate the two types of skills training, Haffey and Levant (1984) compared a behavioral skills approach to a communication skills approach, using similar training methods and standardized measures. The behavioral skills training was based on behavioral principles of child management, and the communication skills training was based on empathy, congruence or genuineness, and unconditional positive regard. Parents who completed communication skills training demonstrated significantly greater communication skills, and parents who completed behavioral skills training demonstrated greater knowledge of behavioral principles. The findings pointed to the efficacy of a combined approach, since the parents who acquired the behavioral skills began to initiate concern for their children's feelings and to request information on communicating better with their children. The conclusion is that once parents' concerns about behaviors are addressed, the parents are more receptive to discussing feelings.

A systematic skills approach focusing on communication skills was used in a program for fathers of school-aged children (Levant & Doyle, 1983). The program emphasized communication skills because fathers are thought to have more difficulty in the expressive role. The program did result in an improvement in fathers' communication skills, as well as in children's perceptions of their relationships with their fathers. A particular strength of the program was its ability to encourage fathers to apply their skills to their relationships with their children.

Hetrick (1979) attempted to assess the effectiveness of communication skills training with parents of learning disabled children. It was hypothesized that the training would result in positive attitudinal changes in parents and students and in higher achievement of the students whose parents received training. The only significant finding, however, was the total subscale on the parents' survey for irritation problems, suggesting more tolerance by the parents toward the students in areas of hyperactivity and dependence.

It is clear that parent education programs can be delivered and content areas developed in many ways. An obvious bias is toward programs for parents of young children. When children are small, parent education programs are readily available. After children enter elementary school, it is uncommon to find a corresponding parenting curriculum, and programs for parents of adolescents are even more rare (Strom, 1985). Parents are a child's only continuous source of guidance throughout the years, and the parents need to acquire a broad understanding of human development that encompasses birth to late adolescence. Although there are many excellent programs, there is definitely a need for programs that are continuous and sequential.

In reviewing exemplary programs of parent involvement, it is evident that most of these programs are being developed with parents of young children. Even among this group, however, parents of gifted children are usually minimally involved. Are the needs of gifted children, and the needs of their families, being met?

Educating Parents of Gifted Children

The rights of children and their parents under PL 94–142 do not extend to gifted children or their parents unless the child is both gifted and handicapped. Although some states do provide programs for gifted students, federal legislation does not, nor does it assure the parents of any rights to involvement in the education of their children.

As with all children, parents and the home play a significant part in every phase of the gifted child's growth and influence the outcome of every educational decision. Clark (1983, p. 386) emphasizes the influence of the home in maximizing the potential of the gifted child:

> I am firmly convinced that the home is the true cradle of eminence. Whatever we find in our world that we would like to change, we must begin at the starting

place with parenting. Some have tried to show that other influences are equally or even more important; however, they have yet to account for the powerful effects of motivation, self-image, and attitudes toward self and others—the factors that find their definition in the home.

It is frequently assumed that the parents of gifted children are, themselves, gifted and that they will know how to deal with the giftedness of their children. Although this is true for some parents, there is no evidence that they will necessarily have the skills required to make the most of their child's abilities (Callahan & Kauffman, 1982). Actually, parents are frequently frustrated, like the parent who wrote:

God sent us a gifted one, but He forgot to enclose a book of instructions. (Goertzels & Goertzels, 1962, p. 290)

Parents of gifted children have organized to influence political action, to help each other understand and manage their children effectively, and to

☐ **Like parents of handicapped children, parents of gifted children play an important role in their children's education program.**

influence school programs for their children. As yet, however, there is little evidence that parents are systematically involved in the schooling of their gifted children. The findings of one study revealed that mothers of gifted children had positive reactions to being told that their child was gifted but negative reactions to their lack of opportunity to become involved in educational planning and to the lack of information and guidance provided by the schools (Dirks, 1979).

Based on the evidence that high achievement of gifted children is associated with parental involvement with their child's learning at home, the following assumptions should guide parents' involvement in the education of their gifted children: (1) parents will represent the interest of their child, (2) parental participation in decision making will enhance the appropriateness of their child's education, and (3) parents' participation will increase the school system's accountability (Callahan & Kauffman, 1982). These are the assumptions underlying parental participation in education of the handicapped under PL 94–142.

More specific assumptions may underlie special services for gifted children. The following four assumptions are derived from a program at the University of Wisconsin–Madison aimed at improving parental roles and achieving desirable school system changes through parental involvement:

1. Parents have a vital interest in their gifted child's education.
2. Even though they have mutual interests and concerns, parents often do not agree with each other, their children, or the school about what is most appropriate for the child.
3. To be successful, a parent consultation program must have earned credibility.
4. A power base is necessary to establish appropriate attitudes and practices in the education of gifted children. (Schatz & Sanborn, 1980)

Although the goals and problems may be somewhat different, the basic approaches to educating parents of gifted children are similar to those used in educating parents of handicapped children. The principles essential in establishing and maintaining a good working relationship are the same. The components of good program planning are also the same: assessing parental needs (Chapter 8), developing goals, and choosing an appropriate program model.

Program Goals

☐ The five major goals for the professional are to help parents (1) understand their gifted child, (2) acquire skills that will enable them to advocate for their child, (3) acquire the knowledge and skill to help their child develop abilities fully, (4) learn appropriate ways of child management, and (5) use resources in the interests of their gifted child (Karnes, 1980).

In an early instructional program (Malone, 1975), parents identified their own educational goals in the areas of counseling and teaching methods. Counseling was requested in the areas of discipline, developing strengths, guiding sensitivity, and determining the rights of parents. Teaching methodology was requested so parents could supplement areas in which they felt the schools were not succeeding.

Karnes (1980) stresses the importance of flexibility and individualization in working with parents of gifted children. She offers ten guidelines that seem likely to ensure successful parent involvement:

1. Professionals working with parents of the gifted must be committed to the notion of parent involvement. Involvement will not be successful unless professionals sincerely believe that parents have something to offer that will enhance the program.

2. Professionals working with parents of the gifted must know how to work with parents. Parents have more confidence in professionals who convey the impression that they know what they are doing.

3. Parents of the gifted are, as a rule, vitally interested in their child's educational program and want to become involved. They want to help the school set goals and to reinforce what the school is doing to facilitate the child's growth.

4. Parents of the gifted involve themselves more readily when they have a part in determining their own needs and in deciding how they will become involved. Parents must be given information with which to make these decisions.

5. Parents of the gifted can acquire new knowledge and skills important to fostering the development of their children. Parents of gifted children usually need more knowledge of what gifted children are like and what methods are particularly suited to working with these children.

6. Parents of the gifted will become more involved when there is good communication between the school and the home and when they are aware of the effects of their efforts. A feedback system is essential if parents are to continue to be involved or to increase their involvement.

7. Training parents of the gifted to assess the development of their children will facilitate realistic and appropriate planning. Parents can bring meaningful information to the attention of the teacher because children often manifest different behavior at home and at school.

8. Flexibility is one of the keys to effective involvement of parents of the gifted child. No two parents enter an involvement program in exactly the same way, have the same talents to contribute, or express the same concerns about their gifted child. One of the reasons parent involvement programs fail is because the professional decides what the parent's needs are.

9. Parents of the gifted have a right to expect professionals to provide them with information and to train them to acquire the skills they need to work with their gifted children. Someone in the school setting must be able to provide the parents with training. Availability of community resources is another kind of information that the teacher provides the family of the gifted child.

10. A parent involvement program for the gifted should encourage independence. In the beginning parents may rely heavily on the teacher and other professionals to train them and to provide knowledge, but the teacher should work toward helping parents develop their own plans for enhancing their child's development. (Karnes, 1980, pp. 128–130)

Administrators and teachers of programs for gifted students have been challenged to provide parents with relevant information and training. Such training, although not extensive, has been provided through a variety of formats.

Models for Educating Parents of Gifted Children

☐ For many years, parents of gifted children have been asking questions and deriving information through professional journals, formal classes, conferences, and meetings. In an investigation of alternative formats, Mathews (1981) reported that parents can be effective supplemental educators when provided with adequate reading materials only, but that they would prefer a personal approach supported by printed materials and audiovisual aids. Another survey (Debinski & Mauser, 1978) indicated that parents generally prefer to receive information through personal interaction with teachers rather than by reading materials about gifted children. It is apparent that a combination of methods should be used to educate parents of gifted students.

Mathews (1981, p. 207) recommends including four components in a parent training program:

> 1. A booklet or packet of informational materials about the program offerings should be sent home at the beginning of each school year or as soon as the child is identified for entrance into a special education program.
>
> 2. A parent newsletter should be sent home at least once each month with descriptions of the units or projects underway. This is a useful method of asking for parent input or for soliciting the help of parent experts or mentors for particular subjects of study.
>
> 3. A parent-awareness meeting is a must for parents of all recently identified children, as well as for the entire parent population of the school in which a special program for the gifted has been recently instituted. This meeting should include a description of the history of the field, the variety of definitions of the gifted and talented used throughout the United States, identification measures, types of program options, and a thorough description of the curriculum.

Structured courses are frequently suggested to help parents understand the problems of the school, the program, and their gifted children. Discussions revolve around alternative programs and strategies to use at home and at school to build self-concept, to facilitate communication, and to develop all areas of functioning. Clark (1983, p. 388) suggests five sessions to present a parent inservice course:

> 1. Understanding Giftedness—Who are the gifted? How do you nurture giftedness?
> 2. Emotional and Social Development of the Gifted—Developing self-esteem, values, and creativity.
> 3. Meeting the Needs of the Gifted—Program alternatives, differential curriculum, learning and challenges, integrating all areas of learning, and evaluation.

4. Effective Teachers at Home and at School—The nurturing home, growth, families, communication, the teacher in the classroom as a part of the learning community.
5. What Can You Do Now?—Planning with the school, student-parent-teacher interaction, legislative possibilities and provisions, becoming active in your community for gifted education.

Parents of gifted children are valuable resource people. Fujita (1984) describes a parent participation cooperative preschool in which parents assist trained teachers in their child's class as well as attend evening parenting meetings, serve on committees, repair toys, cut out name tags, type, and maintain grounds or buildings. Such a program is described as a continuing parenting class—a laboratory school for parents. The cost of tuition for co-op schools is lowered in direct proportion to the amount of time and energy the parents supply.

Parents can cooperate with the schools in providing quality education for their gifted learners in many ways. They can serve as teachers, helping with material development, running individualized learning labs, providing transportation for special events, and arranging for field trips. Parents should organize, become informed, and work cooperatively with school personnel to provide the best possible education for their gifted children (Clark, 1983).

Malone (1975) contends that parents of gifted children can be the greatest source of support or the biggest headache for school districts, depending on how well they understand what is happening to their children. A small investment in parent education can result in support most school districts need.

Given the individual differences among parents of children who are gifted, uniform involvement is not reasonable. School systems should encourage parents to participate in the educational decisions affecting their children, offer parents training in how to be effectively involved, and allow them a wide range of alternatives.

The special needs of gifted children deserve national recognition. Attempts to address their needs and those of their parents should be no less urgent than attempts to provide appropriate education for the handicapped and their parents (Callahan & Kauffman, 1982).

Any program designed to train parents of exceptional children and young people ought to be examined for its effectiveness. Evaluation should be a strong, ongoing component of every program.

Evaluating Parent Education Programs

In a comprehensive review of parent education programs, Dembo, Sweitzer, and Lauritzen (1985) found that differences in the goals and methods of program approaches appeared to influence researchers' selection of both evaluation instruments and specific program outcomes. A number of research problems interfered with accurate program evaluation. Problems identified in many of the studies reviewed included not selecting subjects at random, absence or inappropriate use of control groups, failure to collect process data, and lack of long-term follow-up designs. Measurement problems included the reliance on self-report data and the use of measures validated for clinical rather than educational purposes. The authors suggest careful assessment planning before, during, and after the parent education program is undertaken.

Professionals and parents who are planning programs need to be aware of the reasons for evaluation. According to Huberty and Swan (1977), evaluation (1) is expected and/or mandated, (2) can lead to an examination of program worth, (3) can lead to program improvement, (4) can enhance intraprogram communication, and (5) can add to the knowledge base pertaining to exceptional child education. Appropriate evaluation is usually expected by the funding agency and may be expected by community groups, school board members, school administrators, teachers, and parents. Accountability is expected not only in terms of what is being done, but also how effectively it is being done.

In addition to outcome measures, an evaluation plan should yield information on which decisions may be based at interim points of a program. The following five questions might provide valuable feedback in an ongoing program:

1. How does the instructor teach the skills and present the information?
2. How do the parents interact with the instructor?
3. What problems do the parents raise in class regarding the program?
4. How does the instructor modify the program to deal with parent differences?
5. Is there formative evaluation of the program by the parents and the instructor? (Dembo, Sweitzer, & Lauritzen, 1985, p. 192)

Relatively few program evaluation studies have attempted to measure aspects of program implementation and relate the resulting data to program outcomes (Wang & Ellett, 1982).

A number of measures have been developed to assess the efficacy of parent involvement in intervention programs. Indirect measures of parent involvement include changes in child performance, parent attendance, and compliance with program requirements. Interviews and paper-and-pencil tests have been used to assess parent attitudes, satisfaction with the program, and knowledge of child care and child development (Rosenberg, Robinson, & Beckman, 1984).

Other evaluation needs should be addressed. More attention needs to be paid to the individual goals parents have for participating in a program, leading to program evaluation based on individual goals rather than on group or trainer goals. It would also be helpful to identify parents' behavior and perceptions during their participation in a program. For example, Espinoza (1980) found that the program's impact depended on the cultural beliefs, values, personal experiences, and expectations an individual brought to a program. Understanding parents' motivation and perceptions of the program is important for future planning.

A program evaluation model should be devised in the initial planning stage. The following eleven questions provide guidelines for evaluating the outcome of a program:

1. Do the parents acquire the knowledge and skills?
2. Do the parents use the skills in their interaction with their children?
3. Do parents' attitudes toward their children change?
4. Do parents' attitudes toward child-rearing change?
5. Do children's attitudes toward their parents change?
6. Is the children's behavior assessed through the observation of persons besides their parents before and after treatment?
7. Are any observed changes sustained over time?
8. Are child characteristics related to parent outcome measures?
9. Are there adverse effects of the program?
10. Is attendance related to outcome effects?
11. Do certain parents benefit more from the program? (Dembo, Sweitzer, & Lauritzen, 1985, p. 192)

The importance of a serious commitment to evaluation cannot be overemphasized. A program evaluation system can facilitate the improvement of a particular project's model as well as provide information needed to maintain support for the project.

Parents have confidence in programs that can show success; this confidence in turn helps perpetuate the parent-professional relationship and maintain parent participation. Furthermore, parents are entitled to complete information about any program in which they are to be involved. This right is one of the ethical considerations in any parent education program.

Ethical Issues

☐ ☐ The concept of parent education is offensive to some people. Westin (1981, p. 54) rejects the influence of professional input into the process of parenting:

> Parents have been brainwashed for a quarter of a century into thinking that the closer they can come to adopting professional techniques of dealing with their children's behavior, the better parents they are apt to be.

She contends that such a philosophy has led to feelings of ineptness among parents and therefore the need for parent education:

> From the beginning, professionals implied that parents needed more than on-the-job training for parenthood. They implied that child-rearing, like everything

else, responded to proper technique, which, of course, they alone knew and they alone could teach. (Westin, 1981, p. 56)

A steady increase in the number of parent training programs and the growing number of parent training books demonstrate the value that educators and clinicians attach to training parents to be teachers for their own children. A concern for ethical professional behavior arises when professionals begin to share parenting responsibilities with parents.

Behavior modification programs, in particular, have been criticized for selecting inappropriate goals, for enforcing untenable contingencies, and for creating situations in which a conflict arises between the role of the experimenter attempting to ascertain scientific validity and the role of the therapist attempting to bring about changes in the behavior of parents and their children. Ethical considerations require evaluation that looks beyond target behaviors and includes parental attitudes toward children as well as children's attitudes toward their parents and toward their new forms of management (Sapon-Shevin, 1982).

People who are planning parent education programs should be concerned with the adoption of basic ethical standards. Such standards would include the provision of complete, factual information about the program, its goals, its participants, and its outcome. Credentials of the program directors and participants should be available at the outset. Parents should be made aware of their choice in being involved in programs, their degree of input, and the research basis and rationale of the particular program under consideration.

Many ethical questions raised will be resolved if parents are active participants in the goal-setting and the planning of programs. If active participation is maintained throughout the program, additional problems can be dealt with on a cooperative, ongoing basis.

Successful parent education programs can be organized and conducted if such variables as whom to teach, what to teach, and how to teach are considered. Because parenting is such a dynamic, ongoing concern, it is important to evaluate, modify, and upgrade parent education programs continually (Wyckoff, 1980).

Planning and implementing a successful parent education program are difficult tasks. They require leadership, resources, time, and energy. Such efforts are warranted, however, when the program results in improved family relationships, increased skill development, and a strong parent-professional partnership.

In viewing the family as a system, parent education takes on a broader meaning. This philosophy is projected by Hobbs, Dokecki, Dempsey, Moroney, Shayne, and Weeks (1984, p. 5) in their defense of the concept:

> We examine not only alternative approaches to helping families care for their children, but also the utility of parent education and the notion that all services for families and children should include the component of parent education. We

do not define parent education as instruction in caring for children in the narrow sense, but extend it to include the enhancement of parental competence in all areas that affect the family. To be sure, parent education may provide increased understanding of children and a heightened competence in caring for them. But it may also provide instruction and experience in enhancing the community, in strengthening the family as a mediating structure, and in perfecting the rights and well-being of each family member.

Conclusion

The parent-professional partnership can be facilitated through the design and implementation of programs to meet the needs of parents as well as the needs of their children. When parents are involved in such a partnership, three processes are involved. First, information is exchanged between the partners. Second, the parents are encouraged to grow in their role. The third process is building a trusting, productive relationship between the parents and teachers (Northcott & Fowler, 1976).

Programs designed to educate parents of exceptional students are based on various needs. Ideally, the programs are designed to meet the individual needs of parents and their children. On a functional level, they are usually designed to present information, to teach behavior management and tutoring skills, and to provide emotional support and counseling.

Although the programs for parents of young handicapped children have flourished, there is an acute need for programs designed to meet the needs of parents of handicapped students and gifted students of elementary, secondary, and postsecondary ages. With the current focus on the transitional stage, hopefully this need will receive attention.

As parents of exceptional students become more involved in their own education and in the education of their children, teacher education takes on new meaning. If programs for parents are to succeed, teachers must be in tune with the individuality of parents as well as with the diversity of their children. The challenge in teacher education is the topic of Chapter 10.

References

ACCEPT (1984). Newsletter of The Advocacy Center for Children's Education and Parent Training, *1* (2). Raleigh, N.C.

Angney, A., & Hanley, E. M. (1979). A parent-implemented shaping procedure to develop independent walking of a Down's Syndrome child: A case study. *Education and Treatment of Children, 2* (4), 311–415.

Ball, T. S., Coyne, A., Jarvis, R. M., & Pease, S. S. F. (1984). Parents of retarded children as teaching assistants for other parents. *Education and Training of the Mentally Retarded, 19*(1), 64–69.

Becker, W. C. (1971). *Parents are teachers.* Champaign, Ill.: Research Press.

Bergan, J. R., Neumann, A. J., & Karp, C. L. (1983). Effects of parent training on parent instruction and child learning of intellectual skills. *Journal of School Psychology, 21*(1), 31–39.

Berger, E. H. (1981). *Parents as partners in education.* St. Louis: C. V. Mosby Co.

Berne, E. (1964). *Games people play.* New York: Grove Press.

Bessent, H., & Webb, R. (1976). The role of the parent. In I. J. Gordon & W. F. Breivogel (Eds.), *Building effective home-school relationships,* 93–110. Boston: Allyn and Bacon.

Boyd, R. D. (1979). Systematic parent training through a home based model. *Exceptional Children, 45*(8), 647–648.

Bricker, D., & Casuso, V. (1979). Family involvement: A critical component of early intervention. *Exceptional Children, 46*(2), 108–116.

Brightman, R. P., Ambrose, S. A., & Baker, B. L. (1980). Parent training: A school-based model for enhancing teaching performance. *Child Behavior Therapy, 2*(3), 35–47.

Bronfenbrenner, U. (1975). Is early intervention effective? In B. Friedlander, G. Sterritt, and G. Kirk (Eds.), *Exceptional infant: Assessment and intervention,* Vol. 3. New York: Bruner/Mazel.

Callahan, C. M., & Kauffman, J. M. (1982). Involving gifted children's parents: Federal law is silent, but its assumptions apply. *Exceptional Education Quarterly, 3*(2), 50–55.

Cansler, D. P., & Martin, G. H. (n.d.). *Working with families.* Chapel Hill Training–Outreach Project. Winston-Salem: N.C.: Kaplan School Supply Corp.

Clark, B. (1983). *Growing up gifted* (2nd ed.). Columbus, Oh.: Charles E. Merrill.

Clark, D. B., & Baker, B. L., (1982). Behavioral training for parents of mentally retarded children: Prediction of outcome. *American Journal of Mental Deficiency, 87*(1), 14–19.

Connor, F. P. (1981). Perspectives on early childhood programs. *The Exceptional Parent, II*(1), S3–S6.

Debinski, R. J., & Mauser, A. J. (1978). Parents of the gifted: Perceptions of psychologists and teachers. *Journal for the Education of the Gifted, 1*(2), 5–14.

Dembo, M. H., Sweitzer, M. & Lauritzen, P. (1985). An evaluation of group parent education: Behavioral, PET, and Adlerian programs. *Review of Educational Research, 55*(2), 155–200.

Dinkmeyer, D., & McKay, G. (1976). *Systematic training for effective parenting.* Circle Pines, Minn.: American Guidance Services.

Dirks, J. (1979). Parents' reactions to identification of the gifted. *Roeper Review, 2*(2), 9–11.

Dreikurs, R., & Soltz, V. (1964). *Children: The challenge.* Des Moines, Ia.: Meredith Press.

Enzer, N. (1976). Parent-child and professional interaction. In D. L. Lillie & P. L. Trohanis (Eds.), *Teaching parents to teach,* 17–31. New York: Walker and Co.

Espinoza, R. (1980). Parent education and cultural change in American families. Austin, Tex.: Southwest Educational Development Laboratory. (ERIC Document Reproduction Service No. ED 187478).

Fine, M. J. (1980). The parent education movement: An introduction. In M. J. Fine (Ed.), *Handbook on parent education,* 3–26. New York: Academic Press.

Fotheringham, J. B., & Creal, D. (1974). Handicapped children and handicapped families. *International Review of Education, 20*(3), 353–371.

Fredericks, H. D., Baldwin, V. L., & Grove, D. (1976). A home-center based parent training model. In D. L. Lillie & P. L. Trohanis (Eds.), *Teaching parents to teach,* 107–129. New York: Walker and Co.

Fujita, S. R. (1984). Preschools that teach parenting. *Gifted Children Newsletter, 5*(10), 7.

Ginott, H. (1965). *Between parent and child.* New York: MacMillan.

Goertzels, V., & Goertzels, M. (1962). *Cradles of eminence.* Boston: Little, Brown and Co.

Goldberg, P., & Goldberg, M. (1979). PACER center: Parents learn about special education laws. *Education Unlimited, 1*(4), 34–37.

Gordon, T. (1970). *Parent effectiveness training.* New York: Peter H. Hayden.

Haffey, N. A., & Levant, R. F. (1984). The differential effectiveness of two models of skills training for working class parents. *Family Relations, 33*(2), 209–216.

Hayden, A. H. (1976). A center-based parent-training model. In D. L. Lillie & P. L. Trohanis (Eds.), *Teaching parents to teach,* 89–105. New York: Walker and Co.

Hetrick, E. W. (1979). Training parents of learning disabled children in facilitative communicative skills. *Journal of Learning Disabilities, 12*(4), 70–72.

Heward, W. L., Dardig, J. C., & Rossett, A. (1979). *Working with parents of handicapped children.* Columbus, Oh.: Charles E. Merrill.

Heward, W. L. & Orlansky, M. D. (1984). *Exceptional children* (2nd ed.). Columbus, Oh.: Charles E. Merrill.

Hobbs, N., Dokecki, P. R., Dempsey, K. V., Moroney, R. M., Shayne, M. W., & Weeks, K. H. (1984). *Strengthening families.* San Francisco: Jossey-Bass.

Huberty, C. J., & Swan, W. W. (1977). Evaluation of programs. In J. B. Jordan, A. H. Hayden, M. B. Karnes, & M. M. Wood (Eds.), *Early childhood education for exceptional children.* Reston, Va.: Council for Exceptional Children.

Karnes, M. B. (1980). Elements of an exemplary preschool/primary program for gifted and talented. In *Educating the preschool/primary gifted and talented* (National/State Leadership Training Institute on the Gifted and the Talented), 120–140. Ventura, Calif.: Ventura County Superintendent of Schools Office.

Karnes, M. B., & Esry, D. R. (1981). Working with parents of young exceptional children. *Educational Horizons, 59*(3), 143–149.

Karnes, M. B., & Lee, R. C. (1980). Involving parents in the education of their handicapped children: An essential component of an exemplary program. In M. J. Fine (Ed.), *Handbook on parent education,* 201–225. New York: Academic Press.

Karoly, P., & Rosenthal, M. (1977). Training parents in behavior modification: Effects on perceptions of family interaction and deviant child behavior. *Behavior Therapy, 8*(3), 406–410.

Kroth, R. L. (1980). The mirror model of parental involvement. *Pointer, 25*(1), 18–22.

Kroth, R., & Otteni, H. (1983). Parent education programs that work: A model. *Focus on Exceptional Children, 15*(8), 1–16.

Levant, R. F., & Doyle, G. F. (1983). An evaluation of a parent education program for fathers of school-aged children. *Family Relations, 32*(1), 29–37.

Lillie, D. L. (1976). An overview to parent programs. In D. L. Lillie & P. L. Trohanis (Eds.). *Teaching parents to teach,* 3–15. New York: Walker and Co.

Malone, C. E. (1975). Education for parents of the gifted. *The Gifted Child Quarterly, 19*(3), 223–225.

Mathews, F. N. (1981). Effective communication with parents of the gifted and talented: Some suggestions for improvement. *Journal for the Education of the Gifted, 4*(3), 207–210.

McLoughlin, J. A., Kershman, S., & Netick, A. (1984). Parents and teachers of young exceptional children: Meeting training needs. *The Pointer, 28*(3), 41–47.

Moran, M. A. (1985). Families in early intervention: Effects of program variables. *Zero to Three,* (June), 11–14.

Northcott, W. H., & Fowler, S. A. (1976). Developing parent participation. In D. L. Lillie & P. L. Trohanis (Eds.), *Teaching parents to teach,* 65–73. New York: Walker and Co.

Rettberg, D. F. (1980). Infants in need—an insight on parenting. *Education Unlimited, 2*(1), 39–42.

Rosenberg, S., Robinson, C., & Beckman, P. (1984). Teaching skills inventory: A measure of parent performance. *Journal of the Division for Early Childhood, 8,* 197–213.

Sadler, O. W., Seyden, T., Howe, B., & Kaminsky, T. (1976). An evaluation of "Groups for Parents": A standardized format encompassing both behavior modification and humanistic methods. *Journal of Community Psychology, 4*(2), 157–163.

Sandler, A., Coren, A., & Thurman, S. K. (1983). A training program for parents of handicapped preschool children: Effects upon mother, father, and child. *Exceptional Children, 49*(4), 355–358.

Sapon-Shevin, M. (1982). Ethical issues in parent training programs. *The Journal of Special Education, 16*(3), 341–357.

Schatz, E. M., & Sanborn, M. P. (1980). Some pragmatics of parent consultation. *Roeper Review, 3*(1), 40–43.

Shapero, S., & Forbes, C. R. (1981). A review of involvement programs for parents of learning disabled children. *Journal of Learning Disabilities, 14*(9), 499–504.

Shea, T. M., & Bauer, A. M. (1985). *Parents and teachers of exceptional students.* Boston: Allyn and Bacon.

Shearer, M. S. (1976). A home-based parent-training model. In D. L. Lillie & P. L. Trohanis (Eds.), *Teaching parents to teach,* 131–147. New York: Walker and Co.

Simmons-Martin, A. (1976). Facilitating positive parent-child interactions. In D. L. Lillie & P. L. Trohanis (Eds.), *Teaching parents to teach,* 75–85. New York: Walker and Co.

Snell, M. E., & Dunkle, M. (1979). A review of established programs for training parents of young handicapped children. *Education Unlimited, 1*(5), 54–58.

Southwest Lincoln Sun. (1979). Lincoln, Neb. 7(44), 1.

Steinert, Y. E., Campbell, S. B., & Kiely, M. C. (1981). A comparison of maternal and remedial teacher teaching styles with good and poor readers. *Journal of Learning Disabilities, 14*(1), 38–42.

Stevens, S. H. (1980). *The learning-disabled child: Ways that parents can help.* Winston-Salem, N.C.: John F. Blair.

Strenecky, B. J., McLoughlin, J. A., & Edge, D. (1979). Parent involvement: A consumer perspective—in the schools. *Education and Training of the Mentally Retarded, 14*(1), 54–56.

Strom, R. D. (1985). Developing a curriculum for parent education. *Family Relations, 34*(2), 161–167.

Townes, B. D., Trupin, E. W., & Doan, R. N. (1979). Parent-directed remediation for LD children. *Academic Therapy, 15*(2), 173–184.

Walker, J. E., & Shea, T. M. (1984). *Behavior management: A practical approach for educators* (3rd ed.). St. Louis: C. V. Mosby.

Wang, M. C., & Ellett, C. D. (1982). Program validation: The state of the art. *Topics in Early Childhood Special Education, 1*(4), 35–49.

Westin, J. (1981). *The coming parent revolution.* Chicago: Rand McNally.

Wiegerink, R., & Parrish, V. (1976). A parent-implemented preschool program. In D. L. Lillie & P. L. Trohanis (Eds.), *Teaching parents to teach,* 149–162. New York: Walker and Co.

Wilson, W. (1979). Parent training: Some observations. *Academic Therapy, 15*(1), 45–51.

Wyckoff, J. L. (1980). Parent education programs: Ready, set, go! In M. J. Fine (Ed.), *Handbook on parent education,* 294–316. New York: Academic Press.

10

Teacher Education Programs

The Education for All Handicapped Children Act of 1975, PL 94–142, has presented a tremendous challenge to school systems. It mandated an assessment of the learning environment, the establishment of a closer home-school relationship, and greater responsibility on the part of all school personnel. A resultant challenge also was created in institutions of higher education, specifically teacher training programs.

Before the enactment of PL 94–142, traditional teacher education programs provided instruction and practical experience for preservice teachers in discrete areas of specialty. Classroom teachers were trained to work with students who would perform within the broad range of normalcy; special education teachers were trained to work in segregated environments with students who did not fit the norm.

The concepts of least restrictive environment and the education of severely and profoundly handicapped children have demanded a reform in traditional teacher education; they have called for changes in teacher attitudes and skills. Educators and administrators concerned with the implementation of PL 94–142 have been required to take a close look at teacher education and to initiate some reforms in objectives, programs, and experiences designed to prepare teachers to carry out the intent of PL 94–142.

Teacher Preparation

Educators have been severely criticized by other professionals and by the public in general for lack of professional competence. A number of causes have been cited for these claims of inefficiency, including poor teacher salaries, parent apathy, the low social status of teachers, lack of administrative support, overloading of the schools with social responsibilities, overemphasis on interscholastic sports, and even student nutrition (Gubser, 1980). One source of blame common to most critics is the charge that teacher preparation programs are deficient and thus produce incompetent personnel for the nation's schools.

The quality of teacher preparation has been under attack by educators, administrators, and the general public for a number of years. A report issued by the American Association of Colleges for Teacher Education observed that "all of us have known for decades that teacher education has never been adequate . . . that changing conditions have made teaching progressively more difficult. . . . For too long, teachers and teacher education have proclaimed their professional status, knowing that it was more aspiration than reality" (Howsam, Corrigan, Denemark, & Nash, 1976).

The requirements of PL 94–142 created even greater areas of deficiency in the preparation of teachers. With the knowledge that teacher preparation in general had not met expectations, it became obvious that teachers did not have the kind and level of preparation to accommodate the broad range of learners found in their classrooms as a result of PL 94–142. It was also clear that they did not have the attitudes and skills that would enable them to work effectively with parents of exceptional students and in collaboration with other professionals.

There has been a concerted effort to improve the quality of teacher education in general. In determining responsibility for quality control in teacher education, Meyen (1979) points out that quality teacher education is a dynamic process subject to a variety of forces, including teacher trainers, students, consumers, society in general, and fluctuations in resources. A major shift in any of these forces could cause the quality of a program to suffer or to be enhanced. The enactment of PL 94–142 produced such a force. Corrigan and Howey (1980, p. 199) stated the positive nature of this influence in claiming that

> PL 94–142 could be the most important piece of legislation in the history of the country. Furthermore, since it calls for a new kind of teacher education to produce a new kind of teacher for schools that must meet the learning needs of *all* children, it could be the vehicle through which teaching emerges as a "real" profession.

Although legislation and court orders are powerful forces for change, they do not, by themselves, bring about change. The interactive forces of public opinion, schools, and institutions of higher education contribute to the degree of change that will occur. These forces affect the preparation of personnel destined to carry out the provisions of the law. Funding is a critical force; federal funding is a major consideration in determining program capabilities and objectives.

As noted in Chapter 4, the federal government has increased its support of public school programs from the mid-1960s to the present. Most of this increase resulted in funding programs dealing with children who were disadvantaged, bilingual, handicapped, or migrant. Except for preparing these specialists, few schools of education were concerned with the effect of these special populations on their teacher preparation programs. In fact, the federal support required that such programs, as funded, be separate and distinct from the general program for teachers (Reynolds, 1982). The provisions of PL 94–142 were in direct opposition to this practice.

It became apparent to many educators that the law required fundamental changes in the concept of education and that comparable changes would be required in the preparation of teachers (Reynolds, 1982). As defined by Meyen (1979), quality teacher education results in a good fit between the skills of the trained teacher and the needs and/or expectations of consumers. Since expectations had changed drastically, skills of teachers would have to be augmented. Reforms were necessary in the education of special education teachers, classroom teachers, and administrators as they assumed new roles.

Preparation of Special Educators

As one program that had been separate from general education, special education had to change rapidly to meet the specifications of least restrictive environment. The role of the special educator assumed a broad range of competencies. These ranged from the ability to work with general educators in regular classrooms in teaching mildly handicapped students or gifted students in states in which such programs were mandated, to the ability to work with groups of children whose needs demanded special (and frequently segregated) programming.

Teachers of Severely and Profoundly Handicapped Children Perhaps the greatest challenge to special educators was the education of severely and profoundly handicapped children. Since this group of students was given top priority in the implementation of PL 94–142, the challenge was immediate. Very few college programs were qualified to prepare teachers for this new field, and children who qualified were being identified rapidly through Child Find procedures. The resultant problem educators faced was expressed by leaders in the field of mental retardation:

> The implications of Public Law 94–142 . . . reflect our dilemma in meeting the demand for services while we are as yet unready to provide sufficient numbers of well trained personnel to work with the severely and profoundly handicapped. (McDowell & Sontag, 1977, p. 4)

Thus, the preparation of teachers of severely and profoundly handicapped children is a fairly recent endeavor in the field of special education. Since many people had not believed that severely handicapped people could benefit from educational services, the idea of training professionals to serve this population in public school settings did not seem to be realistic (Umbreit,

Karlan, York, & Haring, 1980). In fact, as of 1976, only four states offered a categorical certification in the area of severely and profoundly handicapped (Mori & Masters, 1980).

As this new field emerges, the implications for teacher education programs are critically important. Given the relatively small numbers of children to be served, colleges and universities must examine their purposes and resources before planning for training programs. The process requires a knowledge of the population to be served, the kind of teacher who will be attracted to the field, the skills required to teach the population, and the teacher preparation program necessary to fulfill the training needs.

The Population A major problem in planning for severely and profoundly handicapped students has been functional definition of the range of behaviors discussed under the category. The population includes, within the school-age population, long-term institutionalized, nonambulatory, multiply handicapped persons who show little response to stimuli; children with observable biological defects traditionally associated with retarded development; and ambulatory, close to moderately retarded individuals (Tawney & Smith, 1981).

Rather than defining severely and profoundly handicapped students in terms of intellectual, physical, and emotional characteristics, a more meaningful definition can be provided in terms of educational needs. Sailor and Haring (1977, p. 4) present this concept as it applies to referral:

> If the diagnosis and assessment process determines that a child with multiple handicaps needs academic instruction, that child should not be referred to the severely/multiply handicapped program. If the child's service need is basic skill development, the referral to the severely/multiply handicapped program is appropriate. Basic skill development consists of: (1) self-help skills, (2) fine and gross motor skills, (3) beginning communication development, (4) beginning social skill development, and (5) beginning cognitive or preacademic skills.

Bricker (1979) defines the population in terms of needed educational resources. In this framework, the severely handicapped student can be defined as "one requiring significantly more resources for making systematic educational progress than are available in programs for the mildly or moderately handicapped individual" (p. 60).

A major issue in defining and identifying severely and profoundly handicapped students deals with the educability of the population. The resolution of the issue lies in the definition of the term *educability,* which has changed considerably from when it referred to the students' ability to deal with academic studies. In a review of research on the educability of profoundly retarded persons, Stainback and Stainback (1983) conclude that significant progress has been made during the past decades in teaching profoundly handicapped persons meaningful behaviors. The results support maintaining a positive attitude about the educability of this group of students and continuing the search for educational procedures that can produce results. With increased expectancies for severely and profoundly handicapped students, the demand for teachers has also increased. A major consideration in planning for this population is identifying qualities required to teach severely handicapped students.

Teacher Characteristics The director of a program for severely handicapped students was approached by teachers and paraprofessionals in the program who asked for a visit by some experts. The director responded, "*You are the experts!*" Good teachers in this field have emerged in the same way that good programs have emerged. People who demonstrated success have become the experts.

As the field grows, efforts continue to be made to identify characteristics of good teachers. Mori and Masters (1980) enumerate four qualities that appear to be important. The first quality is the desire to work with and help others; the second is a positive attitude toward the work—the belief that teaching severely retarded students is as important and significant as teaching nonhandicapped students. The third factor is a lack of concern about a large salary; the fourth quality is emotional stability, requiring the ability to deal with stressful situations and small increments of improvement.

In an effort to identify factors that motivate career choice among teachers of severely and profoundly handicapped children, Marozas and May (1980) surveyed a large group of teachers. Their findings indicated that challenge and practicum experiences were the two most influential factors underlying their choice of a career. Table 10.1 presents the reasons stated.

Because the demands of teachers of severely handicapped students are very different from those of teachers of mildly handicapped students, not all special education teachers are either interested in or capable of teaching this group. The skills required are highly individualized and comprehensive.

Teaching Skills Special educators are required to demonstrate higher levels of competence than the field has ever seen. The ultimate goal of teaching may be the "process of creating or arranging an environment in ways that produce specified changes in a student's behavior" (Umbreit, Karlan, York, & Haring, 1980, p. 58). Many skills that teachers must acquire involve the ability to make quick and accurate responses and to react positively to the severely handicapped child during an emergency. At another level, teachers must apply and practice these skills in the classroom, achieving the ability to generalize and integrate skills into sequences maintained over time. At the highest level, the teacher must develop the skills needed to adapt to a wide variety of instructional settings, including the classroom, the community, and the home.

In identifying specific skills, Haring (1978, p. 412) suggests that competencies can be categorized into nine general areas:

TABLE 10.1 Stated Reasons for Choice of Career as a Teacher of Severely and Profoundly Mentally Retarded Children

Response	Number* (N = 121)	Percentage
Psychological needs		
Rewarding	46	22.87
Challenge	25	12.44
Feel needed	10	4.98
Interest/curiosity	8	3.98
Desire to help	6	2.99
Empathy for the less fortunate	3	1.49
Use special education knowledge	3	1.49
Precertification experiences		
Work with exceptional persons	18	8.96
Characteristics of occupation		
Only position available	19	9.45
Availability of positions	13	6.47
Favorable working conditions	4	1.99
Geographical location	3	1.49
Freedom	3	1.49
Personal characteristics	11	5.47
Miscellaneous	13	6.47
Unable to categorize	10	4.98
Total	201	100.00

*Respondents may have indicated more than one response.

Source: Marozas, D. S. & May, D. C. (1980). Factors which motivate job acceptance among teachers of severely and profoundly mentally retarded children. *Education and Training of the Mentally Retarded, 5*(4), p. 295. Used with permission.

1. Techniques for managing severe behavior problems;
2. Procedures for developing teacher-made instructional materials;
3. Engineering physical properties of a classroom;
4. Basic principles of the acquisition of operant behavior;
5. Basic principles and techniques of measurement;
6. Basic principles of imitation training generalization, discrimination, and maintenance;
7. Basic principles of task analysis;
8. Development and implementation of instructional programs; and
9. Procedures used to develop curriculum sequences.

In addition to providing direct instruction in major curriculum areas, the teacher for severely handicapped students is viewed as an instructional manager or coordinator of instructional activities. Burton (1981) contends that curriculum development is one primary responsibility of the teacher. It can be determined only by the teacher's detailed observation and assessment of the specific behaviors of the group and by writing clearly stated objectives for each class member.

The teacher's responsibilities also include tasks related to parent and professional training, administration, and community involvement (Escudero & Sears, 1982). Because the students' needs are so pervasive, the abilities to coordinate services and to facilitate cooperative efforts are important skills for the teacher of severely and profoundly handicapped students to develop. Preparing teachers for such unique roles has been extremely challenging for colleges and universities.

In addition to the challenges entailed in teaching severely handicapped children and in preparing teachers for this position, another dramatic change has occurred in the role of the special educator. This challenge resulted from the requirements to deliver services to mildly handicapped children who were integrated into regular classrooms and to plan for such services with other teachers and school personnel. A number of models have been developed to enable special educators to function in the broad range of service delivery programs.

Teaching Mildly Handicapped Students Because of the diversity of children served by special educators, the broad range of alternatives available under the concept of least restrictive environment, and the varying service delivery resources of specific communities, there are a number of special education models. The most common are full-time special class, part-time special class, regular class with supportive instructional services, regular class placement with consulting services for regular teachers, and regular classroom placement.

Special Class As stated in the previous section, severely and profoundly handicapped students are frequently educated in segregated classrooms because of the nature of their needs. Until the passage of PL 94–142, this was the most popular style of educating mildly and moderately handicapped children also. In this environment, students spend their entire school day in the classroom with a special education teacher who is responsible for all aspects of the education program. The assumption behind special classes was that the homogeneity in grouping was of substantial educational benefit (Cartwright, Cartwright, & Ward, 1981). Lack of evidence to support this assumption was one factor in promoting the concept of least restrictive environment, or mainstreaming. Although this model is still in existence the population of special classes has changed from mildly handicapped to more severely handicapped students. Another change has occurred through the interaction of students in self-contained, special education classes with students in regular classes.

Part-time special classes accommodate students who have severe disabilities but who benefit from regular classroom placement as well. Frequently, these students need specialized training, such as learning braille, sign language, behavioral training, or physical therapy. This model is also useful for providing stimulating opportunities for students who are gifted but who still need to have social interaction with their peers.

Consulting Services for Regular Teachers Many special educators consult with regular class teachers in planning instruction for exceptional students. Resource teachers and itinerant teachers usually function in this role.

Many handicapped and gifted students receive individual or small-group instruction from a special education resource teacher. These students may leave the regular class to receive instruction in the resource room for a specified period of time each day or each week, or the resource teacher may come into the regular class and instruct exceptional students in the classroom setting. One function of the resource teacher is to provide suggestions, techniques, or curriculum adaptations that are appropriate for students when they are in the regular class (Schulz & Turnbull, 1984).

Itinerant teachers function like resource teachers who serve more than one school. This model is expedient in rural settings or in providing services to children who have low incidence handicaps, such as blindness, where the small numbers do not justify a full-time resource teacher. Many speech, occupational, and physical therapists are employed on an itinerant basis.

Other roles for special education consultants include provision of inservice training to classroom teachers, support to other special educators, availability in crisis situations, coordination of services, and parent involvement and education. Clearly the role of consultant demands the abilities to work with other professionals and to communicate well with educators and parents.

Regular Classroom The least restrictive environment for exceptional students is the regular classroom. Wang and Birch (1984) propose an educational alternative to the resource room that accommodates the instructional and special service needs of a broad range of individual students in regular class settings. This model, the Adaptive Learning Environments Model, supports (1) early identification of learning problems, (2) delabeling of mainstreamed students and description of learning needs in instructional terms, (3) individually designed educational plans that accommodate each student's learning strengths and needs, and (4) teaching self-management skills that enable students to take increased responsibility for their learning. Researchers hope that investigations of this model in a number of states will provide a research-based approach to merging the best in regular and special education.

Another model that increases the use of indirect special education services within the regular classroom setting is the prereferral intervention model. This model represents an indirect, consultative model of service delivery in which resources are directed at providing intervention assistance at the point of initial referral. This model is based on the principle of prevention and focuses on preventing inappropriate placements in special education and on preventing future student problems by increasing the skill and knowledge of regular classroom teachers so they might intervene effectively with diverse groups of students (Graden, Casey, & Christenson, 1985). The system's six prereferral stages are comprised of (1) request for consultation, (2) consultation, (3) observation, (4) conference, (5) formal referral, and (6) formal program meeting. Figure 10.1 represents the first four stages schematically. A prereferral intervention model of service delivery is based on a consultation model. The focus is on using school resource personnel in collaborative problem solving with regular classroom teachers to develop classroom interventions for students. Knowledge of consultation principles, processes, and skills is essential to effective implementation of the model.

Teacher education programs in special education have changed considerably in the past decades in order to keep pace with the changing and evolving roles of the special education teacher (Perkins, 1979). Teachers of mildly handicapped students, teachers of gifted students, and teachers of students who are severely handicapped have vastly different roles; teacher education programs must offer wide ranges of training and experiences to prepare personnel for such roles.

Teacher Preparation Programs—Severely Handicapped

☐ In preparing personnel to work with severely and profoundly handicapped students, the South-Eastern Regional Coalition has identified three factors common to the interests of several universities:

☐ *The least restrictive environment for exceptional students is the regular classroom.*

FIGURE 10.1 Prerefferal Intervention

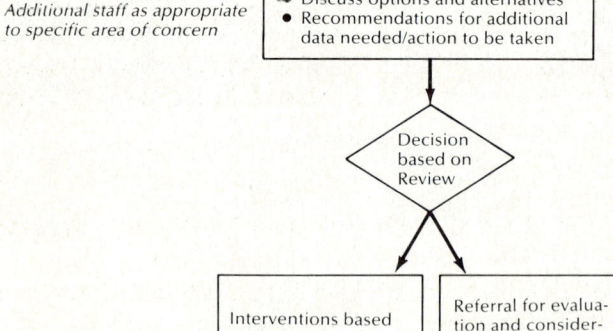

Source: Graden, J. L., Casey, A., & Christenson, S. L., (1985). Implementing a prereferral intervention system. Part I. The Model. *Exceptional Children 51*(5), p. 380. Copyright (1985) by The Council for Exceptional Children. Reprinted with permission.

1. Common development of training models, including college student evaluation.
2. Collaborative in-class research.
3. A behavioral base in teacher personnel preparation. (Tawney & Smith, 1981, p. 13)

This group has suggested a model which requires a two-year master's program, including a full year of internship.

Programs range in quality and depth from comprehensive, integrative sequences to a few isolated courses. Although teacher training programs have been developed at the undergraduate and graduate levels, the most common approach is to provide training for teachers of the severely and profoundly handicapped at the graduate level, reserving the undergraduate level for learning the basic teaching skills (Thomas, 1980). Doctoral level programs have also been developed to train researchers, teacher trainers, school administrators, and consultants.

Institutions of higher education must also consider the adequacy of their resources before developing programs to train teachers of severely and profoundly handicapped students. Colleges and universities wishing to establish training programs should address the need for the program, adequacy of resources to develop and maintain the program, staff needs and instructional integrity, program limitations, and a process for program evaluation (The Southeastern Regional Coalition, 1982, p. 46). Table 10.2 indicates minimum resources for starting a personnel preparation program. It is clear that not all programs have the resources to do the job, even when need and desire are present.

Personnel working with severely handicapped populations need specialized training. McDowell and Sontag (1977) have suggested that the trends and strategies developed for the severely handicapped student have the potential for affecting—or serving as a catalytic agent for improving—the educational services to all handicapped children. The same statement might be made for personnel preparation; strategies and programs developed to train teachers to work with severely handicapped students could improve teacher education in general.

Teacher Education Programs—Mildly Handicapped

☐ Special education teacher preparation programs have changed significantly during the past decade. Changes have been made in response to theoretical questions about labels and assessment, government criteria, and parental demands. Teacher educators reshape their training programs in response to research findings and current practices.

If teacher education programs are to prepare personnel to work in school systems, the service delivery models must influence the type of train-

TABLE 10.2 Minimum Resources for the Initiation of a Personnel Preparation Program in the Area of the Severely Handicapped

I. Program Need
   1. Documented personnel need
   2. Availability and proximity of other training programs
   3. Inservice and/or continuing education needs
   4. Coordination with SEA teacher certification requirements and program approval

II. Minimum Resource Requirements
   1. Availability of population(s) of SH students
   2. Cooperative training agreement with community educational setting(s)
   3. Availability of media and materials
      a. Appropriate assessment instruments
      b. Appropriate curriculum instruments
      c. Instructional materials
      d. Access to adaptive equipment
      e. Library resources

III. Instructional Integrity
   1. At least one PhD level SH faculty member
   2. At least two support faculty members
   3. Core coursework
      a. Population characteristics
      b. Assessment of SH persons
      c. Methods of instruction
      d. Practicum
   4. Availability of instruction in ancillary disciplines
      a. Physical therapy
      b. Physical medicine
      c. Communication therapy
      d. Parent counseling
      e. Occupational therapy

IV. Statement of Program Limitations
   1. Disabilities and levels
   2. Age range
   3. Number of students
   4. Graduate-undergraduate

V. Program Evaluation
   1. Formative evaluation(s)
   2. Summative evaluation(s)
   3. Use of an independent evaluator/consultant

Source: Minimum resources for the initiation of a personnel preparation program in the area of the severely handicapped. The Southeastern Regional Coalition for Personnel Preparation to Work with the Severely/Profoundly Handicapped, (1982). Developing personnel preparation programs to train personnel to teach severely handicapped individuals. *Teacher Education and Special Education,* 5(1), p. 45. Reprinted by permission of the Teacher Education Division and Special Press.

ing. Although specialized (categorical) programs for students with visual impairments, hearing disorders, communication disorders, and severe and profound handicaps have been continued, noncategorical approaches appear to be more appropriate for students designated as educable mentally retarded, emotionally disturbed, orthopedically handicapped, or learning disabled (Blackhurst, 1981). This practice is reflected in the number of institutions offering noncategorical teacher preparation programs.

A noncategorical program provides teacher trainees with knowledge and skills sufficient to provide educational services to exceptional children within two or more of the traditional categories. Teachers with this type of training are prepared to teach children who exhibit a variety of educational characteristics, without use of the traditional labels and stereotypes.

A competency-based model is a common method of preparing special educators to provide a noncategorical service delivery model for mildly handicapped students (Idol-Maestas, Lloyd, & Lilly, 1981). Competencies specified reflect skills that apply to instruction and management of academic and social behavior regardless of categorical label. Such competencies can also serve as an evaluation mechanism for individual teacher performance.

Teacher Education Programs—Gifted

Although programs for gifted children are not provided for under PL 94–142, many states have included this category under the requirements of programs for exceptional children and young people. Despite the increased need for teachers of gifted children, at the beginning of the 1980s less than half of the states had certification requirements for teachers who would be working with these students. Most existing training programs build on an obtained degree in elementary or secondary education and frequently are available only at the graduate level (Gallagher, 1985). Five major program areas appear in standard training programs:

1. Understanding the development of gifted students and the major school adaptations made for them.
2. Understanding how children generate new knowledge, and the special capabilities of gifted students for such knowledge generation; the study of how children think productively and how teachers can enhance those characteristics.
3. Knowledge in depth in a given content field—a content specialty.
4. The ability to understand other social, emotional, and educational needs of the gifted through special courses or experiences in measurement, counseling, curriculum development, etc.
5. Even the teacher who has had many years of experience in a traditional elementary or secondary school program can profit from the special set of experiences learned on site, under supervision, working directly with gifted students. (Gallagher, 1985, pp. 388–389)

The type of training required of teachers of gifted students is strongly influenced by the teaching-learning model advocated. The Renzulli enrichment model, for example, focuses on content knowledge, on a wide range of intellectual skills, and on the development of an investigative attitude. Administrative flexibility is essential; enrichment activities could take place in the regular classroom, in a special resource room, in an independent carrel in the library, or in the community. The Williams model, on the other hand, was developed to enhance creative abilities and to develop thinking and feeling processes. In this model, teaching practices must be related to and built on the children's individual learning modes and abilities (Maker, 1982).

Competencies—Special Educators

☐ Regardless of the model used, or the category of exceptionality served, some competencies should be required of all special education teachers and thus should be part of all teacher education programs. These competencies include functioning as a consultant, as a multidisciplinary team member, and as a liaison to parents.

Consulting Teacher The concept of least restrictive environment necessitates a collaborative relationship between the special educator and the classroom teacher. Another example of service delivery systems leading teacher training institutions has been the use of special education teachers as consultants before they were prepared to serve in that capacity. Because consultation has become such an important part of the special educator's responsibilities, colleges and universities are responding with programs designed to prepare the special educator for this role.

Friend (1985) contends that the definition given to the term *consultation* will determine to a major extent the scope of the training program. Although consultation could refer to special education—classroom teacher interactions, interactions with other school personnel, parents, and students—a narrow definition will allow trainers to concentrate on working with a more discrete group. It is, therefore, important to select models to guide consultation practice.

General consultation models have been identified under the broad descriptors of mental health, clinical, organization, behavioral, program, and education and training consultation. These models differ from each other in terms of problem formulation, methods used in consulting, consultant assumptions about change, and consultant value orientation (Friend, 1985). For example, the choice of a behavioral model requires content stressing the formulation of problems in observable terms, strategies for modifying behavior, and techniques for collecting, recording, and reporting data. When training institutions use a variety of models, teachers have a number of alternatives from which to choose, depending on personal choice, the population served, and the particular consulting situation.

The consultation model requires a number of skills. In a master's level preparation program to enable teachers to become resource/consulting teachers (the University of Illinois at Urbana-Champaign), thirty-four skills have been identified as important for resource/consulting teaching positions. The skills cover referral systems, assessment procedures, behavior management, instructional programs, consultation, interaction with parents, and professional readings and meetings (Idol-Maestas & Ritter, 1985). In a questionnaire sent to program graduates, each skill was rated, using a 5-point scale, on (1) current level of teaching competence, (2) necessity of skill to job, and (3) the degree to which the skill had been developed in the program. Table 10.3 lists the thirty-four items and the three ratings of each item. Even though program graduates felt well-prepared to do their jobs, they encountered some barriers to carrying out their consultative work. The barriers were failure to promote ideas about collaborative consultation, lack of administrative support, and teaching assignments that required primarily direct teaching.

The Consulting Teacher Program of the University of Vermont prepares teachers to provide special education within regular classrooms for mildly handicapped students. Based on a triadic model of consultation, it enables consulting teachers to deliver instruction through the training of classroom teachers (Paolucci-Whitcomb & Nevin, 1985). Applicants for admission into the program as consulting teachers-in-training, in addition to meeting graduate college admission criteria, must be recommended by an immediate supervisor, a colleague or peer with whom they have worked, and a parent of a handicapped student for whom they have provided instruction. Training involves consultation training, workshop training, systems analysis, research, training a change agent, and IEP monitoring.

Six additional skills are identified for people serving as consultants to teachers of gifted students. Berghoff and Berghoff (1979) suggest that they be able to (1) offer strategies for teaching gifted/talented students, (2) offer supplementary materials, (3) provide assistance in developing and implementing IEPs, (4) offer assistance in using community resources, (5) provide direct resource instruction to the students, and (6) conduct staff development. They stress the importance of enhancing the classroom teachers' feelings of self-esteem, adequacy, and competence.

In functioning as a consultant, the special educator must coordinate special and regular educational services for the exceptional student. In collaborating with other school personnel, the consultant is part of an interdisciplinary team.

Team Member Since the passage of PL 94–142, considerable attention has been given to the need for collaboration among professionals involved with evaluation, referral, and team meetings. An interdisciplinary team of professionals shares responsibility for providing services to exceptional students. Even though the team approach has been adopted in a variety of settings, the implications of the team concept have not always been fully

TABLE 10.3 Ratings of Skill Areas by Program Graduates

Skill Area	Current Level of Competence	Necessity of Skill to Job	Skill Developed in Program
1. Manage and use a referral system	4.1 (22)*	3.3 (21)*	3.0 (23)*
2. Assess academic skills	4.7 (24)	4.4 (24)	4.6 (24)
3. Assess study and behavior skills	4.3 (24)	4.5 (24)	4.1 (24)
4. Use behavior assessment techniques	4.2 (24)	4.1 (24)	4.3 (24)
5. Implement curriculum-based assessments	4.8 (24)	3.7 (23)	4.8 (24)
6. Use norm-referenced tests	3.7 (24)	3.7 (23)	2.8 (24)
7. Conduct staffing conferences	4.2 (22)	3.7 (23)	3.1 (21)
8. Participate in staffing conferences	4.7 (24)	4.7 (24)	3.4 (24)
9. Develop written Individualized Educational Plans	4.7 (23)	4.6 (23)	3.9 (23)
10. Include general educators in developing Individualized Educational Plans	3.8 (24)	3.1 (24)	3.3 (24)
11. Accelerate academic performance	4.3 (24)	4.2 (24)	4.2 (24)
12. Accelerate study behaviors	3.8 (24)	4.1 (24)	3.6 (24)
13. Decelerate inappropriate social behaviors	4.1 (24)	4.5 (24)	4.1 (24)
14. Accelerate appropriate social behaviors	4.3 (24)	4.3 (24)	3.9 (24)
15. Generate contingency systems	4.5 (24)	4.2 (24)	4.3 (24)
16. Data collection and charting	4.6 (24)	4.0 (24)	4.6 (24)
17. Make program decisions based on data	4.5 (24)	4.2 (24)	4.5 (24)
18. Teach to specified instructional objectives	4.6 (24)	4.5 (24)	4.0 (24)
19. Locate available instructional materials	4.0 (24)	4.3 (24)	2.9 (24)
20. Serve as consultant to general educators	4.1 (24)	3.8 (24)	4.2 (24)
21. Demonstrate instructional and management techniques in general classrooms	3.7 (24)	2.9 (24)	3.6 (24)
22. Design and implement strategies to teach students in general classrooms	4.1 (24)	3.6 (24)	4.0 (24)
23. Design and implement instructional programs to facilitate transfer from special to general classes	3.9 (24)	3.6 (24)	3.9 (24)
24. Adapt instructional materials	4.3 (24)	4.2 (24)	4.0 (24)
25. Generate methods/activities for specified objectives	4.2 (23)	4.5 (24)	3.7 (23)
26. Describe special education services to other educators	4.3 (24)	4.1 (24)	3.9 (24)
27. Describe special education services to parents	4.5 (24)	4.2 (24)	3.7 (24)
28. Evaluate special education services based on data accumulation	4.2 (24)	4.2 (24)	4.3 (24)
29. Advocate appropriate special education services	4.0 (24)	4.3 (24)	3.8 (24)
30. Read professional literature	4.0 (24)	3.4 (24)	4.5 (24)
31. Train noncertified personnel	4.5 (24)	3.8 (24)	4.0 (24)
32. Offer inservice sessions for teachers	3.9 (24)	2.6 (24)	3.9 (24)
33. Involve parents in instructional planning	3.9 (24)	3.5 (24)	3.4 (24)
34. Report progress to parents	4.6 (24)	4.4 (24)	3.8 (24)

*The first number indicates mean score, and the number in parentheses indicates number responding to that item.

Source: Idol-Maestas, L. & Ritter, S. 1985. A follow-up study of resource/consulting teachers. *Teacher Education and Special Education, 8*(3), 121–131. Reprinted by permission of the Teacher Education Division and Special Press.

understood. In some cases, early enthusiasm has been followed by disillusionment as the difficulties inherent in the team approach have become apparent (Golin & Ducanis, 1981).

Although consultation and team collaboration skills have been a part of most programs for medical and health personnel, institutions preparing educators traditionally have not provided training for interdisciplinary skills (Courtnage & Healy, 1984). Without a commitment by training institutions, practicing educators are left to develop these skills by chance. Shortly after the implementation of PL 94–142, Egbert (1978, p. 14) emphasized the importance of college preparation in working with other people:

> Any professional education program that is designed to prepare personnel to work in schools providing a least restrictive environment should emphasize, through classwork and practical experience, the formation of effective, interpersonal working arrangements. Prospective teachers and principals must work through their own anxieties in joint planning and implementation sessions. They also must learn to understand and live with the anxieties and idiosyncrasies of others.

Before planning for skill development, educators need to clarify the concept of the team approach. Golin and Ducanis (1981, pp. 6–8) have identified nine characteristics that seem to be common to interdisciplinary teams in a variety of settings:

> A team consists of two or more individuals.
> Communication may be direct and face to face or indirect.
> There is an identifiable leader.
> Teams function both within and between organizational settings.
> Roles of participants are defined.
> Teams collaborate.
> There are specific protocols of operation.
> The team is child centered.
> The team is task oriented.

The operation of an interdisciplinary team is the result of a complex interaction of variables associated with the team members, the child, and the context in which the team functions.

The most common team dealing with exceptional students and their teachers is the building-based staff support team. This team is described as follows:

> A staff support team is a school-based problem solving group whose purpose is to provide a vehicle for discussion of issues related to specific needs of teachers or students and to offer consultation and follow-up assistance to staff. The team can respond to staff needs in a variety of ways. It can provide

> immediate crisis intervention, short-term consultation, continuous support, or the securing of information, resources, or training for those who request its service. (Stokes, 1982, p. 3)

One model adopted in North Carolina to provide building support for teachers is the Cooperative Assistance for Results in Education (CARE). CARE teams function on two levels, the first level concerns teacher-to-teacher support, and the second level concerns a group process for solving problems. At the first level, the team provides help with identifying problems, gathering information, and exploring alternatives. At the second level, the team uses a group process to help teachers identify problems, gather information, and explore alternatives. The CARE teams are carefully trained in communications and problem-solving skills and promise to improve school climate substantially (McDowell County Schools, 1985).

Although there appears to be consensus that the interdisciplinary process is important, many problems are associated with it. Among these problems are differing levels of participation by different occupational groups, lack of meaningful discussion in team meetings, problems in implementing team recommendations, lack of training and guidance in the team process, and the inability of professionals to work together in a truly integrative fashion. Bailey (1984) proposes a comprehensive conceptual model that facilitates an understanding of team process and team dysfunction. With the acknowledgment that teams are comprised of unique individuals in unique settings, the model allows consultants, administrators, or team members to pinpoint the specific nature and type of dysfunction within a given team and to identify strategies for improving team performance.

The policy statement of the American Association of Colleges of Teacher Education regarding the preparation of professionals for educating handicapped students clarifies the challenge to colleges and universities. This statement claims changes in professional roles require that educators be

> trained as a member of a differentiated instructional team, able to utilize both human and technological resources, able to function as a team member—sometimes in a leadership role, other times as a supportive observer, sometimes as a catalyst, and other times as a consumer of technical assistance. (AACTE, 1978, p. 45)

Teachers and other professionals can be trained for teamwork in three ways: preprofessional training, continuing education programs, and team development. Each approach has advantages as well as disadvantages. Combinations of these approaches may be most appropriate, with teachers and other professionals getting an initial introduction to teamwork at the preprofessional level and additional input through continuing education, combined with team development activities where feasible (Golin & Ducanis, 1981).

At the University of Northern Iowa (Cedar Falls), an interdisciplinary team training program has been developed on a competency- and procedure-based training approach. The program has three major features.

1. The program is competency-based. Each competency indicates the desired outcomes or exit skills expected of student trainees.

2. The program is procedure-based. Procedures are defined as a sequentially ordered series of progressive and interdependent steps found in the referral/staffing process.

3. The program includes the important affective skills needed for successful interpersonal relationships with other individuals or with teams. The professional behaviors characterized by positive personal interaction with colleagues, parents, administrators, and others are important skills that are interwoven throughout the training activities. (Courtnage & Healy, 1984, pp. 5–6)

A program at the University of Pittsburgh developed a course entitled *The Interdisciplinary Team*. As a result of the course development and other experiences, six recommendations were made for anyone undertaking the education of professionals for work in interdisciplinary settings.

- Programs should include students from a variety of human service professions as well as other school personnel, so that problems associated with interprofessional relationships can be appropriately addressed.
- Insofar as possible, an interdisciplinary team of faculty with diverse expertise and backgrounds should be involved in planning and implementation of the program or course. Adequate time for the team to collaborate in the planning process is essential.
- Training in interdisciplinary teamwork should be affective and experiential as well as cognitive and didactic. Students cannot learn to be team members merely by talking and reading about teams. Neither can they learn to use teams effectively by small group exercises or team activities alone. There should be opportunities to observe functioning teams in schools and other agencies.
- Both direct and indirect costs should be considered in developing such programs. High cost programs with no particular home base do not last long in periods of resource reduction. If outside funding is requested to start a program, then some institutional commitment for continuation of the program beyond the period of external funding should also be sought.
- Because of the complexity of interdisciplinary educational programs, on-going evaluation to insure that program or course objectives are being met is essential and should be an integral part of the program design. Both formative and summative evaluation should be employed.
- At the present time, solid research on the use of the team approach with exceptional children is quite limited. Comprehensive research programs in this area are sorely needed and should be given high priority in program development. Such research will ultimately provide a much firmer foundation for the preparation of professionals as effective team members. (Golin & Ducanis, 1981, p. 30.)

Interdisciplinary team training should be required of all educators, regardless of the model or approach used. The skills acquired through training as consultants and team members are valuable assets to the teacher in working with other professionals and with parents of exceptional students.

Liaison to Parents   As presented in Chapter 4, the role of parents and the schools' perception of that role have changed over the last several decades from passive on-lookers to active participants. Part of the rationale for parent involvement is PL 94–142's specification that special education placements should be based on the understanding and input of all team members, including parents (Witt, Miller, McIntyre, & Smith, 1984).

Educators' acceptance of parents as members of the interdisciplinary team is a prerequisite of effective teacher-parent collaboration. Educators will not be successful in working with parents unless they are convinced that parent-educator communication and cooperation will help the student and that parents legitimately can make decisions that directly affect their children's education (Simpson, 1982a).

Although educators have adopted the philosophy of the parent-teacher partnership, they have not actively pursued it. Attitudes toward parental involvement in the education of their children have run the gamut from total disassociation to active participation and commitment (Clements & Alexander, 1975).

Teachers' attitudes toward parents vary but tend to lean heavily in a negative direction (Seligman, 1979b). In a discussion of the "teacher's predicament," Grant (1984) states that "many teachers no longer feel that either the law or parents are behind them" (p. 34). He points out, however, that the great majority of parents want to keep in touch with teachers and want to be consulted about their children's progress. What has changed is that parents as a group may now be more educated relative to teachers and thus likely to be more critical of a teacher's performance.

The teacher who successfully works with parents demonstrates respect for them and confidence in their ability. Paramount among the attitudes a professional must exhibit is the belief that the school supplements rather than assumes the responsibilities of the home (Karnes & Esry, 1981).

Parents are moving both physically and intellectually into the mainstream of American education. Special education, in particular, has come to exemplify parent-teacher interactions and has, in many cases, presented a model for the parent-teacher partnership (Clements & Alexander, 1975).

Teachers and parents working together can bring about positive changes in the school and can facilitate the formal education of children and young people. This idea of partnership is not only viable; it is also essential. Findings emanating from special projects, educational research, and knowledge about human growth and learning emphasize the critical role of the home in children's education (Suchara, 1982). Strom (1981) presents substantive evidence that educational efforts focusing on both parent and child register the greatest long-term gains.

Research on parent involvement programs delineate the following results:

1. There are effects on teachers from parent involvement at the school. Teachers who had active parents at school tended to feel more comfortable about asking other parents to help with learning activities at home. The parents at school assist the teacher, which may make classroom management of instruction more effective, or increase supervision, order, and safety in the school.

2. There are effects on parents from teacher practices that request parent involvement in learning activities at home. Parents who are asked to assist their child on learning activities are more aware of the teachers efforts, know more about the school program, and rate the teachers as better teachers overall.

3. There are effects on students from teacher practices of parent involvement in learning activities at home and from parent support, encouragement, and assistance. Teacher practices that involve parents in helping students with school-related skills improve students' reading scores, attitudes toward school, and feelings about the positive connections between their teachers and their families. (Epstein, 1985, pp. 22–23)

In spite of the universal approval of the concept of parent involvement and increasing evidence that teachers can affect parent and student achievement, attitude, and behavior, relatively few teachers make frequent or systematic use of parent involvement activities. This is due primarily to the lack of attention to parent involvement theories and practices in teacher training programs (Epstein, 1985).

Many educators have been required to work with parents without being trained to do it. Historically, colleges and universities have not provided educators with training in parent-related matters; and when such competencies have been developed, they have been developed more slowly than other teaching competencies. A productive and mutually beneficial relationship between parents and educators depends on appropriate training of both groups (Simpson, 1982a).

The idea of preparing teachers for effective interaction with parents has introduced a new and challenging task for colleges and universities. The concept of interacting with families is as complex as are families themselves. In addition to working with parents of children who are handicapped or gifted, teachers should have knowledge in the area of single parenting, foster parenting, step-parenting, cultural diversity, and the impact of socioeconomical status and educational level. Kroth and Krehbiel (1982, p. vii) suggest four reasonable objectives for a teacher education program:

1. Preparing teachers who understand the role and importance of parents in the education process.
2. Preparing teachers who are knowledgeable of and sensitive to family dynamics.
3. Preparing teachers who are aware of and sensitive to their own values regarding parents, particularly parents of different ethnic or cultural back-

grounds, who have special problems, who have different attitudes toward schools, who have handicapped children.
4. Preparing teachers who are skillful at techniques that increase and improve parent-teacher interactions.

Preservice and in-service training is needed to give teachers information about the potentials and the problems of parent involvement. Teachers need to be able to view their role as an instructional manager of many types of resources, including parent involvement (Epstein, 1985).

Specific skills teachers need to be able to work with parents have been identified in the areas of communication and counseling (Seligman, 1979b; Sawyer & Sawyer, 1981). Since parents and teachers may lack the necessary interpersonal skills required to communicate in a productive manner, comparable training is necessary. McLoughlin (1981, p. 47) proposes a joint training model to train both groups in the communication and program involvement:

A. Communication
1. To know the basis for the parent-teacher relationship and how to establish it.
2. To know the major concerns of parents and teachers.
3. To know how to interview parents.
4. To know how to conduct parent-teacher conferences, especially placement conferences.

☐ *Preservice and in-service training is needed to give teachers information about the potentials and problems of parent involvement.*

    5. To know how to solve home and school problems with parents.
    6. To know how to share information with parents and supply materials.
  B. Program Involvement
    1. To know the major responsibilities and activities of parents of the handicapped.
    2. To know how to involve parents in assessment activities.
    3. To know how to involve parents in academic remediation.
    4. To know how to involve parents in behavioral remediation.
    5. To know how to organize and conduct parent education sessions.
    6. To know how to support parent advocacy and parent organization.

The training formats used for the joint program were minilectures, role playing, panels, direct interviews, and simulations and modeling.

Another simulated experience was developed as part of a unit on conferencing and communicating with parents of handicapped children at the University of Minnesota (DeBerry, 1980). The simulation directly involved participants in assuming parenting roles and in making choices about their children. In playing the game, the participants discovered the frustrations parents experience from the logical, rule-following reactions of schools, hospitals, and social service agencies. Although real experiences with families of handicapped children would be ideal, role playing and simulated experiences can be substituted or added to practicum experiences.

Simpson (1982a) suggests that teachers are in a position to improve the parent-professional relationship and to avoid many problems and frustrations experienced by other professional groups who interact with parents (see Chapter 5). One reason for this opportunity is that parents usually have more opportunities to establish rapport with their children's teachers than they do with other professionals. Also, parents may perceive teachers more positively than they do professionals involved in initial diagnostic evaluations. Regardless of this perception, the quality of teacher-parent involvement relies heavily on the teacher's skills.

Policy makers and the administrators of special education programs have recognized as a priority the need for well-prepared special educators (Haring & McCormick, 1986). PL 85–926, passed in 1958, provided funds for training teachers to work with mentally retarded students. This act, together with other acts, has provided funds to support the training of personnel to work with handicapped children and young people. PL 94–142 also addresses the need for professional preparation by requiring that states develop comprehensive plans for training special educators and regular educators.

Preparation of Regular Educators

□ □ The concept of least restrictive environment provides multiple programing options in which handicapped children can be enrolled in a regular class for none, part, or all of the day and conversely in a special class all, part, or none of the day (Egbert, 1978). The many options for interaction with nonhandicapped students require a different kind of school environment—a school environment in which all personnel are comfortable with and skilled in working with handicapped students. Personnel-preparation programs must, therefore, prepare regular teachers and administrators, as well as special educators, to function in such an environment.

Regular Teachers

In 1975, the U.S. Department of Education instituted the Dean's Grant Program to encourage teacher-education institutions to adapt their preparation programs to conform to the principles and conditions set forth in PL 94–142. Through this program, college and university deans of education throughout the United States were awarded grants to support faculty development and curricular change activities in an effort to improve teacher education (Reynolds, 1982).

Educators working within the framework of the Dean's Grant Program looked at a number of issues facing teacher educators. These issues revolved around such questions as: Who is a competent teacher? What must a teacher know and be able to do in order to teach in a mainstream classroom that includes one or more handicapped children? Is there an adequate knowledge base for making major changes in teacher education? What is the state of the art in training teachers? Who should conduct the training? What is the role of special education? Must teacher education be restructured and must the roles of teacher educators be renegotiated? (Sharp, 1982).

Many educators tried to delineate competencies essential to successful accommodation of handicapped students. A Texas survey identified needed areas as attitudinal change knowledge of the mainstreaming process, skills needed to facilitate the process, and strategies for the implementation of skills. Specific training programs were designed to deal with attitudes, the mainstreaming process, educational implications of various handicapping conditions, individualized instruction, materials development and evaluation, behavior management, career education, informal and formal assessment techniques, integration and self-concept development, and communication skills (Haughton & Cochrane, 1978).

Another approach to determining needed competencies was the survey of a program's weaknesses as perceived by its graduates. A report of such a survey in Kentucky suggested that program graduates seemed to be having the greatest difficulty in measuring, planning for, and dealing with individual differences. The most frequent program improvement recommendation was more field work or practical experience (Middleton, Morsink, & Cohen, 1979). It became obvious that if all teachers were to be trained to work with handicapped students, the attitudes and skills necessary for such a task must be identified.

A primary goal of the Dean's Grant Projects became the identification of a common body of professional knowledge, skills, behaviors, attitudes, and values that characterized the teaching profession. The following ten clusters of capabilities were developed to provide a map of the domains of professional competence important to teachers participating in the design and implementation of individualized instruction:

1. *Curriculum*. The addition of handicapped students to regular classrooms increases the breadth and variety of students' learning needs and skills which, in turn, requires a sound general knowledge of curriculum at a number of levels.

2. *Teaching Basic Skills*. All teachers should be able to teach skills of *literacy* (reading, writing, spelling, arithmetic, study and speaking); skills of life *maintenance* (health, safety, consumerism, and law) and *personal development skills* (value clarification, goal setting, decision-making and problem-solving).

3. *Class Management*. All teachers should be proficient in class management procedures, including applied behavior analysis, group alerting, guiding transitions, materials arrangement, crisis intervention techniques and group approaches to creating positive affective climate.

4. *Professional Consultation and Communications*. All teachers should be able to establish and maintain responsible interactions with colleagues and administrators. The ability to function as members of a team should be taught and experienced. (Investigations of the resource room model indicate that many teachers lack the interpersonal skills essential for cooperative planning.)

5. *Teacher-Parent-Student Relationships*. All teachers should have skills and sensitivity for dealing with parents and siblings of handicapped students; they should have had opportunities to practice skills in this area as part of their practicums in teacher preparation.

6. *Student-Student Relationships*. All teachers should be able to teach pupils how to relate to each other in ways that produce satisfaction and self-improvement. When teachers have the skill to take command of the social structures of their classes, they find that they have a powerful tool with which to construct individualized learning situations.

7. *Exceptional Conditions*. All teachers should have a knowledge of basic procedures for the instruction of students with limited sight or hearing, emotional problems, limited cognitive abilities or outstanding abilities and talents. It is not reasonable to expect all teachers to know everything about exceptional conditions, but they should have rudimentary knowledge in all areas and know that additional help is available, how to get it, and how to use it.

8. *Referral*. Teachers need to learn the procedures for referrals, the responsibilities involved, and the ways to capitalize on referral resources in behalf of better education for individual pupils.

9. *Individualized Teaching*. All teachers should be competent in the assessment of the individual student's educational needs and in adapting instruction to the individual.

10. *Professional Values*. All teachers, in their personal commitments and professional behavior with pupils, parents, and colleagues, should exemplify the same

consideration for all individuals and their educational rights as are called for in PL 94–142. These include the right of individual students to due process in all school placement decisions, to education in the least restrictive environment and to carefully individualized education. (Reynolds, Birch, Grohs, Howsam, & Morsink, 1980)

In-service and preservice programs must focus on attitudinal aspects of teachers as well as on skills and competencies. Zand (1977, p. 52) claims that teachers have a social identity, in which they are expected to demonstrate almost perfect attitudes and abilities, as if they were supernatural agents sent to deal with children. It is assumed that teachers are:

- ☐ kind and warm to each child;
- ☐ accepting of all types of children; therefore accepting of those children with problems;
- ☐ able to provide each child with all the skills he needs, within the area of their own professional competence;
- ☐ able to provide each student with a positive attitude toward self;
- ☐ able to provide a positive group attitude of warmth and acceptance toward those youngsters who vary significantly from the majority of youngsters in the class.

In spite of their social identity, it is not logical to assume that all teachers have positive attitudes toward all children. Many factors and conditions contribute to teachers' attitudes toward children who are atypical. The sources of negative attitudes are not easily identified; they may be related to lack of exposure to exceptional children or to lack of knowledge about specific areas of exceptionality. Negative attitudes may also be reactions to differences in language, ethnic origin, behavior, and/or socioeconomic status. Target areas for change can be identified as teachers' attitudes toward handicapped students, gifted students, and minority students.

Handicapped Students In a measure of regular classroom teachers' attitudes toward teaching handicapped children, Stephens and Braun (1980) identified four variables related to teachers' willingness to accept handicapped students into their classrooms. Teachers who had taken courses in special education, those confident of their abilities to teach exceptional children, those who believed handicapped children can become useful members of society, and those who believed public schools should educate exceptional children were more willing to integrate handicapped students than were other teachers.

Other factors contribute to positive attitudes of classroom teachers toward handicapped students. Larrivee (1981) found an important factor is increased experience and contact with handicapped children in conjunction with knowledge attainment and specific skill acquisition. The availability of supportive personnel also enhances the development of a positive attitude toward handicapped students.

Schools and universities planning programs designed to deal with teachers' attitudes toward handicapped students can learn a great deal about their participants and their attitudes from the administration of a preassessment. Figure 10.2 is a model for assessing attitudes toward mildly handicapped students.

Since regular classroom teachers are in a unique position to help maximize the integration of severely handicapped students into regular schools, their attitudes toward these students are important. Stainback and Stainback (1982) have demonstrated that the attitudes of prospective teachers can be significantly influenced by the presentation of information about severely handicapped students and their education in an exceptional child course. It has also been found that the presentation of reading materials and subsequent small group discussions can modify the attitudes of practicing regular classroom teachers toward the integration of severely handicapped students (Stainback, Stainback, Strathe, and Dedrick, 1983).

Gifted Students Teachers' attitudes toward gifted students is of equal concern. Gallagher (1985) refers to the hostility some teachers frequently show toward gifted students. He refers to the "That will show Mr. Smartypants" syndrome (p. 390) expressed by giving the gifted student more work. Such an attitude is probably a reaction to threat, brought about by the student's inadvertant challenge to the teacher's role of master authority in the classroom by an evidence of advanced knowledge or skill. When teachers examine their feelings, they may see a reflection of their own insecurities.

Teachers' attitudes toward gifted students vary greatly. Some teachers may favor these students, or reject them for behaving in nonconforming ways, or fail to notice their talent. Better training of teachers in listening and asking questions, as well as practical experiences, might improve the readiness of teachers to accept gifted students in their classrooms (Strom, 1983).

Minority Students Educators have come to realize that students can be handicapped in many ways—by physical and mental impairments, by poverty, or by alienation from the predominant culture (Moore, 1976). Many children and young people who are identified as handicapped experience the double jeopardy of more than one handicap by nature of their social, racial, and/or economic status.

Minority students have been, and still are, overrepresented in special education placements. Mercer's (1973) social system view of the learning environment offers some insight into the reason. According to this theory, every teacher has standards and expectations for acceptable classroom behavior. When children do not meet these expectations, they are considered for special education.

In addition to instructional considerations, teachers may need to examine their own value systems and to evaluate their attitudes toward specific minorities. As a start toward attitudinal change regarding minority students,

FIGURE 10.2 Teacher's Attitude

Module I Pre-Assessment
Let's Try on a Learning Problem

1. Should the regular classroom teacher be responsible for the education of mildly handicapped students?
   a. Yes
   b. No
   c. Yes, only if support services are available.

2. Rate the following disability groups as to their acceptability into regular classroom settings using 3 to indicate not acceptable, 2 to indicate only limited placement as acceptable, and 1 to indicate acceptable with appropriate support services.
   ___ Educable Mentally Retarded   ___ Orthopedically Handicapped
   ___ Emotionally Disturbed   ___ Blind
   ___ Learning Disabled   ___ Deaf
                                       ___ Trainable Mentally Retarded

3. Rate the problem areas which you might expect as a result of mainstreaming mildly handicapped students.

	Not an Additional Problem Area	Only Small Additional Problem Area	Considered to Be Major Problem Area
Structuring classroom space	1	2	3
Management of time	1	2	3
Behavior or discipline problems	1	2	3
Individualization of instruction	1	2	3
Motivation	1	2	3
Peer acceptance	1	2	3
Classroom involvement	1	2	3
Teaming with supportive staff	1	2	3

4. What apprehensions do you have in working with handicapped students?

   Are these apprehensions based upon
   (1) inadequate training   Yes   No
   (2) lack of experience   Yes   No
   (3) other (specify)

Put an X on top of the response which most accurately represents your current opinion about the statement. There are *no* correct answers.

Key: SD Strong Disagree   N No Opinion   A   Agree
      D   Disagree   SA Strongly Agree

5. I believe that placing a handicapped student in a typical classroom would damage the student's self-concept.	SD	D	N	A	SA
6. A handicapped child will be motivated to learn in a regular classroom.	SD	D	N	A	SA
7. As a result of placement in a regular classroom, a handicapped child will develop a more positive attitude toward school.	SD	D	N	A	SA
8. Placement of a handicapped child in a regular classroom will likely result in his becoming socially withdrawn.	SD	D	N	A	SA
9. I think that the integration of handicapped students into the regular classroom will harm the educational achievement of average students.	SD	D	N	A	SA
10. The experience of being in a regular classroom will increase the chances of a handicapped child attaining a more productive and independent place in society.	SD	D	N	A	SA
11. Given my current understanding, I believe that "mainstreaming" will benefit the teacher as well as all children.	SD	D	N	A	SA
12. Assignment of a handicapped child to a regular classroom is a wise administrative decision.	SD	D	N	A	SA

Source: From "Attitude toward Mainstreaming," Dean's Grant, the University of Arkansas. Used with permission.

Simpson (1982) suggests that teachers complete a self-assessment survey of attitudes toward minority groups (see Figure 10.3). After completing the survey, respondents should ask a colleague to evaluate them on the same scale. Areas of discrepancy might be reflected on and discussed, as might a consideration of attitudes that may require modification.

Although attitudinal changes are important, they must be accompanied by appropriate changes in instructional strategies. Brantlinger and Guskin (1985) claim that "simply desegrating diverse populations without adopting effective methods of teaching them can have a negative impact on the minority student" (p. 10).

Teachers must become aware that they have to adapt instruction to children's backgrounds at the same time children begin to adapt to school standards and expectations (Esquivel & Yoshida, 1985). Although local school districts are becoming more sensitive to the instructional implications of cultural diversity, there is little evidence that teacher training programs are placing emphasis on cultural diversity as a generic skill (Rodriguez, 1982).

Multicultural education is education that values cultural pluralism. Education for cultural pluralism includes four major thrusts:

FIGURE 10.3 Minority Attitude Self-Assessment Survey

	Strongly Agree	Agree	Mildly Agree	Neutral	Mildly Disagree	Disagree	Strongly Disagree
1. I am uncomfortable in conferences with individuals with skin colors different from my own.							
2. I consider minority student educational problems basically to be a funciton of a lack of parental emphasis on doing well in school.							
3. I am intimidated by individuals from cultures that I do not fully understand.							
4. I believe that the dominant language of the home, even if not English, should be accommodated in public schools.							
5. I believe that the dominant language of the home, even if not English, should be taught in public schools.							
6. I believe that certain minority groups are innately inferior in educational potential to the majority culture.							
7. I am uncomfortable in conferences with parents who are unable to speak standard English.							
8. I frequently become angry in conferences with parents who are unable to speak standard English.							
9. I experience many similarities with the minority pupils and families with whom I am associated.							
10. I am usually as satisfied with my conferences with minority parents as with those including nonminorities.							

	Strongly Agree	Agree	Mildly Agree	Neutral	Mildly Disagree	Disagree	Strongly Disagree
11. I would prefer to work in a school serving children and families from cultures and backgrounds similar to my own.							
12. I believe that most minority social problems could be solved if groups made up their minds to improve their conditions.							
13. I do not believe that schools can solve many of the problems experienced by minorities.							
14. I am surprised when minority parents show an interest in their child's school-related performance.							
15. I resent certain groups of parents calling me at home more than others.							
16. I am equally at ease in accepting a dinner invitation to the homes of my minority and nonminority students.							
17. I find it easier to empathize with parents whose background is similar to my own.							
18. I am more inclined to give advice to minority parents than to other groups.							
19. I find it easier to admit to a minority parent than a nonminority parent that I was wrong.							
20. I am more inclined to ask minority parents to participate in home-based programs.							

Source: R. L. Simpson (1982). *Conferencing parents of exceptional children.* Reprinted with permission of Aspen Publishers, Inc., copyright 1982.

1. The teaching of values which support cultural diversity and individual uniqueness.
2. The encouragement of the qualitative expansion of existing ethnic cultures and their incorporation into the mainstream of American socio-economic and political life.
3. The support of exploration in alternative and emerging lifestyles.
4. The encouragement of multiculturalism, multilingualism and multidialectism. (American Association for Colleges of Teacher Education, 1973, p. 4)

Rodriguez (1982) presents guidelines for multicultural education that are not aimed at training teachers to work exclusively with handicapped children from particular minority backgrounds. The guidelines are intended to assist in the training for teachers for exceptional children that will provide meaningful education regardless of the ethnic composition. The concept of multicultural education is based on the premises that there are differences in students within any classroom and that all students live in a pluralistic society.

It is interesting to note that the National Council for Accreditation of Teacher Education (NCATE) has approved and implemented two standards relevant to the skills and attitudes mentioned in the previous section. A standard requires that all teachers have the knowledge and skills necessary to provide an appropriate education for exceptional learners (Haring & McCormick, 1986), and another standard requires that prospective teachers must be provided with some knowledge and skills related to multicultural concepts (Chinn & McCormick, 1986).

The task is tremendous: since classroom teachers serve the needs of nonexceptional and exceptional children, they must be trained in their usual skills, knowledge, and attitudes. In addition, they must be trained in the competencies required to teach atypical children. The importance of appropriate training for teachers who work with exceptional students cannot be overemphasized.

The mandate for least restrictive environment suggests changes in both teacher education and teacher certification of regular classroom teachers. In an investigation of certification requirements, Patton and Braithwaite (1980) found that most states did not require regular classroom teachers to complete courses in special education for initial certification or for certification renewal. Alternatives to special course work at the university level have been integration of concepts dealing with exceptional students into the regular curriculum and in-service training for teachers already in the field.

To meet this need, PL 94–142 mandates a Comprehensive System of Personnel Development to provide appropriate preservice and in-service education for classroom teachers. Under this provision, each local education agency must specify in writing the procedures to be used in the local implementation of the comprehensive system of personnel development established by the state education agency (Hayes & Higgins, 1978). The federal law requires that in-service training be provided to both regular and special educators. Teachers must have input into the planning and designing of the personnel development activities, assuring that the training will be relevant to teacher needs.

In-service training is essential to the realization of any significant education reform (Powers, 1983). If any change in the public schools is to be effective, a viable in-service format must be devised that addresses the needs of those who are to serve as change agents. Needs assessments provide a starting point. Figure 10.4 depicts a simple form used to determine the needs of university personnel before in-service training involvement.

Crisci (1981) contends that in-service training of regular educators must be given priority status if they are to be expected to accept the increased responsibilities of teaching exceptional children and young people. To help accomplish this task, a number of federal and state projects have been funded to provide such training and technical assistance to school systems and universities engaged in training efforts.

Implementing the personnel development section of PL 94–142 requires unprecedented collaboration among state education agencies, local education agencies, and institutions of higher education (Burrello & Baker, 1980). An example of a collaborative planning style is the joint effort of the New Jersey State Department of Education, fifty local school districts, and five

FIGURE 10.4   Needs Assessment

**Western Carolina University:
Mainstreaming Needs Assessment, Dean's Grant**

Staff _____ Faculty _____ Administrator _____ Student _____
Department/Major _____

Please indicate in rank order your needs relative to preservice training in teaching handicapped children in the least restrictive environment.

1. Knowledge of the law _____
2. Knowledge of handicapping conditions _____
3. Attitudes toward handicapped people _____
4. Identification and referral procedures _____
5. Behavior management _____
6. Assessment techniques _____
7. Curriculum _____
8. Methods and materials _____
9. Individualized Education Programs _____
10. Practicum experience with handicapped children _____
11. Other: _____

Source: J. Schulz (1981). *Dean's Grant.* Cullowhee, N.C.: Western Carolina University.

institutions of higher education. This group has planned a number of activities, including ongoing seminar groups, statewide workshops, individual consultation, and dissemination of written information (Nadler, Merron, & Friedel, 1981). Through a program of this nature, participants develop understanding and skill in planning and evaluation, implementing educational innovation, and knowledge of resources for serving exceptional students.

Many models have been developed for planning and delivering in-service training. From a review of the literature related to in-service training, Powers (1983, pp. 433–434) gathered nine guidelines applicable in many situations:

1. While there does not appear to be any single superior method for the delivery of inservice training, the use of a variety of activities within an inservice program is probably more effective than the use of a single activity for all participants.

2. The extensive variety of potential formats should be considered in the design of inservice programs. The wide range of format possibilities includes campus courses, on-site courses, workshops, conferences, retreats, consultations, projects, modules, laboratory experiences, travel, independent study, guided research, literature reviews, materials development, and others.

3. Activity-based experiences, those which engage the learner in direct participation, appear to be particularly effective.

4. Live demonstration of techniques, materials, or strategies contributes to learner comprehension.

5. When inservice goals are associated with the acquisition of new skills and behaviors, supervised trials with feedback provide an effective strategy.

6. When inservice goals are associated with attitude changes, particularly attitudes toward handicapped children, the use of simulation techniques may be especially effective.

7. Within the inservice experience, teachers should be encouraged to construct and generate new ideas, to share these ideas with each other, and to assist each other in the development and revision of their ideas.

8. Teachers learning from other teachers is a potentially valuable approach to inservice. As a form of peer training, this process may be operationalized in a number of creative ways, such as release time to observe other teachers and videotapes.

9. A number of more innovative inservice formats and methods have involved a redefinition of the traditional relationship between trainer and trainee. Examples are teams comprised of university faculty and public school teachers and inservice trainers teaching demonstration lessons in trainees' classrooms.

In exploring teachers' skills, attitudes, and training needs, it becomes apparent that the education of special educators is not very different from that of regular educators. The quality of all education must be improved if the broad range of individual differences found in today's classrooms is to be served. As Corrigan (1978, p. 28) states:

The key to making the concepts in PL 94–142 come alive in the schools of this country is a new commitment to the pre-service and inservice education of America's teachers. Reform must move in both directions to *universities* as well as to schools.

Administrators

☐ Crisci (1981) declares that "the school administrator is the key to success in mainstreaming" (p. 180). In bringing about change in teacher education, the administrator's training needs must be given serious consideration. To meet the requirements of PL 94–142, educational administrators need to develop knowledge and skills related to exceptional students and also additional competencies in the business and financial aspects of education.

In the delivery of services for exceptional students, the primary administrators are directors of special education and school principals. In a delineation of roles for these two administrators, Robson (1981, p. 378) describes as follows administrative behavior relative to delivery of special education services:

> 1. Directors of special education are expected to provide minimal amounts of direct service in pupil functions or personnel administration. The only personnel area in which directors are expected to play a role is in relation to certain consultative aspects in a helping capacity. No major line relationship is perceived by directors or expected of directors by others in the role set. Regular classroom teachers, however, appear to want more in this area from directors than all other groups in the role set.
>
> 2. Directors of special education are expected to play their major role in functions that involve boundary spanning activities. That is, dealing with parents or groups beyond the school building or between schools is universally considered to be the director's job. In addition, maintenance of the special education organization, which provides such boundary spanning functions as referrals to and from other agencies, transportation, diagnosis, and placement, is also allocated to the director.
>
> 3. The principal is expected to take major responsibility in direct service to pupils and in all supervisory and evaluation aspects of personnel administration. All that takes place within the building is generally conceded to be the major responsibility of the principal. Internal operational functions are perceived by all members of the role set except regular classroom teachers to be almost the exclusive province of the principal. Organizational maintenance of special education functions and extrabuilding activities are seen universally as minor functions of the principal.

Most states recognize special education administration, and more than half the states require separate certification. Although the role of the special education administrator and that of the school principal have been defined by local school systems, there is some logic to the notion that all educational administrators should become "special" administrators through training in special education competencies (Stile & Pettibone, 1980).

A survey conducted to determine administrators' competency requirements and training needs indicated the need to acquire and maintain current knowledge of research, trends, and programs for the effective education of exceptional students. Other needs were in the areas of keeping data-based records, planning programs, interpreting mandates, assisting in program redesign, assessing needs of the exceptional student, and using evaluation data for program revision (Nevin, 1979).

A further attempt to define training needs of principals was directed toward attitudes and knowledge of principals in a large school district (Cline, 1981). Although the study found that principals' attitudes toward exceptional students were not entirely negative, their lack of knowledge about handicapped students was apparent. The indication is that a major emphasis by teacher trainers and inservice programs must be on educating principals.

Although education programs have appropriately focused on the teacher as the facilitating person in the exceptional student's school experience, it is clear that all personnel involved in the school system should have

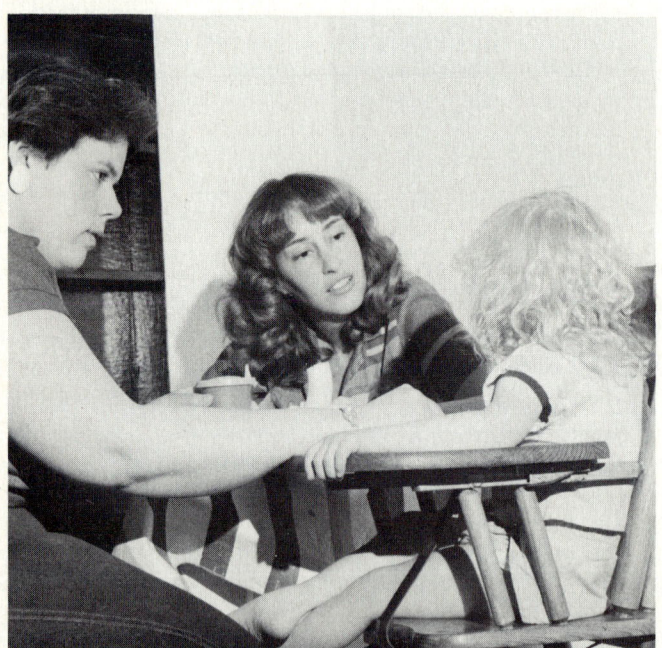

☐ *Teacher education programs are changing to accommodate the increasingly important role of parents as highly visible, active participants in their children's education.*

training to prepare them to function on the interdisciplinary team and to be knowledgeable about the exceptional student. Corrigan and Howey (1980, p. 211) state the challenge:

> Society now demands a new breed of teacher for a new breed of school—a well prepared, highly motivated professional, capable of understanding a broad range of learning problems and of designing and implementing curricular and instructional strategies to solve them. If the school of the future is to become a vehicle for social progress then a sense of social purpose must pervade every level of the educational system and the teaching profession.

Conclusion

Shortly after the passage of the law for education of handicapped children, the president of the National Education Association declared that "PL 94–142's challenge for the education profession is incalculable, as is its promise for those handicapped students whose educational needs have been neglected or ignored by the public school" (Ryor, 1977, p. 24). Since that time, the challenge has permeated every level of education.

Schools and universities concerned with teacher education have been required to examine their purpose, strategies, and programs. The field of special education has changed drastically to accommodate the changing population of exceptional children and young people and therefore the changing role and environment of the educator.

Perhaps more challenging has been the changing role of general educators. Teachers and other personnel have been required to change their attitudes and increase their repertoire of competencies to enable them to understand and teach children whom they may not have expected to teach.

The increasingly important role of parents has also impacted teacher education. As participants on the interdisciplinary team, parents have become visable and active in today's school. This role has also added a new dimension to the training needs of educators, as they are required to interact with parents and other family members.

Although the role of the educator appears to be overwhelming at times, there are also positive changes. Technological advances promise to alleviate some of the paper work and to expedite communication between home and school. Community resources are becoming involved in schools and providing opportunities to students and teachers for extended experiences. Administrators are discovering the advantages of volunteer programs and the unlimited possibilities that develop through school-community interaction.

The greatest promise lies in the increasingly stronger bond between home and school. With appropriate training for parents and for teachers, the hypothesized partnership can become a reality.

References

American Association for Colleges of Teacher Education. (1973). No one model American. *Journal of Teacher Education, 4,* n.p.

American Association of Colleges for Teacher Education. (1978). Beyond the mandate: The professional imperative. *Journal of Teacher Education, 29*(6), 44–46.

Bailey, D.B. (1984). A triaxial model of the interdisciplinary team and group process. *Exceptional Children, 51*(1), 17–25.

Berghoff, B. K., & Berghoff, P. J. (1979). Communication techniques for gifted/talented support teachers. *Journal for the Education of the Gifted, 3*(2), 105–107.

Blackhurst, A. E. (1981). Noncategorical teacher preparation: Problems and promises. *Exceptional Children, 48*(3), 197–205.

Brantlinger, E. A., & Guskin, S. L. (1985). Implications of social and cultural differences for special education with specific recommendations. *Focus on Exceptional Children, 18*(1), 1–12.

Bricker, D. (1979). Educating the severely handicapped: Philosophical and implementation dilemmas. *Teacher Education and Special Education, 2*(3), 59–65.

Burrello, L. C., & Baker, K. T. (1980). Developing a CSPD through a peer planning and dissemination network. *Teacher Education and Special Education, 3*(1), 5–10.

Burton, T. H. (1981). Deciding what to teach the severely/profoundly retarded student: A teacher responsibility. *Education and Training of the Mentally Retarded, 16*(1), 74–80.

Cartwright, G. P., Cartwright, C. A., & Ward, M. E. (1981). *Educating special learners.* Belmont, Calif.: Wadsworth Publishing Company.

Chinn, P. C., & McCormick, L. (1986). Cultural diversity and exceptionality. In N. G. Haring & L. McCormick (Eds.), *Exceptional children and youth* (4th ed.), 95–118. Columbus, Oh.: Charles E. Merrill.

Clements, J. E., & Alexander, R. N. (1975). Parent training: Bringing it all back home. *Focus on Exceptional Children, 7*(5), 1–12.

Cline, R. (1981). Principals' attitudes and knowledge about handicapped children. *Exceptional Children, 48*(2), 172–174.

Corrigan, D. C. (1978). Public Law 94–142: A matter of human rights; a call for change in schools and colleges of education. In J. K. Grosenick & M. C. Reynolds (Eds.), *Teacher education: Renegotiating roles for mainstreaming,* 17–29. Reston, Va.: The Council for Exceptional Children.

Corrigan, D. C., & Howey, K. R. (1980). The future: Creating the conditions for professional practice. In D. C. Corrigan & K. R. Howey (Eds.). *Special education in transition.* Reston, Va.: The Council for Exceptional Children.

Courtnage, L., & Healy, H. (1984). Inter-disciplinary team training. *Teacher Education and Special Education, 7*(1), 3–11.

Crisci, P. E. (1981). Competencies for mainstreaming: Problems and issues. *Education and Training of the Mentally Retarded, 16*(3), 175–181.

DeBerry, J. (1980). Choice or chance. *Teacher Education and Special Education, 3*(4), 37–45.

Egbert, R. L. (1978). Reflections on the past, present, and future of special education. In J. K. Grosenick & M. C. Reynolds (Eds.), *Teacher education: Renegotiating roles for mainstreaming,* 9–16. Reston, Va.: The Council for Exceptional Children.

Epstein, J. L. (1985). Home and school connections in schools of the future: Implications of research on parent involvement. *Peabody Journal of Education, 62*(2), 18–41.

Escudero, G. R., & Sears, J. (1982). Teachers' and teacher aides' perceptions of their responsibilities when teaching severely and profoundly handicapped students. *Education and Training of the Mentally Retarded, 17*(3), 190–195.

Esquivel, G. B., & Yoshida, R. K. (1985). Special education for language minority students. *Focus on Exceptional Children, 18*(3), 1–8.

Friend, M. (1985). Training special educators to be consultants. *Teacher Education and Special Education, 8*(3), 115–120.

Gallagher, J. J. (1985). *Teaching the gifted child* (3rd ed.). Boston: Allyn and Bacon.

Golin, A. K., & Ducanis, A. J. (1981). *The interdisciplinary team.* Rockville, Md.: Aspen Systems.

Graden, J. L., Casey, A., & Christenson, S. L. (1985). Implementing a prereferral intervention system: Part I. The model. *Exceptional Children, 51*(5), 377–384.

Grant, G. (1984). The teacher's predicament. *American Educator, 8*(1), 30–36.

Gubser, L. (1980). Special education and national accreditation. *Teacher Education and Special Education, 3*(2), 3–12.

Haring, N. G. (1978). Conclusion: Classroom two. In N. G. Haring (Ed.), *Behavior of exceptional children* (2nd ed.). Columbus, Oh.: Charles E. Merrill.

Haring, N. G., & McCormick, L. (1986). Contemporary changes in special education. In N. G. Haring & L. McCormick (Eds.), *Exceptional children and youth* (4th ed.). Columbus, Oh.: Charles E. Merrill.

Haughton, D. D., & Cochrane, P. (1978). Modular instructional system development. In J. K. Grosenick & M. C. Reynolds (Eds.) *Teacher education: Renegotiating roles for mainstreaming,* 223–235. Reston, Va.: The Council for Exceptional Children.

Hayes, J., & Higgins, S. T. (1978). Issues regarding the IEP: Teachers on the front line. *Exceptional Children, 44*(4), 267–273.

Howsam, R., Corrigan, D., Denemark, G., & Nash, R. (1976). *Educating a profession.* Washington, D.C.: American Association of Colleges for Teacher Education.

Idol-Maestas, L., Lloyd, S., & Lilly, M. S. (1981). A noncategorical approach to direct service and teacher education. *Exceptional Children, 48*(3), 213–220.

Idol-Maestas, L., & Ritter, S. (1985). A follow-up study of resource/consulting teachers. *Teacher Education and Special Education, 8*(3), 121–131.

Karnes, M. B., & Esry, D. R. (1981). Working with parents of young exceptional children. *Educational Horizons, 59*(3), 143–149.

Kroth, R., & Krehbiel, R. (1982). Parent-teacher interaction. Washington, D.C.: American Association of Colleges for Teacher Education.

Larrivee, B. (1981). Effect of inservice training intensity on teachers' attitudes toward mainstreaming. *Exceptional Children, 48*(1), 34–39.

Maker, C. J. (1982). *Teaching models in education of the gifted.* Rockville, Md.: Aspen Systems.

Marozas, D. S., & May, D. C. (1980). Factors which motivate job acceptance among teachers of severely and profoundly mentally retarded children. *Education and Training of the Mentally Retarded, 15*(4), 293–297.

McDowell, F. E., & Sontag, E. (1977). The severely and profoundly handicapped as catalysts for change. In E. Sontag (Ed.), *Educational programming for the severely and profoundly handicapped.* Reston, Va.: The Council for Exceptional Children.

McDowell County Schools. (1985). Enhancing instructional program options. Grant proposal. McDowell County, N.C.

McLoughlin, J. A. (1981). Training together to work together. *Teacher Education and Special Education, 4*(4), 45–54.

Mercer, J. R. (1973). *Labelling the mentally retarded.* Los Angeles: University of California Press.

Meyen, E. L. (1979). Quality teacher education. *Teacher Education and Special Education, 2*(3), 34–40.

Middleton, E. J., Morsink, C., & Cohen, S. (1979). Program graduates' perception of need for training in mainstreaming. *Exceptional Children, 45*(4), 256–261.

Moore, E. R. (1976). Foreword. In R. L. Jones (Ed.), *Mainstreaming and the minority child*, ix. Reston, Va.: The Council for Exceptional Children.

Mori, A. A., & Masters, L. F. (1980). *Teaching the severely mentally retarded.* Germantown, Md.: Aspen Systems.

Nadler, B., Merron, M., & Friedel, W. K. (1981). Public Law 94–142: One response to the personnel development mandate. *Exceptional Children, 47*(6), 463–464.

Nevin, A. (1979). Special education administration competencies required of the general education administrator. *Exceptional Children, 45*(5), 363–365.

Paolucci-Whitcomb, P., & Nevin, A. (1985). Preparing consulting teachers through a collaborative approach between university faculty and field-based consulting teachers. *Teacher Education and Special Education, 8*(3), 132–143.

Patton, J. M., & Braithwaite, R. L. (1980). P.L. 94–142 and the changing status of teacher certification/recertification: A survey of state education agencies. *Teacher Education and Special Education, 3*(2), 43–47.

Perkins, S. A. (1979). Emphasis and re-emphasis in teacher education. *Teacher Education and Special Education, 2*(3), 12–15.

Powers, D. A. (1983). Mainstreaming and the inservice education of teachers. *Exceptional Children, 49*(5), 432–439.

Reynolds, M. C. (1982). *Foundations of teacher preparation: Responses to Public Law 94–142.* Minneapolis: University of Minnesota.

Reynolds, M. C., Birch, J. W., Grohs, D., Howsam, R., & Morsink, C. (1980). *A common body of practice for teachers: The challenge of Public Law 94–142 to teacher education.* Washington, D.C.: American Association of Colleges for Teacher Education.

Robson, D. L. (1981). Administering educational services for the handicapped: Role expectations and perceptions. *Exceptional Children, 47*(5), 377–378.

Rodriquez, F. (1982). Mainstreaming a multicultural concept into special education: Guidelines for teacher trainers. *Exceptional Children, 49*(3), 220–227.

Ryor, J. (1977). Integrating the handicapped. *Today's Education,* (Sept./Oct.), 24.

Sailor, W., & Haring, N. (1977). Some current directions in education of the severely/multiply handicapped. *AAESPH Review, 2*, 3–23.

Sawyer, H. W., & Sawyer, S. H. (1981). A teacher-parent communication training approach. *Exceptional Children, 47*(4), 305–306.

Schulz, J. B., & Turnbull, A. P. (1984). *Mainstreaming handicapped students.* Boston: Allyn and Bacon.

Seligman, M. (1979a). *Strategies for helping parents of exceptional children.* New York: The Free Press.

Seligman, M. (1979b). The teacher as a facilitator in parent-teacher conferences. *Education Unlimited, 1*(4), 23–25.

Simpson, R. L. (1982a). Future training issues. *Exceptional Education Quarterly, 3*(2), 81–88.

Simpson, R. L. (1982b). *Conferencing parents of exceptional children.* Rockville, Md.: Aspen Systems.

The Southeastern Regional Coalition for Personnel Preparation to Work with the Severely/Profoundly Handicapped. (1982). Developing personnel preparation programs to train personnel to teach severely handicapped individuals. *Teacher Education and Special Education, 5*(1), 46–51.

Stainback, S., & Stainback, W. (1982). Influencing the attitudes of regular class teachers about the education of severely retarded students. *Education and Training of the Mentally Retarded, 17*(2), 88–92.

Stainback, S., Stainback, W., Strathe, M., & Dedrick, C. (1983). Preparing regular classroom teachers for the integration of severely handicapped students: An experimental study. *Education and Training of the Mentally Retarded, 18*(3), 204–209.

Stainback, W., & Stainback, S. (1983). A review of research on the educability of profoundly retarded persons. *Education and Training of the Mentally Retarded, 18*(2), 90–100.

Stephens, T. M., & Braun, B. L. (1980). Measures of regular classroom teachers' attitudes toward handicapped children. *Exceptional Children, 46*(4), 292–294.

Stile, S. W., & Pettibone, T. J. (1980). Training and certification of administrators in special education. *Exceptional Children, 46*(7), 530–533.

Stokes, S. (1982). *School based staff support teams: A blueprint for action.* Reston, Va.: The Council for Exceptional Children.

Strom, R. D. (1981). Accountability and educating the handicapped. *The Educational Forum, 45,* 337–350.

Strom, R. D. (1983). Expectations for educating the gifted and talented. *The Educational Forum, 47*(3), 279–303.

Suchara, H. T. (1982). Parents and teachers: A partnership. *Childhood Education, 58*(3), 130–133.

Tawney, J. W., & Smith, J. (1981). An analysis of the forum: Issues in education of the severely and profoundly retarded. *Exceptional Children, 48*(1), 5–18.

Thomas, M. A. (1980). Current trends in preparing teachers of the severely and profoundly retarded: A conversation with Susan and William Stainback. *Education and Training of the Mentally Retarded, 15*(1), 43–49.

Umbreit, J., Karlan, G., York, R., & Haring, N. G. (1980). Preparing teachers of the severely handicapped: Responsibilities and competencies of the teacher trainer. *Teacher Education and Special Education, 3*(2), 57–72.

Wang, M. C., & Birch, J. W. (1984). Comparison of a full-time mainstreaming program and a resource room approach. *Exceptional Children, 51*(1), 33–40.

Witt, J. C., Miller, C. D., McIntyre, R. M., & Smith, D. (1984). Effects of variables on parental perceptions of staffings. *Exceptional Children, 1*(1), 27–32.

Zand, C. R. (1977). American attitudes toward handicapped children. In P. Bates, T. L. West, & R. B. Schmerl (Eds.), *Mainstreaming: Problems, potentials, and perspectives,* 43–53. Minneapolis: National Support Systems Project.

Name Index

Abramson, M., 118, 127
Ackerman, J., 118
Adler, M. M., 154
Affleck, G., 239
Agard, J. A. 180, 181, 183, 184
Ahr, A. E., 244
Albert, R. S., 47, 222
Alexander, R. N., 316
Algozzine, B., 103
Allen, D., 239
Ambrose, S. A., 269
Anderson, R. S., 80–81
Anderson, W., 128, 129, 159, 191, 192
Angney, A., 281
Anthony, M., 236
Apolloni, T., 228
Arick, J., 105
Atwater, E., 147, 151, 152, 154

Bailey, D. B., 314
Baker, B. L., 269, 281
Baker, C., 147
Baker, K. T., 329
Baldwin, L. M., 4
Baldwin, V. L., 269
Ball, T. S., 270
Ballard, J., 103
Ballering, L. D., 81
Bane, M. J., 6
Barabas, G., 42
Barbe, W. B., 222
Barker, L. L., 147
Barry, S. L., 180, 181, 183, 184
Bas, B. A., 124
Bauer, A. M., 266
Beal, E. W., 7, 18
Beale, A. 172, 211
Beavers, W., 12
Becker, W. C., 279
Beckman, P., 3, 17, 22, 57, 260, 288
Beckman-Bell, P., 57, 65, 82
Beers, C. S., 172, 211
Begab, M. J., 66
Bell, C., 248
Bell, R. Q., 245
Berdine, W. H., 94
Bergan, J. R., 281

Berger, E. H., 20, 133, 247, 248, 259, 270, 271
Berger, M., 122, 218
Berghoff, B. K., 311
Berghoff, P. J., 311
Berlin, I., 117, 124
Berne, E., 272
Bessent, H., 260
Bienvenu, M. J., 244
Birch, J. W., 304, 322
Birdsong, C. W., 7, 18
Birney, D., 188
Bishop, D. S., 4
Blacher, J., 69
Blackham, G. J., 229
Blackhurst, A. E., 94, 309
Boersma, F. J., 42
Boggs, E. M., 92
Boll, T. J., 70
Bolton, R., 159, 169, 186, 187, 188, 189
Bommarito, J. W., 246
Bowen, M., 23
Boyd, D., 66
Boyd, R. D., 265
Bradley, R. H., 239
Braithwaite, R. L., 328
Brantley, J. C., 98, 181
Brantlinger, E. A., 325
Brassard, J. A., 83
Braun, B. L., 322
Bricker, D., 264, 278, 300
Bridges, S., 81
Brightman, R. P., 269
Brim, O. G., 230
Bromwich, R. M., 36
Bronfenbrenner, U., 62–63, 130, 278
Brotherson, J. J., 39
Brown, F. F., 243
Brownstone, J. E., 156, 157
Buros, O. K., 246
Burrello, L. C., 329
Burton, T. H., 302
Buscaglia, L., 67, 69, 134
Byalick, R., 127, 149

Cain, L. F., 94, 119
Caldwell, B. M., 239, 244

Callahan, C. M., 103, 283, 284, 287
Callahan, R., 120, 135
Campbell, S. B., 280
Canady, R. L., 177, 190, 196
Canino, D. J., 19, 20, 69
Cansler, D. P., 153, 261
Carter, E. A., 13–14, 15, 18, 23
Cartwright, C. A., 303
Cartwright, G. P., 303
Casey, A., 304, 306
Casuso, V., 264, 278
Cauble, A. E., 39
Cervone, B. T., 106, 108
Chalfant, J. C., 151, 156
Chapman, J. W., 42
Chinitz, S. P., 77, 126
Chinn, P. C., 4, 6, 8, 9, 11, 22, 29, 30, 146, 158, 328
Chitwood, S., 128, 129, 152, 191, 192
Christenson, S. L., 304, 306
Ciccone, J., 220, 221
Ciha, T. E., 46
Clark, B., 282, 286, 287
Clark, D. B., 281
Clark, J., 148, 150
Clements, J. E., 316
Cline, D., 116, 332
Coan, D. L., 148, 253
Cochran, M. M., 63
Cochrane, P., 319, 328
Coffey, K., 229
Cohen, S., 320
Colangelo, N., 44–45, 46, 47, 81, 206
Coleman, D., 44
Coleman, M. C., 106
Colon, F., 16
Cone, J. D., 225, 244
Connor, F. P., 278
Coren, A., 281
Cornell, C. J., 117
Corrigan, D. C., 96, 298, 330, 333
Courtnage, L., 313, 315
Cox, M., 17, 18, 19
Cox, R., 17, 18, 19
Coyne, A., 270

Name Index

Crawford, D., 101
Creal, D., 56, 58, 60, 63, 276
Crisci, P. E., 329, 331
Critchey, D., 117, 124
Crnic, K. A., 56–57
Croft, D. J., 205
Cromwell, R. L., 244
Cross, A. H., 3, 17, 22
Cruickshank, D. R., 120, 135
Cummings, S. T., 69
Curry, L., 105
Cushing, P. J., 65

D'Alonzo, B. J., 67
Dardig, J. C., 127, 226, 253, 271, 279
Davis, D. H., 196
Davis, D. M., 196
Davis, R. E., 56, 74
Dean, W. S., 154
DeBerry, J., 319
Debinski, R. J., 286
Dedrick, C., 323
Delawyer, D. D., 225
Delisle, J., 235
Delp, J. L., 95
Dembo, M. H., 222, 223, 243, 276, 278, 287, 288, 289
Dembrowsky, C., 91
Dempsey, K. V., 290
Denemark, G., 298
DesJardins, C., 154
Dettmann, D. F., 44–45, 46, 47, 81, 206
DeWert, M., 119
Diament, B., 145, 149, 163
Dickson, R. L., 104
Dinkmeyer, D., 272
DiPaola, 104
Dirks, J., 284
Doan, R. N., 267
Doris, J., 93
Doyle, G. F., 281
Dreikurs, 272
Drew, C. J., 31, 33, 40, 41, 44, 60
Drews, E. M., 244
Ducanis, A. J., 120, 313, 314, 315
Dukecki, P. R., 290
Dunkle, M., 262, 272
Dunlap, W. R., 70
Dunn, N. J., 70
Durham, G. H., 119

Dye, C. J., 156, 157
D'Zamko, M., 101, 102

Edge, D., 99, 100, 295
Egan, M. W., 33, 34
Egbert, R. L., 313, 320
Eheart, B. K., 220, 221
Elardo, R., 239
Ellett, C. D., 288
Emmerich, W., 244
Enzer, N., 262
Epanchin, B. C., 131, 132
Epstein, N. B., 4
Epstein, J. L., 317, 318
Escudero, G. R., 303
Eshleman, J. R., 4, 8, 9, 18, 19
Espinoza, R., 288
Esquivel, G. B., 325
Esry, D. R., 276, 316
Evans, J., 169

Faerstein, L. M., 41, 60, 65
Fairfield, B., 126
Fanning, P., 93, 101
Farber, B., 34, 38–39, 55, 56, 57, 90, 244
Featherstone, H., 31, 33, 69, 70
Feldman, M. A., 127, 149
Fenton, K. S., 105
Ferrari, M., 42
Fine, M. J., 46, 220, 259, 261
Fiscus, E., 91
Fisher, E., 46
Fishler, K., 74
Flake-Hobson, B., 139
Flugman, B., 139
Folkman, S., 61
Forbes, C. R., 280
Forman, B. D., 241, 242, 243
Forman, S. G., 241, 242, 243
Foster, M., 122, 218
Fotheringham, J. B., 56, 58, 60, 63, 276
Fowler, P. C., 241, 243
Fowler, S. A., 291
Fox, D. C., 115
Fox, R., 243
Fredericks, A., 194
Fredericks, H. D., 269
Freund, J. H., 239
Friedel, W. K., 330
Friedrich, W. L., 56
Friedrich, W. N., 56–57, 61

Friend, M., 310
Frye, V. H., 161, 162
Fujita, S. R., 287

Gallagher, G. G., 118
Gallagher, J. J., 3, 17, 22, 46, 64, 65, 91, 95, 103, 118, 136, 205, 220, 309, 323
Gallup, G. H., 135, 248
Gardner, R. A., 43
Gargiulo, R. M., 153, 190
Gath, A., 34, 74
Gibbs, H., 99, 105
Gibran, K., 12
Gilles, J., 11
Gilliam, J. E., 106
Ginott, H., 270
Ginsberg, G., 229
Glass, J., 29, 30
Glasser, L. N., 16, 23
Glasser, P. H., 16, 23
Gliedman, J., 109, 115, 118, 122, 125
Goertzels, M., 283
Goertzels, V., 283
Goldberg, M., 265
Goldberg, P., 265
Goldman, L., 126
Goldstein, S., 105, 194, 226
Golin, A. K., 120, 313, 314, 315
Gordon, I. J., 145
Gordon, T., 188
Gorham, K. A., 116, 117, 154
Gottlieb, J., 104
Gotts, E. E., 248, 253
Gradin, J. L., 304, 306
Graliker, B. V., 74
Grana, G. M., 41, 68
Grant, G., 316
Greenbaum, J., 190, 192
Greenberg, M. T., 56–57
Griswold, D., 221
Grohs, D., 322
Grossman, F. K., 74, 75
Grove, D., 269
Gubser, L., 297
Guskin, S. L., 325
Guthrie, D., 55, 57

Haac, L. A., 33
Hackney, H., 47, 48
Haffey, N. A., 228, 281

Name Index

Hagerty, G., 118, 127
Hall, E. G., 95
Halpern, R., 102, 115
Hanley, E. M., 281
Hanson, D. A., 22
Hanson, R. A., 34, 37
Hardman, M. L., 20, 33, 34, 60
Hareven, T. K., 14, 19
Haring, N. G., 95, 299–300, 301, 319, 328
Harman, D., 230
Harrington, A., 194
Harris, K. G., 134, 164, 180, 224
Harris, R., 46
Harrison, R. P., 146
Hart, N. W., 68, 69, 120
Hatfield, E., 57
Haughton, D. P., 320
Hayden, A. H., 269
Hayden, D., 128, 129, 152, 191, 192
Hayes, J., 328
Healy, H., 313, 315
Helsel, E., 119
Henderson, R. A., 64
Henderson, R. W., 213
Henley, C., 129
Heron, T., 134, 164, 180, 224
Hetherington, E. M., 17, 18, 19
Hetrich, E. W., 282
Heward, W. L., 127, 222, 226, 253, 268, 271, 279
Higgins, S. T., 328
Hill, R., 21, 22, 23
Hobbs, N., 131, 132, 133, 290
Hocutt, A. M., 109
Hoffman, C., 50
Hohenshil, T. H., 125, 126
Hollinsworth, J. S., 70
Holmes, T. H., 22
Holroyd, J., 55, 57
Howe, B., 280
Howey, K. R., 298, 333
Howsam, R., 298, 322
Huber, C. H., 66, 126
Huberty, C. J., 288
Hulnick, H. R., 125
Humes, C. W., 125, 126
Hunter, M., 194
Hurley, J. R., 64

Idol-Maestas, L., 149, 309, 311, 312

Jarvis, R. M., 270
Jedrysek, E., 208–209
Jenne, W. C., 244
Johnson, O. G., 246
Johnson, S. B., 183
Jordan, T. E., 56

Kagan, J., 37
Kaminer, R., 208–209
Kaminsky, T., 280
Kanigher, H., 104
Karlan, G., 299–300, 301
Karnes, F. A., 48
Karnes, M. B., 267, 276, 284, 285, 316
Karnes, M. R., 48
Karoly, P., 280
Karp, C. L., 279
Karpowitz, D. H., 5, 10, 14
Katz, D., 126
Kauffman, J. M., 103, 283, 284, 287
Kaufman, M. J., 105
Kershman, S., 219, 222, 274, 276, 277
Kiely, M. C., 280
Kirk, S. A., 46, 91, 95, 103
Klein, S. D., 137, 152, 195
Knapp, D., 227
Knapp, M. L., 148
Knox, L., 148, 150
Koch, A., 81
Koch, R., 81
Kraft, S. P., 127, 130
Krehbiel, R., 317
Kroth, R. L., 188, 194, 222, 224, 226, 270, 272, 273, 317
Küubler-Ross, E., 34

Larrivee, B., 322
Larson, L., 243
Lauritzen, P., 222, 223, 243, 276, 278, 287, 288, 289
Lawrence, K. M., 55
Lazar, A. L., 67
Lazarus, R. S., 61
Lee, R. C., 267
LeMasters, E. E., 9
Leonard, J., 92
Lerner, J. W., 43
Leslie, G. R., 3, 5
Lester, C. F., 80–81
Levant, R. F., 228, 281

Levin, H., 246
Levinson, R. M., 61
Licence, C., 235
Lichter, P., 188
Lieberman, M. A., 58
Lightfoot, S. L., 126
Lillie, D., 16, 274, 275
Lilly, M. S., 309
Lim, P., 124
Liversidge, E. B., 41, 68
Lloyd, S., 309
Lockhart, C., 228, 229
Loesch, P., 194
Logan, D. R., 31, 40, 41, 44, 60
Long, E. W., 161, 162
Long, J. D., 161, 162
Losen, J. G., 134, 145, 201, 203, 208, 211
Losen, S. M., 134, 145, 149, 165, 201, 203, 208, 211
Lowe, J. P., 180
Luscomb, R. L., 70
Lusthaus, C. S., 99, 105, 192
Lusthaus, E. W., 99, 105, 192
Luthman, S. G., 4
Lyon, H. C., 46
Lyon, S., 39

Maccoby, E. E., 246
Maeroff, G., 46
Magnusson, F. J., 162, 163, 168
Maker, C. J., 310
Malone, C. E., 80, 220, 284, 287
Mandell, C. J., 91
Marcus, L. M., 69, 70
Margalit, M., 58
Marion, R. L., 20, 72, 106, 146, 148, 156, 202, 203, 204, 218
Markel, G., 190, 192
Marozas, D. S., 301, 302
Marsh, G. E., 190, 192, 196, 201
Martin, G. H., 153, 261
Martinson, R. A., 95
Maslow, A. H., 161
Mathews, F. N., 127, 286
Matthews, W. S., 42
Mauser, A. J., 286
Maxwell, J. P., 105
May, D. C., 301, 302

Name Index 341

McArthur, D., 57
McCarney, S. B., 162, 163, 168
McCartney, D., 229
McCormick, L., 319, 328
McCubbin, H. I., 22–23, 39
McDowell, F. E., 299, 307
McGoldrick, M., 13–14, 15, 18, 23
McGough, E., 145, 146
McGrade, B. J., 239
McIntyre, R. M., 316
McKay, G., 272
McKinney, J. D., 109
McLean, M., 122, 218
McLoughlin, J. A., 99, 100, 130, 274, 276, 277, 295, 318
McLoughlin, R., 130
McQueeny, M., 239
McWilliams, B. J., 126
Menaghan, E. G., 58
Mercer, J. R., 323
Merron, M., 330
Meyen, E. L., 298, 299
Meyers, C. E., 56, 241
Michaelis, C. T., 39, 79, 146, 148, 164, 198
Middleton, E. J., 320
Miller, C. D., 316
Miller, S. M., 17
Mink, I. T., 56, 241
Mitchell, A. R. K., 19-20
Moeller, G. B., 149
Molandro, L. A., 147
Montessori, M., 92
Moore, E. R., 323
Moore, N. D., 48
Moos, B. S., 242, 243
Moos, R. H., 242, 243
Moran, M. A., 278
Morgan, D. P., 99, 101, 107
Mori, A. A., 58, 300, 301
Moroney, R. M., 290
Morris, W., 4, 11, 187
Morsink, C., 320, 322
Mullin, J. T., 58
Murray, D. G., 136
Murray, J. N., 117

Nadler, B., 330
Nash, L, 243
Nash, R., 298
Nathan, C., 229

Needle, N. A., 169
Neeley, M. A., 125, 219
Netick, A., 274, 276, 277
Neumann, A. J., 281
Nevin, A., 311, 332
Nihara, K., 56, 241
Nimkoff, M. F., 3, 9
Nirenberg, J. S., 158
Northcott, W. H., 291

O'Leary, K., 106, 108
Olshansky, S., 34
Olson, D. H., 11, 12
O'Neill, K. K., 149, 172
Opirhory, G., 34, 35, 220
Oppenheim, A. N., 245
Orlansky, M. D., 222, 268
Osman, B. B., 41
Otteni, H., 222, 226, 272, 273

Padden, C., 147
Page, R., 154
Pagel, S. 116, 133, 134
Paolucci-Whitcomb, P., 311
Parrish, V., 269, 271
Pasztor, J., 194
Patterson, J., 22–23, 39
Patterson, M., 119
Patton, J. M., 328
Paul, J. L., 40, 92, 96, 131, 132
Payne, H., 55
Pearlin, L. I., 58
Pease, S. F., 270
Perls, F. S., 12
Perosa, L. M., 60, 126
Perosa, S. L., 60, 126
Peters, G. A., 34, 35, 220
Peterson, D., 81
Pettibone, T. J., 332
Pettis, E., 154
Phelps, N., 105
Pieper, E., 79
Pierce, J. R., 152
Porcella, A., 101, 104
Porter, B. R., 245
Porter, P. B., 96
Potok, C., 47–48
Potter, M. W., 50
Powell, D. R., 62, 63, 131
Powell, G. J., 124
Powell, M. L., 230, 231, 238, 239, 240
Powell, T. H., 167
Poznanski, E. O., 60, 64

Preis, A., 39
Prescott, M. R., 125
Price, B. J., 190, 192, 201
Price, J., 116, 133, 134
Pysh, M. V. D., 151, 156

Rabbitt, J. A., 180, 190
Rabkin, J. G., 22
Rahe, R. H., 22
Raiser, L., 101, 102
Raymond, G., 185, 201
Rees, R., 221, 223, 237
Reeve, R. E., 19, 20, 69
Reiss, I. L., 6, 17, 19
Rettberg, D. R., 264
Reynolds, R., 34, 37
Ricci, C. S., 64
Rice, F. P., 37
Riggs, G. G., 128
Ritter, S., 311, 312
Rizzo, J. V., 29, 73
Roberds-Baxter, S., 178–179
Robinson, C. C., 235, 260, 288
Robinson, H. B., 32, 43, 66, 73
Robinson, N. M., 32, 43, 66, 73
Robson, D. L., 331
Rodriguez, F., 325, 328
Rodriguez, R. F., 212, 223
Rollins, B. C., 10
Roos, P., 116
Rose, E., 20
Rosedale, M. P., 127, 149
Rosenberg, S. A., 235, 260, 288
Rosenthal, M., 280
Ross, A. O., 40, 42, 43, 44, 47, 80, 81
Rossett, A., 127, 226, 253, 271, 279
Roth, W., 109, 115, 118, 122, 125
Russell, C. S., 11, 12
Ryckman, D. B., 64
Ryor, J., 333

Sadler, O. W., 280
Sailor, W., 300
Sanborn, M. P., 49, 284
Sandler, A., 281
Sapon-Shevin, M., 290
Sarason, S., 93
Sawyer, H. W., 318
Sawyer, S. H., 318
Scanlon, C. A., 105

Schaefer, C., 61
Schaefer, E. S., 9, 245
Schatz, E. M., 284
Scheiber, B., 154
Schleifer, J. J., 137
Schleifer, M. J., 152
Schuck, J., 191
Schulz, J. B., 38, 68, 98, 101, 107, 152, 159, 185, 304, 329
Schwartz, C. G., 123
Searl, S. J., 57, 64
Sears, J., 303
Sears, R. R., 246
Seligman, M., 40, 66, 72, 74, 78, 123, 160, 209, 210, 316, 318
Seyden, T., 280
Seyfarth, J. T., 177, 190, 196
Shapero, S., 280
Shayne, M. W., 290
Shea, T. M., 131, 228, 229, 266, 279
Shearer, M. S., 265, 266
Shevin, M., 103, 105, 106
Shillinburg, D. H., 72
Silberman, A., 229
Silverman, L. K., 95, 103, 104
Simmons-Martin, A., 262, 263
Simms, S. R., 194
Simons, B., 244
Simpson, R. L., 148, 151, 178, 189, 195, 202, 316, 319, 325, 327
Skinner, N., 95
Slaughter, H., 221, 223, 237
Smith, D., 316
Smith, J., 116, 317
Snell, M. A., 127, 130
Snell, M. E., 262, 272
Soffer, R. M., 102, 105
Soles, B., 208–209
Solnit, A. J., 33
Soltz, V., 272
Somers, P. A., 124
Sonnenshein, P., 116, 117, 118, 137
Spicknall, H., 129
Sprenkle, D. H., 11, 12
Stainback, S., 300, 323
Stainback, W., 300, 323

Stark, M. H., 33
Steinert, Y. E., 280
Stephens, I. M., 103
Stephens, T. M., 322
Stevens, S. H., 127, 196, 199, 281
Stewart, W., 130
Stile, S. W., 332
Stinnett, N., 7, 18
Stokes, S. 314
Straithe, M., 323
Strenecky, B. J., 99, 100, 280
Strickland, B., 98, 105, 181, 226
Strom, R. D., 206, 207, 235, 237, 246, 248, 253, 282, 316, 325
Struening, E. L., 22
Suchara, H. T., 316
Sullivan, O. R., 226
Suran, B. G., 29, 73
Swan, W. W., 288
Swap, S. M., 148, 150
Sweitzer, M., 222, 223, 243, 276, 278, 287, 288, 289
Swick, K. J., 185, 201

Tavormino, J. B., 70
Tawney, J. W., 300, 307
Taylor, D., 12
Taylor, J. R., 70
Teahan, J. E., 244
Tew, B. J., 55
Thomas, D. L., 10
Thomas, M. A., 307
Thornburg, K., 199
Thurman, S. K., 281
Torgoff, I., 246
Townes, B. D., 267
Trevino, F., 275
Troup, J., 194
Trout, M. D., 34
Trupin, E. W., 267
Tulkin, S. R., 37
Turnbull, A. P., 39, 79, 91, 92, 96, 98, 105, 106, 107, 119, 130, 181, 185, 194, 226, 304
Turnbull, H. R., 3, 96, 106, 107
Tuttle, F. B., 149, 172

Umbreit, J., 299–300, 301

Voeller, M. N., 12

Walker, J. E., 228, 229, 279
Walsh, F., 15, 17
Walters, R. H., 4, 8, 9, 29, 30, 146, 158
Wang, M. C., 288, 304
Ward, M. E., 303
Warren, F., 43
Wasow, M., 57
Webb, R., 260
Webster, E. J., 42, 123, 126, 132
Weeks, K. H., 290
Weitz, S. E., 237, 238
Wentworth, E. H., 72
Werner, M. S., 205
Westin, J., 129, 260, 272, 289, 290
Whitford, E. M., 42
Wiegerink, R., 295
Wikler, L., 57, 61
Willson, V., 118, 127
Wilson, W., 279
Winn, J., 4, 8, 9, 29, 30, 146, 158
Witt, J. C., 316
Wolf, J. S., 194
Wolfe, V. V., 225
Wood, K., 229
Wright, B., 60, 124
Wurster, S., 221, 223, 237
Wyatt, G. E., 124
Wyckoff, J. L., 272, 290

Yorburg, B., 6, 7, 9, 17
York, R., 299–300, 301
Yoshida, R. K., 105, 118, 127
Ysseldyke, J. E., 103

Zand, C. R., 322
Zettel, J. J., 103
Zevon, M., 243
Zorman, R., 81, 132
Zuk, G. H., 31

Subject Index

Adaptability, 11–13
Adaptation, to gifted children:
  parental attitudes, 81
  sibling relationships, 81
Adaptation, to handicapped children:
  extended family and, 78–79
  model for, 56–63
  patterns of, 64–70
  siblings and, 70–78
Assessment:
  of behavior management, 228–230
  of environment, 237–243
  of instructional skills, 235–237
  of knowledge of child development, 230–235
  of knowledge of legal rights, 226–228
  of parental needs, 218–226
  techniques and models, 243–254

Behavior management, 228–230
Birth:
  abnormal, 31–34
  impact on marital relationship, 30–34
  normal, 30–31

Child abuse, 19–21
Cohesion, 11–12
Communication process, 148–160
Coping strategies:
  acceptance, 66–69
  adjustment, 69–70
  rejection, 64–66

Development:
  gifted child and adolescent, 44–45
  mildly handicapped child and adolescent, 40–44
  normal child and adolescent, 36–37
  severely handicapped child and adolescent, 37–40

Divorce, 17–19

Environment, 237–243
Extended family, 4, 6, 78–80

Family:
  adaptation to gifted children, 80–81
  adaptation to handicapped children, 56–79
  changes, 10–11
  dynamics, 11–13
  ecology, 62–64
  environment, 237–243
  extended, 6, 78–79
  functions, 7–10
  impact of exceptional children on, 30–50, 55–56
  life cycle, 13–15
  nuclear, 4–6
  one-parent, 6–7, 203–205
  reconstituted, 4
  stress, 22–24
  structure, 4–7
  systems, 3–4
Family Environment Scale (FES), 241

Gifted children:
  development of, 44–49
  family adaptation to, 80–81
  and legislation, 103–104
  and parent education, 282–287
  and parent-teacher conferences, 205–208
  teachers of, 309–310, 323

Home Observation of Measurement of the Environment (HOME), 238–241
Home-school relationships (*see* Parent-school communication)

Individualized education program (IEP), 98–102

Legal rights, 226–228

Legislation:
  confidentiality, 97
  consent and notice, 97
  due process, 97–98
  and gifted children, 103–104
  and individualized education program (IEP), 98–102
  and levels of parent participation, 104–106
  monitoring progress, 102–103
  Public Law 94–142, 96–104
Life cycle, 13–21

Nuclear family, 4–6

Parent advocacy:
  concern, 92–93
  groups, 93–95
  pressure, 93
Parent education:
  and ethical issues, 289–291
  evaluation of, 287–289
  models, 264–272
  for parents of gifted children, 282–287
  program goals, 261–264
  program planning, 272–282
  rationale, 259–261
Parent involvement in special education:
  and legislation, 104–106
  levels of, 104–106
  as participants, 91–92
  as providers, 89–90
  as recipients, 90–91
Parent-professional relationship:
  clinical model, 123–125
  counseling model, 125–126
  ecological model, 130–132
  educational model, 126–130
  future trends, 136–137
  parental expectations, 134–136
  professional expectations, 133–134
Parent-school communication:
  attitudes, 151–153
  barriers, 148–150

Parent-school communication: (cont.)
  nonverbal, 146–148
  process, 148–160
  skills, 153–160
  strategies, 160–162
  techniques, 162–172
  verbal, 146
Parent-teacher conferences:
  conducting, 196–199
  evaluating, 199–201
  postconference activities, 201
  purposes, 178–190
  special situations, 202–211
  structuring, 190–196
Parentalplegia, 117
Parenthood, 8–9
Parents:
  educational level, 222
  ethnic background, 222–223
  and family experience, 223
  individuality, 217
  intellectually limited, 208–209
  and knowledge of child development, 230–234
  and participation in educational planning, 223–226
  relationships with professionals, 115–138
  socioeconomic level, 221–222
Public Law 94–142, 96–104

Sibling relationships, 70–78, 81
Single parents, 4, 203–205
Socialization, 9–10
Special education:
  legislation, 96–104
  parents as advocates, 92–95
  parents as participants, 91–92
  parents as providers, 89–90
  parents as recipients, 90–91
  teacher preparation programs, 297–319
Stress, 22–24, 57–58
Stressor, 22
Systems theory, 4

Teacher preparation programs:
  for administrators, 331–333
  competencies, 310–319
  of gifted, 309–310
  of mildly handicapped, 307–309
  for regular education, 319–331
  of severely handicapped, 305–307
  special educators, 299–305